CW01183099

RICHARD FITZRALPH: HIS LIFE, TIMES AND THOUGHT

Richard FitzRalph

His life, times and thought

Michael W. Dunne and Simon Nolan O.Carm.
EDITORS

FOUR COURTS PRESS

This book was set in 10.5 on 12.5 point Ehrhardt by
Mark Heslington, Scarborough, North Yorkshire for
FOUR COURTS PRESS
7 Malpas Street, Dublin 8, Ireland
www.fourcourtspress.ie
and in North America for
FOUR COURTS PRESS
c/o ISBS, 920 N.E. 58th Avenue, Suite 300, Portland, OR 97213.

© the various authors and Four Courts Press 2013

A catalogue record for this title
is available from the British Library.

ISBN 978-1-84682-369-5

All rights reserved. No part of this publication may be reproduced,
stored in or introduced into a retrieval system, or transmitted,
in any form or by any means (electronic, mechanical,
photocopying, recording or otherwise), without the
prior written permission of both the copyright
owner and publisher of this book.

Printed in Great Britain
by Antony Rowe Ltd, Chippenham, Wilts.

Contents

LIST OF CONTRIBUTORS   vii

INTRODUCTION AND ACKNOWLEDGMENTS   1

OXFORD

1   Accidents without a subject: Richard FitzRalph's question on the Eucharist from his *Lectura* on the *Sentences*   11
  Michael W. Dunne

2   The influence on FitzRalph of Bishop Grandisson of Exeter, with a critical edition of Sermons 62 and 64 of FitzRalph's sermon diary   30
  Michael Haren

3   Is it better for the king of England to be a king of England than a duke of Aquitaine? Richard FitzRalph and Adam Wodeham on whether beatific enjoyment is an act of the intellect or an act of the will   56
  Severin V. Kitanov

4   Adam Wodeham and Robert Holcot as witnesses to FitzRalph's thought   79
  Katherine H. Tachau

AVIGNON

5   The rhetoric of Richard FitzRalph's *Defensio curatorum*   99
  Terence Dolan

6   Conversion, vision and faith in the life and works of Richard FitzRalph   103
  William O. Duba

7   Richard FitzRalph on the *Filioque* before and after his conversations with Barlaam the Calabrian   128
  Chris Schabel

REPUTATION AND AFTERMATH

8 Richard FitzRalph and John Wyclif: untangling Armachanus from the Wycliffites 159
   Stephen Lahey

9 De Vitoria on FitzRalph: an adequate assessment? 186
   Graham McAleer

10 John Foxholes OFM Armachanus (†1474): a note on his logical treatises formerly attributed to FitzRalph 199
   Michael W. Dunne

   BIBLIOGRAPHY 204

   INDEX OF ANCIENT, MEDIEVAL AND RENAISSANCE NAMES 214

   INDEX OF MODERN NAMES 216

Contributors

TERENCE DOLAN is Emeritus Professor of Old and Middle English at University College Dublin.

WILLIAM O. DUBA lectures in Medieval Philosophy at the Université de Fribourg.

MICHAEL W. DUNNE is Head of the Department of Philosophy at the National University of Ireland, Maynooth and President of the FitzRalph Society.

MICHAEL HAREN edited the Calendar of Papal Registers for the Irish Manuscripts Commission.

SEVERIN V. KITANOV is Assistant Professor in the Department of Philosophy at Salem State University.

STEPHEN LAHEY is a Professor in the Department of Classics and Religious Studies at the University of Nebraska-Lincoln.

GRAHAM MCALEER is a Professor of Philosophy at Loyola University, Maryland.

SIMON NOLAN O.CARM. lectures in the Department of Philosophy at the National University of Ireland, Maynooth.

CHRIS SCHABEL is an Associate Professor in the Department of History and Archaeology at the University of Cyprus.

KATHERINE H. TACHAU is a Professor in the Department of History at the University of Iowa.

Introduction and acknowledgments

MICHAEL W. DUNNE AND SIMON NOLAN O.CARM.

In November 2010, a conference was held at Maynooth to commemorate the 650th anniversary of the death of Archbishop Richard FitzRalph, which took place at Avignon on or around 16 November 1360. It was the first conference dedicated to *Armachanus* and a variety of papers were presented by an international group of experts on different aspects of FitzRalph's life, times and thought. The fruits of that conference are gathered together in the essays contained in this volume. The conference was held under the patronage of FitzRalph's two successors, H.E. Cardinal Seán Brady, the Catholic archbishop of Armagh, and the Most Reverend Alan Harper OBE, the Church of Ireland (Anglican Communion) archbishop of Armagh. A highlight of the conference was that on the afternoon of 16 November through the kindness of the rector, Revd Sandra Pragnell, and the congregation of the parish church of St Nicholas at Dundalk, part of the conference was held in that church, where FitzRalph was baptized and confirmed, where he preached on four occasions, and to where his bones were brought back from Avignon. An exhibition was organized in the Russell Library, Maynooth, by the librarian, Ms Penny Woods, of a number of books contained in the library with an association with FitzRalph, including the Russell Library's copy of the *Defensorium curatorum* (Paris, 1633). One outcome of the conference was the founding of the FitzRalph Society and the setting up of a webpage at www.fitzralph.com. Michael Dunne was elected president and Stephen Lahey secretary. The committee of the FitzRalph Society then agreed to the setting up and organization of a FitzRalph Texts project with the idea of making available as many of FitzRalph's texts as possible.[1]

Michael Dunne's topic in the opening essay of the volume is Richard FitzRalph's question on the Eucharist from his *Lectura* on the *Sentences*, the text of which is based on his original lectures at Oxford in 1328–9. Dunne begins by noting the importance of paying scholarly attention to the relationship between

---

[1] See http://philosophy.nuim.ie/projects-research/projects/richard-fitzralph. There are early printed editions of works such as the *Defensio curatorum* (a critical edition of which is nearing completion by Prof. Terence Dolan); the 1512 edition of the *Summa in questionibus Armenorum* is available on the website of the Bayerische Staatsbibliothek. The completion of the nineteenth-century edition of the *De pauperie Salvatoris* or the bringing together of the separately edited parts is being carried out by Stephen Lahey on his webpage '14th-century Oxford Theology Online' (only book I is currently available). Some parts of the *Lectura* on the *Sentences* have been published; namely, the *Principial sermon* by Michael Dunne; a section on the Trinity by Schabel and Friedman and texts on future contingents by Jean-François Genest.

FitzRalph and Adam Wodeham. Wodeham is an extremely important early witness to the reception of FitzRalph's thought among his contemporaries and is also a precious source for understanding how FitzRalph's thought developed and changed over time. This important relationship between FitzRalph and Wodeham is a theme addressed by a number of essays in this volume. FitzRalph's question on the Eucharist is entitled 'Is all of Christ to be found in the Eucharist under the appearance of bread and wine' and it contains a single article: 'Are the accidents in the Eucharist (those of bread and wine) there without inhering in anything (since because of transubstatntiation the substance of the bread and wine no longer exists)'. Dunne places FitzRalph's discussion of the Eucharist within the context of eucharistic theology in the early fourteenth century. While FitzRalph is discussing a matter of theology, he characteristically dwells on the more philosophical aspects of the question. Trying to explain and justify transubstantiation, Dunne notes, can lead thinkers to consider something they might have just passed over: the nature of accidents in themselves and how they are interrelated. If we take the common view that all qualities inhere in quantity, then we have the interesting idea that the qualitative aspects of things are reduced to their measurable properties and that quantity can serve as a subject for all of the qualities; why then would we need substances? Among the modern doctors considered by FitzRalph are Henry of Ghent, Thomas Aquinas and John Duns Scotus. FitzRalph typically seeks to ally himself with Henry, admires the clarity of Aquinas on the matter of Eucharistic presence and identifies Scotus as the thinker with whom he must engage. Dunne concludes his consideration of FitzRalph on the Eucharist by noting that although FitzRalph's *Lectures* on the *Sentences* gained considerable currency in his day, his discussion of the Eucharist was only picked up by Wodeham, whose reference to FitzRalph was later taken up by Henry Totting of Oyta in 1375. Dunne makes the important concluding observation (with the help of William Courtenay) that the consideration of the role of quantity by both Scotus and William of Ockham began a reinterpretation of the Aristotelian categories of time, motion, place and relation, which was fruitful in discussions in the 1320s and 1330s. The reinterpretation of the category of quanity was key, but is rarely dealt with in the English schools after 1332. FitzRalph is, therefore, an important witness to the state of early fourteenth-century debate.

Michael Haren's contribution seeks to trace the influence on FitzRalph of Bishop Grandisson of Exeter. The early part of the essay comprises an informative survey of the available sources for establishing the details of Grandisson's relationship with FitzRalph. Associations between the two can be documented from 1328, but it is possible that they first became acquainted during the time of Grandisson's tenure of the archdeaconry of Nottingham in the period 1312–27; it is conceivable, Haren argues, that Grandisson was an early patron of the young FitzRalph. In 1329, Grandisson appointed FitzRalph as guardian and tutor of his nephew and it is clear that a rapport between the two men continued for many years (even if documentary evidence is patchy). FitzRalph may have been the unknown 'reverend doctor' mentioned in connection with a disputation at Exeter in the 1340s; Grandisson was known to be keen to preserve the old tradition in which a cathedral might aspire to be a centre of higher learning. Grandisson was the principal ordaining prelate at the consecration of FitzRalph as archbishop of Armagh in July 1346. Now a bishop, FitzRalph was commissioned to carry out a number of episcopal functions within the diocese of Exeter in Grandisson's place. The major and most public declaration of sympathy between FitzRalph and Grandisson came with the latter's endorsement in 1359 of FitzRalph's campaign against the privileges of the friars. A large part of Haren's essay is given over to considering Grandisson's influence on FitzRalph principally in terms of what is known of the activity of Grandisson and his circle. Seeking to advance the state of scholarship concerning the affinities between the two men, Haren suggests that there is a 'potentially fertile field' in studying FitzRalph's outlook against that of Grandisson. To this end, Haren provides a critical edition of two sermons of FitzRalph preached on 18 October and on All Saints Day, 1356.

Severin Kitanov's contribution is a comparative study of Richard FitzRalph's *Lectura* and Adam Wodeham's *Oxford lectures* on the topic of beatific enjoyment and whether it should be considered to be an act of intellect or of will. Comparative analysis of the *Sentences* commentaries of the two authors gives real insight into the complexity and wealth of medieval scholastic debate at Oxford in the first half of the fourteenth century. FitzRalph is clearly a major influence on Wodeham. Kitanov presents both FitzRalph and Wodeham as responding to the challenge of Thomas Aquinas' account of enjoyment in two ways. First, Aquinas does not really explain the precise nature of the relationship between delight and volition. If beatific enjoyment is considered to be an act of the will, then how might enjoyment differ from delight, which also belongs to the will? Since delight (or pleasure) is generally considered to be a passion, why not call enjoyment a passion rather than an act of the will? Secondly, for many theologians, Aquinas places too much emphasis on the speculative or vision-based aspect of the experience of heavenly beatitude in a way that leads later authors, especially from the Franciscan tradition, to consider it to be important to give more consideration to love and volition in the context of the beatific vision. Comparison reveals FitzRalph to be a more polished and also a more reticent thinker than Wodeham in his careful consideration of noble faculties, pleasure and the different senses of beatitude. FitzRalph explicity rejects Aquinas' view that ultimate human happiness consists primarily in the vision of the divine essence. For FitzRalph, *pleasure* is the noblest of the simple goods integrated in beatitude; only pleasure brings satisfaction to the rational human mind with respect to God. For Kitanov, Wodeham is a more original thinker than FitzRalph in his use (under the influence of Ockham) of logical and semantic analysis in a theological context. Wodeham espouses, according to Kitanov, a 'well-rounded nominalism' in his defence of the view that intellect and will are fundamentally inseparable, even as they have distinct perfections. Wodeham is keen to insist on the substantial unity of the human soul, which should not be compromised by prizing intellect over will or will over intellect. Wodeham's analytic approach pays dividends in giving him certain tools for discussing the relationship between intellect and will. For Kitanov, a consideration of the discussion of *fruitio beatifica* in fourteenth-century scholastic thinkers such as FitzRalph and Wodeham can help philosophers in the modern era to think more deeply about philosophical issues of human enjoyment, fulfilment and consolation.

Katherine Tachau's essay is a study of Adam Wodeham and Robert Holcot as witnesses to FitzRalph's thought. Tachau begins by pointing to the burgeoning of scholarly interest in FizRalph in the 1930s associated with figures such as Louis Hammerich, Aubrey Gwynn and Konstanty Michałski. Tachau notes how Michałski tends to view Wodeham as a hostile witness to FitzRalph's views, a view that is repeated and extended by later historians such as John Robson. While paying tribute to the pioneering work of Michałski, Tachau nevertheless points to errors in his transcription of Wodeham's manuscripts, which contributed to his misinterpretation of FitzRalph as somehow siding with Thomas Aquinas against Wodeham on the vexed question of the relationship between the intellect and the will. Tachau also surveys the views of Gordon Leff, who was largely unsympathetic to FitzRalph's 'derivative' thinking, which tended (in Leff's view) to evade commitment. By the late 1970s, William Courtenay had begun to point out that Wodeham's response to FitzRalph was more nuanced and varied than Michałski and Robson realized. In her study, Katherine Walsh shows the influence of both Michałski and Robson in her reflection on the 'ecclecticism' of FitzRalph's position on intellect, will and their acts. Walsh also suggests that FitzRalph is trying to negotiate a 'middle way' between Aquinas and Scotus. Here, for Tachau, Walsh continues to be influenced by Robson but also by Leff. Having also read William Courtenay, Walsh was aware that warmer relations might have existed between FitzRalph and Wodeham than were previously appreciated among scholars. Moving on from the historiographical background, Tachau proceeds to an examination of relevant sources with the aim of establishing (against the trend that began with Michałski) that what Wodeham has to say about FitzRalph is neither hostile nor critical. Tachau insists that removing Wodeham from the camp of hostile critics to lodge him with the friendly witnesses of FitzRalph leads to the reappraisal of the views of both. What to previous scholars might have looked like denunciation on Wodeham's part is revealed instead to be a recognition that FitzRalph's views had evolved. Tachau makes the important point that one should always be aware in reading FitzRalph and Wodeham of the context of scholastic disputation where it was normal to take on the role of *respondens* and *opponens*. She

Introduction and acknowledgments 5

refers to her own reappraisal of the *sermo finalis* of Robert Holcot (a fellow *bachalarius* of FitzRalph), once seen as evidence for mutual antagonism among Dominican *socii* housed, lecturing and disputing in the same convent, but now correctly understood to be an example of a genre of jocular speeches, delivered at the end of one's years as *Sententiarius*. Tachau makes an important final observation in noting that whenever Wodeham quotes FitzRalph the citations are reasonably exact.

Turning to the Avignon period of FitzRalph's life and work, Terence Dolan addresses the topic of the rhetoric of FitzRalph's *Defensio curatorum*. In the *Defensio*, FitzRalph's preference is for proof and clarity of presentation rather than bombast. Dolan's essay assesses the limited range of rhetorical devices, which are nevertheless employed by FitzRalph to very good effect. FitzRalph reveals himself to be skilled in his use of quotation and illustrative example designed to capture the imagination of his listeners. For Dolan, the *Defensio* 'is a model of forensic, epideictic and deliberative oratory, an outstanding Philippic in the anti-mendicant tradition'.

In his contribution to this book, William Duba considers conversion, vision and faith in the life and works of FitzRalph. With reference to the celebrated 'autobiographical prayer' within which FitzRalph claims to have undergone a conversion during his six years at Avignon, Duba notes and begs to differ with the common opinion that FitzRalph came to reject scholasticism. Duba's essay pursues two lines of enquiry. First, he examines the scholastic structure, content and intent of a number of FitzRalph's post-conversion works with the aim of showing that FitzRalph did not abandon the scholastic approach in favour of a 'non-scholastic' methodology. Duba does, however, identify a certain change in FitzRalph's approach from one engaged in Aristotelian philosophy of the arts faculty to one engaged more and more in theological controversy. Second, continuing the theme of conversion, Duba considers FitzRalph's doctrine concerning knowledge of God, a doctrine inspired by Henry of Ghent but which emphasizes the experience of Paul in the rapture. That FitzRalph maintains a consistent and coherent doctrine, from the time of his university lectures on theology to his autobiographical prayer, is revealed on reading the first question (article 2) of his *Sentences* commentary and his account of the beatific vision in book XIV of the *Summa de quaestionibus Armenorum*. Midway through his life, FitzRalph underwent a religious conversion under the influence of his reading of Paul, Augustine and Pseudo-Dionysius. For Duba, this conversion was a conversion not away from scholastic theology, but towards it. FitzRalph skillfully seeks to bolster the authority of Paul through the application of his reading of Henry of Ghent. He also uses Henry's distinction between faith, abstractive knowledge and knowledge of vision to interpret the writings of Pseudo-Dionysius. FitzRalph's thoroughly scholastic epistemology can even be seen to permeate the very prayer in which he describes his conversion. For

Duba, FitzRalph's post-university career involved the application of scholasticism to the burning issues confronting Latin Christianity.

Chris Schabel's essay considers the topic of FitzRalph's thinking concerning the *Filioque* before and after his conversations with Barlaam the Calabrian. Schabel's essay gives us a fascinating insight into a case of serious exchange of ideas between a Latin and a Greek theologian in the fourteenth century. FitzRalph came into contact with Barlaam at Avignon. A close study of FitzRalph's *Sentences* commentary and his *Summa de quaestionibus Armenorum* reveals a certain change in tone and argumentation between the two works. Of course, FitzRalph consistently professes the *Filioque* throughout his career. While he condemns as heresy what the Greeks actually believed (unbeknownst to him at the time) in his *Sentences* commentary, however, in his *Summa*, FitzRalph is altogether more conciliatory in continuing to maintain that the Greeks are wrong but at the same time avoiding a renewal of the charge of heresy. His conversations with Barlaam, an eminent Greek theologian, had clearly left their mark. FitzRalph's stay at Avignon and his encounter with Barlaam forced him to reevaluate the issue of the *Filioque* comprehensively. Both theologians learned from one another, as Schabel attests. In the end, each adhered to the party line but no longer in ignorance.

In his essay, Stephen Lahey undertakes a reexamination of the relationship between FitzRalph and John Wyclif. For Lahey, it is necessary to 'untangle' the archbishop from the Wycliffites in order to shed light on the issue. Lahey takes time to consider the important fourteenth-century Carmelite theologian, Thomas Netter of Walden. Written in 1426, Netter's *Doctrinale* was a three-volume compendium of all the errors associated with Wyclif and Wycliffism. FitzRalph figures as an unwitting accomplice to Wyclif in the writings of the Carmelite master, Lahey notes. In some instances, for Netter, FitzRalph's errors are taken up and magnified by Wyclif, and, in others, Wyclif departs from them in favour of even greater ones. Curiously, Netter avoids connecting the two thinkers in relation to the debates concerning the mendicants and concerning just dominion. Lahey's main concern is to demonstrate that Wyclif's opposition to the friars is nothing like FitzRalph's, that FitzRalph's anti-mendicant arguments are as similar to Wyclif's as chalk to cheese. Both theologians are notable for basing their arguments against the friars almost exclusively on scripture, but FitzRalph's antifraternal arguments are ecclesiastically centred and directed explicitly at the privileges the friars enjoy. In contrast, for Lahey, Wyclif's arguments are chiefly metaphysical and are aimed at the very nature of sectarianism itself. Lahey concludes his contribution with the assertion that FitzRalph can be understood as having never advocated the absolute dissolution of the friars; FitzRalph's argument was for the restriction of their privileges, their preaching, their shriving and their mendicancy. Wyclif, on the other hand, cannot countenance the allowing of factions within the Christian religion, be

Introduction and acknowledgments 7

they monastic or fraternal. Lahey contends that FitzRalph's arguments are based in ecclesiology, while Wyclif's are grounded in a formal theology of ideas.

In his contribution, Graham McAleer reconsiders the assessment of FitzRalph by the sixteenth-century Dominican theologian, Francisco de Vitoria. McAleer argues that de Vitoria fails to appreciate the originality of FitzRalph's views concerning legitimate authority and property, views that stem from a theological anthropology that is unusal for its time. McAleer situates the thought of FitzRalph within the context of fourteenth-century debates about the legitimacy of property before going on to critique de Vitoria's unsympathetic reading of FitzRalph. He pays particular attention to de Vitoria's *On the American Indians*, and points to the many misrepresentations of FitzRalph's views on lordship within that work. For McAleer, de Vitoria fails to engage with the deeper ontological and normative insights at the heart of FitzRalph's thought. For example, FitzRalph denies, according to McAleer, what de Vitoria assumes: the ontological fixity of the capacity for self-mastery.

Finally, Michael Dunne turns his attention to the purported logical works of FitzRalph. In the concluding contribution to the volume, Dunne argues that the attribution of these works to FitzRalph is in fact a mistake, that they were authored by an Armachanus but not by FitzRalph. These texts are to be attributed to another archbishop of Armagh, the Franciscan John Foxholes, and Dunne sets out the reasons for this.

One overall impression that we formed from the conference is that we are at a turning point in the study of FitzRalph's writings and thought. Whereas before now, soundings or samplings of FitzRalph's texts had been made, from now on a more serious attempt will be made to comprehensively explore the many features and developments of his thought.

Our thanks go to the NUI Publications Fund, the Maynooth Scholastic Trust, Revd Martin Baxter O.Carm. and H.E. Cardinal Sean Brady for their financial support towards the publication of this book. Thanks are also due to Ms Kate FitzPatrick, NUI Maynooth, who copy-edited the manuscript for publication and to Dr Yinya Liu, NUI Maynooth, who prepared the bibliography. The editors also express their sincere gratitude to Dr John Flood of the University of Groningen and to Dr Catherine Kavanagh of Mary Immaculate College (University of Limerick) for their support and advice.

Finally, the editors and the contributors to this volume would like to mark the passing of Prof. Katherine Walsh, who died on 21 March 2011, and to whose scholarship we are all indebted.

Michael W. Dunne & Simon Nolan O.Carm.
17 March 2012
Department of Philosophy
National University of Ireland Maynooth

Oxford

Accidents without a subject: Richard FitzRalph's question on the Eucharist from his *Lectura* on the *Sentences*

MICHAEL W. DUNNE

Richard FitzRalph gave his lectures on the *Sentences* at Oxford in the years 1328–9.[1] In the course of his lectures, FitzRalph dealt with topics drawn mainly from the first two books of the *Sentences*, devoting one question only to book III and perhaps two questions to book IV, of which only one has survived: the question on the Eucharist. It must be supposed that it was with a certain amount of relief that the 29-year-old FitzRalph came to the end of his lectures and had the prospect of spending a year at the University of Paris as a paid tutor to the nephew of the bishop of Exeter. The text that has come down to us with the title *Lectura in Sententias* is not exactly the content of the lectures that FitzRalph gave but the partial reworking of his text, which he was engaged in after his return from Paris in 1330 and presumably abandoned after he became chancellor of the University of Oxford from 1332 to 1334. These years, 1330–4, when FitzRalph was regent master and then chancellor, were extremely important, since a number of exceptionally talented thinkers were reading the *Sentences*; namely Adam Wodeham, Robert Holcot and Walter Chatton, and, as a senior and influential member of the university, FitzRalph figures prominently in their debates. On the other hand, it does not seem that his contemporaries figure directly in FitzRalph's discussions of his *Sentences* questions – firstly, because, unlike Wodeham and Holcot, he preserves the older courtesy of not naming contemporaries and, secondly, because the *Sentences* commentaries of his contemporaries such as Reppes and Skelton have not survived. Indeed, information regarding the debates between FitzRalph and his contemporaries may have to be gleaned from the next generation, such as in the writings of Wodeham, and so on. As Courtenay points out,[2] Wodeham set out to challenge two of the *magistri regentes* while he was giving his Oxford *lectura* on the *Sentences* (in 1332–4), namely, Chatton, who had left for Avignon in late 1332,

---

1 For an overview, see M. Dunne, 'Richard FitzRalph's *Lectura* on the *Sentences*' in P. Rosemann (ed.), *Medieval commentaries on the* Sentences *of Peter Lombard* (Leiden), 2, pp 405–38; M. Dunne, 'A fourteenth-century example of an *Introitus sententiarum* at Oxford: Richard FitzRalph's inaugural speech in praise of the *Sentences* of Peter Lombard', *Medieval Studies*, 63 (2001), 1–29.   2 W.J. Courtenay, *Adam Wodeham: an introduction to his life and writings* (Leiden, 1978), p. 77.

11

and FitzRalph, who in May 1332 had become chancellor of the University of Oxford. Courtenay describes FitzRalph as Wodeham's major opponent and, on occasion, ally. And Courtenay concludes by stating that:

> Except for Ockham, FitzRalph was the most frequently cited *modernus* in Wodeham's Oxford lectures, appearing in the margins or text of over forty of Wodeham's seventy questions.[3]

Clearly, the relationship between FitzRalph and Wodeham is an important one and highly relevant to various research projects. On the one hand, Wodeham is an extremely important early witness to the reception of FitzRalph's thought among his contemporaries and also a unique source for an understanding of how Fitzralph's thought developed or changed on certain points between the text as given in the original *Lectura* in 1328–9 and the partial revision of the same into the text we now have, the *opus correctum* as edited by the author between roughly 1330 and 1332. On the other hand, from the point of view of editing Wodeham's Oxford *Lectura*, FitzRalph's text will be of some importance in identifying precisely what Adam is quoting and to the contextualization of Wodeham's discussion of certain arguments. We will return to this relationship in the context of their discussions of the Eucharist at the end of this essay.

EUCHARISTIC THEOLOGY IN THE EARLY FOURTEENTH CENTURY

FitzRalph's question on the Eucharist is entitled 'Is all of Christ to be found in the Eucharist under the appearances of bread and wine' and contains a single article: 'Are the accidents in the Eucharist (those of the bread and wine) there without inhering in anything (since because of transubstantiation the substance of the bread and wine no longer exists)'.[4] FitzRalph was lecturing on the Eucharist at the end of a very innovative period in Eucharist theology, which had been inaugurated by the *Commentary on the* Sentences of Thomas Aquinas. In fact, Thomas' views ultimately became the common view of most theologians, but this was only after decades of debate in which a variety of positions were put forward; for example, consubstantiation by Jean Quidort. It was, of course, transubstantiation that won the allegiance of the majority of theologians, but if it solved one problem (namely, how to explain the real presence of Christ in the Eucharist), it inevitably created another one: given the real persistence of the

---

3 Ibid., p. 75. 4 For an overview of the historical development of the doctrine of transubstantiation, see E. Yarnold, 'Transubstantiation' in R. Forrai, G. Geréby and I. Perczel (eds), *The Eucharist in theology and philosophy: issues of doctrinal history in East and West from the Patristic Age to the Reformation* (Leuven, 2005), pp 381–94.

accidents of the bread and wine, what kind of reality was to be accorded to them? Again, given that at the moment of consecration the substance of the bread and wine disappears, the accidents of the bread and wine remain unchanged – they cannot belong to the body of Christ, they cannot it seems remain on their own since they are accidents. The accidents have to inhere in something, so what then is the subject in which the accidents inhere?[5]

Generally, theologians of the thirteenth and fourteenth centuries followed Peter Lombard, who asserted that the accidents of the bread and wine subsist without any subject at all (*sine subiecto*). Commentaries on this in the thirteenth and fourteenth centuries gave rise to two different questions. The first concerned the possibility for an accident in general to be separated and to subsist independently of its subject. The second question is that of the real mode of the subsistence of the Eucharistic accidents. Aquinas, in fact, gives a very clear answer to both, something that FitzRalph will acknowledge in his text as well.[6]

Aquinas is one of the great defenders of transubstantiation, but this forces him to accept that in the Eucharist there are accidents without a subject. This is at variance with Aristotle's teaching and with what Thomas accepts elsewhere: namely, that the definition of an accident includes that of its substance, the notion of accidents subsisting without a subject is contradictory. How then can this be justified, by a direct intervention of God? Aquinas chooses to redefine the notions of subject and accident. 'Inherence' does not constitute the being of an accident but only one mode of being. This mode of being – namely inherence – belongs to an accident in relation to its immediate cause, the substance. In its relation to the First Cause, however, an accident does not possess the mode of inherence but only that of dependence. Thus, Aquinas can argue that the separability of an accident from its subject does not imply the contradiction of the separability of a being (*ens*) from its 'to be' (*esse*), but only that of the separability of a being from one of its modes of being. An accident is to be defined in terms of its potential inherence and not in terms of its actual inherence; its potential inference remains intact even if sometimes by a miracle it subsists without a subject.[7]

Having shown the possibility of the subsistence of accidents without a subject, Aquinas now moves on to consider the real mode of the subsistence of the accidents. Aquinas assigns a particular role to one of the nine categories of accidents – quantity. According to Thomas, after the substance of the bread has disappeared only the quantity of the bread really subsists without a subject.[8] It is quantity that assumes the role or mode of being of substance with regard to the other accidents.

5 I am indebted to the detailed discussion of these themes by P.J.J.M. Bakker in *La raison et le miracle: les doctrines eucharistiques (c.1250–c.1400): contribution à l'étude des rapports entre philosophie et théologie* (Nijmegen, 1999), i, ch. 4, pp 293–430. 6 See below, p. 22. 7 Thomas Aquinas, *Commentary on the* Sentences, book IV, dist. 12, q. 1, a. 1, q. 1. 8 Ibid.

Opinion was divided on this explanation of the separability of accidents through the mediation of quantity. One reaction was that of Peter John Olivi, who argued that quantity has its foundation in quantity rather than the other way round. It is a view that we will see again in William of Ockham. Richard Middleton OFM argued against Olivi that quantity has an independent status; it is really distinct from substance and from quality. After his criticism of Olivi's understanding of what an accident is, however, Middleton introduces a distinction between three types of accidents: relative, absolute and mixed. An accident is relative when it has the status of a pure relation (the accidents that belong to the category of relation as well as the other six categories); an accident is absolute which does not have the status of being a relation but that of an absolute thing (this is the case of the categories of quantity and quality). It is a distinction that we will find in FitzRalph but mediated through Scotus.[9]

The second view on the Eucharistic accidents that gets most attention from FitzRalph is that of John Duns Scotus. While maintaining that it is proper for an accident to inhere in a subject, Scotus considers how it would be possible for an accident to exist separately. For Scotus, an accident taken as something absolute can be and not be actually in a subject but it necessarily is in a subject potentially. It would be contradictory to state that a relative accident could subsist without inherence since a relative accident is nothing other than a relation and for which two terms are required, both an '*ad quem*' and a '*cuius*'; without one or the other the relation ceases. An absolute accident when separated from its subject is such because of its dependence on the First Cause which can carry out in an eminent way (*eminentius*) all that secondary causality can. When it comes to the question of which of the two absolute accidents (quantity or quality) assumes the role of immediate subject (only a substance can be the ultimate subject of accidents),[10] however, Scotus is happy to juxtapose the two opposing views of Aquinas/Giles of Rome and Peter John Olivi without, it seems, declaring himself for any side, even if he in fact favours the common opinion. However, the possibility of the separability of accidents does force Scotus to rethink the relation between subject and accident. As Bakker states, in affirming that inherence does not belong to the essence of an accident, Scotus stands out from other Parisian theologians at the end of the thirteenth century.[11]

These are the views that FitzRalph had to take into account when it came to drawing up his lectures on the Eucharist. There was, however, one more view and that was the view of William of Ockham. For Ockham, as it had been for Olivi, quantity is not a thing (*res*) which is really distinct and independent from substance and from quality; quantity, in fact, is seen as nothing other than the parts of substance or of quality. Ockham recognized that his position was

---

9 See below, p. 23.   10 The distinction between immediate and ultimate subjects goes back to Peter of Tarantaise. See Bakker, *La raison et le miracle*, i, p. 379.   11 Ibid., p. 305.

contrary to that of the *doctores moderni* (FitzRalph will find himself in a similar situation, but for the opposite reason), but held that no one can prove through authority or reason that quantity is a different thing from substance and quality. In his *Tractatus de corpore Christi* (*c*.1324), Ockham concluded that only the quality of the bread subsists without a subject; its quantity is not really distinct from its quality.

All of these matters might remain purely theoretical were it not for the fact that Ockham fled Avignon on 26 May 1328 and FitzRalph began lecturing on the *Sentences* that autumn. Pope John regarded Ockham's act of fleeing Avignon together with Michael of Cesena and Bonagratia as proof of his heresy and excommunicated them on 6 June 1328. Another piece of the jigsaw that we need to consider is that after the second (inconclusive) report on Ockham was delivered to John XXII, the documents were turned over to Jacques Fournier, the future Pope Benedict XII, for his opinion, and friend of Bishop Grandisson, who would soon become FitzRalph's patron. The young FitzRalph must have known that he would have to tread warily when it came to the question on the Eucharist.

EXAMINATION OF THE TEXT[12]

The principal question
The principal question is, in fact, a typical one: Is all of Christ to be found in the Eucharist under the appearances of bread and wine? Paul Bakker, for example, has edited a threefold edition of a question of Durandus of Saint Pourçain to which he has given a title that is more or less the same as the one we are dealing with here: *Utrum totus Christus sit in sacramento eucharistie*.[13] As Bakker points out, the topic could be quite a controversial one. Two of the views that Durandus expressed on this question got him into trouble and two catalogues of his errors were compiled, the first dating from 1314 and the second dating from 1316 or 1317, where errors meant where he deviated from Aquinas. Durandus was censured for giving an explanation of the Eucharist in terms of a relation (*habitus* or *ordo*) between the body of Christ and the species of the consecrated bread. The second error was Durandus' opinion according to which Christ's sacramental body does not have quantity.[14] The problem of Eucharistic presence for the medieval theologian was not, it seems, helped by the confession that Berengar of Tours was forced to make at the Council of Rome in 1059:

12 A critical edition of the text of the question on the Eucharist has been edited by the present author and is to be found on the webpage of the FitzRalph Critical Edition Project: http://philosophy.nuim.ie/projects-research/projects/richard-fitzralph/.   13 P.J.J.M. Bakker, 'Durandus of Saint-Pourçain on Eucharistic presence: with a threefold edition of Durandus' question *Utrum totus Christus sit in sacramento eucharistie* (Sent. IV, d. 10, q. 2)' in Forrai et al. (eds), *The Eucharist in theology and philosophy*, pp 229–79.   14 Ibid., p. 230: *quod corpus Christi potest esse in altari sine hoc quod quantitas sua sit ibi* ...

that the bread and wine, placed on the altar, are not only a sacrament, but also the real body and blood of our Lord Jesus Christ and that this body and blood are touched and broken by the hands of the priest and chewed by the teeth of the faithful.[15]

This statement found its way into the collections of canon law and especially the *Decretum* of Gratian and then in the *Book of Sentences* of Peter Lombard, IV, dist. 12, c. 3, where it is attached to the opinion that 'that the body of Christ is essentially broken and divided and yet remains complete and incorruptible'. The opinion implies that the real body of Christ, both substance and accidents, is really contained within the consecrated host. Now, how is one to explain that a human body with its own quantity is contained within a small piece of bread? Again, as Bakker points out, from the time of Alexander of Hales theologians agree that the whole body of Christ with its own quantity is present, not only in the consecrated host as a whole, but also in every single part of it.[16] Thus, a theological problem related to Eucharistic presence needs to be clarified in relation to quantity, position and place, which are philosophical themes.

This is some of the background at least to what is happening when FitzRalph frames his thirteen principal arguments at the beginning of the *quaestio* and to which, unfortunately for us, he never responded. We might regard these thirteen arguments as thought-experiments devised to test how we think about a particular matter and then to come up with better arguments for a position where the conclusion is already decided as it is in this case by Peter Lombard, whose authority is invoked to state that those who hold that Christ is not fully present in the Eucharist are heretics, therefore all of Christ is present under the appearances of bread and wine. Nonetheless, the thought-experiments are quite striking and we will look at one or two in a moment. The question is where did these arguments come from? Did these form part of his teaching? Perhaps the *argumenta principalia* came from the classroom in either Oxford or Paris? That FitzRalph composed them himself is perhaps suggested by the fact he writes '*arguo*' at the beginning of the *quaestio*, whereas at the beginning of the article it is '*arguitur*'.

The principal arguments
The reader is directed to the text for an understanding of all of the principal arguments that FitzRalph puts forward. In what follows, I have simply concentrated on some *notabilia* and have selected some of the arguments to examine.

The first argument is typical of the kind of thought experiment that FitzRalph constructs. Since the Eucharist was instituted before Christ's passion, one of the apostles at the time of the crucifixion could have consecrated the

---

15 Ibid., p. 231. 16 Ibid.

Eucharist in the temple at Jerusalem. If this had happened, then all of Christ would have been present under the species of bread and wine. Therefore, Christ's passion and death would also take place there in the temple because they were taking place in Christ's body. Therefore, the crucifixion took place in the temple and so, reaching the limits of absurdity, the cross was also in the temple.[17]

Arguments 2–4 continue the theme of what would have happened if one of the apostles said mass at the time when Christ was on the cross, the central idea being that if Christ's body is really present in the Eucharist then Christ's body is in two places simultaneously:

> 2 Would the vinegar he drank and the nails in his hands be in the temple and then in heaven?[18]
> 3 Those crucifying Christ must be physically present to Christ's body; therefore, they too must be in the temple.[19]
> 4 If mass was said at the moment Christ died, it would be false to say in the person of Christ 'this is my body', since Christ's soul was no longer united to a body.[20]

---

[17] Et arguo quod non, quia ex quo modus consecrandi fuit institutus ante passionem Christi sic quod tempore passionis Christi in monte Calvarie aliquis apostolorum consecrasset in templo in Ierusalem, quo facto, arguitur sic: si Christus totus fuit sub speciebus panis et uini in templo, ergo passio Christi et eius mors tunc fuit ibi, quia illa passio fuit subiectiue in corpore Christi; ergo fuit ubi<cun>que corpus Christi <fuerit>. Et ulterius sequitur quod Christus tunc moriebatur in templo, quia ibi anima eius separabatur a corpore, et per consequens Christus fuit crucifixus in templo; quod falsum est. Et consequencia patet, quia Christus non moriebatur nisi per crucifixionem, ergo ubi<cun>que Christus moriebatur, ibi fuit eius crucifixio per quam moriebatur; et ubicunque fuit crucifixio Christi, ibi Christus fuit crucifixus; et ita sequitur quod Christus fuit crucifixus in templo. Set manifestum est quod Christus non fuit crucifixus nisi ibi fuit eius crux; ergo crux Christi tempore passionis fuit in templo; quod falsum est.   18 Preterea, retento casu priori, scilicet quod tempore passionis aliquis apostolorum consecrasset in templo, sequitur, si totus Christus sit in sacramento altaris, quod Christus tunc fuit in templo; ergo quicquid fuit in Christo, tunc illud fuit in templo; set acetum quod Christus bibit et claui suarum manuum tunc fuerunt in Christo, ergo acetum et claui tunc fuerunt in celo; quod falsum est.   19 Preterea, retento priori casu, sequitur quod Christus tempore passionis fuit in templo sub speciebus panis et vini, et per consequens sua passio fuit tunc in templo; ergo tempore passionis accio Iudeorum fuit in templo, cum sua accio fuit passio Christi; set inpossibile est aliquam accionem agentis alicui esse nisi ubi agens agit; ergo Iudei crucifigentes Ihesum tempore passionis egerunt in templo; et ita sequitur quod ipsi tunc fuerunt in templo, uel quod aliquod agens egit in distans ab illo et non prius in medium, quod est inpossibile, quia nec Deus potest sic agere.   20 Preterea, retento casu priori, scilicet quod aliquis apostolorum consecrasset in templo in instanti mortis Christi in cruce, tunc illud pronomen «*meum*» cum apostolus ille dixit consecrando «hoc est corpus meum» aut significabat Christum aut illum consecrantem; non illum consecrantem, quia tunc ipse dixisset «hoc est corpus meum» quia sarcerdos numquam dicit illa verba nisi in persona Christi; nec illud pronomen tunc significabat Christum, quia similiter tunc ille consecrans dixisset falsum tunc, quia illud corpus tunc non fuit corpus Christi, quia Christus tunc non fuit homo, cum anima fuerit separata a corpore; ergo tunc nec habuit animam nec corpus.

Other problems are now raised in arguments 5, 8, 10 and 11:

> 5 Let us say that all of the blood that was spilt from the cross was collected and kept in a church until the day of judgment; since priests are consecrating the blood of Christ every day, either they are consecrating the same blood as Christ did at the Last Supper or other blood; if other blood the sacrament then and the sacrament now is not the same ... if the priests consecrate the same blood as that of the Last Supper, then since Christ converted the wine into the same blood as was shed on the cross, so the priests who now consecrate that blood, that is, the blood that is being kept in the church until the day of judgment, which is impossible because it is not now part of Christ's body.[21]
>
> 8 When the host moves does Christ move as well? And if two or more priests were moving hosts at the same time that means that the body of Christ is moving simultaneously in different directions.[22]
>
> 10 On the different types of bread used in the Eucharist (something that is dealt with below by Chris Schabel).[23]
>
> 11 The form of words instituting the Eucharist in the gospel of Luke is not that used by the Church.[24]

---

[21] Preterea, supposito quod totus sanguis qui effusus erat in cruce, fuisset collectus et positus in aliqua ecclesia usque ad finalem iudicium; istud enim, etsi non sit uerum, est tamen possibile; quo supposito, non minus adhuc cotidie possent sacerdotes consecrare; ergo <aut> conficerent de uino illum sanguinem quem Christus ex uino conficit in cena Domini, aut alium sanguinem; si alium, ergo non esset nunc idem sacramentum quod tunc, nec uerba usitata nunc haberent eandem uim nec eandem significationem sicud in cena Domini: que omnia falsa sunt. Si dicatur quod sacerdotes nunc conficerent eundem sanguinem quem Christus confecit in cena Domini, posito casu priori, cum Christus in cena confecit sanguinem suum tunc effundendum in cruce, sicud patet per uerba consecrata que tunc Christus dixit «hic est sanguis, et cetera, qui pro multis effundetur», sequitur quod sacerdotes illum sanguinem effusum nunc conficerent, posito predicto casu, scilicet quod ille sanguis fuisset conservatus in aliqua ecclesia usque ad finalem iudicium. Consequens inpossibile, quia tunc in sacramento altaris nunc esset aliquod corpus quod nec esset Christus nec pars Christi scilicet ille sanguis qui nunc non esset pars Christi; manifestum est, si esset predicto modo conseruatus. [22] Preterea, si totus Christus sit sub speciebus sacramenti, aut ergo mouetur corpus Christi quando hostia consecrata defertur localiter a sacerdote, aut non. Si sic, ergo corpus Christi simul mouetur motibus contrariis, et simul accedit ad aliquem locum et recedit ab illo; quod non uidetur intelligibile. Si dicatur quod Christus non mouetur nec eciam eius corpus, quando hostia consecrata defertur localiter, _ contra: quando sacerdos deffert hostiam consecratam ad aliquem infirmum, tunc corpus Christi continue magis appropinquat illi infirmo et magis; ergo sequitur necessario quod corpus Christi tunc mutatur localiter. [23] See below, p. 133 and n. 17. [24] Preterea, si Christus sit sub speciebus sacramenti panis et uini tunc per uerba sacerdotis uinum conuerteretur in sanguinem Christi; et si hoc, tunc illa conuersio fieret per certa uerba, sicud conuersio panis fit per certa uerba, ita quod per alia fieri non potest. Set consequens est falsum, quia Luce 22 dicitur quod Christus in consecrando dixit «hic est calix noui testamenti in meo sanguine»; ergo per ista uerba potest esse consecracio; et ecclesia utitur in consecrando hiis uerbis «hic est sanguis meus»; et per illa uerba precise fit conuersio sicud dicit Augustinus in libro *De sacramentis*, omelia quarta, et habetur *De consecracione*, dist. secunda, et allegat illud dictum Magister, 4 libro, dist. 8, cap. 6: «omnia autem

In the ninth principal argument, the matter of the Eucharistic accidents is referred to. FitzRalph raises the objection that if all of Christ is in the Eucharist, then since there is no other substance under the accidents of bread and wine other than Christ's body and blood, the accidents do not inhere in a subject. This is impossible and involves contradictories, since the definition of an accident is to inhere in another. In fact, this is what the word 'accidens' (falling into) means. Therefore, if the accidents have no subject, they are not accidents but substances, which is false.[25]

The division of the question
The division of the question (*decisio quaestionis*) follows:

> In this question I will proceed as follows: firstly, I will examine whether the accidents of the Eucharist are there without a subject; then I will state what are the opinions of the doctors; and finally I will reply to the question.[26]

There was, as it happens, no reply to the question, but there is an article that examines the accidents of the Eucharist and the opinions of some recent doctors, namely, Thomas Aquinas, Henry of Ghent and Duns Scotus. Their views are examined in detail by FitzRalph, before he gives his answer to the article.

The article
Now FitzRalph proposes the unique article of this question: 'Whether the accidents in the Eucharist are there without a subject' (*Vtrum accidencia in sacramento altaris sint ibi sine subiecto*). Many of the arguments that are put forward relate to the fact that to the senses the accidents of the Eucharist seem like they are in any other kind of composed body: they have weight (arg. 1), they act and are acted upon (arg. 2), and they are affected by heat (arg. 3, 5). Other changes seem to affect the consecrated host: the host is the body of Christ; if it rots and a worm is produced, where did the matter come from? Is there another matter in the host besides the body of Christ, which produces the worm and allows it to eat and be nourished? (arg. 4).[27] If a consecrated host is received by

---

reliqua non sunt nisi laudes et oraciones», sicud dicitur ibi; ergo uidetur quod non sit aliqua certa forma consecrandi uinum. **25** Preterea, si totus Christus sit in sacramento altaris, cum sub speciebus panis non sit alia substancia, sequitur quod accidencia panis ibi sint sine subiecto. Consequens inpossibile et includens contradictoria cum diffinitio accidentis sit «inesse alteri»; et eciam hoc inportatur per hoc nomen «accidens»; ergo si sint sine subiecto, sequitur quod non sint accidencia set substancie, quia per se subsistunt, sicud angeli; ergo species panis in sacramento sunt substancie abstracte; quod falsum est. **26** In ista questione sic procedam: primo tractabo utrum accidencia in sacramento altaris sint ibi sine subiecto, et recitabo opiniones doctorum circa hoc; et postea dicam ad questionem. **27** Preterea, ex hostia consecrata potest per putrefaccionem generari aliquod conpositum naturale sicud vermis; ergo in hostia est aliqua materia

a communicant, it is digested and so ceases to exist as the sacrament of the body of Christ; therefore, a natural body is now in the place where the body of Christ was. Is this a new body or is it the old one back again? It must be a new body produced from the pre-existent matter and not from the matter of Christ; therefore there is another matter alongside the body of Christ and this is what the accidents of bread and wine inhere in (arg. 6).[28] Further arguments follow that suggest there is another matter in the host alongside the matter of the body of Christ and this is shown by the fact that men and animals can be nourished by eating consecrated hosts (arg. 7);[29] that the host can be crushed, bent, heated and broken[30] by a natural agent shows there is ordinary matter there (arg. 8 and 9).

Against these arguments, according to FitzRalph, is the position of the church, which does not hold that the accidents of bread and wine inhere in the Eucharist in the manner of a composed body. Again, Peter Lombard states in book IV, distinction 12 that the accidents of the bread and wine – namely taste, weight, smell and the other accidents – are there without a subject; that is, they do not inhere in anything because they are not in the body of Christ; nor is there another subject, and so they are not in any subject.[31]

In what follows, we shall see, as often happens in FitzRalph, that he will go for the philosophical aspects of a problem rather than the theological or spiritual.

prima, saltem que potest remanere in generato; et per consequens accidencia sacramenti sunt in illa materia. 28 Preterea, hostia recepta ab uno communicato tandem digeritur et non semper manet in illo remanente. Accepto ergo in primo instanti in quo hostia est corrupta, tunc in illo instanti est aliquod corpus naturale in loco illo in quo hostia prius fuit, quia ibi in illo instanti non est aliquod sacramentum; ergo tunc in illo situ est aliquod corpus naturale, uel locus ille est uacuus, quod est inpossibile. Et si in illo instanti sit in illo toto situ aliquod corpus naturale, aut ergo est ibi corpus de nouo generatum, quod esse non potest ubi prefuisset materia et tunc fuerunt accidencia in illa materia, aut in illo situ in illo instanti est corpus sicud prius fuit circumstans. Et si hoc, cum <in> illo instanti corrumpitur, et alia pars hostie sequitur secundum se totam, quia est aliqua minima quantitas istius naturaliter sicud aliarum rerum naturalium, sequitur quod corpus circumstans illam partem mouetur ad centrum illius partis, et per consequens motus localis sit in instanti a corpore naturali, quod est inpossibile. Relinquitur ergo quod quando hostia degeritur in homine communicato quod generatur tunc in situ illius unum corpus naturale ex materia preexistente in illo situ et non ex materia Christi; ergo ibi est alia materia cum materia Christi; et per consequens accidencia sunt in illa materia. 29 Preterea, homo potest nutriri ex hostiis consecratis sicud multi sunt experti, ergo hostia potest conuerti in materia membri animalis. Et per consequens in hostia consecrata est aliqua materia; aliter enim per hostias consecratas <non> posset aliquod deperditum de corpore animali restaurari. Hugh of St Cher was concerned with the question as to whether the accidents of the bread and wine can still nourish and accepts the view of Prepositinus of Cremona, who held that they did just as if the substance of the bread and wine were still present even if for Hugh this is miraculous. However, for Hugh although the accidents can satiate hunger and thirst, they cannot nourish. See Bakker, La raison et le miracle, i, p. 292. 30 William of Auxerre concentrated upon the problem of the breaking of the host in the Summa aurea, IV, tract. 7, c. 6, 162. See. Bakker, La raison et le miracle, i, p. 294. 31 Oppositum tenet fides ecclesie, sicut patet in legenda novi testamenti de hoc sacramento. Et Magister declarat dist. 12, quarti libri, quod accidencia panis et uini, scilicet sapor, pondus, et odor et alia accidencia, sunt sine subiecto quia non sunt in corpore Christi; nec est ibi aliud subiectum; et ideo non sunt in alico subiecto.

Trying to explain and justify transubstantiation forces thinkers to consider something they might have just passed over – the nature of accidents in themselves and how they are interrelated. Indeed, if we take the common view that all qualities inhere in quantity, then we have the interesting idea that all of the qualitative aspects of things are reduced to their measurable properties and that quantity can serve as a subject for all of the qualities. At this stage, one might raise the question as to why then do we need the notion of substance at all?

The opinions of the doctors
FitzRalph now examines the opinions of three doctors: Henry of Ghent, Thomas Aquinas and Duns Scotus. Here, as elsewhere, FitzRalph seems to demonstrate a loyalty to Henry as a secular master; he regards Aquinas as the one whose views are the clearest on the matter, and Scotus as the one he has to engage with.

FitzRalph explains Henry's position as follows. Henry, he writes, holds that all of the accidents of the Eucharist have the same potency to act and to be acted upon just as if they were in matter and this by a miracle. If, then, we take this miracle as given, then no new miracle is needed in order to explain how these accidents nourish, or that a worm can be generated from them. Henry puts forward two ways in which we can envisage how a worm or any body can be produced from these accidents. Firstly, since these species have been altered (through the consecration) inasmuch as the body of Christ lies under them, then at the first instant in which the body of Christ no longer lies under them, the substantial form of the worm or any other thing is produced without there being any matter at all. The same is true of the food that the worm eats, which must also, like the worm, be composed of matter and form. For Henry, all of this happens according to nature and no new miracle is needed if the first is accepted. For this is better than saying that a completely new miracle happened or that is was partly by nature or partly be a miracle, since God disposes all things – as Augustine says, 'he lets each one have its own movement'.[32] The *second way* is that the accidents were not only in potency to the substantial forms but also in

---

32 Et ponit duos modos subtiles quibus ymaginatur quod ex illis speciebus generetur uermis uel aliquod corpus. Quorum <modorum> primus est quod cum fuerint ille species alterate in tantum quod corpus Christi debeat esse sub eis, tunc in primo instanti in quo corpus Christi non est sub illis speciebus, generatur forma substancialis uermis uel alterius rei sine materia aliqua. Et est ibidem conpositum unum secundum accidens ex forma substanciali et accidentibus; et postea, adueniente cibo, per uirtutem nutritiuam alteratur ille cibus quousque corrumpatur eius forma substancialis, qua corrumpta, materia illius cibi substernitur forme substanciali uermis et eius dimensionibus et accidentibus; et fit uermis conpositum uere unum ex forma substanciali et materia que prefuit sub forma cibi habens sua accidencia propria, ita, dicit ipse, ut ponatur hoc totum fieri uirtute nature, primo miraculo presupposto. Hoc enim melius est quam ascribere hoc nouo miraculo totaliter, aut partim nature et partim miraculo, quia Deus sic administrat res, dicit ipse, ut dicit Augustinus quod sinit eas habere motus proprios.

potency to a *compositum*, such that matter is produced out of them just like a form, so that there is no miracle nor an act of creation.[33]

FitzRalph produces nine arguments against the first way. In the sixth argument, FitzRalph turns Henry's argument against him: Henry says that you cannot understand what a man is without his bones and flesh; thus, the worm cannot be a form only together with the accidents of the eucharist [therefore, there must be another matter there acting as a subject].[34] In the seventh, FitzRalph puts forward an argument to the effect that the accident of quantity, it seems, would be sufficient to support all natural forms just like matter; and in the eighth argument, quantity and the other accidents could be substances because they are a sufficient subject.[35] Against the second way (that from the species not only can substantial forms be produced but also the matter in a natural fashion), FitzRalph states that it does not seem convincing to him, but it is more probable, as Henry himself acknowledges.[36]

FitzRalph now moves on to examine the opinion of Thomas Aquinas. Thomas, he states, holds that quantity in the Eucharist remains without a subject and that all of the other accidents exist in quantity just as if it were a subject. Aquinas also holds that these accidents can act as both matter and substantial forms and so can be corrupted, such that a worm is produced or ash or another substance, just as if they were in the substance of the bread.[37] FitzRalph

---

33 Secundus modus, dicit ipse, est magis congruus; et est quod illa accidencia non solum fuerunt in potencia ad formas substanciales, set eciam ad conpositum, scilicet ad hoc quod materia producatur ex eis sicud forma illa, ita quod non erit aliquod miraculum neque noua creacio. Nec est hic alia difficultas nisi quod ponitur quod substancia materie ita reciperet nouum esse in conposito sicud substancia forme, quod non contingit in aliis generacionibus naturalibus. Hec iste doctor sub conpendio, 8 Quodlibet, q. 36.   34 Preterea, 5 Quodlibet, q. 14 «Vtrum homo possit esse sine quantitate», dicit quod non, quia partes quantitatiue, sicud caro et os, sunt necessaria de sua essencia; ymmo dicit quod inpossibile est intelligere hominem sine carnibus et ossibus; ergo nec uermis ille potest esse sola forma cum accidentibus sacramenti, ut dicit.   35 7. ... ex quo quantitas ita sufficit ad sustentandum formas naturales sicud materia ... 8. Preterea, sequitur quod quantitas et cetera accidencia sint substancie, quia subsunt accidentibus sicud sufficiens subiectum; ergo, cum hoc sit proprium substancie, ut patet in *Predicamentis* sequitur quod sunt uere substancie et non amplius accidencia.   36 Quantum ad secundum modum ponendi, scilicet quod ex illis speciebus potest generari non solum forma substancialis, set <eciam> materia per generacionem naturalem, non uidetur michi rationabile; hoc tamen est probabilius michi quam primum dictum, et hoc ipse fatetur.   37 Doctor Communis, quarta parte *Scripti*, dist. 12, art. 1, q. 1, tenet quod quantitas in sacramento altaris manet sine subiecto et quod omnia alia accidencia existent in quantitate sicud in subiecto. Et questione secunda, dicit quod illa accidencia agunt et materiam et formas substanciales et ita possunt corrumpi, ita ut generetur uermis uel cinis uel alia substancia eodem modo sicud si essent in substancia panis. Set tunc, dicit ipse in responsione quarta, quamuis quod hoc fuit sic quod generacione alterius substancie simul per comitantiam generetur noua materia aut quod quantitati interminate que prefuit in pane tribuatur a Deo natura materie propter eius propinquitatem ad materiam ita ut generatum sit conpositum ex materia et forma. Et sic dicit in questione quinta illius questionis secunde, quod species sacramenti nutriunt per modum eundem quo ex eis aliquid generetur ita quod non solum hominem set eciam sustentant corpus.

produces nine arguments against Thomas' position, including the following points:

> **arg. 1** Fire acting on the host causes heat naturally and so transmits its accidents and its substantial form; thus there is a different substantial form in the Eucharist than Christ;[38]
> **arg. 3** Aristotle says that one accident cannot be in another, so quality cannot be in quantity;[39]
> **arg. 5** If this is the case then it is useless to posit the existence of matter [at all], since quantity can sustain any form; indeed, no philosopher could prove the necessary existence of matter;[40]
> **arg. 6** Following this line of argumentation would lead us to concede that quantity is a substance.[41]

It seems to me that FitzRalph deals with the opinion of Scotus in more detail than the opinions of the previous two doctors because of its obvious impact on the contemporary discussions, overshadowed as they must have been by the flight of Ockham from Avignon and his condemnation as well as the presence of Ockham's supporters in Oxford at the time when FitzRalph was lecturing. As regards Scotus, FitzRalph goes straight to the point: Scotus holds that quantity can be without a subject if it is a thing (*res*) other than a substance, but whether it is or not, Scotus never said.[42] A discussion begins which focuses on the distinction between relative and absolute accidents: an absolute accident is one that has some kind of reality besides that of being a mere modification of a substance, and Scotus concedes that there are two such absolute accidents – namely quantity and quality – that can exist without a subject. FitzRalph examines five arguments against Scotus' position and concludes that it has been disproved by the modern doctors; but as regards the rest, he agrees with Scotus – namely that in the sacrament of the Eucharist the accidents remain without a subject properly speaking, that is, a substance; 'even if some accidents which are extraneous are attributed to others as subjects just like secondary qualities are

---

38 Secundum illud sequitur quod ignis agens in hostiam causet suam caliditatem naturaliter agendo, set naturaliter accione eius non separatur eius accidens a forma sua substanciali; ergo causat simul suam formam substancialem et erit in sacramento alia substancia quam pars Christi uel Christus, quod ipse dicit hereticum quia tunc esset falsum «hoc est corpus meum». 39 Preterea, Philosophus, 4 Metafisice, expresse dicit quod accidens non accidit accidenti nisi quia ambo accidunt alicui eidem subiecto quia nichil hoc illi magis accidit quam illud huic; ergo nulla qualitas est subiectiue in quantitate. 40 Preterea, si sic tunc frustra ponatur materia aliqua, cum quantitas sufficienter posset sustenere quamcunque formam; ymmo nullus philosophus posset probare eius necessitatem. 41 Preterea, tunc quantitas esset substancia, quia uere substaret accidentibus quod est proprium substancie secundum Philosophum in *Predicamentis*. 42 Doctor Subtilis, 4 libro, dist. 12, q. 2, tenet quod quantitas est sine subiecto si sit alia res a substancia; set utrum sit alia res uel non ipse non diffinit.

attributed to primary qualities and all qualities are reduced to quantity'. He continues:

> whether quantity is something other than substance and quality, I will say nothing [more] for the moment; I do not say that if quantity is posited there that it has a being in itself like a substance, so that it is properly speaking the subject of the qualities as Aquinas states; on the contrary ... it is not the subject of quality except in an improper way of speaking just like a quality is [said to be] the subject of another quality.[43]

Response to the article

Finally, we come to the response, and FitzRalph refers to two opinions: that of Aquinas and that of Scotus (Henry of Ghent's has disappeared along the way in the unfinished editorial process and some manuscripts do not contain the text we examined above).[44] He concedes that Aquinas' opinion that quantity is something other than substance or quality is something that is commonly held by the majority of teachers. Thus, all of them hold that all of the accidents of the Eucharist (except quantity of course) inhere in quantity, and that they are there without a subject, and have the potential through the power of God to receive accidents just as if they were in a substance. If we follow the opinion of Aquinas, FitzRalph states, many arguments and difficulties are avoided, and could not be solved if we did not hold that quality is something other than quantity.[45]

Then he states that there is another opinion, that of the contemporary teachers who hold that quality is extended in itself (*quanta*), and so also is any natural thing; nor do they posit any quantity other than substance and quality.

---

[43] Oportet multa argumentare contra istam posicionem quia satis inprobata est a uenerabilibus doctoribus modernis. Quo tamen ad aliud quod iste doctor dicit in isto articulo uidetur michi dicendum esse cum illo, scilicet quod in sacramento altaris accidencia manent sine subiecto proprie dicto, scilicet substancia, licet aliqua accidencia ibi extranea attribuuntur aliis tanquam subiectis sicud qualitates secundarie attribuuntur primis et omnes qualitates sic attribuuntur quantitati. Set quantitas est aliud a substancia et a qualitate de quo nichil dico ad presens; non tamen dico quod quantitas si ponatur ibi habet esse per se sicud substancia ut sit subiectum proprie dictum qualitatum, sicud ponit Doctor Communis, ymmo si ponatur ibi quantitas alia a qualibet qualitate, illa non est subiectum alicuius qualitatis nisi inproprie quomodo qualitas est subiectum alterius. [44] In fact, the opinion of Henry is to be found only in the Worcester and Oriel College manuscripts, which preserve the 'Oxfordian' tradition of the text of the *Lectura* and not in the other manuscripts, which preserve the Parisian tradition. [45] In isto articulo ergo ut uidetur est duplex opinio. Vna opinio est opinio Thomae scilicet quod quantitas est alia res a substancia et a qualitatibus et est communiter omnium doctorum. Et secundum hoc ponunt quod omnia accidencia sacramenti preter quantitatem sunt subiectiue in quantitate, et quod ipsa est sine subiecto, et habet uirtutem per potenciam. Dicitur simili modo recipiendum accidencia sicud habuit quando fuit in substancia. Et secundum istam opinionem euacuantur argumenta multa et plures difficultates que non ita soluuntur ponendo quod quantitas non est aliud a substancia et a qualitate. Et hanc opinionem dicit Doctor Communis, 4 libro, dist. 12, art. 1, q. 1.

Following this opinion, we have to state that all of the accidents of the Eucharist remain without a subject properly speaking, as Scotus states. However, both opinions agree that in the Eucharist there is no substance in which the accidents of bread and wine inhere. FitzRalph concludes: 'But whether we should hold that quantity is something other than substance or quality, I do not think that I should deal with at the moment since this is something which should be dealt with in another faculty'.[46] How should we interpret this closing statement of FitzRalph? Might it have been the case that he was lecturing in the arts faculty in philosophy at the same time and would deal with the problem there, or was he merely indicating that it was not a theological problem but one for the philosophers to sort out? Or was he fluffing it and refusing to deal with what was one of the burning issues in theology of the day, namely the views of Ockham? FitzRalph's words are a curious echo of a similar statement made by Ockham himself, however: '*Sed quia hoc* [the debate on the nature of quantity] *pertinent a logicum magis quam ad theologum, ideo pertranseo*'.[47] Perhaps FitzRalph was using Ockham against Ockham's supporters?

As Gabriel Buescher wrote in his classic 1950 treatment of Ockham on the Eucharist,

> For Ockham, the reality of quantity as an entity separate from substance and quality can be disposed of without embarrassment. He insists that everything which can be explained by the hypothesis that quantity is a distinct entity can be salvaged equally well without postulating a distinct entity for quantity.[48]

He goes on to make the point, as many commentators have done in this regard, that for Ockham quantity is a connotative term that signifies either a substance or a quality; an absolute term signifies some entity as such; a connotative term signifies some thing and tells us something about it. Here, Ockham was, of course, going against the common opinion, for most scholastic philosophers and theologians taught that quantity is a reality distinct from substance and quality. As regards the question of the inherence of the accidents of the bread and wine, most of the scholastics agree that the accidents that remain after the consecration do not inhere in any substance as in a subject.[49] That these remaining

---

46 Alia est opinio modernorum ponencium qualitatem est quantam per se, et similiter quamlibet rem materialem, nec ponit aliquam1 quantitatem preter substanciam et qualitatem. Et secundum istam opinionem oportet dicere accidencia omnia in sacramento altaris manere sine subiecto proprie dicto, sicud dicit Doctor Subtilis. Vtramque tamen opinio concordat in hoc quod in sacramento eukaristie non est aliqua substancia subiecta accidentibus sacramenti. Set utrum quantitas alia sit ponenda quam substancia uel qualitas non uidetur michi nunc esse insistendum, quia hoc magis pertinet ad alias scolas.   47 *De corpore Christi*, c. 31; quoted in G. Buescher, *The Eucharistic teaching of William Ockham* (New York, 1950), p. 74.   48 Buescher, *The Eucharistic teaching of William Ockham*, p. 67.   49 Ibid., pp 119–20.

accidents cannot inhere in the substance of the bread and wine is clear from Ockham's definition of transubstantiation, which postulates the annihilation of these two substances. Thus, Ockham is forced into a different opinion from the common one. He needs to postulate that God causes each of the remaining accidents to exist per se, without a subject. Applying his notion that quantity is a connotative term to the Eucharist, he is logically obliged to teach that the quantity of the bread does not remain after the consecration, since its substance is annihilated. Each of the qualities, insofar as it was extended before the consecration and remains so afterwards, is quantity. But these qualities do not inhere in quantity as in a subject, but subsist per se, without any subject of inherence.[50]

As Buescher points out,

> The logic of Ockham's position is this: Quantity is not a distinct entity separate from the substance and the qualities of the unconsecrated host. Consequently, after the consecration the absolute qualities of the host cannot be subjectively in quantity as in a subject, since quantity is not a reality with a distinct and individual existence. Before the consecration, of course, these various quantified qualities inhere in the substance of the bread as in their proper subject. After the consecration, however, these same extended qualities continue to exist as previously, save for this that now each, by divine intervention, exists per se and without any subject of inherence.[51]

Ockham seems, however, to have had a certain misgiving as to its authenticity. Writing in the *Summa totius logicae* (p. 1, c. 44, 17v) he states:

> There is another opinion which, it seems to me, is in accordance with the thought of Aristotle, but since it is unclear whether it is heretical or orthodox, I will recount it rather than assert it ... The opinion, namely, which many Catholics put forward and many theologians hold and have held in the past is that no quantity is really distinct from substance and quality.[52]

Although FitzRalph does not deal directly with Ockham's views, it should, of course, be kept in mind that many of the people with whom FitzRalph was directly involved did hold views such as these and defended Ockham on this point and on others.

---

50 Ibid., p. 124. 51 Ibid. 52 Quoted by Buescher, *The Eucharistic teaching of William Ockham*, p. 124.

The replies to the principal arguments
Very lengthy replies now follow to eight of the nine arguments put forward at the beginning of the question. Among the replies, the following points are worthy of note:

> **Resp. ad 1** FitzRalph begins by stating that Thomas holds that a natural power in everything apart from God is something other than its substance, proving by this that the powers of the human mind are really distinct. If we accept this, then it can be stated that weight (*gravitas*), which is the immediate principle of the movement of an element, is not the substantial form of an element but rather quality is; but Aristotle sometimes calls heaviness and lightness the substances of the elements and sometimes accidents. However, he states that the opinion of Thomas was disproved by him in the questions of the *Lectura* dealing with the parts of the image of the Trinity. FitzRalph concludes that in the host there is some formal principle other than God, according to which the host resists upward movement and that this principle is its hardness and its continuative principle.[53]
>
> **Resp. ad 2** FitzRalph gives two replies to the second argument; one is based on Thomas and the other on Scotus. While admitting that Scotus' view makes it more difficult to solve the question, he concludes after a long and exhaustive treatment of the various positions by stating: 'You have heard two answers, choose whichever one you wish!'[54]
>
> **Resp. ad 4** FitzRalph states that the corruption of the host is only possible if God creates the contrary qualities to cause putrefaction; therefore, God recreates the matter that was previously in the host before the consecration and makes this into the matter of the worm. FitzRalph concludes by stating that he cannot see how it is possible otherwise for a worm to be produced out of a consecrated host by means of putrefaction, whether one holds that quantity exists as a subject or not.
>
> **Resp. ad 6** When a host is digested, the aggregate of accidents that were in the bread is digested; at the first instant in which the host is corrupted, there is a natural body in the place of the host and this is created by God.

---

53 The term 'continutatiua uirtus' is to be found in the *Sentences Commentary* of Franciscus de Marchia (ed. Schabel, IV, q. 1), who lectured on the *Sentences* in 1320: Quod etiam potest declarari ex parte caeli sic: quanto aliquod mobile est magis oboediens moventi et non resistens sibi, tanto magis est susceptivum influentiae moventis ex parte sua, quia 'actus activorum sunt in patiente praedisposito,' II *De anima*;17 sed caelum est magis oboediens intelligentiae moventi quam sit lapis vel medium ipsi manui moventi, quia minus caelum resistit motui quam lapis vel medium manui; sed a manu relinquitur aliqua virtus in medio vel in lapide, secundum Commentatorem ubi prius [*In Physicam* VIII, comm. 82]; ergo multo magis ab intelligentia causari potest in caelo aliqua virtus continuativa motus.   54 Audistis duas responsiones, eligatis quem uolueritis.

The text ends abruptly at the beginning of the answer to the eighth principal argument (no answers to arguments nine to thirteenth have been preserved). It seems, as I have already mentioned, that the principal arguments were introduced later, when FitzRalph was editing his text for publication rather than when he was actually lecturing on the *Sentences* in 1328-9. At a distance of some years, and now a regent master listening to the views expressed in their own *Lecturae* by students such as Adam Wodeham, FitzRalph had the occasion to think again regarding some of the arguments that he had dealt with previously. The ongoing debates in the early 1330s seem to have pushed him in the direction of a more critical and analytical attitude towards his material than before. However, it also seems to have disenchanted him and left him somewhat sceptical regarding the possibility of these debates coming to a successful end.

CONCLUSION

FitzRalph's *Lectures* on the *Sentences* clearly had an influence, judging from the number of manuscript copies that survive and from the number of extracts made. He was quoted by some of his contemporaries and throughout the fourteenth century by other authors commenting on the *Sentences*. On the particular topic of the Eucharist, however, I have not yet identified anyone who refers to this question, apart from a reference made by Wodeham that was then picked up by Henry Totting of Oyta when he composed his abbreviation of Ockham in 1375. Wodeham dealt with the Eucharist in two questions in his commentary on book IV of the *Sentences*: Q. 4: Whether the body of Christ is really contained under the species that belonged to the bread and wine (*Vtrum corpus Christi realiter sub speciebus que fuerunt panis et uini contineatur*); and Q. 5: Whether the quantity describing [*terminata*] the bread to be consecrated is some real thing outside of the soul and reality distinct from the substance and quality to which it belongs (*Vtrum quantitas terminata panis consecrandi sit aliqua res extra animam distincta realiter a substancia et qualitate cuius est*). As Paul Bakker notes, the first question is expedited quite quickly by Wodeham, who follows Lombard on the matter.[55] The second question, however, is made up of seven articles and constitutes a long discussion with a certain number of doctors, particularly Gauthier Chatton, on the ontological status on quantity. In effect, FitzRalph is only mentioned by Wodeham once, and this is repeated by Oyta, who mentions him in the company of Ockham: *Et ita eciam repondet Adam, et dicit idem tenere Scotum, Hokam, Syraf et alios doctores multos*. The context is a discussion of how the body of Christ can be in various places at the same time and, this being the case, can God through his absolute power cause another body to be present in

---

[55] Bakker, *La raison et le miracle*, ii, p. 96.

various places at the same time? Wodeham mentions that Skelton had argued this against him and had held that, for example, if God can cause the same vase to exist in different places, then all kinds of contradictions would become true, that something could be broken and not broken at the same time, that a man could sin and yet merit eternal life and so on. Wodeham's response was to state that he did not hold that Christ was present in different places in a quantitative manner. Thus, it seems that there is no contradiction and that FitzRalph was one of those who agreed with him. All of this is very well, but there is no trace of such a discussion in FitzRalph's text! It may, however, be elsewhere in the *Lectura* of course, and this is something that may emerge when the edition is completed.

Courtenay comments that the consideration of the role of quantity by both Scotus and Ockham began a reinterpretation of the Aristotelian categories – of time, motion, place and relation – which was so fruitful in discussions in 1320s to early 1330s.[56] He goes on to state that the reinterpretation of the category of quantity and the corresponding adjustment in the understanding of transubstantiation was one of several points on which the views of Ockham and Wodeham made a common front against Chatton and others.[57] Quantity, however, is rarely dealt with after 1332 and Eucharistic theology was almost phased out in the English schools between Wodeham and Wyclif.[58]

---

56 W.J. Courtenay, *Schools and scholars in fourteenth-century England* (Princeton, 1987), p. 305.
57 Ibid.   58 Ibid. and note: 'Eucharistic questions do not appear in the Sentences commentaries of Halifax, Rosetus, Kilvington, Buckingham, Went, Monachus Niger, Langeley, Stuckeley or Aston, although Pickingham included one (q.7)'.

The influence on FitzRalph of Bishop Grandisson of Exeter: with a critical edition of Sermons 62 and 64 of FitzRalph's sermon diary[1]

MICHAEL HAREN

INTRODUCTION

My subject is conviction – in the case of Grandisson (1292–1369) a conviction that despite its quality and intensity has only recently begun to attract the attention that it merits historiographically. As late as 1955, in Roger Highfield's still fundamental review of the English hierarchy under Edward III, John Grandisson was claiming hardly more than respectable regard in terms of the categories to which he belonged – the aristocratic bishop[2] who was notably learned[3] and who in carrying on the work of his predecessor in the see of Exeter, to which he was provided in 1327 and which he held until his death in 1369, was 'for a short while ... able to command the services of the outstanding theologian, Richard FitzRalph'.[4] In the interval, it has been possible to appreciate Grandisson's outlook, government and impact more expansively, not precisely because the sources have been augmented – for the basic corpus of evidence has always been there, at least in the form of *disiecta membra* – but because the discovery of new connections between that evidence has forced at once a concentration on the whole and deductions from the whole that have enhanced understanding both of substance and of context. If the results seem obvious in terms of what was previously known, they serve merely to restate as a feature of historical inquiry that it does often arrive at what should have been obvious from the beginning. That the process of arrival is apt to appear laboured illustrates a point worth stressing, even at the risk of triteness. Overt statements of the sources are more readily absorbed than is the import of the sources' implicit content in its own right. Lively as has been the controversy over the conclusions of K.B. McFarlane's famous exposition of the wills of the so-called Lollard

---

[1] This paper was given to a session of the conference in the parish church of St Nicholas, Dundalk. I am most grateful for the hospitality shown by Revd Sandra Pragnell and the members of the congregation who attended and for their encouraging interest in the strands that combined to form the outlook of a figure, St Richard of Dundalk, in whose honour the church incorporates a chapel. [2] J.R.L. Highfield, 'The English hierarchy under Edward III', *Transactions of the Royal Historical Society*, 5th ser., 6 (1956), 115–38 at 120. [3] Ibid., 131. [4] Ibid., 124.

The influence on FitzRalph of Bishop Grandisson of Exeter

knights, those documents are unlikely perhaps to have been subjected to intensive scrutiny at all had not the chroniclers, Knighton and Walsingham, variously drawn suspicion of heterodoxy on the heads of the ten members of that debated group.[5] No chronicler tells us that Grandisson was unusual in himself, or that he attracted, sought out, patronized, putatively stimulated and in turn was stimulated by his association with figures of unusual, even extreme, persuasion. One of his critics – probably no less than the chancellor of his own cathedral – did, evidently, characterize his régime as eccentric in its 'immoderate rigour'.[6] Another, his cousin by marriage, Hugh de Courtenay, earl of Devon, not long after his entry on his diocese upbraided his 'singularity'.[7] But to notice these stray pointers the historian needs already to be looking closely. They fall into place in a pattern that has already begun to take shape. Once the pattern is discerned, however, the sources for estimating Grandisson prove ample and eloquent. The effect is twofold, at once edifying and disconcerting. As to the first, Grandisson emerges as a reforming prelate of first rank by the standards of any age. As to the second, his heightened profile raises questions about how much else the historian may be missing under the pedestrian records of administration that are often the only evidence for the quality of late medieval episcopacy.

SOURCES FOR THE CHARACTER OF GRANDISSON'S EPISCOPACY

The most important sources for the character of Grandisson's episcopacy and outlook may be conveniently listed under separate heads, not all of which, however, bear directly upon my present subject.

First, there are his episcopal acts. They were edited (1894–9) by Prebendary F.C. Hingeston-Randolph, of whom the late Dom David Knowles commented mordantly that 'His name is kept in memory, if not in benediction, by students of the Exeter episcopal registers'.[8] The judgment is too harsh, certainly in the case of Grandisson's register. The major mistake that Hingeston-Randolph made was to rearrange the register entries chronologically, thus losing the sometimes crucial connections that can be inferred from the quiring and other physical aspects of the manuscripts. (For these, there is no alternative to working on the original, as would probably be necessary, in any case, on the finer points, however faithfully the editor had proceeded.) But Hingeston-Randolph was a Latinist of his time – which is to say that by our all too often dismal modern

---

5 See K.B. McFarlane, *Lancastrian kings and Lollard knights* (Oxford, 1972), pp 139–206, 227–32. 6 *The register of John de Grandisson, bishop of Exeter (AD1327–1369)*, ed. F.C. Hingeston-Randolph (London, 1894), i, p. 224 (the unnamed correspondent's criticism must be reconstructed from Grandisson's reply). 7 Ibid., 203. 8 D. Knowles, *Great historical enterprises and problems in monastic history* (London etc., 1962), p. 114.

standards he was superb: his text is generally careful and reliable. His dedication rendered accessible in three volumes both Grandisson's record of his personal correspondence and the attentively registered general memoranda, as well as the institutions, that were his official business. Hingeston-Randolph also edited Grandisson's will, which is an important source in general, though since FitzRalph predeceased him it is not of immediate concern to me here.

Second, there is the evidence of Grandisson's ruminations on his extensive reading, witnessed to by copious annotations in the large number of surviving books known to have been owned or used by him. These have been studied minutely by Dr Margaret Steele, in a ground-breaking, richly documented, Oxford doctoral thesis, completed in 1994,[9] and with minute focus on his concern with St Augustine's *Confessiones* by Linda Olson.[10] To that literary category of witness may be loosely annexed Grandisson's own writing: he was an ardent admirer of St Thomas of Canterbury, and wrote an as yet unedited history of the martyr whose unyielding stand for ecclesiastical independence, it is not too fanciful to suggest, stiffened his own resistance to compromise. (In a happy – I believe altogether well-founded – extension of this motif, Katherine Walsh has depicted FitzRalph as 'the Becket of the Irish church'.)[11]

As a loose extension of this aspect may be noted Grandisson's appreciation of the *beaux arts*: he was a connoisseur of artistry, visual and musical, and a notable patron of ecclesiastical architecture. Several aspects of this dimension have been the subject of particular study[12] and it is strikingly illustrated in the magnificent eagle lectern bearing his arms, which he presented to his collegiate foundation of Ottery St Mary.[13] Though particular stimulus need not be invoked, the fact that Grandisson was so active a builder at Exeter may have been a factor in the plans evidently entertained by FitzRalph himself for a restoration of the cathedral fabric of Armagh.[14]

Third, within my present subject's terms, there is the potential of arguing from the particular influence upon Grandisson of Jacques Fournier, under whom, in an unusual attachment – for a secular clerk – to the Cistercian school at Paris, he had studied theology during the latter's regency there (*c*.1313–17). On the one hand we have a record of Grandisson's regard for his former mentor

9 M.A. Steele, 'A study of the books owned or used by John Grandisson, bishop of Exeter (1327–1369)' (DPhil, Oxford, 1994).   10 L. Olson, 'Reading Augustine's *Confessiones* in fourteenth-century England: John de Grandisson's fashioning of text and self', *Traditio*, 52 (1997), 201–57.   11 K. Walsh, 'Der Becket der irischen Kirche: der "Armachanus" Richard FitzRalph von Armagh (+1360), Professor – Kirchenfürst – "Heiliger"', *Innsbrucker historische Studien*, 20/21 (1999), 1–58. See especially 12–13.   12 F. Rose-Troup, *Bishop Grandisson, student and art lover* (Plymouth, 1929).   13 See H.B. Clarke and J.R.S. Phillips (eds), *Ireland, England and the Continent in the Middle Ages and beyond: essays in memory of a turbulent friar, F.X. Martin OSA* (Dublin, 2006), pl. 10.1.   14 As surmised, very plausibly, by Katherine Walsh, who refers also to the Coventry and Lichfield context in this respect in *A fourteenth-century scholar and primate: Richard FitzRalph in Oxford, Avignon and Armagh* (Oxford, 1981), p. 273.

in the highly personal letter of congratulation that he wrote him on Fournier's elevation to the papacy as Benedict XII in 1334.[15] Even with allowance for the expedience of fostering so advantageous a connexion, the terms in which he addresses him are persuasive of the impression left on the pupil by his erstwhile master: 'talem doctorem ... talem theologum' ('such a teacher ... such a theologian').[16] That this was no empty compliment is suggested by the putative testimony to the nature of Fournier's teaching provided by his voluminous Postill on the Gospel of St Matthew extant principally in Biblioteca Apostolica Vaticana, MSS Barberini Latini 600–602 and Troyes, Bibliothèque Municipale, MS 549. (The former set of manuscripts, which preserve the first eighty-nine treatises into which the work is divided, are the product in part of redaction during Benedict's pontificate, but it is a plausible hypothesis at the least that proceedings in the classroom are at their core. The Troyes manuscript, which, though palaeographically to be dated to the late fifteenth century, is by provenance from the master's old college of St Bernard in Paris, has a specific claim to witness to those proceedings.)[17] I have calculated that this Postill, though in its major transmission[18] it gets no further than the first seven chapters of the Gospel, runs to something in the order of more than a million words. (The Troyes manuscript, the most complete, has 1,687 folios – a count, however, that includes tabular apparatuses – which at their most dense contain over one thousand words per folio.) In that statistic we have surely an element of what might be termed the ferocious application to which Fournier's career as a prelate amply attests. Fournier, of course, is now immortalized for historians of all epochs by Emmanuel Le Roy Ladurie's study of the inquisition conducted by him, while bishop of Pamiers, into late Catharism in the Pyrenean uplands of the southern reaches of his diocese. That proceeding is symbolized historiographically by the single village of Montaillou, whose inhabitants Fournier summoned to appear before him and interrogated systematically while meticulously recording and collating their evidence. Le Roy Ladurie catches well Fournier's unremitting persistence and single-mindedness as an investigator and interlocutor:

> What drove him on was a desire (hateful though it was in this form) to know the truth. For him it was a matter first of detecting sinful behaviour and then of saving souls. To attain these ends he showed himself 'pedantic as a schoolman' and did not hesitate to engage in lengthy

15 *The register of John Grandisson*, ed. Hingeston-Randolph, i, pp 110–11.   16 Ibid., p. 110.
17 For a passage that seems especially pertinent to the teaching context, see M. Haren, 'Montaillou and Drogheda: a medieval twinning' in A. Meyer, C. Rendtel and M. Wittmer-Butsch (eds), *Päpste, Pilger, Pönitentiarie: Festschrift für Ludwig Schmugge zum 65. Geburtstag* (Tübingen, 2004), pp 435–56 at p. 447.   18 On the case presented by A. Maier, 'Der Kommentar Benedikts XII. zum Matthaeus-Evangelium', *Archivum Historiae Pontificiae*, 6 (1968), 398–405, Biblioteca Apostolica Vaticana, MS Borghese 32, witnesses to a further section of the commentary.

discussion. He spent a fortnight of his precious time convincing the Jew Baruch of the mystery of the Trinity, a week making him accept the dual nature of Christ and no less than three weeks of commentary explaining the coming of the Messiah.[19]

The proceeding at Pamiers and the rigour of the unpragmatic idealism that Fournier brought to the papal office can be shown from the Postill to be rooted in a radically Augustinian analysis of the human condition and the requirement that spiritual rule be on guard against the 'elation'[20] that besets fallen man: the incapacity spontaneously to maintain right order on the moral plane and the perverse resistance to its imposition from without. 'The vice of elation', says Grandisson the bishop, confronting a disputed incumbency, 'seething in the lust of domination, twists down every crooked path and more ardently seeks that which is forbidden than that which is lawful'.[21] I do not maintain that the insight was owed entirely to Fournier, but if Grandisson the student's bent was Augustinian, and one is fortunate to be able to follow how heavily engaged, precisely during his Paris sojourn, he was with Augustine's *Confessiones*, he would have found nothing in Fournier's lectures that did not solidly reinforce it.

Fourthly, and very largely, there are the clues to Grandisson's outlook offered by the views current within his circle. Grandisson was an able talent-spotter. We can see this most explicitly in the case of FitzRalph himself.[22] I do not propose to engage in the circular argument of using FitzRalph's own writings as a means of illuminating Grandisson's mind and thence of arguing for the nature of Grandisson's influence on FitzRalph. But there are no grounds for thinking that FitzRalph's views even at their most controversial and polemical would have been unacceptable to Grandisson and some grounds for thinking that they were indeed highly congenial. The issue of the friars' privileges I will deal with later. For the moment, I will repeat the suggestion that I have made elsewhere[23] that the John who is Richard's probing partner in FitzRalph's dialogue *De pauperie salvatoris* is intended to represent the engagement of Grandisson himself. Though FitzRalph began as a protégé of Grandisson, the mature relationship between them must have been one of mutual intellectual exchange and it is worth remembering that, both as a distinguished theologian of European-wide reputation and as an archbishop and metropolitan, FitzRalph was finally the

19 E. Le Roy Ladurie, *Montaillou: Cathars and catholics in a French village, 1294–1324* (London, 1980), p. xv. 20 See Haren, 'Montaillou and Drogheda', pp 450–1. 21 'Elacionis vicium estuans in libidine dominandi ad omnem tortum tramitem se divertit, et quod est prohibitum ardencius appetit quam quod licet'. *The register of John Grandisson*, ed. Hingeston-Randolph, ii, p. 1052. 22 See ibid., pp 1, 173 and M. Haren, *Sin and society in fourteenth-century England: a study of the Memoriale presbiterorum* (Oxford, 2000), pp 61–2. 23 See Michael Haren, 'Richard FitzRalph of Dundalk, Oxford and Armagh: scholar, prelate and controversialist' in James McEvoy and Michael Dunne (eds), *The Irish contribution to European scholastic thought* (Dublin, 2009), pp 88–110 at p. 105.

'senior' party. In the early development of FitzRalph's views, however, the flow of ideas on certain crucial points emerges from the evidence as having been from patron – with the latter's influence taken to include the episcopal circle as a whole[24] – to client.

The origin of FitzRalph's antagonism to the friars was recognized as a central problem by his most comprehensive biographer, Katherine Walsh, in these terms:

> One of the most problematic aspects of FitzRalph's career is his apparently sudden change of heart with regard to the four orders of mendicant friars and their role in later medieval society. This change of heart affected FitzRalph's attitude both to the friars' position as academic teachers in the universities and above all to their participation in pastoral work through preaching, hearing confessions and burying those members of the laity who so wished in their churches – for all of which activities the friars received some financial remuneration – while at the same time continuing to profess allegiance to the mendicant ideal and the obligation of charity of their fellow men to contribute to their support through almsgiving and pious bequests. The question has often been raised as to how it came about that FitzRalph, who, initially through his childhood acquaintance with the Franciscans in his native Dundalk, subsequently as student, master, and chancellor of Oxford University, but most especially during his long years of residence at Avignon as supplicant, litigant and as papal theological adviser on a wide range of topics, was in close and friendly contact with leading members of the mendicant orders, should suddenly become their most bitter opponent and should devote the last years of his life to a systematic attempt to undermine their privileges, their way of life, even their *raison d'être*.[25]

Katherine Walsh found the solution to this puzzle in the problems encountered by FitzRalph as archbishop:

> The most likely explanation for FitzRalph's sudden and total opposition to the friars is that on acquiring a large diocese to administer he was faced in an acute form with the problem of enforcing episcopal authority. The problem of the exempt religious who exercised a pastoral ministry was made more difficult by the tensions of a racially divided community and FitzRalph showed an intense awareness of this situation. It can be argued that his previous experience of the mendicant orders had been limited to

---

24 On Grandisson's circle, see Haren, *Sin and society*, pp 57–63. 25 Walsh, *A fourteenth-century scholar and primate*, p. 349.

the atypical situations of the schools at Oxford and the cosmopolitan convents at the papal curia, whereas in the course of his duties as archbishop he encountered the practical problems caused by exempt religious in general, linked with the specific issues which arose when mendicant confessors might abuse the confessional in excessive support for one 'nation' or the other.[26]

As I have argued in detail elsewhere,[27] a close reading of FitzRalph's sermon-diary against the evidence for views developed to an advanced and trenchant level within the Grandisson circle well before FitzRalph's becoming archbishop both provides an alternative and coherent explanation for the departure and renders it less a sudden change than the result of an evolution in sensitivity. On the issue that Katherine Walsh identified as central to FitzRalph's emerging reservations about current confessional practice – deficiencies in imposing the obligation of restitution[28] – it is possible to document particularly heavily what may licitly be termed a Grandissonian preoccupation with the subject.

THE *MEMORIALE PRESBITERORUM*

The anonymously transmitted treatise, *Memoriale presbiterorum* ('Handbook of parish priests'), one of a thriving genre in fourteenth-century England of handbooks for parish clergy, concentrates centrally on penance as a mechanism of restorative justice within society.[29] It uncompromisingly inculcates the obligation of restitution as a defining characteristic of true penitence where the sinner's conduct has caused damage to another and the confessor's duty both to impose restitution and to make it effective. It fiercely criticizes the perceived shortcomings particularly of mendicant confessors in that regard, whether acting from basely corrupt motives or from misplaced consideration for the

---

[26] Ibid., p. 363. [27] M.J. Haren, 'Richard FitzRalph and the friars: the intellectual itinerary of a curial controversialist' in J. Hamesse (ed.), *Roma, magistra mundi: itineraria culturae medievalis: mélanges offerts au Père L.E. Boyle à l'occasion de son 75e anniversaire* (3 vols, Louvain-la-Neuve, 1998), i, pp 349–67 at pp 352–61. [28] For an instance of particular topicality, the paper as delivered included quotations from Sermon 33 of FitzRalph's 'Sermon diary', to the people of Drogheda in the town's Carmelite church on Lady Day, 1349, illustrating FitzRalph's interweaving of the doctrine of restitution with an analysis of dominion and the application of both themes to the problems of a divided society. The relevant text is in Haren, 'Richard FitzRalph of Dundalk, Oxford and Armagh', pp 89–91. Here and at subsequent references the sermons are numbered according to the listing in A. Gwynn, 'The sermon-diary of Richard FitzRalph, archbishop of Armagh', *Proceedings of the Royal Irish Academy*, 44C1 (1937). [29] For an account of the manuscripts, see Haren, *Sin and society*, pp 6–8, 217–23. For excerpts illustrating the social focus, see M. Haren, 'The interrogatories for officials, lawyers and secular estates of the *Memoriale presbiterorum*' in P. Biller and A.J. Minnis (eds), *Handling sin: confession in the Middle Ages* (Woodbridge, 1998), pp 122–63.

penitent's peace of mind. Attention was first drawn to the author's perspective by the late Dr W.A. Pantin in his Birkbeck lectures given in the University of Cambridge in 1948 and subsequently published in his seminal book *The English church in the fourteenth century*.[30] Pantin reflected on the fact that the treatise anticipated by a short interval FitzRalph's attitude and from a connection, attested by one of the manuscripts, between the treatise and Avignon (where FitzRalph was long resident at the relevant time), suggested that the author might have helped to inspire FitzRalph as a polemicist on the shared concerns.[31] This shrewd perception, overlooked in intervening scholarship, is confirmed by a convergence of evidence now permitting the *Memoriale presbiterorum* to be dated in its original form with high probability to the years 1337 to 1338, but at latest by 1344, and assigned to the Exeter context – to the authorship specifically of Mr William Doune. At the date of the treatise's composition, Doune – later, in his combination of the archdeaconry of Leicester with the officialty of the dioceses of Lincoln and Worcester, to become arguably the most influential figure at sub-episcopal level in the contemporary English church – was Grandisson's registrar.[32] Doune was a clerk of Exeter origin, who – though he may have had a family connection with Grandisson – must certainly have been recruited by him as evincing the signs of high moral seriousness that mark him as an administrator, testator[33] and putative author. Although the other evidence for his outlook demonstrates that the views expressed in the *Memoriale presbiterorum* must have been deeply laid in his consciousness, so that his personal input to them is likely to have been substantial, their articulation in the treatise may properly be characterized as the source of a 'Grandissonian' influence on FitzRalph. Doune accompanied Bishop Grandisson to the papal curia at Avignon in 1343,[34] where FitzRalph had by then been resident for some six years, litigating as dean on behalf of Lichfield Cathedral.[35] This is the latest date by which Doune may be deemed to have met FitzRalph and if this was their first encounter (as it must certainly have been their first encounter since the compilation of the treatise) the introduction would have been made by Grandisson himself.

Grandisson's relationship with FitzRalph can be documented from about 1328, the likely date of a letter in which the bishop declared his satisfaction in respect of a doubt that he had entertained, on account of which he had 'for certain causes which then affected our thinking, the truth of which being more completely known we are heartily consoled' denied FitzRalph access to him.[36] The matter evidently affected Grandisson's estimate of FitzRalph's suitability as

30 W.A. Pantin, *The English church in the fourteenth century* (Cambridge, 1955). 31 Ibid., p. 206. 32 For details of his career, see Haren, *Sin and society*, pp 39–44, 190–207. 33 See A.H. Thompson, 'The will of Master William Doune, archdeacon of Leicester', *Archaeological Journal*, 72 (1915), 233–84; Haren, *Sin and society*, pp 10–18, 207–9. 34 See Haren, *Sin and society*, p. 30. 35 See Walsh, *A fourteenth-century scholar and primate*, pp 115–29. 36 'Quamquam

a candidate for major orders, for he now invites him to receive at his hands should he wish.[37] Though this is the first notice, the implication is that the two were already acquainted. FitzRalph's earliest known academic affiliations, as a fellow of Balliol and later of Mickle University Hall, were northern – in terms of the administrative organization of the university of Oxford – somewhat surprisingly given that the Irish were classified as part of the southern nation.[38] I have surmised that this aspect of the young scholar's career may reflect associations developed by Grandisson during his tenure of the archdeaconry of Nottingham in the period 1312–27, and thus be an incident of early patronage.[39] In the same way may perhaps be explained the young Richard Rauf's adoption of the 'Fitz' prefix: as an aristocrat, Grandisson will have been conscious of such nicety, and might well have approximated his protégé to the minor Devonian family of 'filius Radulfi', which gave its name to the manor of Aysshraf, later known as Roseash. If so, we could push the acquaintanceship back to at least 1325, when the new name was current.[40] By 1329, confidence was sufficiently strong for Grandisson to send FitzRalph as guardian and tutor to the bishop's nephew, John de Northwode, embarking in October of that year on the Parisian university scene. In that connection, Grandisson introduced FitzRalph as 'a man both of marked knowledge and honourable conduct; ... a master of arts and eminent bachelor of theology, he is distinguished among all students and teachers of the university of Oxford as outstandingly acute and discriminating'.[41] Although fitfully documented, it is beyond doubt that the rapport continued strong for the rest of FitzRalph's career. On 24 May 1331, Grandisson guaranteed FitzRalph, whom he described as a member of his 'household' and as having elected permanent residence in Exeter diocese, an annual pension of one hundred shillings, in lieu of ecclesiastical benefice, until he might make more competent provision for him.[42] By September he had collated to him the precentorship of Crediton, which office FitzRalph exchanged within the month for the prebend 'de Cruce' of that church.[43] On 27 September of the same year, FitzRalph had papal provision to a canonry and prebend of Exeter Cathedral.[44] During this time, however, it is evident that his principal activity was at Oxford,

---

nuper vobis scripserimus de non veniendo ad nos illa vice, certis ex causis que nostrum animum tunc movebant; earum, tamen, veritate lacius sciscitata visceraliter consolamur'. *The register of John Grandisson*, ed. Hingeston-Randolph, i, p. 173.   37 Ibid.   38 See A.B. Emden, 'Northerners and southerners in the organization of the university to 1509' in *Oxford studies presented to Daniel Callus* (Oxford, 1964), pp 1–30 at pp 2, 9.   39 For this and the following, see Haren, 'Richard FitzRalph and the friars', pp 350–2.   40 See H.E. Salter, *The Oxford deeds of Balliol College* (Oxford, 1913), no. 570.   41 'Virum utique preclare scientie et conversacionis honeste... et eo gracius quo Magister in Artibus et in Sacra Pagina egregius Bacularius, inter omnes studentes et legentes Universitatis Oxoniensis eminenter dinoscitur intelligens et subtilis'. *The register of John Grandisson*, ed. Hingeston-Randolph, i, p. 233.   42 Ibid., ii, p. 616. 43 Ibid., iii, p. 1286.   44 *Calendar of entries in the papal registers relating to Great Britain and Ireland: papal letters*, ii, ed. W.H. Bliss (London, 1895), p. 355.

for he was regent when Bishop Burghersh of Lincoln confirmed him as chancellor of the university,[45] which office he held until May 1334. The deduction is that Grandisson, who was, as I have remarked, a notable talent-spotter, intended initially to recruit FitzRalph perhaps to his administration and that events intervened. Shortly after his tenure of the Oxford chancellorship, FitzRalph sojourned briefly at the Roman curia, evidently on university business, and that initial stay ended with his provision by Grandisson's old mentor Benedict XII to the deanery of Lichfield Cathedral in December 1335.[46] As regards his continuing physical contact with Exeter, an interesting line of speculation is provoked by the account of a question debated there between Thomas Buckingham (who had formally a local link, being chancellor of the cathedral until 1349) and an unknown 'reverend doctor', 'Whether all adults and children who died before Christ died in mortal sin and without the grace of present justification and remission, being bound to perpetual loss of the vision of God'. We know from an apologetic letter to the king in 1349[47] that Grandisson was keen to preserve the old tradition – antedating the primacy of the universities and the friars' schools – in which a cathedral might aspire to be a centre of higher learning. The account of what took place on this occasion is contained in the text of Thomas Buckingham's *Quaestiones* preserved in Oxford, New College, MS 134, where he is described as 'showing the finding of a catholic middle way between the errors of Pelagius, Cicero[48] and Scotus, [and] that predestination, preordinance, eternal forewilling and the unfolding course of God stand with free-will and merit of the creature'.[49] Pantin suggested that the unnamed disputant, who, as is evident from the report of the exchange, took a rigorously high Augustinian position, might have been FitzRalph. Given FitzRalph's general Augustinianism, this seems altogether plausible. FitzRalph was provided archbishop of Armagh on 31 July 1346 and – following negotiations with the king and the papal camera leading to restoration of the temporalities and the grant of the *pallium* respectively – he was consecrated on 8 July 1347 by Grandisson, with assisting bishops, in Exeter.[50] Presumably as a special mark of the metropolitan standing of the new prelate, he then rode in rather grand parade through the city mounted on a palfrey accoutred in cloth of white 'as has been used to be done in the Roman curia'.[51] The ceremony would

---

45 *The registers of Henry Burghersh, 1320–1342*, ed. N. Bennett (Woodbridge, 2003), p. 83, no. 1828; *Snappe's formulary*, ed. H.E. Salter (Oxford, 1923), p. 75.   46 See Walsh, *A fourteenth-century scholar and primate*, pp 108–10.   47 Pantin, *English church*, pp 115–16. *The register of John Grandisson*, ed. Hingeston-Randolph, i, pp 307–8.   48 On the model of Thomas Bradwardine's *De causa Dei contra Pelagianos*, Pelagius must be taken to represent the Ockhamist position, Cicero a generally naturalistic, humanistic one.   49 Oxford, New College, MS 134, fo. 324r, as edited in Pantin, *English church*, pp 263–6. See also B.R. de la Torre, *Thomas Buckingham and the contingency of futures: the possibility of human freedom* (Notre Dame, IN, 1987), p. 151.   50 See *The register of John Grandisson*, ed. Hingeston-Randolph, ii, p. 1022. See also Walsh, *A fourteenth-century scholar and primate*, pp 227–31.

have accorded with Grandisson's pronounced sense of episcopal dignity, which he would have been glad to impress on his diocese. It may also be a reflection of consciousness of FitzRalph's archiepiscopal status that in the aftermath of his consecration Grandisson commissioned him, with specific reference in the address to his primacy of Ireland, to perform a list of episcopal functions in his stead. Although the editor in presenting the entry gives it the title '[sc. appointment of a] Suffragan Bishop' Grandisson himself does not use a term that would imply inferiority.[52] It is specifically noted that the new prelate did indeed tour 'nearly all the diocese' carrying out confirmations and dedicating churches, among other acts.[53] 'Nearly all the diocese' is remarkable: Grandisson himself was assiduously resident and it is difficult to believe that in thus deputing he was doing other than using the opportunity maximally to advertise to his diocesans a figure of major distinction.

While subsequent relations between the two men are largely inferential, the defect plausibly derives from the character of the source material. Grandisson's register of memoranda would not be expected to reveal contact of the kind and there are few records of his private letters after 1340. There is stray evidence from his reading of Trevet's commentary on Augustine's *De Civitate Dei* that he meant to relay matter from it to FitzRalph.[54] But the major manifestation of sympathy for the latter's later onslaught on the friars' privileges is the fact that Grandisson, after decades of official inscrutability, suddenly – at the point when the FitzRalph campaign was at its height – emerges as nothing short of apocalyptic in his fulminations. A mandate issued by him on 10 February 1359,[55] directed against 'the heralds of Anti-Christ' – *gyrovagi*, hermits, pardoners and pretended penitentiaries and confessors – in the course of a trenchantly forthright statement of a bishop's pastoral responsibility, suggestively echoes the text used by FitzRalph as the *locus* of his great polemical sermon preached at St Paul's Cross on 12 March 1357: *Nemo vos seducat inanibus verbis* (Eph. 5. 6).[56] It is impossible to suppose that Grandisson here was unaware of the resonance. The English bishops were under considerable constraint in this phase of the anti-mendicant controversy, which it was known that the king outrightly discountenanced. Grandisson's pulse of support is the more noteworthy for the reticence that was general elsewhere. The campaign on which FitzRalph engaged can be seen as integral to the perspective of Grandisson's circle. It was

---

51 'Et idem consecratus postea equitavit per medium Civitatis Exonie, indutus Pontificalibus, super palefridum albo panno coopertum, prout in Romana Curia fieri consuevit'. *The register of John Grandisson*, ed. Hingeston-Randolph, ii, p. 1022.   52 Ibid., pp 1021–2.   53 'Circumivit fere totam Diocesim Exoniensem'. Ibid., p. 1022.   54 The evidence, from MS Bodley 691, fo. 211ra, is noted by Steele, 'A study', p. 166.   55 *The register of John Grandisson*, ed. Hingeston-Randolph, ii, p. 1197. For a fuller review of the implications in context, see M.J. Haren, 'Bishop Gynwell of Lincoln, two Avignonese statutes and Archbishop FitzRalph of Armagh's suit at the Roman curia against the friars', *Archivum Historiae Pontificiae*, 31 (1993), 275–92 at 277.   56 Sermon 68 in the Gwynn listing.

not, from that perspective, a mere protectionism of the rights or economic interest of the secular clergy – though those rights and economic interest were rigorously insisted on as divinely ordained. Grandisson's object was the imposition upon recalcitrant humanity in its post-lapsarian degradation of a disciplinary programme that could not be short-circuited by preferential recourse to moral leaders whose counsels differed. He had a clear and urgent perception of a bond between the efficacy of moral authority and its unity and homogeneity.[57]

SERMON 62

So far I have considered Grandisson's influence on FitzRalph principally in terms of what is known of the activity of Grandisson and his circle. As suggested already, however, there is a potentially fertile field in studying FitzRalph's outlook against Grandisson's. By way of illustration of this approach, I select two sermons, preached by FitzRalph on 18 October and about a fortnight later on All Saints Day 1356.[58] They are among three sermons recorded as delivered during that intermission between his meteorically polemical appearances on the London scene in the summer and again in the early winter of that year. All three of these intervening sermons were understood to have been delivered in the parish church of Deddington, some sixteen to seventeen miles as the crow flies north of Oxford, from which it was deduced that he was resident in Oxford at this time – though no source survives to place him in so public a setting and there is some other reason for supposing that he was not in direct communication with the Oxford scene. In fact, though two of the sermons – those preached on 16 October (the third Sunday of the month)[59] and on All Saints[60] – were certainly preached in Deddington, the second of the series chronologically[61] was equally certainly preached elsewhere: as the manuscript evidence stands, putatively at nearby Thame.[62] Though this location does not in the least diminish the inference to FitzRalph's Oxford base, it is possible to suggest an alternative explanation for his activity in the area, for both Deddington and Thame (if that is indeed the other location) were both equally easily reached from a small hamlet on the Buckinghamshire/Oxfordshire borders, called Quainton. Quainton has, in controversialist terms, an engaging literary aftermath as the preferred retreat of that fictional pamphleteer, well known to the student scene of the late 1960s, Hugh Trevor-Roper's Mercurius

---

[57] See M. Haren, 'Confession, social ethics and social discipline in the *Memoriale presbiterorum*' in Biller and Minnis (eds), *Handling sin*, pp 109–22 at pp 119–20.   [58] Sermons 62 and 64 respectively in the Gwynn listing. For the text, see below.   [59] Sermon 63 in the Gwynn listing.   [60] Sermon 64 in the Gwynn listing.   [61] Sermon 62 in the Gwynn listing.   [62] See Haren, 'Richard FitzRalph and the friars', pp 363–4.

Oxoniensis. In my reference, it has the claim to attention that its parish church was held actually (not, for technical reasons, formally) by none other than Mr William Doune. We know that Doune's archdeaconry of Leicester had no dwelling attached and, from his will – by whose date he had changed from Quainton to the neighbouring parish of Swalcliffe – that he kept personal possessions at the rectory there.[63] Quainton would have been an ideal location in which our fourteenth-century Mercurius might have escaped the pack, and its name may well underlie the peculiar difficulty witnessed to by the manuscripts. The date of the sermon here, 18 October, was the feast of St Luke – as it happens, the dating of Grandisson's consecration, from which his episcopal year ran. It would have been a most suitable occasion for the bishop's former clients to mark specially. The sermon itself is for the major part a subtle disquisition on spirituality and spiritual direction, taking its cue from the text of Ezechiel 1:12: *Ubi erat spiritus impetus illuc gradiebantur et non revertebantur* ('Where was the impulse of the spirit there went they up and did not regress'). The instruction of the more prudent, the more potent, the more loving and more attentive leader or director is to be preferred to the counsels of all others. 'At which point it was set forth overall how the spirit of good impetus or impulse can be distinguished from the impetus of malign spirits, in as much as the angel of Satan frequently transforms himself into an angel of light'.[64] He may thus appear in various guises with plausible promptings – to almsgiving corrupted by ostentation; to prayer turned into an occasion of lust; to the taking of impractical vows (including mendicancy, for man is born to work, not to the life of leisure, even aimed at salvation, or to spontaneous begging); to the construction of chantries and chapels whose effect is to divert the faithful from the church [sc. their parish church] that is ordained for them and whose result is very frequently in such places that the populace is led to idolatry.[65] These are for the most part themes that are readily recognized as in keeping with FitzRalph's ingrained preoccupations. They are also readily recognized as Grandissonian. Grandisson too has deeply absorbed the warning of Second Corinthians that the angel of Satan has the facility to transform himself into an angel of light and (an image of the English countryman rather than of St Paul) 'to cheat the skill of the hunter with the assumed simplicity of a guileful vixen'.[66] Accordingly, not every spirit is worthy of credence.[67] Instability was abroad.[68] Underpinning Grandisson's

[63] Ibid., pp 364–6. [64] Sermon 62, p. 47, ll 26–7. [65] Ibid., p. 50, ll 6–8. [66] 'Qualiter angelus Sathane, secundum Apostolicam doctrinam, transfigurare se in Lucis Angelum consuevit, atque sub adumbrata simplicitate dolose vulpis astucia ingenium fallere venatoris'. *The register of John Grandisson*, ii, p. 942. See also ibid., p. 1157, where the angels of Satan (this time thus in plurality) deceive the souls of the unwitting under the appearance of the good (to stray from the parish church again). [67] Ibid. [68] Ibid., p. 1158: 'Nonnulli, tamen, fide, prochdolor, instabiles, ecclesiis Collegiatis vel Parochialibus derelictis, ad capellas sepe seu oratoria prophana, nedum pro Divinis audiendis set, quod dampnabilius est, Ecclesiasticis Sacramentis tractandis, hiis temporibus, quod displicenter dicimus, nimis voluntarie se convertunt'.

opposition to private chapels was an ingrained distrust of where choice in moral matters might lead. Their discouragement where practical was an evidently general part of his regime.[69] Instability is readily recognized as the near cousin of the formidable vice of 'elation'.[70] The case of the chapel built by the Augustinian priory of Frithelstock is particularly noteworthy in present context:[71] in 1351, he ordered its demolition, stigmatizing it precisely as 'a house of idolatry' those having resort to which were in consequence sacrificing to idols and practising sorcery.[72] The perspective gives context to a passage in the other of FitzRalph's sermons that I have singled out for attention here.

SERMON 64

The text of the All Saints' Day sermon is that from Revelation 7:4: *Audivi numerum signatorum* ('I heard the number of those sealed'). The progression is rapid, breathless even. Several categories of the sealed are distinguished. The first category are the saintly still alive:

> who although they be saints, yet because their sanctity is not known by others and to others too is uncertain – to themselves, even, as to final perseverance – *In that no one knows whether he be worthy of love or hatred* (Eccles 9.[1]),[73] for a doer of howsoever much good can in the blink of an eye fall into mortal sin ... the honour that is rendered this day to the saints ought not to be rendered to those only sealed in this way.

---

69 See Haren, *Sin and society*, pp 55–6. 70 Addressing in 1348 an alleged conspiracy among the parishioners of Paignton, within whose parish there was a chapel at Marldon, the bishop bemoaned the consequences even of chapels duly founded in response to problems of distance and terrain: 'dum illi qui parochianos Capellarum abusive se vocant, erecta elataque cervice contra eorum Matricem Ecclesiam et vere Parochialem, variis viis et exquisitis coloribus ac persuasionibus periculosis, ac contra ipsius Ecclesie Parochialis honorem et libertatem, ut filii degeneres, studiose moliuntur, seipsos verius doctrinis variis et peregrinis, contra doctrinam Apostoli [the reference is to Heb. 13.9], periculose seducentes'. *The register of John Grandisson*, ii, p. 1056. 71 The episode has been illuminatingly presented in context of Grandisson's general outlook by N. Orme, 'Bishop Grandisson and popular religion', *Reports and Transactions of the Devonshire Association for the Advancement of Science, Literature and Art*, 134 (1992), 107–18 at 110–13. 72 'Et, quamvis domus ipsa, quam, non pro devocione fidei set questu cupiditatis, ut exitus rei geste manifeste declarat, edificatam, prophanamus et dampnamus, et, quantum ad nos attinet, prophanam et dampnatam reputamus et eciam declaramus, non Capella set ydolatrie domus pocius sit censenda; nonnulli, tamen, parochianorum nostrorum, quod dolencius referimus, quos iidem Prior et Conventus a recta fide, per asserciones vanas, nepharias, et dampnatas fecerant deviare, dimissis Ecclesiis suis Parochialibus et aliis Locis sacris rite per Pontifices Deo consecratis, ad locum ipsum prophanum peregrinacionis causa confluentes, ydolis sacrificium, immo verius sortilegium, impendere non formidant'. *The register of John Grandisson*, ed. Hingeston-Randolph, ii, pp 1110–11. 73 The form of quotation from the Vulgate is not exact.

The second are the saints in purgatory. What then of the third group, the truly beatified? Do they have knowledge of us? The question prompts a disquisition on the question whether knowledge of our condition and our changing wills is compatible with true beatitude. There are competing considerations. As if the preacher realizes that he is leading his audience in too deep, he abruptly terminates: 'No more of that now'. On to the church's honouring of them, this day being appointed on account of their innumerable multitude. Suddenly the preacher seems to have forgotten his recent glimpse of how quickly the garden path may lead to a swamp. We have food for thought in the extirpation of the images and idols from the Pantheon, the temple of all the demons in Rome, and the veneration in their place of all the saints.

> And there was comment on a number of dangers concerning the veneration of images, which they commonly call by the name of the subjects depicted, and perniciously – such like: St Mary of Lincoln, St Mary of Walsingham, St Mary of the New Work and so on – since St Mary, the mother of God, is in heaven all the time, never in those and other similar places here on earth. Wherefore those who venerate such images for themselves and offer to them for the procuring of remedies or various advantages are seen as true and patent idolaters, since they are adoring the image not just as an image, only that is as thing imagined, but in part on account of the image itself. Wherefore it is beyond doubt but that they are rendering service to a block of wood or a picture, as being a picture, and it is a reprehensible superstition; and if children so informed by their parents were led into captivity with Jews or Saracens they would adore such images forever as being idolaters, wholly ignorant of the subjects depicted by the images. [The point here is presumably that they would remain in arrested development without prospect of better instruction in Christianity. The preacher might from a modern perspective be expected to allow for their being corrected against image-worship in their new culture. But though the author of the *Summa de questionibus Armenorum* is of interest for his acquaintance with the Koran, his determination in respect both of Islam and Judaism was to demonstrate their inferiority to Christianity. Moreover the premiss here that what is ill-found among Christians must axiomatically be worse or not less ill-found among Jews and Saracens is in keeping with the general truculence which marked FitzRalph's later career.[74]] That idolatry the greed for offerings introduces daily – greed on the part of the ministers of church, say rather of Satan, for the offerings which are made to such

---

74 As justly commented on by Walsh, *A fourteenth-century scholar and primate*, pp 176–7.

images on account of fabricated and fictitious miracles, in respect of which remedy ought to be applied by the prelates.[75]

Grandisson for his part did apply remedy, recurringly, to feigned miracles for which his register shows him to have been on lively guard.[76] Whether or not we need invoke him as an inspiration of this censure he would certainly have served as a model of its aspiration to reform. To recur to idolatry, a term which must have sounded exotically startling in fourteenth-century English country context: it too is Grandissonian. The idolatry and sorcery practised by those having resort to the chapel of Frithelstock was the cult of an image of St Mary the Virgin.

CONCLUSION

Dignity, prelacy, decorum, authority separate Grandisson and FitzRalph, on the point of such strictures, from that ascetic version of Jude the Obscure, William the Smith of Leicester.[77] Having failed in love, according to Knighton, he renounced the flesh (becoming vegetarian and teetotal, eschewing linen and footware too) and learned to read and write. Archbishop Courtenay proceeded against him in 1389[78] for having (with much ribaldry in Knighton's account)[79] used a statue of St Katherine, wooden evidently, to boil his kale and for deriding the Virgin's two local images as the 'wyche of Lincolne' and the 'wyche of Walsyngham'.[80] If the collation seems unavoidable, there is no implication that Grandisson and FitzRalph are proto-Lollards.[81] One aspect of the Lollard programme especially would have been anathema to Grandisson, whose jealousy of the church's independence of lay encroachment is strident.[82] The approximation of views is enough, however, to surmise that in another generation the preacher at Deddington would not have spoken as he did. What impact may be attributed to the pulpit articulation as ultra-orthodoxy of such ideas in the previous generation or the more general raising of moral consciousness at which the critique of the Grandisson circle aimed is imponderable. At the level of the professional élite, there is, however, one particular focus of attention. I have

---

[75] Sermon 64, p. 53, ll 8–23. [76] It was his proceeding against a feigned miracle at Exeter in 1341 that evoked the warning about the vulpine angel of Satan, quoted above. For the circumstances and the bishop's careful and structured inquiry into them, see *The register of John Grandisson*, ii, pp 942–3. [77] Although both Knighton and Courtenay use 'Smyth' as a surname, Knighton is explicit in its derivation directly from avocation: 'ab artificio sic vocatus'. *Chronicon Henrici Knighton vel Cnitthon, monachi Leycestrensis*, ed. J.R. Lumby(London, 1895), i, p. 180. [78] See J.H. Dahmus, *The metropolitan visitation of William Courteney, archbishop of Canterbury, 1381–1396* (Urbana, AR, 1950), pp 164, 166–7, 168–9, 170–2. Smith performed his penance with an image of St Katherine in his hand. [79] *Chronicon*, p. 182. [80] Ibid., p. 183. [81] Wyclif cited FitzRalph with approval of his stance. See G.A. Benrath, *Wyclifs Bibelkommentar* (Berlin, 1966), pp 34–5. [82] See Haren, *Sin and society*, pp 46–7.

observed in another context how the administration of the diocese of Lincoln in the early Lollard period was in the hands of a figure who on ideological pedigree might be reckoned Grandisson's grandson. The highly developed moral sensitivity of Mr John de Belvoir, William Doune's own official in the archdeaconry of Leicester and successor as official of the diocese, is evident from his will, proved in 1391.[83] During much of his tenure, Lollardy enjoyed what K.B. Macfarlane described as 'the obscurity of the tolerated and ignored'.[84] In the phase of Lollard or quasi-Lollard organization and dissemination before dogmatic formulation became a crucial solvent – while to the fore, in J.A.F. Thomson's terms, were issues of 'conduct rather than belief' and 'personal morality'[85] – a degree of empathy may have been the stay on effective persecution. That in itself could be considered an important, if unintended, delayed effect from the episcopal programme of Grandisson and FitzRalph.

APPENDIX

The text of Sermons 62 and 64 from the Sermon Diary of Richard FitzRalph is critically edited below from the four manuscripts designated by sigla as follows: *J* Oxford, St John's College, 65; *N* Oxford, New College, 90; *B* Oxford, Bodleian Library, Bodley 144; *L* London, British Library, Lansdowne 393. Editorial emendation is shown within angle brackets < >. Although there is no certain critical basis for the choice, as a presentational device the expanded form of scriptural citation of roman numeral followed by the word *capitulo* generally found in *BL* and less consistently in *N* has been preferred to the simple arabic numeral normally found in *J*.

Sermon 62 (B fo. 87r; J fo. 71r; L fo. 101v; N fo. 117v)
In nomine patris et filii et spiritus sancti. Amen. Sermo eiusdem Ricardi apud Dacmexton in vulgari in festo sancti Luce ewangeliste, anno Domini millesimo CCCmo[86] lvi.[87]

Ubi erat spiritus impetus illuc gradiebantur et non revertebantur. Eze<chielis> primo[88] capitulo[89] et in lectione epistolari festi presentis. Premissa oracione cum[90] introductione ipsius oracionis dominice et salutacionis angelice introductio thematis facta fuit per hoc quod per multa annorum curricula[91] antequam

---

83 See M.J. Haren, 'The will of Master John de Belvoir, official of Lincoln (d. 1391)', *Mediaeval Studies*, 58 (1996), 119–47. 84 McFarlane, *Lancastrian kings and Lollard knights*, p. 224. 85 See J.A.F. Thomson, 'Orthodox religion and the origins of Lollardy', *History*, 74 (1989), 39–55 at 45. 86 CCCmo: ccc *L*. 87 In nomine patris et filii et spiritus sancti. Amen. Sermo eiusdem Ricardi apud Dacmexton in vulgari in festo sancti Luce ewangeliste, anno Domini millesimo CCCmo lvi: Sermo in vulgari in festo sancte [*sic*] Luce evangeliste *J* In nomine Patris. Ricardi apud Dami Oxon' in vulgari in festo sancti Luce evangeliste anno lvi[to] *N*. 88 primo: 1 *BL (?)*ii *N*. 89 Cf. Ezech. 1.12. 90 cum: cuius *N*. 91 curricula: curicula *N*.

isti[92] quatuor ewangeliste[93], Matheus, Marcus[94], Lucas et Johannes nati fuerant hec[95] prophetica Ezechielis visio[96] de ipsorum modo vivendi seu regula fuit illi exhibita non solum pro eis set eciam et pro nobis qui eis succedimus ut nos homines iam exigui temporis et infirmi qui in quatuor quasi hominum genera que diffuse fuerant[97] descripta / (fo. 71rb *J*) simus partiti[98] iuxta quatuor animalium condiciones significancium ewangelistas[99] predictos scilicet hominis, leonis, bovis et aquile, regulam in verbis istis expressam imitaremur[1] indeclinabiliter in vivendo[2], implentes *ubi erat spiritus impetus illuc gradiebantur et non revertebantur*, ubi propheta utiliter nobis[3] ostendit sancte vivendi regulam[4] *ubi erat spiritus impetus*, vite sequelam *illuc*[5] *gradiebantur* et recidivi[6] cautelam *et non revertebantur*. Quo ad regulam sancte vivendi[7] fuit ostensum quod illa est regula nobis utilior, quam spiritus[8] sanctus ingerit, habita deliberacione[9] humana, iuxta illud Domini salvatoris, *Ponite in cordibus vestris non premeditari quomodo aut quid dicetis*[10], *dabitur enim vobis in illa hora quid loquamini*. Matt. x capitulo[11].[12] Et iuxta Aristotelem in libro suo de bona fortuna affirmantem[13] quod illi qui reguntur ab illo principio tocius mundi felicius cuncta agunt quam illi qui omnia consilio operantur.[14] Talis ibi est sensus. Et est simile quasi in x^{o}[15] Ethicorum.[16] Racio illud[17] affirmat, supposito illo principio Apocalipsis[18] iii capitulo[19],[20] *Ecce sto ad hostium vestrum et pulso. Si quis aperuerit*[21] *michi intrabo ad eum et cenabo cum eo et ipse mecum*, quia prudencioris, potencioris[22], amancioris[23] et diligencioris ducis sive rectoris instructio preferenda est cunctorum aliorum consiliis et utilioris exitus est credenda. Spiritus Dei nos semper peculiariter gubernantis impetus sive instructio[24] est huiusmodi. Igitur talis[25] instructio sive im/(fo. 87v *B*) pulsus aut impetus est cunctis humanis consiliis preferenda. Ubi consequenter fuit suasum qualiter agnosci poterit spiritus boni impetus sive impulsus[26] ab impetu seu impulsu spirituum malignorum ex quo angelus Sathane in angelum lucis se sepius transfigurat. Et fuerunt[27] data tria signa aut quatuor, ymmo verius raciones. Primo debet quisque attendere[28] finem principalem (fo. 102r *L*) quem intendit ex impetu et si sit bonus et[29] Deo acceptus nisi aliud optinet[30] signum est impetus[31] spiritus boni impellentis ad illud agendum.

92 isti: iste *J*. **93** ewangeliste: evangeliste *N*. **94** Marcus: Marchus *L*. **95** *om*. hec *N*. **96** visio: vicio *N*. **97** fuerant: fuerat *JN*. **98** descripta simus partiti: decerpta sumus preteriti *N*. **99** ewangelistas: evangelistas *N*. **1** imitaremur: mutaremur *N*. **2** in vivendo: in mundo *N*. **3** *om*. nobis *N*. **4** *om*. ubi erat spiritus impetus illuc gradiebantur et non revertebantur ubi propheta utiliter nobis ostendit sancte vivendi regulam *J*. **5** illuc: illic *J* illud *N*. **6** recidivi: residui *J* recedivi *N*. **7** sancte vivendi: vivende sancte *N*. **8** *add*. sp *per errorem L*. **9** deliberacione: de liberacione *L*. **10** dicetis: dicitis *N*. **11** x capitulo: 10 *J*. **12** Cf. Matt. 10.19. **13** affirmantem: affirmantis *BN*. **14** Aristotle, *Eudemian ethics*, 8.2.22–3. **15** x^{o}: x *B* 10 *J* Christo *N*. **16** Aristotle, *Nicomachean ethics*, 10.7.8. **17** illud: id *BLN*. **18** Apocalipsis: Appocalipsis *N*. **19** iii capitulo: 3*J*. **20** Apoc. 3.20. **21** aperuerit: apparuerit *BL* apparuit *N*. **22** potencioris: retencioris *N add*. et *BL*. **23** amancioris: amaricioris *J* amacioris *LN*. **24** instructio: instructo *BL*. **25** *om*. sive instructio est huiusmodi. Igitur talis *N*. **26** impulsus: impulsa *N*. **27** fuerunt: fuerant *BN*. **28** Primo debet quisque attendere: debet primo attendere quisque *N*. **29** *add*. a *N*. **30** optinet: opti [*sic*] *J* obtinet *L* optinent *N*. **31** *add*. et

Secundo[32] attendenda est intencio operantis precipua, numquid principalis intencio sit[33] ad laudem Dei aut eius lege directa, et est signum[34] secundum. Set hec duo signa possunt deficere. Ideo tercio debet homo attendere numquid in exercendo actum ad quem quis eo modo impellitur ad aliud incitetur[35] / (fo. 71v *J*) noxium sue saluti, et, si non, valde probabiliter potest homo inferre quod[36] a bono spiritu erat primus impulsus et continuacio subsecuta. Si vero econtra, si[37] senserit in exercendo actum illum ad aliquod[38] illicitum stimulari ex visis <aut> auditis aut aliter noviter in[39] exercendo actum, occurrentibus non antea cogitatis, signum est caliditatis spiritus fraudulenti sub specie boni ad[40] malum conantis adducere. Verbi gracia, incedens in publico inter multos cernit pauperem indigentem. Nonnumquam[41] hoc modo a Sathana ad ei dandum[42] (fo. 117vb *N*) elemosinam excitatur et cum fortassis manum extendit ad pauperem excitatur ut multitudinem circumstantem attendat et ex hoc alliciatur[43] ut eorum commendacionibus extollatur et est factus primus impulsus ab angelo perdito qui secundum perversum immittit. Pariter nonnumquam[44] homo vel mulier ut[45] vadat ad ecclesiam ad orandum ex recta intencione ad opus Deo[46] acceptum impulsus interius <i>bi[47] in loco oracionis mulierem pulcram solam fortassis repperiens[48] ad concupiscenciam ipsius antequam oracionem inceperit excitatur. Unde sicut iste ultimatus impulsus a spiritu nequam efficitur ita presumi[49] potest verisimiliter quod primus impetus sive impulsus ab eo fiebat[50]. Item sic puto plures a spiritu nequam[51] impelli ad vota grandia emittenda[52] eo quod talium observancia magni est meriti apud Deum set cum ad[53] observanciam pervenitur obstat difficultas actus[54] promissi et nichilominus a Sathana[55] consideracio difficultatis fortassis immittitur aut augetur et torpor[56] per eum retardativus adicitur aut timor destruccionis[57] complexionis[58], abbreviacionis[59] proprie sue vite aut aliud simile[60] ita ut homo transgrediendo votum graviter[61] valde peccet qui sine voto ageret innocenter. Hoc de voto ieiunii, de voto peregrinacionis sepe contingit et de voto castitatis satis frequenter ita ut homo experiatur sepissime illud Salomonis[62], *Non placet Deo infidelis et stulta promissio*.[63] Unde videntur Deum temptare qui huiusmodi difficilia[64] vota emittunt cum casus facile possit contingere quod compellantur votum dissolvere, sicuti est de istis fatuis ancoritis[65] inclusis qui seu que[66] certam sustentacionem (fo. 71vb *J*) non habent set elemosinas solas pro sustentacione

---

N. 32 secundo: secunda *J*. 33 sit: potest *J*. 34 *om*. signum *N*. 35 incitetur: visitetur *N*. 36 quod: quia *N*. 37 si: et se *N*. 38 aliquod: aliqua *N*. 39 *om*. in *N*. 40 ad: os *N*. 41 nonnumquam: ideo numquam *N*. 42 *om*. dandum *J*. 43 alliciatur: aliciatur *N*. 44 nonnumquam: non numquid. 45 ut: et *N*. 46 Deo: Dei *N*. 47 <i>bi: ubi *BJLN*. 48 repperiens: reperiens *BLN*. 49 presumi: precium *N*. 50 *om*. fiebat *J*. 51 nequam: inquam *N*. 52 emittenda: eminenda *N*. 53 *om*.ad *N*. 54 *om*. actus *J*. 55 Sathana: samia *N*. 56 torpor: toporum *N*. 57 destructionis: destruxcionis *N*. 58 complexionis: complexcionis *J*. 59 *om*. complexionis abbreviacionis *N*. 60 simile: simille *N*. 61 *om*. graviter *J*. 62 Salomonis: Salamonis *BJ*. 63 Cf. Ecclesiastes 5.3. 64 difficilia: visibilia *N*. 65 ancoritis: auctoritate *N*. 66 seu que: suam *N*.

expectant, quoniam si elemosine, quod facile posset contingere, subtraherentur ab eis, paucis diebus aut tamquam homicide sui penitus inter/(fo. 88r B)irent[67] aut providenciam divinam Deum temptando inprovide expectarent. Quamvis enim tales nonnumquam zelum sanctum habuerint in voto forsitan mendicitatis emisso[68] non tamen est dubium quin non secundum scienciam[69] ita ag<a>nt[70] cum homo ad laborem sit natus non ad solitarium[71] ocium aut ad mendicitatem gratuitam cum possit manibus laborare, dicente apostolo, *Qui non vult[72] operari nec[73] manducet*. ii[74] ad Thessalonicenses iii capitulo[75].[76] Et forte non est nisi rarissime in talibus heremitis vocatis – inprovide[77], quoniam non sic[78] nisi quia colunt heremum sunt vocati – sancta intencio, quia volunt heremite vocari et colere civitates, qui ob hoc[79] civimite sunt verius appellandi[80]. Unde non sancte in civitatibus eligunt mendicare aut certis locis includi. Immo[81] quia non est caucior modus congregandi di(fo. 102v L)vicias, elemosinas extrahendo a bursis[82], quam per titulum sanctitatis, videtur, ex gestis istorum qui communiter secrete plura congregant quam plures divites reputati, quod intencionem habent omnino distortam, quorum facta sepissime id[83] ostendunt, quoniam vix quivis[84] talis moritur sic inclusus aut in heremitico habitu, quoniam[85] pocius propter latrocinium et homicidium et sacrilegium et incestum detruncacione[86] capitum aut suspendio finem accipiunt, ut infra dies[87] paucos de uno recluso accepi;[88] quod multis annis[89] sic vixit et iam tanquam princeps latronum apud Coventr'[90] captus carcere latronum[91] sancte includitur. An non tales fuerant a principio a spiritu nequam ad huiusmodi fatuam professionem impulsi[92] non puto quod oportet ambigere[93]. Item quid[94] meriti amplioris quam sancta loca construere[95], quam cantarias[96] pro cuncto populo Christiano fulciendo fundare? Unde Sathanas ex hac causa se in lucis angelum (fo. 118r N) transfigurans interius hominem ita alloquitur: 'Videsne tu, qui actus devotos libens exequeris – huiusmodi actus seu opera quanti sunt meriti apud Deum[97] – construere[98], ibi[99] in / (fo. 72r J) cimiterio talis ecclesie, unam capellam ad quam populus facile possit confluere; ibi ordina perpetuam cantariam cuius capellanus pro devotis hominibus ipsius[1] parochie summo mane celebret omni die. Fac ibi crucis aut virginis gloriose gloriosam ymaginem ut veniencium devocio excitetur[2] et grandem mercedem a Deo recipies'. Facta sunt omnia iuxta angeli[3] perditoris[4]

---

67 interierint: interiorent *N*. 68 emisso: emisse *N*. 69 scienciam: conscienciam *J*. 70 ag<a>nt: agunt *BJL*. 71 solitarium: salutarium *J*. 72 vult: wult *BJ*. 73 nec: non *N*. 74 ii: 2 *J* ill<ud> *N*. 75 iii capitulo: 30 *J*. 76 Cf. 2 Thess. 3.10. 77 inprovide: improvide *BL*. 78 sic: sit *N*. 79 *om*. hoc *J*. 80 verius appellandi: appellati *N*. 81 immo: ymmo *BLN*. 82 a bursis: ab ursis *N*. 83 id: *(?)illud J*. 84 quivis: quamvis *N*. 85 quoniam: qui *J*. 86 detruncacione: detractacione *N*. 87 *add*. per *N*. 88 accepi: accipiunt *J*. 89 annis: aliis *N*. 90 Coventr': Coventro *BL*. 91 *om*. apud Coventr' captus carcere latronum *N*. 92 impulsi: inpulsi *N*. 93 ambigere: abigere *N*. 94 quid: Christi *N*. 95 construere: constituere *N*. 96 cantarias: grantarias *N*. 97 Deum: sanctum *N*. 98 construere: constituere *J*. 99 ibi: ergo *N*. 1 ipsius: ipsi *N*. 2 excitetur: exitetur *N*. 3 angeli: anglis *B* angelis *L* angli *N*.

impulsum.⁵ Venit ad missam populus summo mane. Subtrahitur meritum minuendo a missa per ecclesiam ordinata. 'Una', inquit iste hominum inimicus, 'missa pro uno die tibi potest sufficere'. Devocio brevis⁶ misse pro devocione maioris misse cum⁷ nota, eciam⁸ meritum minuendo, mutatur. Locus in quo orans minus meretur, cum non sit institutus ab ecclesia set extortus⁹, pro loco maioris meriti commutatur et fit¹⁰ reversio in sequendo spiritum – ambulando si non ad ydolatriam¹¹ populus adducatur, quod tamen sepissime in huiusmodi locis¹² contingit – contra secundam nostri thematis¹³ particulam, *et non revertebantur*, et contra illud a nostro Salvatore assertum, *Nemo mittens manum ad aratrum*¹⁴ *et respiciens retro aptus est regno Dei*. Luc. ix⁰¹⁵ capitulo.¹⁶,¹⁷ Quo ad reversionem, duplex fuit, scilicet modo ultimo nunc pretacto et peccando mortaliter. Ubi fuit obiectum¹⁸ de David, de sancto Petro et¹⁹ de sancta Maria Magdalena, ex hoc quod eorum peccata eis profuerunt,²⁰ de quorum²¹ primo post / (fo. 88v B) commissum adulterii et homicidii²² Urie peccatum a Deo est dictum,²³ *Inveni virum*²⁴ *iuxta*²⁵ *cor meum*.²⁶ De secunda²⁷ est dictum, *Dimissa sunt ei peccata*²⁸ *multa quoniam dilexit multum*.²⁹ Et de tercio³⁰ erat dictum, *Tibi*³¹ *tradite sunt claves*³² *regni celorum*. Matt. xvi capitulo.³³,³⁴ Ubi fuit responsum quod peccatum fuit utile eis³⁵ solum per accidens, eo quod postmodum propter enormitatem delictorum suorum gravius penitebant. Et ob hoc non inde consequitur³⁶ quoniam per eorum peccata revertebantur a loco in quo erat impetus spiritus. Sic enim dicit apostolus³⁷ ad Romanos viii capitulo,³⁸ *Quoniam*³⁹ *diligentibus Deum omnia cooperantur*⁴⁰ *in bonum*,⁴¹ intelligendo per se sive per accidens, cum tamen multis in⁴² locis affirmet quod peccans mortaliter reliquit⁴³ viam iusticie. Et fuerant dicta aliqua pauca inpertinencia, quia videbantur utilia michi,⁴⁴ et fiebat finis sermonis.

Sermon 64 (B fo. 91r ; J fo. 74r; L fo. 105r; N fo. 118r)
Sermo eiusdem Ricardi in vulgari apud Datyngton' in festo omnium sanctorum anno domini millesimo CCC^{mo} quinquagesimo sexto.⁴⁵

---

4 perditoris: proditoris *N*.   5 impulsum: impulsam *N*.   6 brevis: pronis *N*.   7 cum: causa *N*.   8 eciam: iter<um> (?) *N*.   9 *add.* sic *N*.   10 fit: sic *N*.   11 ydolatriam: idolatriam *N*.   12 locis: legis *N*.   13 thematis nostri: nostri thematis *J*.   14 aratrum: matrem *N*.   15 ix⁰: ix *BN* 11*J*.   16 Luc. 9. 62.   17 *add.* quomodo *N*.   18 obiectum: *corr. ex* abiectum *N*.   19 *om.* et *N*.   20 profuerunt: profuerim *N*.   21 quorum: quo *N*.   22 adulterii et homicidii: homicidium et dusterii *N*.   23 dictum: ducum *N*.   24 virum: vir *N*.   25 iuxta: secundum *N*.   26 Cf. (?) 1 Reg. 13.14.   27 De secunda: se seran' *N*.   28 peccata: ppeccata *N*.   29 Cf. Luc. 7. 47.   30 de tercio: detorcio *N*.   31 *add.* et *N*.   32 claves: clavis *N*.   33 xvi capitulo: 16 *J* xvi *N*.   34 Cf. Matt. 16. 19.   35 utile eis: eis utile *N*.   36 inde consequitur: indicio sequitur *N*.   37 dicit apostolus: apostolus dicit *N*.   38 viii capitulo: 8 *J* viii quarto *N*.   39 quoniam: quod *BL* quia *N*.   40 cooperantur: cooperiuntur *N*.   41 Rom. 8. 28.   42 multis in: in multis *N*.   43 reliquit: reliquid *N*.   44 *om.* michi *BLN*.   45 Sermo eiusdem Ricardi in vulgari apud Datyngton' in festo omnium sanctorum anno domini millesimo CCC^{mo} quinquagesimo sexto: Sermo in wulgari in festo omnium sanctorum *J* Sermo eiusdem Ricardi in vulgari apud Datyngton' in festo omnium sanctorum anno domini millesimo CCC^{mo} lvi⁰ *L* Sermo eiusdem

Audivi numerum signatorum. Apocalipsis vii^{mo}[46] capitulo et in epistolari lectione festi istius. Premissa oracione introductum fuit thema per tria genera[47] signatorum Dei gracia salvatrice. Primum est viatorum sanctorum. Secundum est actualiter purgatorum seu in purgatorio actualiter punitorum. Tercium est in celestibus beatorum. Primi, licet sint sancti, quia tamen eorum sanctitas ab aliis ignoratur ac eciam aliis – quo ad permanenciam sibi ipsis eciam – est incerta, quia[48] *Nemo novit utrum odio an amore sit dignus,*[49] Ecclesiastes ix capitulo[50/51] (potest enim quisque[52] quantumcumque[53] sit bonus in ictu oculi in mortale peccatum incidere cum non solum in rebus prohibitis sit mortale peccatum factum prohibitum exercere set eciam ex[54] deliberacione[55] et voluntatis assensu factum huiusmodi affectare, iuxta illud omnium salvatoris, *Qui viderit mulierem ad concupiscendam eam*[56] *mechatus est eam in corde suo.* Matthei xix capitulo[57]),[58] nemo potest certus esse[59] / (fo. 118rb *N*) de altero quod est sanctus nec eciam quod in sanctitate perseverabit in finem et ob hoc honor[60] qui ab ecclesia isto die sanctis impenditur sic[61] signatis[62] tantummodo non debet impendi. Secundi licet sint Dei gracia in purgatorio sicut fuerant in vita signati et preter hoc careant maculis peccatorum, quia[63] tamen debitum[64] ibi ab eis exigitur pro seipsis non sunt congrui adhuc mediatores pro nobis ad Deum. Ideo eis non impendimus hunc honorem nec eis ab ecclesia exhibetur. Tercii vero quia[65] habent non tantum stolas albas[66] ob graciam candidantem et eciam[67] palma<s>[68] in manibus triumphale<s>[69] tanquam victrices omnium peccatorum ita ut amodo nec peccare[70] poterunt[71] nec pro peccatis puniri set insuper stant ante tronum[72] Dei, eius[73] faciem intuentes, iuxta illud Johannis in[74] nostra leccione pretacta, *Post hec,* inquid, *vidi turbam magnam quam nemo dinumerare*[75] *poterat stantes ante thronum*[76] *in conspectu agni amicti stolis albis et palme in manibus eorum,* Apocalipsis vii capitulo[77,78] ob hoc eis tanquam perfecte signatis ac nostris patronis isto die simul impendimus hunc honorem et eos – quia propter[79] ipsorum multitudinem quam, ut dicit, nemo dinumerare potest, non divisim set simul – oracionibus , ieuniis et elemosinis / (fo. 74rb *J*) ac aliis nostris obsequiis veneramur, ad quod faciendum sanctus Johannes, edoctus ab angelo, ut affirmat, volens nos utiliter excitare, expressit verba premissa, *Audivi numerum signatorum,*[80] ubi supra. In quibus verbis tres causas probabiles, immo[81] iustas, impendendi eis honorem, ut

---

Ricardi in vulgari apud Dadyngton' in festo omnium sanctorum anno lvi^{to} *N*.   46 vii^{mo}: 7 *J*.
47 *add.* hominum *N*.   48 quia: *(?)*cena *N*.   49 sit dignus: dignus sit *J*.   50 *om.* capitulo *J*.
51 Ecclesiastes 9.1.   52 *om.* quisque *J*.   53 quantumcumque: quantum quandoque *N*.   54 ex: de *BN*.   55 deliberacione: laboracione *N*.   56 eam: illam *N*.   57 xix capitulo: 19 *J*.   58 *recte* Matt. 5.28.   59 certus esse: esse certus *J*.   60 honor: onor *N*.   61 sic: *(?)*sicut *J*.
62 signatis: signanter *N*.   63 quia: quod *J*.   64 debitum: debiti *N*.   65 *add.* non *N*.   66 albas: alias *N*.   67 et eciam: eciam et *N*.   68 palma<s>: palmam *B J cum abbrev. LN*.
69 triumphale<s>: triumphalem *BJ cum abbrev. LN*.   70 nec peccare: peccare non *J*.
71 poterunt: potuerunt *BL*.   72 thronum: tronum *BJ*.   73 eius: cuius *N*.   74 in: iii *N*.
75 dinumerare: dinu merare *N*.   76 thronum: tronum *JN*.   77 vii capitulo: 7 *J*.   78 Apoc. 7.9.
79 *om.* propter *N*.   80 signatorum: signarum *N*.   81 immo: ymmo *BLN*.

ex hoc nobis commodum[82] acquiramus, ostendit, videlicet eorum sanctitatem sive bonitatem,[83] eorum facultatem sive potestatem et eorum gratam voluntatem. Bonitatem probat signacio. *Signatorum*, inquit,[84] id est beatorum. Potestatem[85] affirmat / (fo. 105v *L*) collectio, quia multi[86]. *Numerum* inquit.[87] Et voluntatem gratam propalat instructio. *Audivi*,[88] inquit,[89] uno eorum, scilicet angelo, me docente. Ex quibus possumus fidenter inferre quod sunt a nobis honorandi et quod sunt nobis proficui quia alias essent, quod beati non possunt nobis esse,[90] ingrati. Set hic dices,[91] 'In quo nobis proficiunt isti iam[92] vere beati[93] cum loqui non possunt – sunt enim anime separate sine corporibus, domino nostro Ihesu,[94] matre eius et hiis qui surrexerunt cum Christo resurgente[95] exceptis?' Et si dixerimus quod habent ut angeli linguas[96] spirituales iuxta illud apostoli, 1^a ad[97] Corinthios xiii[98,99] *Si linguis hominum loquar[1] et angelorum* et cetera, quam loquelam ita Deus intelligit et exceptat[2] ac si linguis corporalibus verba sonarent, artamur ostendere qualiter non solum hic in terris per nos gesta agnoscunt set qualiter[3] novas habent voluntates et vicissitudines voluntatum et cogitaciones eciam variatas,[4] iuxta hominum voluntates varias, quibus orando sive petendo Deum debent et possunt[5] eis succurrere. Ubi si dixerimus quod sicut[6] nobis ministrantes angeli vident que gerimus, sic et ipsi, et eciam cogitaciones et voluntates variatas[7] et varias, sicut[8] ipsi angeli, sine detrimento sue beatitudinis, ipsi habent – non enim omnis cuiuscumque[9] cogitacionis aut voluntatis innovacio[10] sive variacio beatitudinem veram auget aut minuit[11] – forte insurget dubietas de delectacione annexa. Ita[12] enim videntur gaudere de nostro profectu sive[13] affectare de novo nostrum futurum profectum sicut et angeli, de quibus salvator affirmat, *Maius gaudium est in celo coram angelis Dei super uno*[14] *peccatore penitenciam agente quam super nona<ginta> n<ovem>*[15] *iustis*[16] *qui non indigent*[17] *penitencia*.[18] Luc. xv° capitulo.[19/20] Et sic videntur beatitudinis augmentum[21] aliquando accipere et pariter ex causa seu occasione contraria[22] (fo. 118v *N*) illud / (fo. 74v *J*) amittere,[23] nisi fortassis dixerimus quod huiusmodi gaudia ad beatitudinem omnino non pertinent et ob hoc nec essencialiter nec accidentaliter eam minuunt[24] aut augmentant[25] sicuti nec huiusmodi passiones in capite nostro Christo suam beatitudinem non minuerunt neque[26] auxerunt cum erat conversatus in terra. Set non amplius de hiis modo.

82 commodum: comodum *N*.   83 sive bonitatem: sanitatem *N*.   84 inquit: inquid *BL*.
85 potestatem: bonitatem *N*.   86 *om*. multi *BN*.   87 inquit: inquid *BL*.   88 Audivi: Adam *N*.
89 inquit: inquid *BL*.   90 *om*. esse *BLN*.   91 set hic dices: nec dices hic *N*.   92 iam: alii *N*.
93 beati: beate *N*.   94 *add*. Christi *N*.   95 resurgente: surgente *N*.   96 linguas: ligulas *N*.
97 1^a ad: 1 *BL*.   98 xiii: 13 *J*.   99 1 Cor. 13.1.   1 loquar: loquor *N*.   2 exceptat: acceptat *J*
expectat *N*.   3 qualiter: an aliter *N*.   4 variatas: veritas *N*.   5 possunt: possent *N*.   6 sicut: si
N.   7 variatas: contrarias *N*.   8 sicut: sicud *JL*.   9 cuiuscumque: cuiusque *N*.   10 innovacio:
invencio *N*.   11 aut minuit: et minuet *N*.   12 *om*. ita *N*.   13 sive: sicut *BLN*.   14 *om*. uno *N*.
15 nona<ginta> n<ovem>: 19*J*99*N*.   16 *om*. iustis *JN*.   17 indigent: egerint *B* ege<nt>*J*
egent   *L*.   18 penitencia: penitenciam   *B*.   19 xv° capitulo: 15*J*.   20 Luc.   15.7.
21 augmentum: aumentum *N*.   22 *add*. et pariter *canc. L*.   23 amittere: emittere *N*.
24 minuunt: minuant *N*.   25 augmentant: aumentant *N*.   26 neque: videlicet *N*.

/ (fo. 92r B) Set racio prima quare debemus eis honorem impendere est signacio eorundem: si enim Deus eos honorat nos eos honorare debemus. Item[27] ex quo ecclesia eos statuit[28] honorandos simul[29] hoc die propter eorum multitudinem innumerabilem[30] nobis, ut dicit Johannes, merito obediencie nos agere sic debemus. Ubi fit[31] narracio[32] de extirpacione simulacrorum[33] et ydolorum de Pantheon, templo omnium demonum in Roma, et veneracione omnium sanctorum pro istis[34] per dominum papam Urbanum et ecclesiam[35] ordinata. Dicta fuerant aliqua pericula[36] de veneracione ymaginum quas communiter nomine ymaginatorum appellant et male, videlicet, sanctam Mariam de Lincoln,[37] sanctam Mariam de Walsyngham,[38] sanctam Mariam in novo opere, et ita de ceteris, cum sancta Maria, mater Dei, sit semper in celo, numquam in locis illis aut aliis illis similibus hic in terra. Unde qui tales ymagines venerantur pro seipsis et eis offerunt pro medelis aut commodis[39] aliquibus procurandis videntur veri et patentes ydolatre, quoniam[40] non solum ymaginem tanquam ymaginem, scilicet solum ymaginatum, adorant set parcialiter propter ipsam ymaginem. Unde non dubium quin racionale[41] ob/(fo. 106r L)sequium trunco exhibent aut picture propter picturam. Et est[42] supersticio reprobanda. Et si pueri a parentibus sic informati ad Iudeos vel[43] Saracenos ducentur captivi[44] ipsi perpetuo tales ymagines tanquam ydolatre adorarent, res ymaginatas per eas[45] penitus ignorantes. Istam ydolatriam introducit cotidie[46] cupiditas oblacionum, que offeruntur[47] talibus ymaginibus propter fabricata ac ficta miracula, ministrorum ecclesie, ymmo verius Sathane, super quo excessu expedit per prelatos remedium adhiberi. Secundo fuit ostensum qualiter sancti isti tripliciter nobis proficiunt, remedium ut[48] a peccatis resipiscamus sepius procurando, iustificatos ne cadamus sepius adiuvando et ut grandia[49] opera perficiamus sepius promovendo.[50] / (fo. 74vb J) Quo ad[51] primum fuit ostensum qualiter nos oracionibus, ieiuniis et elemosinis mutuo[52] nos iuvamus et ex hoc fuit suasum qualiter isti sancti beati nobis benivoli similia iuvamenta nobis a[53] Deo per angelos adhiberi procurant. Ubi de elemosina fiebat sermo diffusior,[54] primo[55] ostendendo quod aliter per eam quam per oracionem et ieiunium homines cotidie adiuvantur pro eo quod per elemosinam nobis cotidie impetramus alios oratores et alios qui pro nobis ieiunant: non ita in aliis. Ubi tractatum fuit illud salvatoris: *Facite vobis amicos de mammona*[56] *iniquitatis ut ipsi recipiant vos in eterna*

---

27 item: facto *N*. 28 eos statuit: statuit eos *N*. 29 simul: similis *N*. 30 innumerabilem: innumeratibilem *N*. 31 *om.* fit *J*. 32 narracio: variacio *N*. 33 extirpacione simulacrorum: exstirpacione silanciorum *N*. 34 istis: illis *BJL*. 35 ecclesiam: ecclesiarum *N*. 36 pericula: particula *N*. 37 Lincoln: Lyncoln' *J* Lincolin *N*. 38 de Walsyngham: Walsinham *N*. 39 commodis: comodis *BL* comodum *N*. 40 quoniam: qui *N*. 41 racionale: racionabile *N*. 42 et est: et cetera *N*. 43 vel: aut *BL om. N*. 44 captivi: caponi *N*. 45 per eas: earum *BLN*. 46 *add.* cotidie *per errorem repetit. N*. 47 offeruntur: offerunt *N*. 48 ut: vel *N*. 49 grandia: gaudia *N*. 50 perficiamus sepius promovendo: proficiamus spe movendo *N*. 51 quo ad: qui *N*. 52 *om.* mutuo *N*. 53 a: ad *N*. 54 diffusior: diffusio *N*. 55 *add.* est *N*. 56 mammona: mamona *B* mamonia *L*.

tabernacula. Luc. xvi capitulo.[57,58] Non autem ita est dictum[59] aut ita[60] dici potuit de oracione sive ieiunio. Et quo ad[61] dubium tactum[62] qualiter pauperes quia[63] parum habentes suaderi debent ut elemosinas[64] facerent cum hoc pocius suaderi deberet[65] divitibus, fuit ostensum econtra quod pauperibus in casu sauderi deberet[66] dacio elemosine / (fo. 118vb *N*) ut scire possent quid eis proficeret[67] et ad quantum, quod plures ignorant, et ad hoc expositum fuit illud salvatoris, *Amen, Amen, dico vobis quoniam hec vidua plus omnibus obtulit*[68] et cetera. Luc. xxi[o69] capitulo.[70,71] Et de avaris illud so/(fo. 92v *B*)litum fuit ostensum, scilicet quod utilius est quadrantem ex caritate in vita offerre quam quod[72] executores offerant quantumcumque post mortem et eciam quod <per> factum executorum[73] <pro> talibus, quia sunt avari et ob hoc in peccato mortali decedunt, nullum fructum nec in celo nec[74] in purgatorio consequuntur.[75,76] Et quo ad[77] primum modum quo nos iuvant sancti iam[78] vere beati fuit relata[79] populo narracio una de[80] miraculis sancte Marie virginis, matris Dei,[81] de milite homicida atque predone[82] preservato per xiiii annos ne iugularetur a diabolo,[83] camerario suo tanto tempore sub humana effigie,[84] quia singulis diebus quantumcumque perversus decem salutaciones[85] angelicas beate[86] virgini offerebat, quam rem in publico coram omnibus familiaribus eiusdem militis quidam vir[87] sanctus, ad hoc ab eo spoliari cupiens, spoliatus ac captus ipsum camerarium fateri compulit adiuratum,[88] scilicet quod si uno die de illis xiiii[89] annis illas salutaciones dicere omisisset eum[90] continue iugulasset. Descripto secundo iuvamine, scilicet qualiter sancti beati nos a sceleribus[91] expurgatos ne[92] temptacionibus succumbamus sepe nos[93] adiuvant ministerio angelorum, adiecta fuit narracio de quodam episcopo, devoto sancto Andree / (fo. 75r *J*) apostolo, qualiter diabolus,[94] in specie mulieris pulcherrime, se fingens filiam regis cuiusdam nobilis et heredem, volens[95] castitatem servare, audita fama eius et cetera, sicut in sermone illo, *Rex tuus veniet tibi iustus*.[96] Et tercio quo ad tercium

---

57 xvi capitulo: 16*J*. 58 Luc. 16.9. 59 *add.* qualiter *N*. 60 ita: ibi *N*. 61 quo ad: qua *N*. 62 tactum: tacitum *BLN*. 63 quia: quoniam *BN*. 64 elemosinas: helemosinas *L*. 65 deberet: debent *J*. 66 deberet: debent *J*. 67 proficeret: proficerent *J*. 68 obtulit: optulit *J*. 69 xxi°: xxi *B*. 70 xxi° capitulo: 21*J*. 71 Cf. Luc. 21.3. 72 *om.* quod *N*. 73 executorum: extentorum *N*. 74 nec: vero *N*. 75 consequuntur: consecuntur *BL*. 76 Although an emendation is suggested for the defect in syntax, it may represent a loss of train of thought on the preacher's part – with *avari* substituted for *factum* as the subject – rather than being a corruption of the text. 77 *om.* ad *N*. 78 iuvant sancti iam: istam *N*. 79 relata: narrata *N*. 80 una de: unde *N*. 81 *om.* Dei *N*. 82 *om.* predone *N*. 83 diabolo: dyabolo *BLN*. 84 effigie: figura *N*. 85 salutaciones: salutacionis *N*. 86 beate: beati *N*. 87 quidam vir: quidem vere *N*. 88 compulit adiuratum: compulsit ad iuratum *N*. 89 xiiii: 14*J*. 90 eum: cum *N*. 91 sceleribus: celeribus *N*. 92 ne: in *N*. 93 *om.* a sceleribus expurgatos ne temptacionibus succumbamus sepe nos *J*. 94 diabolus: dyabolus *BL*. 95 See the preceding note. While the syntax strictly requires *volentem*, it is evident that in the train of thought here the reference is to *diabolus*. 96 The reference is to Sermon 43 of the sermon diary, delivered at Athboy [Co. Meath], 30 November 1354, being the first Sunday of Advent and also the feast of St Andrew. There, the story, whose ultimate source is the *Legenda Aurea* (cf. G. Paolo Maggioni, ed., *Iacopo da Varazze Legenda Aurea con le miniature del codice Ambrosiano C 240 inf. Testo critico riveduto e*

iuvamentum a sanctis beatis nobis impensum, scilicet[97] ut in[98] gracia existentes opera grandia efficiamus[99] / (fo. 106v L) illo modo racione ostenso narracio de sancta Lucia[1] et Euticia matre eius fuit relata, scilicet[2] qualiter in sompno per sanctam Agatham[3] roborata, facta est virgo fortissima ita[4] ut matrem suam a fluxu sanguinis sua oracione salvaret. Et recapitulacio dictorum facta ac indulgencia omnibus vere contritis ac vere confessis ibi presentibus et qui[5] de ibi presentibus[6] infra octo dies tales se facere vellent concessa <sc. est>. Finis fuit[7] sermoni impositus.

commento (2 vols, Florence & Milan, 2007), 1, pp 38–42), is expanded slightly, though not recorded at full length. See Oxford, St John's College, MS 65, fos 53r–54r. **97** *om.* scilicet *N*. **98** *om.* in *BN*. **99** efficiamus: faciamus *BJL*. **1** Lucia: Luca *N*. **2** *om.* scilicet *N*. **3** Agatham: Aghatam *J* Aghatham *N*. **4** ita: fiat *N*. **5** The defective syntax here has been allowed to stand without emendation as more probably to be ascribed again to the recording of a train of thought rather than being a textual corruption. **6** *om.* et qui de ibi presentibus *J*. **7** Finis fuit: Fuit finis *J*.

Is it better for the king of England to be a king of England than a duke of Aquitaine? Richard FitzRalph and Adam Wodeham on whether beatific enjoyment is an act of the intellect or an act of the will

SEVERIN V. KITANOV

FITZRALPH AND WODEHAM: SCHOLARS OR THINKERS?

In Thomas Duddy's *History of Irish thought*, Archbishop FitzRalph is mentioned at the end of the chapter devoted to John Scottus Eriugena and treated summarily alongside Aquinas' arts teacher in Naples, Peter of Ireland. Duddy's verdict regarding Peter of Ireland's and Richard FitzRalph's contribution to Irish thought, based in part on Michael Dunne's assessment of the place of Peter of Ireland in the history of Latin Aristotelianism and on Katherine Walsh's comprehensive study of the life, writings and thought of FitzRalph, is that Peter of Ireland and Richard FitzRalph are best understood as scholars rather than as original thinkers, although '[t]he work of most scholars', writes Duddy, 'whether medieval or modern, contributes impressively to the history of research, exegesis, commentary, and interpretation [...]'.[1] According to Duddy, 'the best scholars are not original thinkers, even to a minor degree [...]'.[2] The work of those scholars merits attention mostly on account of the thinkers with whom they are associated. This kind of assessment, although quite sympathetic in tone, seems based on the assumption that the work of thinkers worthy of a lengthy historical narrative appears in an intellectual vacuum. Are we not guilty of a Romantic bias in assuming that originality implies a sort of divine fiat? It may be true that Aquinas was indeed an original thinker, but what would Aquinas have been without Aristotle, Averroës, Augustine and, to no small measure, his own immediate teachers – Master Martin, Master Peter and Master Albert? In any case, Dunne's essay on FitzRalph in Duddy's more recent encyclopedic volume, *Dictionary of Irish philosophers*, adds immensely to our understanding of FitzRalph's role in the history of Irish thought.[3] FitzRalph is no longer a relic of a 'defeated tradition', to use Alasdair MacIntyre's expres-

1 T. Duddy, *A history of Irish thought* (London & New York, 2002), p. 43. 2 Ibid. 3 M. Dunne, 'FitzRalph, Richard' in T. Duddy (ed.), *Dictionary of Irish philosophers* (London, 2006), pp 129–32. See also M. Dunne, 'Richard FitzRalph's *Lectura on the Sentences*' in P.W. Rosemann (ed.), *Medieval commentaries on the Sentences of Peter Lombard*, 2 (Leiden & Boston, 2010), pp 405–37.

sion,[4] an outlived historical curiosity too radically detached from the concern of modern day historians of philosophy to be worthy of any serious consideration, but a part of the living tradition of Irish thought, in particular, and western thought, in general. Just how original FitzRalph's philosophical theology is remains to be seen. The extent of this originality can be judged accurately only on the basis of a comprehensive and open-minded study of FitzRalph's *Lectura*.[5]

To acknowledge the significance of Adam Wodeham's contribution to philosophical theology, on the other hand, we can point to the testimony of the Scottish theologian and philosopher John Mair, who edited Henry Totting of Oyta's *Abbreviation* of Wodeham's Oxford lectures and authored the first biographical notice about Wodeham. According to Mair, Wodeham was Ockham's equal in logic and philosophy. If Ockham was a man of sublime and audacious disposition, Wodeham was to no small measure a man of exceptional and solid character. We should also mention the assessment of the seventeenth-century Irish scholar Luke Wadding, who wrote in his *Annales Minorum* that Wodeham's lectures attracted 'huge crowds' and that afterward many doctors used Wodeham's theological authority in support of their own views.[6] But a more adequate appraisal of Wodeham's originality and place in the history of western thought has been made possible only in the past three decades as a result of William Courtenay's unsurpassed reconstruction of the intellectual context of Wodeham's life, writings and thought,[7] Rega Wood's edition of Wodeham's *Lectura secunda*, and a considerable number of essays and book chapters exploring various aspects of Wodeham's theological and philosophical work.[8]

4 See A. MacIntyre, *Three rival versions of moral enquiry: encyclopaedia, genealogy and tradition* (Notre Dame, IN, 1990), pp 149–69.   5 Gordon Leff's dated study of FitzRalph's *Sentences* commentary is thus far the only attempt at a complete reconstruction of FitzRalph's philosophical theology. In Leff's judgment, FitzRalph's commentary is derivative and sketchy when compared with William Ockham's groundbreaking *Sentences* commentary. Walsh has criticized this judgment mostly on historical grounds. See G. Leff, *Richard FitzRalph: commentator on the Sentences: a study of theological orthodoxy* (Manchester, 1963), pp 12–13; see also K. Walsh, *A fourteenth-century scholar and primate: Richard FitzRalph in Oxford, Avignon and Armagh* (Oxford, 1981), pp 50–5. Walsh also singles out Jean-François Genest's study of FitzRalph's *Quaestio biblica* on 'future contingents' as a turning point in the evaluation of FitzRalph's contribution to philosophical theology. See K. Walsh, 'FitzRalph, Richard (b. before 1300, d. 1360)', *Oxford dictionary of national biography*, Sept. 2004; online ed., May 2010, http://www.oxforddnb.com/view/article/9627, accessed 7 July 2010. As Michael Haren notes, however, a more complete evaluation of FitzRalph's work will have to await the critical edition of FitzRalph's *Sentences* commentary. See Michael Haren, 'Richard FitzRalph of Dundalk, Oxford and Armagh: scholar, prelate and controversialist' in James McEvoy and Michael Dunne (eds), *The Irish contribution to European scholastic thought* (Dublin, 2009), pp 88–110 at p. 100.   6 For Mair's and Wadding's biographical accounts of Wodeham, see R. Wood, 'Introduction' in R. Wood and G. Gál (eds), *Adam de Wodeham, lectura secunda in librum primum Sententiarum* (3 vols, St Bonaventure, NY, 1990), 1, pp 5–49 at pp 7–8.   7 See W.J. Courtenay, *Adam Wodeham: an introduction to his life and writings* (Leiden, 1978).   8 For a bibliography of manuscripts and editions of Wodeham's writings and studies of Wodeham's thought, see the Adam Wodeham Critical Edition Project at http://jeffreycwitt.com/adamwodeham/bibliography/.

FITZRALPH'S AND WODEHAM'S TREATMENTS OF ENJOYMENT

The distinction between enjoyment and use (*frui et uti*), inherited from the writings of Aurelius Augustine and employed by Peter Lombard as a tool for organizing the contents of the *Sentences*, became in thirteenth-century *Sentences* commentaries an appropriate platform for exploring a number of significant epistemological, psychological, ethical and metaphysical problems associated with the relation between human beings and God, in this life (*in via*) and the next (*in patria*). Given the vital importance of the Christian belief in the possibility of personal salvation and everlasting life, on the one hand, and the growing popularity of Aristotelian eudemonism, on the other, many Christian theologians considered it paramount to address concerns about the compatibility between the Christian ideal of beatitude and Aristotle's praise of the activity of philosophical contemplation as the best human lifestyle. More specifically, theologians attempted to articulate a distinctive theological concept such that it could accommodate a purely Christian understanding of the ultimate end and the nature of one's relation to that end. This is the concept of beatific enjoyment (*fruitio beatifica*). In the effort to articulate this concept, theologians asked a number of key questions: What exactly is beatific enjoyment and how does it differ from use? Is it possible to know by natural means alone that God is the sole adequate object of enjoyment? Are there different kinds and degrees of enjoyment? Can one enjoy the divine persons separately from each other, on the one hand, and separately from the divine essence, on the other? Is enjoyment an intellectual or volitional act? Is beatific enjoyment a free or determined act?[9]

---

[9] To my knowledge, the first twentieth-century scholar to have written about the medieval scholastic discussion of the Augustinian concepts of *frui* and *uti* is Ludger Meier. See L. Meier, 'Zwei Grundbegriffe augustinischer Theologie in der mittelalterlichen Franziskanerschule' in *Fünfte Lektorenkonferenz der deutschen Franziskaner für Philosophie und Theologie*, Schwarz in Tirol, 3–7, Sept. 1929 (Werl i. Westfalen, 1930), pp 53–74; Meier, *Dei Barfüsserschule zu Erfurt* [Beiträge zur Geschichte der Philosophie und Theologie des Mittelalters, Band XXXVIII, Heft 2] (Münster Westf., 1959), pp 111–12. The literature dealing with the concept of beatific enjoyment in scholastic theology and philosophy is as follows: S.V. Kitanov, 'Peter of Candia on demonstrating that God is the sole object of beatific enjoyment', *Franciscan Studies*, 67 (2009), 427–89; idem, 'Durandus of St-Pourçain and Peter Auriol on the act of beatific enjoyment' in S.F. Brown, T. Dewender and Th. Kobusch (eds), *Philosophical debates at Paris in the early fourteenth century* (Leiden, 2009), pp 163–78; idem, 'Beatific enjoyment in scholastic theology and philosophy: 1240–1335' (PhD, Helsinki, 2006); idem, 'Peter of Candia on beatific enjoyment: can one enjoy the divine persons separately from the divine essence?' *Mediaevalia Philosophica Polonorum*, 35:1 (2006), 145–66; idem, 'Displeasure in Heaven, pleasure in Hell: four Franciscan masters on the relationship between love and pleasure, and hatred and displeasure', *Traditio*, 58 (2003), 287–340; idem, 'Bonaventure's understanding of *Fruitio*', *Picenum Seraphicum*, 20 (2001), 137–91; K. Georgedes, 'The serpent in the tree of knowledge: enjoyment and use in fourteenth-century theology' (PhD, Wisconsin-Madison, 1995); W.J. Courtenay, 'Between despair and love: some late modifications of Augustine's teaching on fruition and psychic states' in Kenneth Hagen (ed.), *Augustine, the harvest and theology (1300–1650)* (Leiden, 1990), pp 5–20; idem,

The topic of beatific enjoyment became especially well-liked around the turn of the thirteenth and the beginning of the fourteenth century. Commentators on Lombard's *Sentences* tended to spend more time and effort debating the various questions routinely discussed in the context of the first distinction at the expense of some of the other distinctions of Lombard's *Sentences*. This is certainly the case with FitzRalph, who devotes a considerable portion of his *Lectura*[10] to the *frui/uti* distinction (for instance, Paris, Bibliothèque Nationale de France MS 15853, fos 1ra–17rb) before dealing with distinctions 2 and 9 summarily. FitzRalph's treatment of enjoyment consists of two questions. Question 1 asks whether only the Trinity is to be enjoyed. Question 2 is whether beatitude is an act of the intellect or the will? Each of the two questions is neatly divided into four articles, the first three of which focus on specific topics, whereas the last one contains FitzRalph's response to the principal question. The first article of q. 1 is concerned with whether beatitude or the enjoyment of God is possible for a human being. The second article of q. 1 deals with whether the blessed can enjoy one divine person without enjoying another, or God's essence without the persons. The third article of q. 1 examines whether the will enjoys the ultimate end freely on the basis of the liberty of contradiction.[11] The first article of q. 2 is whether the will is a nobler faculty (*potentia*) than the intellect. The second article deals with whether joy (*gaudium*) or pleasure (*delectatio*) is the same as volition. The third article explores whether joy or pleasure is beatitude.[12]

In Wodeham's case, we have two separate treatments of beatific enjoyment – one from Wodeham's *Lectura secunda*, edited by Wood, and a second, longer treatment found in Wodeham's *Oxford lectures*.[13] Wodeham's treatment of enjoy-

Schools and scholars in fourteenth-century England (Princeton, 1987), pp 282–98; A.S. McGrade, 'Enjoyment at Oxford after Ockham' in A. Hudson and M. Wilks (eds), *From Ockham to Wyclif* (Oxford, 1987), pp 63–88; idem, 'Ockham and Valla on enjoyment' in I.D. McFarlane (ed.), *Acta conventus neo-Latini sanctandreani: proceedings of the fifth international congress of neo-Latin studies* (Binghamton, NY, 1986), pp 153–8; idem, 'Ockham on enjoyment:towards an understanding of fourteenth-century philosophy and theology', *Review of Metaphysics*, 33 (1981), 706–28; idem, in A.S. McGrade, J. Kilcullen and M. Kempshall (eds), *The Cambridge translations of medieval philosophical texts*, 2 (Cambridge, 2001), pp 349–417.   10 The *Lectura* dates from the period 1331–2 and is FitzRalph's major work from his university life at Oxford. The text of the *Lectura* is preserved in full and short versions in seven fourteenth-century manuscripts and in the form of extracts in a further set of seven manuscripts. I have used Paris, Bibl. Nat., MS lat. 15853, which is regarded as the most important of the extant codices. For a description of the mentioned codex, see ibid., pp 39–40, 475. For the list of manuscripts of FitzRalph's *Sentences* commentary, the table of questions, the various versions and a provisional stemma, see Dunne, 'Richard FitzRalph's Lectura', pp 407–20. For available texts from the ongoing FitzRalph Critical Edition Project at the National University of Ireland at Maynooth (NUIM), see the website of the FitzRalph Society at http://philosophy.nuim.ie/projects-research/projects/richard-fitzralph/text.   11 Ricardus Fitzralph, *Lectura in sententias* [hereafter *LS*], bk I, dist. 1, q. 1 (Paris, Bibl. Nat., MS 15853, fo. 1va).   12 Ibid., q. 2 (Paris, Bibl. Nat., MS 15853, fo. 12rb).   13 There is a disagreement regarding the exact nature of the relationship between Wodeham's *Lectura secunda*

ment in the *Lectura secunda* does not begin until the fourth and final question of the first distinction. The title of the question is 'whether enjoyment is really distinct from cognition and pleasure'. According to the actual division of the question, however, the first question is whether enjoyment is really distinct from the soul (q. 4), the second question is whether enjoyment is the same as cognition (q. 5), and the third question is whether enjoyment is the same as pleasure (q. 6).[14] Wodeham's discussion of enjoyment in the *Oxford lectures* comprises fourteen questions and extends over sixty-two folio pages in Paris, Sorbonne MS 193 (fos 12vb–74va). The following is the list of enjoyment related questions:

Q. 1 (fos 12vb–16rb): Utrum pro studio sacrae theologiae ex caritate procedente debeatur pro mercede visio Dei et eius fruitio.

Q. 2 (fos 16rb–18ra): Utrum fruitio beatifica differat ab ipsa anima.

Q. 3 (fos 18ra–20ra): Utrum fruitio realiter distinguatur ab omni cognitione.

Q. 4 (fos 20ra–23rb): Utrum fruitio realiter distinguatur a delectatione.

Q. 5 (fos 23rb–24rb): Utrum generaliter omnis delectatio sit dilectio vel odium, seu volitio aut nolitio.

Q. 6 (fos 24rb–35rb): Utrum voluntas necessario vel libere principiet actus suos.

Q. 7 (fos 35rb–37vb): Utrum voluntas sola sit causa effectiva suae volitionis liberae supposita communi Dei influentia vel concausatione.

Q. 8 (fos 37vb–44ra): Utrum voluntas possit simul et subito producere actum voluntarium meritorie et libere dilectionis.

Q. 9 (fos 44ra–48rb): Utrum voluntas libere possit subito suspendere actum suum sive ab actu habito cessare.

Q. 10 (fos 48rb–58ra): Utrum creatura rationalis clare videns Deum necessario diligat ipsum.

Q. 11 (fos 58ra–64ra): Undecimo circa distinctionem primam quaero: Utrum solus Deus sit licite a creatura rationali ultimate fruibilis.

Q. 12 (fos 64ra–69va): Utrum haec sit possibilis: 'creatura rationalis fruitur una persona divina non fruendo alia'.

Q. 13 (fos 69va–72va): Utrum liceat filium Dei plus diligere vel frui eo quam patrem vel spiritum sanctum.

Q. 14 (fos 72va–74va): Utrum fruitio beatifica sit actus intellectus.[15]

---

and the *Oxford lectures*. According to Courtenay, the *Lectura secunda* was written after the *Oxford lectures* and is independent of Wodeham's *London*, *Norwich* and *Oxford lectures*. According to Wood, the *Lectura secunda* precedes the *Oxford lectures* and the manuscript in which it is preserved is a part of Wodeham's *Norwich lectures*. See Wood, 'Introduction' in Wood and Gál (eds), *Adam de Wodeham, Lectura secunda*, i, 30–8. **14** Adam de Wodeham, *Lectura secunda*, i, bk I, dist. 1, q. 4,1. 5–6,1. 23–25, p. 251. **15** See http://jeffreycwitt.com/adamwodeham/text/.

A comparative textual analysis of FitzRalph's and Wodeham's treatments of enjoyment can be especially informative insofar as it can help us identify conceptual nuances and subtle theoretical shifts in the complex history of the scholastic debate regarding the nature and possibility of beatific enjoyment. Both FitzRalph and Wodeham lectured at Oxford at a time when Oxford was taking the lead over Paris in theological studies and research. FitzRalph probably lectured on the *Sentences* in 1326–7, incepted as Doctor of Theology in 1331, and was elected Chancellor of Oxford University a year later, on 30 May 1332. Wodeham completed his lectures on the *Sentences* in 1333 or 1334 and became *magister regens* in 1338.[16] Courtenay tells us that Wodeham may have attended FitzRalph's lectures on the *Sentences*.[17] According to Walsh, Wodeham functioned as a sententiary bachelor under FitzRalph's supervision in 1331–2.[18] Next to Ockham, FitzRalph is the most frequently cited contemporary authority in Wodeham's *Oxford lectures*.[19] Furthermore, FitzRalph may have changed some of his own positions as a result of Wodeham's criticism, and these changes were reflected in FitzRalph's *Opus correctum*, that is, FitzRalph's revised *Lectura*.[20]

BEATIFIC ENJOYMENT: AN ACT OF THE INTELLECT OR OF THE WILL?

In his *Commentary on Peter Lombard's Sentences*, Thomas Aquinas says that beatific enjoyment (*fruitio*) is man's ultimate happiness (*ultima felicitas*). Since, according to Aristotle, happiness is an operation, not a habit, ultimate happiness is found in the operation of the highest human faculty, that is, the intellect, with respect to the noblest of objects, that is, God. It follows that enjoyment is an operation of the intellect. Aquinas adds, however, that the actual union with God accomplished through a sort of (*quasi*) mutual penetration of seer and seen, lover and beloved, is followed by a great delight (*summa delectatio*). Thus, we employ the term 'fruition' to name happiness more so on account of the quality which completes or perfects happiness, that is, delight (*ex parte sui complementi*), rather than on account of happiness as such (*ex parte principii*), since happiness as such already involves some delight (*quamdam delectationem*). One should therefore say, according to Aquinas, that fruition is an act of the will more so than an act of the intellect.[21]

---

16 See Dunne, 'Richard FitzRalph's *Lectura*', pp 405–6; also idem, 'FitzRalph, Richard', 129; Courtenay, *Adam Wodeham*, pp 75–6; Courtenay, 'Wodeham, Adam (*c.*1295–1358)', *Oxford dictionary of national biography* (2004), http://www.oxforddnb.com/view/article/10854, accessed 27 Oct. 2010. For a tabular chronology of the Oxford lectureship of Wodeham and other contemporary theologians, see K.H. Tachau, 'Introduction' in P.A. Streveler and K.H. Tachau (eds), *Seeing the future clearly: questions on future contingents by Robert Holcot* (Toronto, 1995), p. 27. 17 See Courtenay, *Adam Wodeham*, p. 77. 18 See Walsh, *A fourteenth-century scholar*, p. 45. 19 See Courtenay, *Adam Wodeham*, p. 75. 20 Ibid., pp 77–8. 21 Thomas de Aquino,

Aquinas' remarks on beatific enjoyment fit nicely with Aristotle's account of happiness and pleasure in the *Nicomachean ethics*, book X. For Aristotle, pleasure is a good, but not the ultimate good. We would prefer vision, memory, knowledge and virtue even without the pleasure that inevitably accompanies them.[22] Pleasure relates to activity as beauty relates to youth. More precisely, pleasure perfects an activity.[23] Happiness is the operation of the highest human faculty, that is, the speculative intellect.[24] In line with Aristotle, Aquinas holds that happiness is the operation of the highest human faculty, that is, the intellect, and that ultimate happiness consists in the vision of God, which is an intellectual operation. Insofar as it is an operation, the vision of God, if unimpeded, involves a certain kind of pleasure. The great delight (*summa delectatio*), which Aquinas speaks of, is not the same as the pleasure of the unimpeded activity of contemplation and pertains to the activity of the will, not the activity of the intellect. Aquinas articulates this point further in his *Summa theologiae*, I^{a}II^{ae}, q. 3, a. 4, where he explains that beatitude as such (*essentialiter*) is an act of the intellect rather than the will, whereas the delight or joy (*gaudium*) experienced as a result of the actual attainment (*consecutio*) of the beatific object, that is, God, is an act of the will.[25]

Commentum in quatuor libros Sententiarum Petri Lombardi (Parma, 1856; repr. New York, 1948), bk I, dist. 1, q. 1, a. 1, p. 12: 'Respondeo dicendum, quod fruitio consistit in optima operatione hominis, cum fruitio sit ultima felicitas hominis. Felicitas autem non est in habitu, sed in operatione, secundum Philosophum 10 *Eth.* cap. 4. Optima autem operatio hominis est operatio altissimae potentiae, scilicet intellectus, ad nobilissimum objectum, quod est Deus: unde ipsa visio Divinitatis ponitur tota substantia nostrae beatitudinis, Joan. 17, 5: *Haec est vita aeterna, ut cognoscant te solum Deum verum.* Ex visione autem ipsum visum, cum non videatur per similitudinem, sed per essentiam, efficitur quodammodo intra videntem, et ista est comprehensio quae succedit spei, consequens visionem quae succedit fidei, sicut spes quodammodo generatur ex fide. Ex hoc autem quod ipsum visum receptum est intra videntem, unit sibi ipsi videntem, ut fiat quasi quaedam mutua penetratio per amorem. Sed dicitur 1 Joan. 4, 16: *Qui manet in caritate, in Deo manet et Deus in eo.* Ad unionem autem maxime convenientis sequitur delectatio summa; et in hoc perficitur nostra felicitas, quam fruitio nominat ex parte sui complementi, magis quam ex parte principii, cum in se includat quamdam delectationem. Et ideo dicimus quod est actus voluntatis, et secundum habitum caritatis, quamvis secundum ordinem ad potentias et habitus praecedentes' [italics in the original]. 22 Aristoteles, *Ethica Nicomachea* (AL, XXVI 1–3, fasc. quartus), Renatus Antonius Gauthier (ed.) (Leiden, 1973), X.2, l. 20, p. 568, l. 1, p. 569 (74a5–10): 'Et circa multa studium faceremus utique, etsi neque unam inferant delectacionem, puta videre, recordari, scire, virtutes habere. Si autem ex necessitate sequntur his delectaciones, nichil differt. Eligeremus enim utique hec, etsi non fieret utique ab his delectacio. Quoniam quidem igitur neque per se bonum delectacio neque omnis eligibilis, manifestum videtur esse, et quoniam sint quedam eligibiles, secundum se ipsas differentes specie, vel a quibus [...]'. 23 Ibid., X.5, ll 27–8, p. 570 (74b30): 'Perficit autem operacionem delectacio non sicut habitus que inest, sed ut superveniens quidam finis velud iuvenibus pulcritudo'. 24 Ibid., X.8, ll. 10–16, p. 576 (77a10–15): 'Si autem felicitas est secundum virtutem operacio, racionabile secundum optimam; hec autem utique erit optimi; sive igitur intellectus hoc sive aliud quid quod utique secundum naturam videtur principari et dominari et intelligenciam habere de bonis et divinis, sive divinum ens et upsum, sive eorum que in nobis divinissimum, huius operacio secundum propriam virtutem erit utique perfecta felicitas. Quoniam autem est speculativa, dictum est'. 25 Thomas de Aquino, *Summa theologiae* (Madrid, 1985), I^{a}II^{ae}, q. 3, a. 4, p. 27:

Aquinas' account of beatific enjoyment created two different challenges with respect to articulating a coherent theological concept of fruition. Aquinas had not really explained the exact nature of the relation between delight and volition. If beatific enjoyment is an act of the will, then how does enjoyment differ from delight, which also pertains to the will? Since delight or pleasure was generally considered a passion, why not call enjoyment a passion rather an act of the will? Aquinas had also placed too much emphasis on the speculative or vision-based aspect of the experience of heavenly beatitude, which is why later authors, especially Franciscan theologians, believed it was important to give just as much consideration to love and volition in the state of the beatific vision. Since both FitzRalph and Wodeham address the challenges raised by Aquinas' account of enjoyment in their commentaries on Lombard's *Sentences*, a careful comparison of the portions of these commentaries which discuss whether fruition (or beatitude in general) is an act of the intellect or the will can show the extent to which FitzRalph's and Wodeham's work is merely derivative or genuinely innovative.[26]

'Respondeo dicendum quod ad beatitudinem, sicut supra dictum est, duo requiruntur: unum quod est essentia beatitudinis; aliud quod est quasi per se accidens eius, scilicet delectatio ei adiuncta. Dico ergo quod, quantum ad id quod est essentialiter ipsa beatitudo, impossibile est quod consistat in actu voluntatis. Manifestum est enim ex praemissis quod beatitudo est consecutio finis ultimi. Consecutio autem finis non consistit in ipso actu voluntatis. Voluntas enim fertur in finem et absentem, cum ipsum desiderat; et praesentem, cum in ipso requiescens delectatur. Manifestum est autem quod ipsum desiderium finis non est consecutio finis, sed est motus ad finem. Delectatio autem advenit voluntati ex hoc quod finis est praesens: non autem e converso ex hoc aliquid fit praesens, quia voluntas delectatur in ipso. Oportet igitur aliquid aliud esse quam actum voluntatis, per quod fit ipse finis praesens volenti. Et hoc manifeste apparet circa fines sensibiles. Si enim consequi pecuniam esset per actum voluntatis, statim a principio cupidus consecutus esset pecuniam, quando vult eam habere. Sed a principio quidem est absens ei; consequitur autem ipsam per hoc quod manu ipsam apprehendit, vel aliquo huiusmodi; et tunc iam delectatur in pecunia habita. Sic igitur et circa intelligibilem finem contingit. Nam a principio volumus consequi finem intelligibilem; consequimur autem ipsum per hoc quod fit praesens nobis per actum intellectus; et tunc voluntas delectata conquiescit in fine iam adepto. Sic igitur essentia beatitudinis in actu intellectus consistit, sed ad voluntatem pertinet delectatio beatitudinem consequens; secundum quod Augustinus dicit, X *Confess.*, quod beatitudo est *gaudium de veritate*; quia scilicet ipsum gaudium est consummatio beatitudinis' [italics in the original]. It should be noted that Thomas' indication that pleasure is a *quasi per se* accident of happiness means that pleasure is not included in the definition of happiness. Pleasure is understood as an interconvertible or coextensive property. Interconvertible properties are non-essential properties, yet they can be said to 'follow' or 'flow from' their subjects. See P.L. Reynolds, *'Per se* accidents, accidental being and the theology of the Eucharist in Thomas Aquinas', *Documenti e studi sulla tradizione filosofica medievale*, 13 (2002), 198.   26 In her contribution to the present volume, Katherine Tachau corrects the interpretation of FitzRalph's views on the relation of the will, the intellect and their acts as derivative and inconsistent. According to Tachau, this interpretation was advanced by the historians Konstanty Michalski and John A. Robson and restated unchallenged in the works of Gordon Leff and Katherine Walsh, although Walsh, in light of William Courtenay's examination of the sources, acknowledged that FitzRalph and Wodeham influenced each other's work on several occasions. After tracing the origin and evolution of the interpretation, Tachau demonstrates that the assumptions on which the interpretation is based are not supported by the manuscript sources. See Tachau, 'Adam Wodeham and Robert Holcot

Thus, I focus primarily on the discussions of enjoyment contained respectively in dist. 1, q. 2 of FitzRalph's *Lectura* and dist. 1, q. 14 of Wodeham's *Oxford lectures*.

FITZRALPH: NOBLE FACULTIES, PLEASURE AND THE DIFFERENT SENSES OF BEATITUDE

In his response to the first article of the second question, FitzRalph states that the view according to which the intellect is nobler than the will is very probable (*valde probabilis*), yet he concurs with the view of those doctors who hold the opposite, namely, that the will is the nobler human faculty.[27] FitzRalph argues that the activity of the intellect with respect to a given object is naturally ordered toward the activity of the will with respect to the same object. The cognitive acts of brute animals, for instance, are structured so as to function in concert with appetitive acts. An animal is naturally capable of discriminating between convenient and inconvenient nourishment, but without the ability to chase the convenient and shun the inconvenient, the animal's discernment ability would be superfluous. If we apply the same reasoning to the relation between the intellect and the will in humans, we would have to admit that cognitive acts cannot function properly without volitional acts. Furthermore, on the basis of the principle that in the natural order of things something qualitatively higher is never subordinate to something qualitatively lower (*ordine naturali numquam nobilius ordinatur ad vilius*), a principle that FitzRalph attributes to Anselm of Canterbury and claims that Aristotle uses in the *Nicomachean ethics*, book I to defend the motivational priority of happiness, FitzRalph argues that volition is nobler than cognition. If volition is nobler than cognition, it follows that the faculty of the will is nobler than the faculty of the intellect, although that does not mean that the intellect and the will are two different things.[28]

---

as witnesses to FitzRalph's thought', pp 79–95.   27 Ricardus Fitzralph, *LS*, bk I, dist. 1, q. 2, a. 1 (Paris, Bibl. Nat., MS 15853, fo. 13rb): 'In isto articulo tenent alii doctores concorditer, quod voluntas est potentia nobilior ut voluntas est, unde teneo hanc partem, quamvis opposita pars sit valde probabilis'. As Tachau explains, Leff had interpreted the cited text as evidence for FitzRalph's effort to pave a middle way between the positions of Aquinas and Scotus. But it is clear from the text that FitzRalph sides with those doctors who think that the will is nobler than the intellect. Furthermore, the corrected version of FitzRalph's text found in Paris, Bibl. Nat., MS Lat. 6441, fos 62vb–63ra and Troyes, Bibl. Municipale, MS 505, fo. 4rb shows that FitzRalph sides with Duns Scotus. See Tachau, 'Adam Wodeham and Robert Holcot as witnesses to FitzRalph's thought', p. 87, n. 33.   28 Fitzralph, *LS*, bk I, dist. 1, q. 2, a. 1 (Paris, Bibl. Nat., MS 15853, fos 13rb–va): 'Et responsio ad hanc partem potest esse talis praeter praedictas rationes. Actio intellectus circa aliquid obiectum ordinatur naturali ordine at actionem voluntatis circa idem obiectum, sicut cognitio in animali bruto ordinatur ad actionem virtutis appetitivae. Ad hoc enim animal habet sensum tactus ut distinguat conveniens alimentum ab inconvenienti, sicut dicitur II° *De anima*. Sed certe ista distinctio nihil sibi prodest nisi potest appetere et

FitzRalph also cites Aquinas as saying in book I of his *Sentences* commentary, dist. 1, q. 1 that the intellect is the highest potency (*potentia altissima*) in us. FitzRalph asks: Does the term 'highest potency' mean 'noblest potency' or a 'potency prior in origin'? If 'highest potency' means 'noblest potency', then Aquinas contradicts himself because he also says in his response to the first objection of article 1 that of the two parts of the mind – the intellect and the will – the intellect is higher according to origin, whereas the will is higher according to perfection. If, on the other hand, 'highest potency' means not 'noblest' or 'most perfect', then Aristotle's principle – the highest operation is the operation of the highest potency, that is, the intellect – which Aquinas treats as nearly self-evident (*quasi principium per se notum*), must be false since the intellect would turn out on such an interpretation of 'highest' not to be the most perfect potency after all.[29]

In the second article of the second question, FitzRalph asks whether the passions of the intellect and the will are really distinct from their respective acts.

---

prosequi conveniens et fugere disconveniens, et certe simili modo de cognitione intellectus et actione voluntatis, sicut declarat Anselmus II° libro *Cur Deus Homo*, cap. primo: "sed ordine naturali numquam nobilius ordinatur ad vilius, sed econverso", ut patet I° *Ethicorum*, quia per hoc probat Philosophus quod felicitas est actio nobilissima, quia omnes aliae actiones humanae sunt gratia ipsius felicitatis. Sequitur ergo quod actio voluntatis sit nobilior, et per consequens ipsa potentia a qua procedit est nobilior, inqantum talis dictio <intelligitur?> non quod sit res aliquo modo nobilior, cum sint eadem res ut patebit in articulo de hoc'.   **29** Ricardus Fitzralph, *LS*, bk I, dist. 1, q. 2, a. 1 (Paris, Bibl. Nat., MS 15853, fo. 13rb): 'Thomas dicit prima parte *Scripti*, dist. 1, a. 1, q. 1, quod intellectus est altissima potentia in homine. Sed contra hoc dictum <potest argui sic>: aut intelligit per 'potentiam altissimam' nobilissimam potentiam, aut intelligit aliquid aliud, scilicet, potentiam priorem origine, sicut apparet convenienter <ex dictis suis>. Si nobilissimam, tunc contradiceret sibi <ipsi>, quia statim post in responsione ad primum argumentum dicit quod "mens habet intellectum et voluntatem, quorum duorum intellectus est altior secundum originem et voluntas secundum perfectionem; et similis ordo est in habitibus et actibus", haec iste, ubi expresse dicit quod voluntas est altior secundum perfectionem. Si vero per 'altissimam potentiam' non intelligat nobilissimam sive perfectissimam, tunc illud quod accipit pro principio quasi per se noto est falsum, scilicet, quod optima operatio est operatio altissimae potentiae, scilicet, intellectus. Hoc enim capit in positione, quod est falsum, nisi per altissimam intelligatur nobilissimam'. The angle brackets here < > indicate editorial inserts adopted from Tachau's superior rendition of FitzRalph's text in the present volume. See Tachau, 'Adam Wodeham and Robert Holcot as witnesses to FitzRalph's thought', p. 87, n. 33. See also Thomas de Aquino, *Commentum in quatuor libros Sententiarum Magistri Petri Lombardi*, bk I, dist. 1, q. 1, a. 1, ad 1, p. 12: 'Ad primum ergo dicendum, quod appetitus semper sequitur cognitionem. Unde, sicut inferior pars habet sensum et appetitum, qui dividitur in irascibilem et concupiscibilem, ita suprema pars habet intellectum et voluntatem, quorum intellectus est altior secundum originem, et voluntas secundum perfectionem. Et similis ordo est in habitibus, et etiam in actibus, scilicet visionis et amoris. Fruitio autem nominat altissimam operationem quantum ad sui perfectionem'. William Ockham has also commented upon the mentioned text from Thomas' *Sentences* commentary, which is quite significant in itself because it raises the possibility that FitzRalph could have borrowed the remark from Ockham. See Guillelmus de Ockham, *Scriptum in librum primum Sententiarum*, ed. Gedeon Gál et Stephanus Brown (St Bonaventure, 1967), Opera theologica, 1, dist. 1, q. 2, l. 18, p. 402, l. 6, p. 403.

More precisely, FitzRalph explores whether pleasure (*delectatio*) is a volitional passion rather than an act of the will. After presenting a substantial number of arguments on the side of the claim that pleasure is identical with volition, FitzRalph gives three arguments for the opposite side and points out that most modern authors believe that pleasure in the will is indeed an act of the will rather than a passion. FitzRalph does, however, concede a distinction between pleasure as a passion in the will and volition. He appeals to the authority of the Subtle Doctor, John Duns Scotus, and argues that pleasure is a passion because pleasure sometimes precedes volition on account of the apprehension of a delectable object, in which case pleasure is not under the immediate control of the will of the agent since it is caused by the object or the apprehension of the object. In other cases, however, pleasure is not roused by the object itself or by the apprehension of the object but is brought about by means of a volition. This happens especially when one loves something or someone. Love causes pleasure in the will albeit not immediately. Once the pleasure is produced, the agent can augment and intensify it through his/her will.[30]

The third article of question 2 is whether beatitude is pleasure. In his reply to the article, FitzRalph suggests that beatitude can be taken in several different senses: (1) for the beatific object, which is God (FitzRalph does not discuss this sense of beatitude at all), (2) for the vision of the divine essence, (3) for the actual love of the divine essence, (4) for the pleasure and joy obtained through the clear vision of the divine essence, and (5) for the collection of vision, love and pleasure. According to FitzRalph, the fifth sense is the most suitable and inclusive definition of beatitude. Thus, neither vision nor love nor pleasure alone constitute complete beatitude since they are merely parts of beatitude.[31]

30 Ricardus Fitzralph, *LS*, bk I, dist. 1, q. 2, a. 4 (Paris, Bibl. Nat., MS 15853, fo. 15rb): 'Praeter praedicta argumenta videtur mihi esse dicendum sicut dicit Doctor Subtilis et alii doctores concorditer quod delectatio non sit volitio, sed est aliquando passio praecedens volitionem, sicut ubi obiectum est per se apparens delectabile, quia circa tale primi motus, hoc est primae delectationes vel tristitiae, non sunt in potestate nostra secundum Philosophum. Et aliquando sequitur volitionem, ubi obiectum non est tale, quando enim obiectum non est apparens delectabile in prima apprehensione. Tunc voluntas ex aliqua causa aliquando amat illud, et ita ex intentione amoris circa illud aliquando delectatur, et forte non in principio volitionis, et ita auget delectationem aliquando et aliquando eam causat per accidens'. 31 Ibid., dist. 1, q. 2, a. 3 (Paris, Bibl. Nat., MS 15853, fo. 16rb): 'Ad istum articulum nihil asserendo dico sic, quod beatitudo accipitur multipliciter in modo loquendi auctorum. Uno modo pro obiecto beatifico, scilicet Deo, et sic loquitur Boethius III libro *De consolatione*, prosa 10 probans Deum esse summam beatitudinem. Alio modo pro visione clara essentiae divinae, et sic loquitur Dominus in *Evangelio Ioannis*, cap. 17 "haec est vita aeterna" et cetera. Alio modo pro actuali amore illius essentiae divinae, et sic loquitur Augustinus innumerabiles vocans fruitionem Dei beatitudinem. Tertio modo accipitur pro delectatione vel gaudio quod habetur ex visione clara essentiae divinae, et sic loquitur Augustinus in libro *De vera innocentia*, prop. 180, ubi diffiniens beatitudinem dicit quod est "gaudium de veritate quae Deus est". Quarto modo et maxime proprie accipitur beatitudo pro aggregato ex omnibus istis et aliis pertinentibus ad statum beati, qui numerat Anselmus in libro *De similitudinibus*, cap. 49, et sunt septem pertinentes ad animam, et septem ad corpus, et sunt

FitzRalph's understanding of complete beatitude rests on the authority of Boethius and Anselm, but especially so on Anselm. In Anselm's treatise *De humanis moribus*, we are told that there are altogether fourteen parts of beatitude: seven corporeal (beauty, agility, courage, freedom, health, delight and longevity) and seven spiritual (wisdom, friendliness, harmony, honor, power, security and joy). Correspondingly, there are also fourteen parts of misery or suffering: seven corporeal (ugliness, heaviness, feebleness, slavery, sickness, anxiety and short life) and seven spiritual (insensitivity, hostility, discord, dishonour, powerlessness, fear and sadness).[32] Anselm regards perfect joy and ultimate sadness as unobtainable in this life. Perfect joy results from the possession of all parts of beatitude and extreme sadness comes from the sum of all forms of unhappiness.[33] Thus, in agreement with Anselm, FitzRalph defines complete beatitude as a collection of constitutive components. FitzRalph also explains that the reason many authors identify vision with beatitude is that, given the natural law and order of things (*secundum legem statutam*), love and pleasure presuppose vision, and so vision appears to be the more fundamental aspect or part of beatitude.[34]

secundum ipsum ibidem – pulchritudo, agilitas, fortitudo, libertas, sanitas, voluptas, longevitas, – haec ad corpus. Ad animam – sapientia, amicitia, concordia, honor, potestas, securitas, gaudium – ecce septem, et vide ista tria sapientia, amicitia, gaudium. Ideo Anselmus talem beatitudinem describens in libro *De concordia praescientiae et praedestinationis*, cap. 23 dicit quod "beatitudo secundum omnem sensum est sufficiencia competentium commodorum sine omni indigentia", et Boethius describit beatitudinem quod est "status omnium bonorum aggregatione perfectus"'.

32 Anselmus Cantuariensis, *De humanis moribus per similitudines* in R.W. Southern and F.S. Schmitt (eds), *Memorials of Saint Anselm* (London, 1969), pp 57–8: 'Quatuordecim quippe sunt beatitudinis partes, quas boni tunc omnes habebunt, totidemque miseriae genera, quae mali tunc universa sustinebunt. Hae autem beatitudinis partes atque miseriae sic sibi invicem sunt omnino contrariae, quomodo et ipsi qui eas accipiunt in remuneratione. Partes enim beatitudinis sunt pulchritudo, agilitas, fortitudo, libertas, sanitas, voluptas, longaevitas, sapientia, amicitia, concordia, honor, potestas, securitas, gaudium. Partes vero miseriae: turpitudo, ponderositas, imbecillitas, servitus, infirmitas, anxietas, vitae brevitas, insipientia, inimicitia, discordia, dedecus, impotentia, timor, tristitia. Septem denique priores illius beatitudinis partes ad corporis beatitudinem septemque posteriores ad animae pertinent. Sic quoque et septem priores huius miseriae partes corporis septemque ultimae miseriam perficiunt mentis. Quicumque ergo illas omnes beatitudinis partes habere poterit, perfectam corporis et animae beatitudinem possidebit. Quemcumque vero has miseriae partes tolerare contigerit, summae corporis et animae miseriae subiacebit. Verum in hac vita nec unam illius beatitudinis vel huius miseriae partem quisquam potest habere nec rursus ex toto carere. In alia vero vita aut perfectam habens beatitudinem miseriae nullatenus subiacebit, aut summae subiacens miseriae omnino beatitudine carebit. Quod ut totum comprobare possimus, per singulas beatitudinis atque miseriae partes curramus'.

33 Ibid., ll. 26–33, p. 63: 'Quartadecima pars beatitudinis gaudium, miseriae vero tristitia est. Gaudium perfectum solus ille potest habere, qui praedictas omnes beatitudinis partes valet obtinere. Quarum quia nullam nullus hic habere potest, patet quia nec gaudium summum hic valet habere. Sic et ille solus pati potest tristitiam summam, quem praedictae omnes miseriae partes omnino coarctant. Verum quia nullus ex toto hic eas patitur, liquet quia nec in summa tristitia hic habeatur. In saeculo autem futuro aut laetitia aut tristitia quisque replebitur summa'.

34 Ricardus Fitzralph, *LS*, bk I, dist. 1, q. 2, a. 3 (Paris, Bibl. Nat., MS 15853, fo. 16ra): 'Unde

Pleasure, according to FitzRalph, is the best part of beatitude insofar as only pleasure brings ultimate satisfaction to the rational human mind with respect to God.[35] FitzRalph rejects Aquinas' claim that ultimate human happiness is found primarily in the vision of the divine essence.[36] FitzRalph contends that, according to right reason, one seeks pleasure (*delectatio*) more so than any of the other simple goods included in happiness. Similarly, one avoids sadness (*tristitia*) more so than any of the other simple things included in unhappiness. Consequently, pleasure is the noblest of the simple goods integrated in beatitude.[37]

Furthermore, FitzRalph juxtaposes Anselm's and Aquinas' definitions of beatitude. Anselm defines beatitude as a complete satisfaction or as a replenishment without anything lacking (*beatitudo est sufficientia sine omni indigentia*), which, to FitzRalph's mind, is consistent with Boethius' conception of beatitude. The mentioned Anselmian definition is more inclusive than Aquinas' definition. Moreover, Aquinas' definition seems to entail the logical possibility that one can see God without loving Him. For Aquinas, pleasure is not included in the essence of beatitude but is rather an additional extrinsic component of beatitude.[38] Finally, FitzRalph points out that the vision of God is ordered naturally towards the pleasure of the union with God, which, as Aquinas himself says, is what makes the vision of God perfect. Thus, on Aquinas' account, it would follow that, simply speaking (*simpliciter*), pleasure contributes more to one's happiness than the vision.[39]

dico quod isto quarto modo accipitur beatitudo maxime proprie et maxime sufficienter. Dico etiam quod nec visio, nec amor, nec delectatio, quae sunt partes beatitudinis, dicitur beatitudo nisi quando coniungitur cum aliis partibus, et quia ista coniunctio est naturalis posito primo istorum, scilicet visione clara, ideo auctores plures accipiunt unam istarum partium pro tota beatitudine, quia aliae partes coniunguntur secundum legem statutam'. **35** Ibid. (Paris, Bibl. Nat., MS 15853, fos 16rb–va): 'Unde pro articulo in se dico quod inter istas partes ipsa delectatio est pars ultima et optima. Unde Augustinus ubi supra ipsum gaudium ponit ultimam partem beatitudinis, quia per ipsam ultimate satiatur mens rationalis de suo creatore. Unde ista septem argumenta ad istam partem concludunt verum, scilicet quod delectatio est ultima beatitudo et optima loquendo de beatitudinibus partialibus et simplicibus. Tota tamen aggregata est melior, nec aliquod argumentum probat oppositum huiusmodi'. **36** Ibid., dist. 1, q. 2, a. 4 (Paris, Bibl. Nat., MS 15853, fo. 16va): 'Thomas dicit prima parte *Scripti*, distinctione prima, articulo primo, quaestione prima, quod ipsa visio divinitatis ponitur tota substantia nostrae beatitudinis, ut patet dicit ipse Joan. 17: "haec est vita aeterna ut cognoscant te", et cetera, et addit quod cum essentia divina clare videtur, tunc ipsa fit intra videntem et unit ipsum sibi, unde fit mutua penetratio per amorem. Ex unione autem maxime quiescentis sequitur summa delectatio, et ita proficit nostra beatitudo, et istam delectationem fruitio nominat ex parte complementi, haec ipse'. **37** Ibid.: 'Sed contra istum arguitur sic, sicut in ultimo articulo, delectatio inter beatitudines simplices est maxime secundum rectam rationem appetenda, quia tristitia secundum rationem inter miserias simplices est maxime fugienda, et per consequens est beatitudo nobilissima inter simplices'. **38** Ibid.: 'Praeterea, beatitudo secundum Anselmus in *De concordia*, cap. 33, est "sufficientia sine omni indigentia", et similem definitionem ponit Boethius ut est dictum in positione ultimi articuli. Si haec sit vera definitio, ergo claudit contradictoria quod sit vera beatitudo sine amore, quod tamen esse posset si sola visio sit tota beatitudo ut ipse ponit'. **39** Ibid.: 'Praeterea, visio ordinatur naturaliter ad delectationem, ut videtur, vel saltem

In the fourth and final article of the question, FitzRalph repeats distinctions 2–5 introduced in the third article. Beatitude can be now defined from the perspective of four distinct modes: (1) the clear vision of the divine essence; (2) the actual love of the divine essence; (3) the conjoined pleasure; and (4) from the perspective of all three modes jointly. The last fourth mode is again the most adequate mode of considering beatitude. Of the three preceding modes pleasure is most truly called beatitude. Consequently, depending on which mode one uses to define beatitude, one could say that beatitude is an act of the intellect or an act of the will or both. From the point of view of the first mode, beatitude is an act of the intellect. From the point of view of the second and third modes, beatitude is an act of the will. From the point of view of the last mode, beatitude is neither an act of the intellect alone nor an act of the will alone but an aggregate of both.[40]

FitzRalph clarifies the second and third definitions of beatitude by adding that pleasure, as he had said earlier in article 2, is not properly speaking an act of the will but rather a passion. One may thus ask: Since pleasure is a passion rather than an act of the will, why would pleasure be the best and noblest part of beatitude? How can one reconcile the claim that pleasure, as the best part of beatitude, is a passion with Aristotle's dictum that happiness is an activity rather than a passion? How can a passion be better than an activity? Even William of Ockham, who very diligently distinguishes between actions and passions in the will in both his *Sentences* commentary and *Quodlibetal questions*, agrees on this matter with Aristotle and appeals to the authority of Aristotle's commentator Michael Ephesius, who writes that 'we pursue pleasures for the sake of operation and for the sake of life, and not vice versa'.[41] Thus, for Ockham, love (*dilectio*) is nobler than pleasure.[42]

---

delectatio est eius perfectio ut ipse dicit; ergo delectatio est simpliciter magis beatificans quam visio, dico formaliter'. **40** Ibid. (Paris, Bibl. Nat., MS 15853, fos 16va–b): 'Ad quaestionem principalem cum quaeritur utrum beatitudo sit actus voluntatis vel intellectus dico, sicut dixi in positione ultimi articuli, quod beatitudo accipitur quatuor modis: pro visione clara Dei, pro amore eiusdem actuali, pro delectatione coniuncta, et pro omnibus hiis coniunctim, et hoc est maxime proprie, sed inter tres primos delectatio verissime dicitur beatitudo, sicut tunc dixi. Dico etiam quod actus accipitur communiter pro quacumque forma et alio modo magis proprie pro actione. Per hoc dico ad quaestionem, si intelligatur quaestio de beatitudine primo modo, sic est actus intellectus, si secundo modo vel tertio modo, sic est actus voluntatis, et hoc loquendo de actu communiter, quia delectatio non est actus proprie, sed quarto modo nec est actus intellectus nec voluntatis sed aggregatus ex hiis'. **41** Guillelmus de Ockham, *Scriptum in librum primum Sententiarum*, Opera theologica, 1, dist. 1, q. 3, l. 13, p. 426, l. 1. 6, p. 427. **42** It should be noted that Ockham also thinks that heavenly beatitude (or felicity) includes several components: vision, enjoyment, pleasure and, perhaps, security. Nevertheless, enjoyment (*fruitio*) as a species of love is higher than pleasure. See V. Hirvonen, *Passions in William Ockham's philosophical psychology* (Dordrecht, 2004), p. 159, n. 129.

WODEHAM: THE ORIGIN OF A MISGUIDED QUESTION

The question whether beatific enjoyment is an act of the intellect or the will is the last question of the treatment of enjoyment in Wodeham's *Oxford lectures*.[43] The question is divided into five articles: (1) whether the intellect is nobler than the will, pros and cons, (2) that there is no distinction between the intellect and the will, (3) that there is a distinction between the intellect and the will, (4) a corollary solution concerning the distinction or in-distinction between the intellect and the will, and (5) replies to the principal arguments.[44]

Wodeham's text reveals a well-rounded nominalist position. Wodeham believes that any effort to assert the primacy of the intellect over the will or of the will over the intellect distorts the substantial unity of the human soul. He thus maintains that the intellect and the will have unique perfections, but he also insists that they are fundamentally inseparable. He says that, as far as moral goodness and virtue are concerned, the nobility of the human intellectual nature surfaces most clearly through the rightly ordered, virtuous and meritorious acts of the human will in this life as well as through the love and pleasure of the will experienced in the state of beatific bliss.[45] In response to the main question of the article, Wodeham states:

> And the same applies to the corresponding habits, since there is no habit more excellent than charity. Therefore, it is more excellent for the soul to be a will than an intellect, although the intellect and the will are one and

[43] Wodeham's *Oxford lectures* on Lombard's *Sentences* are found complete in four manuscripts. One of the manuscripts – Rome, BAV, MS 955 – is a *reportatio*, examined, it seems, by Wodeham himself. See Wood, 'Introduction', *Adam de Wodeham*, 1, p. 46. For a description of the manuscripts of Wodeham's *Ordinatio*, see Courtenay, *Adam Wodeham*, pp 186–7. For a working draft of Wodeham's *Ordinatio*, bk 1, dist. 1, q. 14 based on Paris, Sorbonne, MS 193, see http://jeffreycwitt.com/adamwodeham/text/textdisplay.php?text=id1q14S.xml. [44] Adam Wodeham, *Ordinatio Oxoniensis* [hereafter *OO*] bk 1, dist. 1, q. 14, a. 4 (Paris, Sorbonne, MS 193, fo. 72va): 'In quaestione ista primo suppono quod fruitio et felicitas beatifica principaliter pertinent ad eandem potentiam, quaecumque sit illa, et quod sint tales potentiae multae in natura eadem beatificabili, et quod fruitio beatifica est perfectio potentiae nobilissimae ex eisdem. Ita enim dicit Philosophus X *Ethicorum*, cap. 8, in principio, ubi dicit quod felicitas est operatio secundum optimam virtutem. Haec autem erit optimi, sive utique intellectus hoc, sive aliud quod utique secundum naturam conatur principare. Hoc supposito, primo prosequenda est dubitatio adducta quae sistit arguendo pro et contra. Secundo ostendetur quod nulla est distinctio intellectus a voluntate, vel e contra. Tertio impugnabitur conclusio secundi articuli et respondebitur ad obiecta. Quarto inferetur conclusio corollaria, et pro solutione quaestionis, et assignabitur intellectus unus verus auctoritate praecedentium. Quinto secundum istum intellectum respondebitur ad argumenta dubitationis primae et argumenta principalia quaestionis'. [45] Ibid. (Paris, Sorbonne, MS 193, fo. 73vb): 'Ad hunc sensum respondeo quod in actibus volendi rectis et virtuosis, meritoriis volitionibus in via et ex dilectione et delectatione fruitiva in patria magis innotescit nobis nobilitas naturae intellectualis et scitur esse nobilis quam ex actibus praecise cognitivis, quia igitur nobilior est operatio animae in ordine ad quem ipsa appellatur voluntas quam operatio alia distincta a volitionibus ex qua ipsa vocatur intellectus'.

the same thing; thus, it is nobler on the part of the King of England to be a king of England than a duke of Aquitaine, but the two are the same, yet not according to the same, that is, from the same cause.[46]

Wodeham claims that the doubt as to whether the intellect is superior to the will or vice versa affects those who believe that the intellect and the will are two really distinct potencies or accidents appended to the substance of the soul. This belief, Wodeham says, is held in common not only by some ancient, but also by modern doctors alike, insofar as FitzRalph, along with Scotus, have argued against Aquinas that the will is nobler than the intellect.[47] According to Wodeham, there is no real distinction between the intellect and the will, on the one hand, and between the intellect and the will and the essence of the soul, on the other. The terms 'intellect' and 'will' are simply used to designate the different manners or ways of being a soul. Moreover, not only are the intellect and the will substantially indistinguishable from each other, they are also indistinguishable from sense in general.[48]

---

46 Ibid. (Paris, Sorbonne, MS 193, fos 73rb–74ra): 'Et similiter etiam de habitibus correspondentibus, quia nullus est habitus nobilior caritate, ideo nobilius est animam esse voluntatem quam esse intellectum. Licet idem sit intellectus et voluntas, sicut nobilius est parte regis Angliae esse regem Angliae quam esse ducem Aquitaniae, licet idem sit utrumque, non secundum idem, idest, ex eadem causa; ita in proposito etc'.   47 Ibid., dist. 1, q. 14, a. 1 (Paris, Sorbonne, MS 193, fo. 72vb): 'Ista dubitatio de nobilitate voluntatis respectus intellectus locum habet apud eos qui ponebant intellectum et voluntatem esse potentias diversas et esse accidentia superaddita substantiae vel aliquo modo distingui ex parte rei cum reali identitate inter se et cum substantia animae. Et hoc non solum doctores aliqui antiqui sed moderni tenuerunt, in tantum etiam quod Hibernicus tenet cum Scoto contra Thomam in *Scripto*, quod voluntas est potentia nobilior quam intellectus. Et arguit contra Thomam dicentem quod intellectus est altissima potentia in anima: "quaero", inquit, <quid intelligit per 'altissimam potentiam'?> "Aut intelligit per 'potentiam altissimam' potentiam nobilissimam aut potentiam priorem secundum ordinem, sicut magis consequenter apparet ex dictis suis. Si nobilissimam", inquit, "contradicit sibi ipsi, quia statim post in responsione ad primum argumentum dicit quod mens habet intellectum et voluntatem, quorum duorum intellectus est altior secundum ordinem et voluntas [perfectione *scr. et del.* Paris] secundum perfectionem, et similis ordo est in habitibus et actibus", haec ille. "Si vero per 'potentiam altissimam' non intelligit nobilissimam seu perfectissimam, tunc illud quod ipse accipit pro principio per se notum est falsum, scilicet, quod optima operatio sit altissimae potentiae, scilicet, intellectus. Hoc enim capit in positione, quod tamen est falsum, nisi per 'altissimam' intelligat nobilissimam, quia potentiae nobilissimae est operatio nobilissima, sicut etiam vult Philosophus X *Ethicorum*, cap. 8"'. The editorial inserts here are also adopted from Tachau's rendition of Wodeham's text in the present volume. I should point out, however, that I have retained 'ordinem' rather than 'originem' because Paris, Sorbonne MS 193 contains twice a clearly written 'ordinem', although the word should be 'originem' as is obvious from the texts of Aquinas and FitzRalph. See Tachau, 'Adam Wodeham and Robert Holcot as witnesses to FitzRalph's thought', p. 85, n. 28.   48 Wodeham, *OO*, bk 1, dist. 1, q. 14, a. 1 (Paris, Sorbonne, MS 193, fos 72vb–73ra): 'Teneo igitur conclusionem contrariam ad vim sermonis eundo, scilicet, quod intellectus non est potentia nobilior voluntate nec econverso, quia idem omnino est intellectus quod voluntas, et econtra, et in eadem substantia intellectualis. Nam omni alio circumscripto ab hac natura intellectuali ipsa nata est intelligere et ipsa eadem nata est velle. Igitur hoc natum velle est

Wodeham rejects any real distinction between the intellect and the will on the basis of the principle of parsimony (*frustra ponitur fieri per plura quod eque faciliter potest fieri per pauciora*). Furthermore, he claims that neither sacred Scripture nor reason pose any obstacle to the elimination of such a distinction. According to Wodeham, the Subtle Doctor himself admits that it is not contrary to reason to think that there is no distinction between the faculties of the soul.[49]

Following Ockham, Wodeham also eliminates any conceptual distinction between the intellect and the will. According to Ockham, there cannot be a conceptual distinction between the intellect and the will because a conceptual distinction presupposes an intellectual act, which in turn presupposes an already existing distinction between intellect and will. If, on the other hand, there is a real distinction between the intellect and the will, then such a distinction is either established on the basis of the dissimilarity of the acts (*propter diversitatem actuum*) or the operational manner (*propter modum principiendi*), namely, necessarily v. contingently. If the distinction is based on the acts, then there would be as many faculties as there are diverse acts, which cannot be the case. If the distinction rests on a difference in the operational manner, then the intellect and the will should operate differently at all times, which cannot be the case either because, although the intellect always acts of necessity, the will acts contigently for the most part but not always, since the will is sometimes necessitated.[50]

---

natum intelligere, et econtra. Ergo intellectus est voluntas, et econtra. Ex hoc enim quod talis natura enim nata est vel potens in intellectivae ordine proterea dicitur intellectus, et ex hoc quod est potens vel nata ad volendum ipsa dicitur voluntas. Et hoc non solum dicerem in homine de intellectu et voluntate, sed de omni sensu, cui consentit auctor *De spiritu et anima*, dicens cap. 3: "Sensus vero unus est in anima, et quod vere ipse est in anima, et quod ipse cum corpus non sit corporeus dicitur, et cum non sit nisi unus verumtamen propter varia exercitia varie nuncupantur. Dicitur namque sensus, imaginatio, ratio, intellectus, intelligentia, et haec omnia in anima nihil aliud sunt quam ipsa", et cap. 10: "Anima est spiritus intellectualis rationalis boneque male voluntatis capax, secundum benignitatem Creatoris atque secundum sui operis officium variis nuncupatur nominibus. Dicitur namque anima dum vegetat, spiritus dum contemplatur, sensus dum sentit, animus dum sapiat, mens dum intelligit, ratio dum dissolvit, dum recordatur memoria, dum vult voluntas, ista tamen non differunt in substantia quaemadmodum in nominibus, quoniam ita omnia una est anima"'. 49 Ibid. (Paris, Sorbonne, MS 193, fo. 73ra): 'Frustra ponitur fieri per plura quod eque faciliter potest fieri per pauciora et salvari ubi nec Scriptura sacra nec ratio obviat, sed per eandem simplicem naturam intellectualem sine omni tali distinctione reali praevia primis actibus, modo quo illam expressit auctor ille, facilimme potuerunt salvari omnia propter quae alii ponunt potentias animae distingui, igitur etc. Quod autem non obviet patet etiam per ipsum Scotum secundo libro, ubi de isto puncto investigatur de *Reportatione Parisiensis*'. Scotus suggests that Aristotle's dictum that the distinction of faculties is based on the distinction of their objects does not apply to the non-organic faculties of the intellect and the will. There is no formal distinction between superior and inferior non-organic faculties or between intellect and will because these faculties have a single common object, namely, being as such (*ens*), which is common to both created and uncreated being. See Ioannes Duns Scotus, *Reportata Parisiensia*, Ludovicus Wadding (ed.) (Lyon, 1939), Opera omnia, 11.1, bk 2, dist. 24, q. 1,1. 12, p. 366. 50 Wodeham, *OO*, bk 1, q. 14, a. 1 (Paris, Sorbonne, MS 193, fo. 73ra): 'Praeterea, si distinguerentur, aut ratione solum, et hoc non, quia talis distinctio

Although Wodeham does not develop any exceptional solution to the problem of the distinction between the intellect and the will and does not seem to think any differently than Ockham, he nevertheless offers some clarifying comments. In the fourth article of the question, Wodeham declares that beatitudo or beatific enjoyment is an act of the 'nude substance of the soul' and not of some faculty really distinct from that substance.[51] One can object by saying that if this is true, then the soul can be said to will through the intellect and understand through the will.[52] In response to the objection, Wodeham points out that statements such as 'the intellect wills' and 'the will understands' are true only *per accidens*, and not *per se*. For instance, the statements 'the human sculpts', 'Policletus sculpts' and 'the musician sculpts' are true *per accidens* only because the actual scultor happens to be simultaneously a human being, a musician and a person called Policletus. In contrast, the statement 'the sculptor sculpts' is true *per se primo modo* and ought to be treated as a proper scientific and skillful discourse (*sermo artis et scientiae*). The statement 'the sculptor sculpts' is true *per se primo modo* because the subject of the statement includes the predicate in its definition.

causaretur per actum intellectus, sed intellectus et voluntas praecedunt omnem actum voluntatis et intellectus, aut ex natura rei, et hoc non, quia illa diversitas aut esset ponenda propter diversitatem actuum aut propter diversus modum principandi. Non propter primum, quia tunc tot essent potentiae intellectivae quot essent actus intelligendi secundum speciem distincti, quod non est verum. Nec propter secundum, quia principare libere et necessario respectu diversorum non opponuntur, ut patet de voluntate divina quae necessario vult se et contingenter creaturam, et Pater etiam necessario producit Filium et Spiritum Sanctum libere'. See Guillelmus de Ockham, *Quaestiones in librum secundum Sententiarum*, ed. Gál and Wood (St Bonaventure, NY, 1981), Opera theologica, 5, q. 20, p. 436, l. 19, p. 437, l. 21. Ockham asserts that when the words or concepts 'intellect' and 'will' are used in reference to the single productive principle of the act of the intellect and the act of the will, there is no distinction whatsoever between the intellect and the will. Thus, one can say neither that the will is nobler than the intellect nor that the intellect is nobler than the will. However, from the perspective of the total nominal definitions of the will and the intellect, the will is nobler than the intellect because the act of love connoted by its definition is nobler than the act of understanding connoted by the definition of the intellect. The intellect, on the other hand, is prior to the will because the act of understanding connoted by its definition is prior to the act of the will, since the act of understanding is the efficient partial cause of the act of the will and can exist without the act of the will. Nevertheless, the priority of the act of the intellect does not imply perfection in what is prior and imperfection in what is posterior. See Guillelmus de Ockham, *Quaestiones in librum secundum Sententiarum*, q. 20, l. 6, p. 441, l. 3, p. 442. For an account of the various modes of considering the distinction between the intellect and the will, see also A. Maurer, *The philosophy of William of Ockham in the light of its principles* (Toronto, 1999), pp 460–70. See also T.M. Holopainen, 'William Ockham's theory of the foundations of ethics' (PhD, Helsinki, 1991), pp 24–6.   51 Wodeham, *OO*, bk 1, q. 14, a. 4 (Paris, Sorbonne, MS 193, fo. 73va–b): 'Ex iam dictis patet corollarie ad principalem articulum quaestionis, quod secundum veritatem, ad proprietatem sermonis eundo, dubitatio ita nulla est. Est enim felicitas seu beatitudo actus immediate receptus in nuda substantia animae sive naturae intellectualis beatae, et non in alia potentia realiter ibi distincta a tali natura vel ab aliqua eius intrinseca potentia'.   52 Ibid. (Paris, Sorbonne, MS 193, fo. 73vb): 'Contra: si praedicta vera essent, tunc vellet anima per intellectum et intellectus per voluntatem, quod non est bene dictum'.

According to Wodeham, statements such as 'the intellect is capable of understanding' or 'the intellect understands' are true in this sense. Statements such as 'the soul is capable of understanding' or 'the soul is capable of willing' are true *per se secundo modo*, which means that the subjects of these statements are included in the definitions of the predicates. Statements such as 'the intellect wills' and 'the will understands' are true neither *per se primo modo* nor *per se secundo modo*. Such statements are indeed banished from proper scientific discourse, but this is not on account of them being strictly speaking false, but rather because they are true only *per accidens*.[53]

According to Wodeham's opponent, the Aristotelian saying that happiness is the most excellent operation of the most excellent faculty leaves it open as to which is the most excellent of the human faculties.[54] Wodeham responds that Aristotle frequently uses hypothetical propositions in place of categorical ones. Thus, the categorical proposition 'every triangle has three angles' can be interpreted in a hypothetical sense: 'if such an entity as a triangle exists, then that entity will have three angles'. Similarly, one could take the proposition 'happiness is the highest operation of the highest human faculty' in a hypothetical sense and argue in the following manner: 'if there are distinct faculties in the soul, then happiness is the operation of the most excellent of those faculties'. One could even say, Wodeham suggests, that Aristotle alludes to multiple equivalent operative principles in the human soul and that, in this sense, one could imagine that there are several portions in the soul with their respective functions – thinking, willing, desiring, seeing, hearing etc.[55]

53 Ibid.: 'Praeterea, potentiae distinguntur per actus et actus per obiecta, ex II *De anima*, igitur dicendum quod sine dubio hoc vere diceretur, sequitur enim "hic intellectus intelligit, hic intellectus est voluntas; igitur voluntas intelligit" et econverso. Tamen modus loquendi non est proprie sermo artis et scientiae, quia est sermo per accidens et non per se, isto modo quo loquitur Philosophus II *Physicorum*, par. 33 et sequentibus, et V *Metaphysicae*, par. 3 dicens quod aliter est Policletus vel homo vel musicus causa statuae et aliter statuae factor. Sic in proposito ille sermo "intellectus intelligit vel potest intelligere" est sermo artis et scientiae, et sermo quodammodo per se. Si enim dicatur quod "intellectus natus est intelligere vel potest intelligere", ipse est sermo primo modo per se vel converso. Si autem dicatur quod "talis natura vel talis anima potest intelligere vel velle", est sermo per se secundo modo. Si autem dicatur quod "intellectus intelligit", hoc non differat ab illa quam dixi esse per se primo modo nisi sicut una <sententia> de inesse a sententia de possibili. Nullo autem istorum modorum est hoc per se sed solum per accidens – "intellectus vult" vel haec "voluntas intelligit". Igitur talis modus loquendi ab artificiali usu scolae dimittendus, non quia falsus, sed sicut nec iste "musicus aedificat", si idem sit musicus et aedificator, igitur'.   54 Ibid.: 'Dices, Philosophus, ut supra recitatum est, dicit quod felicitas est optima operatio secundum virtutem optimam et optimi principiis. Igitur iusta potest esse et rationalis dubitatio cuius optimae potentiae in homine felicitas sit optima operatio'.   55 Ibid.: 'Dicendum quod Philosophus vel loquitur ibi utendo propositione hypothetica pro categorica sententia, sicut saepissime in auctoritatibus philosophiae et scientiarum aliarum, verbi gratia, "omnis triangulus habet tres" etc., "si aliquis sit triangulus in entibus, habet tres", etc.; sic hoc "felicitas est operatio optima", idest, "si essent in anima distinctae vires realiter, tunc felicitas esset optima operatio istarum". Vel dicendum quod Philosophus loquitur ibi modo praeexposito utens unico actu ac simplici principio secundum

In its strongest form, however, the doubt whether there is a single highest or noblest faculty in the human soul arises from the manner in which Aristotle in the *Nicomachean ethics* juxtaposes the rational soul, where the intellect and the will are housed, to the sensitive soul; and Wodeham appeals to the authority of Averroës, who explains that, within the rational soul, one must distinguish between the part that governs and the part that obeys. It is in fact Aristotle's ambiguity regarding the highest faculty in us that gives rise to Averroës' separate agent intellect, as the full text of Wodeham's citation of the passage from Averroës' *De anima* commentary shows.[56]

Wodeham concludes his investigation with the somewhat ambiguous statement that, truly speaking (*veraciter*), neither the will is more excellent than the intellect nor the intellect is more excellent than the will, although it is surely more excellent for the soul to be will than intellect. He also appeals to FitzRalph's separate treatment of the distinction between memory, intelligence and the will in the *Lectura*, book I, q. 5, where FitzRalph denies that there is any partitioning in the sensitive soul as well as in the intellective soul.[57] Wodeham

---

veritatem tamquam multis principiis operationum propter equivalentiam, quia eque perfecte potest anima unica humana simplex natura existens in varias operationes secundum genus ut sunt intelligere et velle, sicut si realiter imaginentur esse in anima distinctae particulae quarum una praecise posset cognoscere et alia appetere et tertia videre et quarta audire, et sic de aliis'. 56 Ibid.: 'Verumtamen imaginabatur etiam alio modo intellectum et voluntatem comprehendi sub eadem particula distinguendo partem intellectivam contra sensitivam, sicut fecit I *Ethicorum* et IV, ubi allegatur in articulis principalibus. Et pro hoc facit auctoritas Commentatoris super I *De anima*, commento 66, ubi super illud Philosophi, quod "intelligere et amare et odire marcescunt quosdam interius corrupto ex parte corporis", dicit quod "amor et odium attribuuntur rationi", et isto modo loquendi utendo est prima dubitatio rationalis quae potentia sit nobilior, intellectus, scilicet, an voluntas, quia hoc non est ad verum intellectum aliud quaerere quam quid genus actuum est nobilissimus, volitiones, scilicet, vel intellectiones, vel ex quibus eius actibus magis innotescit talis naturae nobilitas'. See also Averroes Cordubensis, *In Aristotelis De anima librum primum*, ed. Stuart F. Crawford (Cambridge, MA, 1953), com. 66, ll 33–48, p. 90: 'Et facit hoc ne accidat questio in hoc dixit in intellectu materiali in tertio tractatu, scilicet quomodo intellectus sit ingenerabilis et incorruptibilis, et nos post mortem neque diligimus neque odimus neque distinguimus. Deinde dixit: Distinctio autem et amor et odium, etc. Idest, distinctio autem, que attribuitur virtuti cogitative, et amor et odium, que attribuuntur rationi, scilicet que recipiunt actionem rationis; videtur enim in hac parte anime quod sit aliquod rationabile, quia est obediens intellectui in hominibus bonis. Ista igitur non sunt actiones istius intellectus, sed sunt actiones virtutum habentium hanc actionem secundum quod habent illam actionem. Et addidit hanc conditionem, scilicet secundum quod habent, quia impossibile est ut iste virtutes sunt nisi cum intelligere; sed si attribute fuerint ei, non erit attributio secundum quod sunt'. 57 Wodeham, *OO*, bk 1, q. 14, a. 5 (Paris, Sorbonne, MS 193, fo. 74ra): 'Dico igitur ad articulum quod voluntas veraciter non est nobilior intellectu nec e converso. Et nota quod Siransis tenet hoc idem non [see n. 58 below] in priori loco, ubi tractat praesentem quaestionem, sed in alia quaestione dicens quod tam anima intellectiva est quaelibet sua potentia quam anima etiam sensitiva est sua potentia, et quod denominatur talis vel talis potentia ab actione quam exercet in tali vel tali organo, in isto articulo *Correcti operis*, utrum memoria, intelligentia, et voluntas distinguitur ab invicem. Tenet tamen Magister quod in homine sensitiva distinguitur ab intellectiva, nulla tamen sensitiva potentia ab ipsa vel intellectiva ab intellectiva, sed tamen ulterius dicendum quod

thus points out that FitzRalph's view is in effect the same as Wodeham's own.[58]

If the intellect and the will are not really distinct faculties,[59] but merely different expressions of the soul, then what makes these expressions different? According to Ockham, the intellect and the will are two very different systems. The intellect is a valuational system whereas the will is a motivational system.[60] For Wodeham, on the other hand, these two systems are less sharply diversified. All volitions are cognitions to the extent to which volitions include an act of apprehension and, sometimes, an act of assent or dissent to a propositional content. The key distinctive feature of volitions, in contrast to cognitions, is the non-veridical acceptance or rejection of a cognitive content from the perspective of its desirability or repugnancy.[61] FitzRalph's ingenious proposal is to associate diversity of mental functioning with specific somatic localization and particular organic operation – regardless of whether there are two souls in man, a sensitive and an intellective one, each of these two souls is identical with her own powers, yet she is diversified *per accidens* depending on the bodily organ through which she acts or manifests herself.[62]

licet intellectus sit vere voluntas et econtra. Verumtamen nobilius est sibi esse voluntatem quam esse intellectum, et hoc et non aliud possunt concludere media principalia primi articuli, quae arguunt intellectum esse nobiliorem, et ideo solvam illa'. See also Fitzralph, *LS*, bk I, q. 5, a. 1 (Paris, Bibl. Nat., MS 15853, fo. 27rb): 'Ideo dico ad istum articulum cum quaeritur utrum memoria et cetera, quod quaecumque istarum intellectionum memoria, intelligentia et voluntas accipitur dupliciter: uno modo pro actu et alio modo pro potentia a qua vel in qua est actus. Et sic est ad propositum. Unde sic dico quod memoria, intelligentia et voluntas non sunt distinctae realiter in una mente'. See the full passage of FitzRalph's text cited in Tachau, 'Adam Wodeham and Robert Holcot as witnesses to FitzRalph's thought', p. 90, n. 42. For a discussion of FitzRalph's understanding of the relationship between the intellect and the will, see Leff, *Richard FitzRalph*, pp 99–109, but note also the corrective offered by Tachau in the present volume. **58** Tachau argues that 'Michałski was mislead by an erroneously inserted negative when he renders what Wodeham says here as "note that FitzRalph holds the same [view] *not* in the prior place ... but in another question"'. The negative is found both in Paris, Sorbonne, MS 193, fo. 94ra and Rome, BAV, MS 955, fo. 99v, but if the insertion is erroneous, as Tachau maintains, then Wodeham is indeed saying that FitzRalph holds the same view as Wodeham already within FitzRalph's treatment of the same question. See Tachau, 'Adam Wodeham and Robert Holcot as witnesses to FitzRalph's thought'. **59** Tachau points out that the debate regarding the distinction between the soul and the soul's powers and acts, a debate to which both FitzRalph and Wodeham have contributed, was initially sparked by Richard Campsall at Oxford around 1316. See Tachau, 'Adam Wodeham and Robert Holcot as witnesses to FitzRalph's thought', p. 92, n. 45. **60** See Holopainen, *William Ockham's theory*, p. 26. **61** See S. Knuuttila, *Emotions in ancient and medieval philosophy* (Oxford, 2004), pp 278–9. **62** See Tachau, 'Adam Wodeham and Robert Holcot as witnesses to FitzRalph's thought', p. 90, n. 42.

CONCLUDING THOUGHTS

In conclusion, I hope to have demonstrated that a comparative analysis of FitzRalph's and Wodeham's *Sentences* commentaries is a worthwhile hermeneutic endeavour, which can divulge both the extraordinary complexity and the wealth of medieval scholastic debates at Oxford in the first half of the fourteenth century. I would like to make three observations.

(1) The comparison between FitzRalph's and Wodeham's treatments of enjoyment shows some peculiarities with respect to structure, style and content. In terms of structure, FitzRalph's treatment of enjoyment is perhaps the more elegant and polished one. Each question is neatly divided into four articles, the last of which contains FitzRalph's response to the principal question. In contrast, Wodeham's treatment appears more schematic and raw. With respect to style, FitzRalph's account of enjoyment reveals a perceptive mind and a sympathetic character. Expressions such as 'valde probabilis', 'nihil asserendo', 'videtur mihi' betray caution and reluctance to draw any hasty conclusions.[63] Wodeham, on the other hand, appears much more confident and eager to develop strong and definitive positions. With respect to content, Wodeham's account of enjoyment is perchance the more original of the two. Just as FitzRalph's, Wodeham's positions are firmly rooted in an exegetical practice governed by the scholastic principle of respect for the authority of ancient and modern theological and philosophical tradition. Unlike FitzRalph, however, Wodeham seems much more interested in the articulation and application of logical and semantic tools of analysis in theological context. Wodeham's discussion of the distinction between the faculties of the soul, albeit greatly influenced by Ockham, contains also some rather exceptional ideas regarding, for example, how we can get around the problem of improper discourse once we say that the intellect and the will are the same entity.

(2) FitzRalph's work is clearly essential for a deeper understanding and appreciation of Wodeham's thought. Wodeham's treatment of enjoyment contains ample evidence in support of the claim that Wodeham regarded FitzRalph as an important and influential modern authority. The critical editions of FitzRalph's *Lectura* and Wodeham's *Oxford lectures* will make it possible to determine just how much Wodeham's thought evolved as a result of FitzRalph's influence.

---

[63] And indeed, as Tachau observes, FitzRalph's caution is certainly warranted in light of the difficult philosophical and theological problems one would have to solve once one denies all distinctions between the soul and the soul's faculties, on the one hand, and between the faculties and the faculties' acts and habits, on the other. See Tachau, 'Adam Wodeham and Robert Holcot as witnesses to FitzRalph's thought', p. 92. Michael Dunne suggests that FitzRalph's caution probably 'stemmed partially from his personal insecurity as a secular student'. See Dunne, 'Richard FitzRalph's *Lectura*', p. 427.

(3) Lastly, a diligent and sympathetic reading of the works of scholastic authors can help us overcome to some degree the dangers of oversimplification and anachronism when telling the history of western thought. We can, for instance, avoid treating the theological concept of *fruitio beatifica* as a misnomer simply because we, moderns, do not have the cultural and experiential equivalent or, more generally, the life-form we can rely on in trying to make sense of such a concept. In John Kekes' latest monograph – *Enjoyment: the moral significance of styles of life* (Oxford, 2008) – beatific enjoyment does not find a place of its own, perhaps because religious belief is no longer as dominant and life-transforming as it used to be centuries ago. Kekes maintains that there is indeed a 'rightful enjoyment of our being', but he also points out that philosophers have not told us what it might consist in. Kekes' monograph is an attempt to answer the question about the rightful enjoyment of our being by means of comparing and contrasting human lifestyles. A 'rightful enjoyment', Kekes claims, is one based on a realistic attitude to life and destiny, on the one hand, and on a reasonable evaluation of what matters to us (individually) most, on the other. A genuinely enjoyable lifestyle involves integrity of character, reflectivity and autonomy; it affirms human dignity and is the outcome of ever-increasing self-control.[64] Most importantly, the best human lifestyle (and there are many different forms of it) is one that avoids the pitfalls of 'vacuous consolation' (that is, the optimism associated with religious promises of salvation or the utopia of socialistic ideology) and 'nihilism' (that is, the pessimism stemming from the belief that human life is utterly meaningless).[65] It may be true that medieval scholastic attempts to articulate a coherent theological concept of enjoyment were broadly speaking an expression of a 'vacuous consolation', considering especially the impact of the Black Death on the Christian psyche in the period shortly after FitzRalph and Wodeham lectured on Lombard's *Sentences*. From the point of view of understanding humanity, however, whether a consolation is vacuous or not says little or nothing at all about why humans seek consolation in the first place. Moreover, the question whether religious consolation is vacuous or not is very much an open one and is also very likely a question we may not be able to answer by purely scientific and objective means.

---

[64] See J. Kekes, *Enjoyment: the moral significance of styles of life* (Oxford, 2008), pp 234–51.
[65] Ibid., pp 255–70.

Adam Wodeham and Robert Holcot as witnesses to FitzRalph's thought

KATHERINE H. TACHAU

The 1930s was a decade in which the study of FitzRalph's life and work made enormous advances, thanks to the simultaneous and complementary research of Louis Hammerich,[1] Aubrey Gwynn,[2] and Konstanty Michalski. Michalski's ground-breaking studies of Oxford and Parisian thought in the first half of the fourteenth century alerted historians interested in the lectures and debates at those *studia* to the frequent references to and quotations of Richard FitzRalph's views in the *Sentences* lectures of the Franciscan theologian, Adam Wodeham.[3] Indeed, Wodeham's quotations of FitzRalph and other contemporaries are crucial to the establishment of a relative chronology of an entire academic generation of theologians teaching and debating at Oxford in the years of FitzRalph's regency and immediately following. Michalski saw Wodeham as what we might call a hostile witness as to FitzRalph's views, an approach to their relationship that subsequent historians, most notably John Robson, tended to repeat and extend. The issue that caught Michalski's attention was whether the will and intellect, or their acts, are identical with each other or with the soul; and if distinct, what is the nature of their distinction? Are they really, or formally distinct, or is the distinction instead one made by reason? Because FitzRalph rejected the position of Aquinas, Michalski was not a fully sympathetic reader of FitzRalph; and because he changed what he said from one question of his *Sentences* lectures to another, Michalski wrote that 'one sees with FitzRalph an indecision that str[uck] his successors and for which they reproach[ed] him for adopting sometimes one point of view, and sometimes another'.[4] Thus, Michalski related:

1 L.L. Hammerich, *The beginning of the strife between Richard FitzRalph and the mendicants, with an autobiographical prayer and his proposition* Uniusquisque, in *Det kon: Danskes videnskabernes selskab: historisk-filologiske meddelelser*, 26.3 (Copenhagen, 1938). Hammerich, p. 12, makes clear that he has read A. Gwynn's work on FitzRalph up to 1937.   2 Aubrey Gwynn SJ, 'Richard FitzRalph at Avignon', *Studies*, 22 (1933), 591–607; 'Richard FitzRalph, Archbishop of Armagh', *Studies*, 25 (1936), 81–96; 'Archbishop FitzRalph and the Friars', *Studies*, 26 (1937), 50–67; 'The sermon-diary of Richard FitzRalph', *Proceedings of the Royal Irish Academy*, 44 (1937), 1–57; also Gwynn's later 'Two sermons of Primate Ric. FitzRalph', *Archivia Hibernica*, 14 (1949), 50–65.
3 Konstanty Michalski, 'Le problème de la volonté à Oxford et Paris au XIVe siècle', *Studia Philosophica*, 2 (1937), as repr. in idem, *La philosophie au XIVe siècle* (Frankfurt-am-Main, 1969), pp 281–412 at p. 313 (33).   4 Michalski, 'Le problème de la volonté', p. 312: 'En même temps on voit chez Fitz-Ralph une indécision qui frappe ses successeurs et qui lui attire la reproche

> Adam Wodeham ... had visibly followed the development of the discussion of [this] problem from up close ... for in his Oxford [*Sentences*] commentary, Wodeham recalls FitzRalph's opinion in order to attack it vigorously. FitzRalph, following Duns Scotus, [had] admitted the primacy of the will over reason; Wodeham declares that, formulated and resolved in ... terms [of whether the will is superior to the intellect, or *vice versa*], the very problem itself does not make sense, because [Wodeham holds] there are no faculties distinct from the soul. Instead, the soul itself accomplishes two series of acts, which differ from each other, and which we call 'thought' and 'will'. [Wodeham] explicitly applied the principle of reduction [that is, the principle of economy, or *Ockham's razor*] in combating the theory of [such] faculties, and if he attacked FitzRalph [on this score], it [was] not because Wodeham considered FitzRalph to be a defender of this theory, but only because Wodeham, who recognized that FitzRalph rejected the faculties, found insufficient his expression of that rejection.[5]

Michałski makes several points here worth our notice. He treats Wodeham as having (a) been in a position to know FitzRalph's positions in a developing debate (which is clearly correct), and (b) attacked FitzRalph vigorously because (c) FitzRalph did not go far enough in rejecting faculties of the soul distinct from it, which (d) Wodeham was explicitly willing to do through what we (but not Michałski) usually call the 'principle of economy'. Michałski's evidence in support of this reading is offered in an important footnote. There, he quotes Wodeham's fourth question on the first book of the *Sentences* as follows:

> Hibernicus holds with Scotus against Thomas in [the latter's *Sentences* commentary] (*Scriptum*), that the will is a more noble faculty than the intellect. ... But ... [FitzRalph then] says ... immediately, that the mind has both intellect and will, the intellect being the superior (*altior*) of the two according to order (*sic!*) and the will being superior according to perfection. ... [Against FitzRalph] I hold this conclusion by way of

---

d'adopter tantôt un point de vue, tantôt un autre'. 5 Ibid., p. 313: 'Adam Wodeham. Il a suivi visiblement de près le développement de la discussion sur le problème ici traité, puisque dans son commentaire d'Oxford il rappelle l'opinion de Fitz-Ralph pour l'attaquer avec vigueur. Fitz-Ralph, après J. Duns Scot, admettait le primat de la volonté sur la raison: A. Wodeham déclare que le problème formulé et résolu en ces termes n'a aucun sens, puisqu'il n'y a pas de facultés distinctes de l'âme, mais que cette même âme accomplit seulement deux séries d'actes qui diffèrent entre eux et que nous appelons la pensée et la volonté. Il applique expressément le principe de réduction en combattant la théorie des facultés; s'il attaque à Fitz-Ralph, ce n'est pas qu'il le considère comme le défenseur de cette théorie, c'est uniquement parce qu'il trouve insuffisantes les expressions dont il se sert. Il reconnaît du reste que Fitz-Ralph rejette la théorie des facultés, lorsqu'il vient à s'en occuper de façon spéciale'.

reduction, since I say, namely, that neither is the intellect a more noble power than the will nor the converse, because [the will] is numerically identical to the intellect, and *vice versa*, in the same intellectual substance in which it is innate to know and innate to will. ... And note that FitzRalph holds this same [view] not in the [aforesaid discussion] ... but in another question.[6]

This last statement – that 'FitzRalph holds this same [view] in another question' but not here – is an instance of what had led Michalski, a couple of paragraphs earlier, to announce that FitzRalph's contemporaries 'reproached him for holding sometimes one view, but sometimes another'.[7] Yet, as we shall see below, that is not actually what Wodeham does, as we can discover by turning to Wodeham's manuscripts, which Michalski – I believe honestly but hurriedly – transcribed incompletely, as the elipses in this footnote reveal, and not entirely accurately. Unfortunately, Michalski's elipses in his own transcription of Wodeham's quotation of FitzRalph not only led Michalski to misread the tenor of Wodeham's remarks, but, repeated by Robson without Michalski's elipses,[8] led to further misrepresentation of Wodeham's response to FitzRalph. Thus, on the basis of Michalski's transcription, Robson somehow understood FitzRalph to have sided with Aquinas, and reached the conclusion that FitzRalph earned 'the contemptuous scorn of Adam Wodeham'.[9]

6 Ibid., n. 1: 'Hibernicus tenet cum Scoto contra Thomam in scripto, quod voluntas est potentia nobilior quam intellectus... Sed... statim... dicit, quod mens habet intellectum et voluntatem, quorum duorum intellectus est altior secundum ordinem et voluntas secundum perfectionem... Teneo conclusionem ad viam reductionis, cum dico scil. quod non intellectus est potentia nobilior voluntate nec econverso, quia idem numero est intellectus et econtra in eadem substantia intellectuali... ipsa nata est intelligere et ipsa nata est velle. 1 Sent., q.4. Cod. Vat. lat. 955, fo. 98vo. Nota, quod Firauf tenet hoc idem non in priori loco, ... sed in alia quaestione'. 7 See above, n. 4. 8 Compare Michalski to John A. Robson, *Wyclif and the Oxford schools: the relation of the 'Summa de ente' to scholastic debates at Oxford in the later fourteenth century* (Cambridge, 1966), p. 81, n. 2: 'Hibernicus tenet cum Scoto contra Thomam in scripto, quod voluntas est potentia nobilior quam intellectus ... Sed ... *statim dicit quod* mens habet intellectum et voluntatem, quorum duorum intellectus est altior secundum ordinem et voluntas secundum *perfeccionem*... Teneo conclusionem ad viam *reduccionis*, cum dico *scilicet* quod non intellectus est potentia nobilior voluntate nec econverso, quia idem numero est intellectus et econtra in eadem *substancia* intellectuali... ipsa nata est intelligere et ipsa nata est velle'. At '*Sed ... statim dicit*', Robson omits a crucial elipsis; although he acknowledges Michalski *in this note* as his source, Robson emended the latter's transcription of two words (*perfectionem* and *reductionis*) without any cited manuscript witnesses! Robson's translation of this passage in the text has no elipses at all: 'Hibernicus first admits the supremacy of the will over the intellect, but immediately declares that the mind contains both intellect and will, of which the first is superior secundum ordinem and the second secundum perfectionem. But I support the conclusion that is a matter of reduction, that is, that neither the will nor the intellect is the higher faculty since both are aspects of the same mental substance, which exists both to will and to intuit'. The last of these sentences is especially inaccurate in conveying what Wodeham asserts. 9 Robson, *Wyclif*, p. 81; for Robson's understanding of FitzRalph as having sided with Aquinas, see pp 80–1. See also

Two years after Robson's views were published, Gordon Leff's monograph on FitzRalph appeared, with no mention in it of whether Wodeham scorned FitzRalph's thinking.[10] Rather, any disappointment with FitzRalph's mind was on the part of Leff, who described him as 'a traditionalist of a considerably less searching and original kind' and as 'conventional';[11] as someone who 'evinced little ... participation in, or perhaps more correctly permeation by, contemporary thinking' and 'whose thinking lacks ... authenticity'.[12] On difficult questions according to Leff, FitzRalph 'evaded commitment',[13] and 'had virtually nothing new to add to the traditional positions' that his (mostly Ockhamist) contemporaries had moved beyond, while he instead 'felt constrained to reaffirm them'.[14] 'Both as a conservative and as a thinker', Leff decided as he worked through the future bishop's *Sentences* questions, 'FitzRalph was ill-equipped to grapple with innovations'.[15] 'Ultimately', Leff asserts,

> It was the inability of FitzRalph to penetrate to the heart of contemporary issues, to grasp the full range of issues and to devise solutions to meet them, which makes his Commentary on the *Sentences* so inferior ... and so generally unsatisfactory. It stamps his thinking as essentially derivative and frequently perfunctory.[16]

FitzRalph's views on the relation of the will, the intellect and their acts are among the positions that Leff evidently deemed 'unsatisfactory' and 'derivative' even though he recognized, contrary to Robson, that FitzRalph did not side with Aquinas. Instead, Leff read FitzRalph as taking the course of least resistance; given the fact that, according to FitzRalph, 'the other doctors [of theology] agree that the will is nobler' than the intellect, he also 'came down in favour of the will' in spite of his doubts and 'without great conviction'.[17] On Leff's interpretation,

Robson, p. 78: 'It is noteworthy that this stand earned the disapproval of Adam Woodham' citing in support Michalski, 'Le problème de la volonté', p. 266 (p. 313 in the repr. ed.). **10** Gordon Leff, *Richard FitzRalph, commentator of the sentences: a study in theological orthodoxy* (Manchester, 1963). **11** Leff, *FitzRalph*, pp 11–12; the comparison here is to the theologian Gregory of Rimini. See also p. 50. **12** Ibid., p. 12. On p. 13, Leff suggests as a mitigating factor that FitzRalph's *Sentences* lectures were a youthful work, but the age of Scotus, Ockham, Wodeham, Holcot et al. would not have been significantly different at the time they delivered their lectures on Lombard's work. Unfortunately, William J. Courtenay repeats Leff's assessment. See Courtenay, *Schools and scholars in fourteenth-century England* (Princeton, 1987), p. 138 (footnoting Leff's p.13): 'As late as 1328, when Richard FitzRalph was lecturing on the *Sentences*, one finds no evidence of the newer elements [of Oxford thought]. The Augustinianism of the young FitzRalph is, as Gordon Leff has shown, almost identical with that of Henry of Ghent'. **13** Leff, *FitzRalph*, p. 17; see also Robson, *Wyclif*, p. 80: 'FitzRalph's reply to this question is revealing because his indeterminacy, and indeed undignified hedging ...'. **14** Ibid., p. 50. Throughout this book, Leff alludes to his earlier work on Bradwardine and on Rimini as the *oeuvre* in which he had established the 'radicalism' of Ockhamists (among whom he counted Wodeham and Holcot) against which Leff judges FitzRalph to be 'conservative' and 'traditional'. **15** Ibid., p. 18. **16** Ibid., p. 12. **17** Ibid., pp 96–7, quoting FitzRalph (p. 97, n. 1): 'In isto

FitzRalph reached for a moderate if not mediocre position, rejecting both Aquinas' 'doctrine' of the intellect's superiority and Scotus' decision in favour of the will's 'primacy', instead 'contrapos[ing]' his own *opinio media*.[18]

By the late 1970s, William Courtenay had begun to point out that Wodeham's response to FitzRalph was more nuanced and varied than Michalski and Robson had appreciated.[19] For Courtenay, 'FitzRalph was Wodeham's major opponent and, on occasion, ally'.[20] Thanks to a careful examination of Wodeham's manuscripts, Courtenay had realized that 'in his Oxford lectures, Wodeham challenged the opinions of FitzRalph more than those of any other living author'.[21] Indeed, Courtenay wrote of Wodeham's familiarity with the contents of FitzRalph's lectures as a bachelor of the *Sentences*, surmising that the younger Franciscan had actually attended them. While preparing his own Oxford lectures on the *Sentences*, Wodeham discovered 'that FitzRalph had changed his position on the capacity of the soul for beatitude'.

> The position Wodeham had [earlier] criticized ... was abandoned by FitzRalph in favor of a 'corrected' opinion. It is not clear whether FitzRalph changed his position because of the critique of Wodeham. ... It is certain, however, that FitzRalph was just then in the process of making a new and to his mind improved edition of his *Sentences* Commentary.[22]

Neither here nor elsewhere did Courtenay directly address previous historians' interpretations, which meant that when FitzRalph's next intellectual biographer, Katherine Walsh, took up the exploration of FitzRalph's Oxford teaching, she faced what must have appeared to be a general consensus about the quality of his mind among twentieth-century readers of FitzRalph's *Sentences* lectures. Moreover, the lengthy summary of FitzRalph's arguments by Leff, together

---

articulo tenent alii doctores concorditer quod voluntas est potentia nobilior ut voluntas est. Unde teneo hanc partem quamvis opposita pars sit valde probabilis (I, d.i, q.a, 13rb)'. Although this citation is less than clear as to the manuscript from which Leff here quotes, it must be Paris, Bibliothèque Nationale, MS Lat. 15853 (where the passage is on 13rb), which contains FitzRalph's earlier, uncorrected version, as it does not match the text that Wodeham refers to as corrected. See below, n. 33. 18 Leff, *FitzRalph*, p. 97, quoting FitzRalph (p. 97, n. 4): 'In isto articulo sunt tres opiniones, due extreme et una media (I, q.9, a. 3, 62vb)'. – hardly sufficient to establish which (if any) opinion of the three FitzRalph claimed as his own. 19 W.J. Courtenay, *Adam Wodeham: an introduction to his life and writings* (Leiden, 1978), pp 75–81. 20 Ibid., p. 75. 21 Ibid., pp 77 and, again, 80. 22 Ibid., pp 77–8 (refering to Wodeham's second question of his prologue). As Courtenay graciously noted, he worked out this sequence with my assistance. Having already arrived at his assessment of Wodeham's attitude towards FitzRalph, Courtenay's remarks at this juncture drew in part on my 1975 master's thesis written under his direction, *Richard FitzRalph on the will and the intellect*. As appendices, this work included my first paleographical effort: predictably rough, unreliable editions of FitzRalph's and Wodeham's questions on the will, intellect, their acts, and beatitude upon which Courtenay drew at this juncture.

with his characterization of FitzRalph as intellectually pedestrian, would have discouraged an independent reading of manuscripts of his *Sentences* lectures, especially as his career after Oxford was Walsh's principal focus. Not surprisingly, therefore, she simply restated the Michalski–Robson theme of FitzRalph's 'ecclecticism' – fighting words for a philosopher or theologian – and inconsistency of argumentation, writing that

> He sometimes qualified his own previous statements almost to the point of contradiction. This tendency, which marred his entire *lectura* on the *Sentences* and which originated largely in the author's habit of picking and choosing among a variety of authorities in his quest for a middle way, was criticized by Wodeham as 'hedging'.[23]

The 'middle way' along which FitzRalph was trying to walk was, according to Walsh, the route between Subtle and Angelic Doctors. 'Throughout [FitzRalph's] commentary', Walsh states, 'he is frequently to be found in opposition to the teaching of Scotus, slightly less often does he take issue with Aquinas'. On the issue of which of the two mental faculties (will or intellect) is superior, Scotus' 'view of the will as a power superior to the intellect ... appealed to FitzRalph personally', in Walsh's judgment, but he deemed Aquinas' support for the opposite ranking 'more authoritative'. Walsh's conclusion that FitzRalph sought such a 'middle way' is clearly indebted to Leff, from whom as well as from Robson, Walsh gained the impression that FitzRalph's position was somehow untenable, so much so that 'Wodeham took him to task for trying to have things both ways'.[24] Yet, Walsh had also read Courtenay, so she recognized that 'there are several indications of give and take on the part both of the regent master [FitzRalph] and the Franciscan bachelor, with each prepared to learn from and revise their own opinions in the light of the other's work'.[25] Moreover, Walsh appreciated with Courtenay that Wodeham's evident access to both FitzRalph's original lectures and his *opus correctum* is suggestive of warm relations rather than hostility.[26] Similar evidence has long been the basis for historians' appraisal of Wodeham's relationship with his older, Franciscan

---

23 Katherine Walsh, *A fourteenth-century scholar and primate: Richard FitzRalph in Oxford, Avignon and Armagh* (Oxford, 1981), p. 59. The description of FitzRalph's view as 'hedging' suggests reliance on Robson, *Wyclif*, p. 80 (quoted above, n. 13). It seems to me that, contrary to Walsh's claim that the 'habit of picking and choosing among a variety of authorities' was what Wodeham criticized, this particular 'habit' constituted standard scholarly method in Oxford *Sentences* debates and lectures, so I would argue that it is improbable *prima facie* that any debater would have thrown this particular stone at another. 24 Walsh, *A fourteenth-century scholar and primate*, p. 60, citing Robson, *Wyclif*, p. 78. 25 Walsh, *A fourteenth-century scholar and primate*, p. 62. 26 Ibid., p. 61, where she cites Courtenay, *Adam Wodeham*, pp 75–81. In notes on pp 77–80, Courtenay illustrates the numerous discussions of FitzRalph's views by Wodeham in the latter's Oxford *Sentences* lectures.

teacher, Ockham, as having been not only warm, but that of follower to intellectual leader.[27]

Ad fontes

This, then, is the historiographical context for taking a fresh look at what manuscript copies of Wodeham's *Sentences* lectures have to say. In I *Oxford lectures on the* Sentences, d. 1, q. 14, we find the passage quoted by Michalski in the following context: as a preliminary to rejecting any actual division of the soul into parts, Wodeham speculates on the origin of the very subject of debate, or *dubitatio*, concerning which faculty of the intellectual soul is more noble – and thus, commands – the other. As Wodeham says,

> This subject of debate (*dubitatio*) concerning the nobility of the [faculty of the] will with respect to the intellect had its start among those who posited that the intellect and will are different faculties (*potentiae*) and are accidents added to the essence or substance and in some way distinguished on the part of reality yet with a real identity between them and with the substance of the soul. And not only some of the ancient doctors but also modern ones held this, inasmuch as Hibernicus also holds with Scotus, against Thomas in [the latter's *Sentences* commentary] (*Scriptum*), that the will is a more noble faculty than the intellect.[28]

27 In addition to Courtenay, *Adam Wodeham*, pp 63–4, 160–4: see Gedeon Gál and Stephen Brown (eds), *Venerabilis Inceptoris Guillelmi de Ockham Scriptum in librum primum Sententiarum, Ordinatio*, 1 (St Bonaventure, NY, 1967), introduction, p. 29; Gedeon Gál and Rega Wood (eds), *Adam de Wodeham, Lectura secunda in librum primum Sententiarum* (Binghamton, NY, 1990), 1, intr., pp 5, 12–18. 28 Wodeham, I, *Ordinatio Oxon.*, d. 1, q. 14, Paris, Université MS 193, fos 72vb–74va, Vatican, BAV Lat. 955, fos 98v–100v (pp 196–200); Mazarine MS 915, fo. 60va–vb: 'Ista dubitatio de nobilitate voluntatis respectu intellectus locum habet apud eos qui ponebant intellectum et voluntatem esse potentias diversas et esse accidentia superaddita essentie vel substantie et aliquo modo distingui ex parte rei cum reali idemptitate inter se et cum substantie anime. Et hoc non solum doctores aliqui antiqui sed moderni tenuerunt in tantum etiam quod Hybernicus (Fire<f> mg. *Vat.*) tenet cum Scoto contra Thomam in *Scripto* quod voluntas est potentia nobilior quam intellectus. Et arguit contra·Thomam dicentem quod intellectus est altissima potentia in anima: 'quero' inquit <quid intellegit per 'altissimam potentiam?> 'Aut intellegit per "potentiam altissimam" potentiam nobilissimam aut potentiam priorem secundum originem, sicut magis convenienter apparet ex dictis suis. Si nobilissima,' inquit, 'tunc contradiceret sibi ipsi, quia statim post in Responsione ad primum articulum dicit <Thomas> quod «mens habet intellectum et voluntatem, quorum duorum intellectus est altior secundum originem et voluntas [perfectior *add. Maz*] secundum perfectionem; et similis ordo in habitibus est et actibus.» Haec ille. Si vero per "potentiam altissimam" non intelligit nobilissimam seu perfectissimam, tunc illud quod ipse accipit pro principio per se noto est falsum, scilicet quod optima operatio sit altissime potentie, scilicet intellectus. Hoc enim capit in positione quod tamen est falsum, nisi per "altissimam" intelligatur (*Maz*: intellegat) "nobilissimam", quia potentie nobilissime est operatio nobilissima,' sicut enim (*Maz*. eciam) vult Philosophus 10 *Ethicorum* capitulo 8. Teneo igitur conclusionem contrariam ad vim sermonis eundo, scilicet quod intellectus non est [operatio *scr. et del. Maz*] potentia nobilior voluntate nec econverso, quia idem

Let me pause here to note that one historical issue to which these remarks speak is the question as to how recently a master of theology could have lectured and still have been numbered among the *antiqui* – a categorization that, in the early fourteenth century, continued to advance,[29] but which we know from many sources clearly included Bonaventure, Aquinas and Henry of Ghent. For Wodeham, John Duns Scotus – like Thomas Aquinas – must have been an *antiquus* for the contrast with FitzRalph to make sense, as he sides with one against the other. This passage also tells us, through the use of the reference to 'ancient and modern *doctors*' [of theology], that FitzRalph had already attained that status, so Wodeham was writing these words no earlier than the fall term of 1331 – which is when, as Katherine Walsh established, documents first style FitzRalph *sacra pagina doctor*; for other reasons, Paul Streveler and I have argued for 1332–3, when FitzRalph was chancellor.[30] So far, Wodeham's tone is respectful.

Having reached the point in Wodeham's discussion where he states that 'Hibernicus [that is, FitzRalph] holds with Scotus, against Thomas in [the latter's] *Scriptum* [that is, *Sentences* commentary], that the will is a more noble faculty than the intellect', Michalski began to introduce elipses, quoting Wodeham as follows: 'But ... [FitzRalph then] says ... immediately, that the mind has both intellect and will, the intellect being the superior of the two according to order (*sic*!) and the will being superior according to perfection ...'.[31] On Michalski's reading, Wodeham criticizes FitzRalph for an immediate *volte face*. The manuscripts, however, show us that Wodeham instead quotes in careful detail FitzRalph's critique of Aquinas, writing as follows:

> And [FitzRalph] argues against Thomas, who says that the intellect is the highest power in the soul. 'I ask', [FitzRalph] says, 'whether by "the

omnino est intellectus quod voluntas et econtra, et substantia intellectualis, nam omni alio circumscripto ab hac natura intellectuali ipsa nata est intelligere et ipsa eadem nata est velle; igitur hoc natum velle est natum intelligere et econtra. Igitur intellectus est voluntas et econtra, ex hoc enim quod talis natura est nata vel potens intelligere [quam] dicitur 'intellectus,' et ex hoc quod est potens vel nata ad volendum ipsa dicitur 'voluntas' – et hoc non solum dicerem in homine de intellectu et voluntate sed de omni sensu. Cui consentit auctor *De spiritu et anima*, dicens capitulo 8, 'sensus vero unus est in anima et quod vere ipse est in anima..'. (61ra) Sed contra hanc conclusionem sunt multe auctoritates propter quas (*in Vat*; *om. Maz.*) alias tenet Scotus distinctionem formalem inter potentias. Dicunt enim auctores quod potentie fluunt ab essentia et quod sunt passiones et huiusmodi'. Transcriptions, punctuation and translations from manuscripts are mine, and include some of the more notable variants that could affect sense. Angle brackets < > indicate editorial insertions of words I believe should have been in the manuscript for sense (or that are attested in other witnesses); square brackets [ ] indicate words present in the manuscript that should be deleted for sense; and parentheses ( ) are to indicate variant readings. **29** See William J. Courtenay, 'Antiqui and moderni in late medieval thought', *Journal of the History of Ideas*, 48 (1987), 3–10, esp. 4–6. **30** Paul A. Streveler, K.H. Tachau et al. (eds), *Seeing the future clearly: quodlibetal questions on future contingents by Robert Holcot* (Toronto, 1995), pp 16–21. **31** See above, n. 6.

highest power" [Aquinas] understands "the most noble power" or "that power which is prior by origin", which appears to be more compatible (*convenienter*) with his words. If [Aquinas means] "the most noble" power', [FitzRalph] says, 'then [Aquinas] would be contradicting himself, because *immediately after this* in his "Response" to the first articles, Thomas says that "the mind has intellect and will, of which the intellect is the superior (*altior*) of the two according to its origin and the will according to its perfection; and there is a similar order in [their] habits and acts". That is what [Aquinas says],' [as FitzRalph says].[32]

We have not yet reached the end of Wodeham's quotation of FitzRalph's arguments against Aquinas' position, but it is important to appreciate how this differs from the reading one would have from Michałski's transcription. Michałski construed Wodeham as having accused FitzRalph of 'immediately' (*statim*) contradicting his own – correct – rejection of a distinction between powers (or faculties) of the soul; but the manuscripts make clear that it is *FitzRalph* who so accuses *Aquinas*, and it is *Aquinas*' possible contradiction that is described as occurring 'immediately', not FitzRalph's.[33] Moreover, FitzRalph

---

32 See above, n. 28.   33 In his contribution to the present volume, Severin Kitanov, too, has recognized that FitzRalph is the accuser and Aquinas' the text in which the possible contradiction occurs. See S. Kitanov, 'Is it better for the king of England to be a king of England than a duke of Aquitaine', above, pp 63–4. There are two versions of FitzRalph's discussion in the surviving manuscripts. Except for the precise citation to the passage in Aquinas, Wodeham is quoting a 'corrected text' of FitzRalph, I *Sent*., q. 2, 'Utrum beatitudo sit actus intellectus vel voluntatis', to be found in Paris, Bibliothèque Nationale, MS Lat. 6441, fos 62vb–63ra and Troyes, Bibliothèque municipale, MS 505, fo. 4rb: 'Thomas dicit <prima parte *Scripti*, distinctio prima, articulo primo, questione prima,> quod intellectus est altissima potentia in homine. . Quero: quid intellegit per 'altissimam potentiam?' Aut intellegit per 'potentiam altissimam' potentiam nobilissimam, aut aliquid aliud, scilicet potentiam priorem origine, sicut apparet convenienter ex dictis sui.. Si nobilissimam, tunc contradicit sibi ipsi, quia statim post in Responsione ad primum articulum dicit <Thomas> quod 'mens habet intellectum et voluntatem, quorum duorum intellectus est altior secundum originem, et voluntas secundum perfectionem; et similis ordo est in habitibus et actibus'. Haec ille, ubi expresse vult quod voluntas est altior secundum perfectionem. Si vero per 'altissimam potentiam' non intellegit 'nobilissimam' seu 'perfectissimam,' tunc illud quod accipit pro principio per se noto est falsum, scilicet quod optima operatio sit operatio altissime potentie, scilicet intellectus. Hoc enim capit in positione hac, quod tamen est falsum, nisi per 'altissimam' intellegatur nobilissimam, quia potentie nobilissime est operatio nobilissima certum est. Dico igitur sicut tenet Doctor Subtilis et alii doctores concorditer quod voluntas est potentia nobilior quam intellectus, quamvis alia pars sit valde probabilis'. For FitzRalph's uncorrected (or less completely corrected) version, see Florence, Biblioteca Nazionale MS A.iii.508, fo. 8rb; Oxford, Oriel College MS 15, fo. 111ra; Paris, Bibliothèque Nationale, MS Lat. 15853, fo. 13rb, Vatican, Biblioteca Apostolica Vaticana, Ottob. lat. 869, fo. 122v; Worcester Cathedral Library MS Q71, fo. 84v: 'Thomas dicit prima parte *Scripti*, distinctione prima, articulo primo, questione prima, quod intellectus est altissima potentia in homine. Sed contra hoc dictum potest argui sic: aut intellegit per 'potentiam altissimam' potentiam nobilissimam, aut aliquid aliud, scilicet potentiam priorem origine, sicut apparet convenienter ex dictis suis. Si nobilissimam, tunc contradiceret sibi ipsi, quia statim post

had quoted Aquinas' own edition (*Scriptum*) of his *Sentences* lectures accurately.[34]

This is merely the first horn of the dilemma onto which, FitzRalph thinks, Aquinas has thrown himself by his ambiguous description of the intellect as the mental faculty that is *altissimus*. If Aquinas does mean by this word that the intellect ranks as the highest power in status – as, that is, the noblest – then he immediately contradicts himself. If, however, by *altissimus* Aquinas instead refers to 'earliest in origin',[35] then Aquinas has just shown to be false what he has taken to be a principle that is *per se nota*, namely that the best workings of the mind are those of its best faculty, for this will not be true unless one is taking nobility as the measure. Of course, the point of FitzRalph's argument is that, since neither alternative should be acceptable to Aquinas, the assumption that either faculty is superior to the other should be abandoned.

This, then, is the juncture at which Wodeham states that, taking the conclusion (that a given mental faculty is superior to another) according to the force of its words (its *vis sermonis*), which is its strictest sense,[36] he rejects any distinction

in Responsione ad primum articulum dicit <Thomas> quod 'mens habet intellectum et voluntatem, quorum duorum intellectus est altior secundum originem, et voluntas secundum perfectionem; et similis ordo est in habitibus et actibus'. Haec ille, ubi expresse dicit quod voluntas est altior secundum perfectionem. Si vero per 'aıtissimam potentiam' non intellegat 'nobilissimam' seu 'perfectissimam', tunc illud quod accipit pro principio quasi per se noto est falsum, scilicet quod optima operatio sit operatio altissime potentie, scilicet intellectus. Hoc enim capit in positione quod tamen est falsum, nisi per 'altissimam' intellegatur nobilissimam quia potentie nobilissime est operatio nobilissima certum est. In isto articulo tenent alii doctores concorditer quod voluntas est potentia nobilior ut voluntas est quam intellectus, unde teneo hanc partem quamvis opposita pars sit valde probabilis'. **34** Compare FitzRalph (preceding note) to Thomas Aquinas, *Commentum in quatuor libros Sententiarum Petri Lombardi* (Parma, 1856), I, d. 1, q. 1, art. 1, arg. 1: 'Circa primum sic proceditur. Videtur quod frui sit actus intellectus. Nobilissimus enim actus est nobilissimae potentiae. Altissima autem potentia in homine est intellectus. Ergo, cum frui sit perfectissimus actus hominis, quia ponit hominem in suo fine ultimo, videtur quod sit actus intellectus. ... Respondeo dicendum, quod fruitio consistit in optima operatione hominis, cum fruitio sit ultima felicitas hominis. Felicitas autem non est in habitu, sed in operatione, secundum philosophum. Optima autem operatio hominis est operatio altissimae potentiae, scilicet intellectus, ad nobilissimum objectum ... Ad primum ergo dicendum, quod appetitus semper sequitur cognitionem. Unde, sicut inferior pars habet sensum et appetitum, qui dividitur in irascibilem et concupiscibilem, *ita suprema pars habet intellectum et voluntatem, quorum intellectus est altior secundum originem, et voluntas secundum perfectionem. Et similis ordo est in habitibus, et etiam in actibus*, scilicet visionis et amoris. Fruitio autem nominat altissimam operationem quantum ad sui perfectionem'. (In addition to the 1948 reprint of the Parma edition, one can consult Aquinas' text at: http://www.corpusthomisticum.org/snp1001.html, credited as *Textum Parmae 1856 editum ac automato translatum a Roberto Busa SJ in taenias magneticas denuo recognovit Enrique Alarcón atque instruxit*.) Severin Kitanov suggests, 'Is it better', above, p. 65, n. 26, that FitzRalph might have 'borrowed the remark [of Aquinas] from Ockham' rather than quoting Aquinas directly, but this seems to me unlikely, because FitzRalph's quotation is considerably longer and more complete than Ockham's. **35** Not *order*, as Michalski and, following him, Robson wrote; see above, nn 6, 8. **36** See William J. Courtenay, 'Force of words and figures of speech: the crisis over *Virtus sermonis* in the fourteenth century', *Franciscan Studies*, 44 (1984), 107–28, reprinted in idem, *Ockham and ockhamism:*

between the mind's substance, faculties and acts. Here, by misreading '*ad vim sermonis*' as '*ad viam reductionis*' (not an expression I believe I have ever encountered in a fourteenth-century author), Michałski read Wodeham as 'expressly using the principle of reduction'[37] – presumably, that is, the principle that *frustra fit per plures quod potest per pauciora* – where Wodeham did no such thing.[38] Rather, having used FitzRalph's arguments to demolish any conclusion that the intellect is nobler than the will or *vice versa*, Wodeham adds his own justification for rejecting the very basis for such a conclusion.

Having quoted FitzRalph's views favourably, Wodeham thus reaches the point in the question where arguments from authority that appear to counter a conclusion being defended would at Oxford normally be recited, and Wodeham proceeds to offer almost three more columns (roughly 350 printed lines in the Mazarine manuscript) of such arguments. To defang these requires him to refute or reinterpret numerous authoritative treatments of distinct faculties and acts by the likes of Aristotle, Augustine, Anselm, Peter Lombard and Scotus. Eventually Wodeham reaches what, if he were a master, would constitute the determination of the question at issue in this article; and lest anyone attack him for being at odds with virtually all major authorities on the subject, Wodeham announces that FitzRalph agrees with him. Michałski was mislead by an erroneously inserted negative when he renders what Wodeham says here as 'note that FitzRalph holds the same [view] *not* in the prior place ... but in another question'.[39] Instead, what Wodeham actually says is this:

studies in the dissemination and impact of his thought (Leiden, 2008), pp 209–28.   37 Robson, *Wyclif*, p. 81 repeats Michałski's error; see above, n. 8.   38 A few paragraphs further along Wodeham's text does include an appeal to the principle of economy, but directed chiefly at Aquinas. See Wodeham, I, *Ordinatio Oxon.*, d. 1, q. 14, Paris, Université MS 193, fo. 73ra, Vatican, BAV Lat. 955, fo. 98v (p. 196); Mazarine MS 915, fo. 60vb: '(*Vat. mg.* Contra Thomam) Preterea, non videtur rationabile quod solum per unum accidens mentem sit [ipsa] receptiva beatitudinis, sive per unum quocumque modo a parte rei ab ipsa distinctum, nam tunc unum accidens esset (tunc *add. Maz.*) beatum. Praeterea (*mg. Vat., om. Maz.*) frustra ponitur (*om. Maz.*) fieri (fit *Maz.*) per plura quod eque faciliter potest fieri per pauciora et salvari. Nec *Scriptura Sacra* aut ratio obviat, sed per eandem simplicem naturam intentionalem sine omni tali distinctione rationali previa primis actibus modo quo iam expressit auctor ille facilissime poterunt salvari omnia propter que alii ponunt potentias anime distingui, igitur et cetera. Quod autem ratio non obviet patet etiam per Scotum in II libro <d. 16>, ubi de isto puncto investigatur (investigat *Vat.*) in *Reportatione Parisius*. Auctoritates que oppositum pretendunt faciliter glosari possunt una per aliam, igitur nihil obstat dicte sententie. Hoc etiam (autem *Maz.*) declaratur exemplo de Deo, qui habet potentiam creativam *(om. Maz.)*, gubernativam, reperativam, predestinativam, reprobativam (*mg. Vat., om. Maz.*) que nullo modo distinguuntur in eo, sed eadem omnino Dei essentia vel voluntas varie nominatur a variis effectibus secundum Magistrum sepe libro primo. Similiter potest per omnia (ad propositum *add. Vat.*) dici de intellectu et voluntate' (the words in italicized capitals are omitted in the Mazarine manuscript).   39 See above, n. 6, Michałski, writing 'Nota, quod Firauf tenet hoc idem *non* in priori loco, ... sed in alia quaestione', rather than Wodeham's 'Dico igitur ad articulum quod voluntas veraciter non est nobilior intellectu nec econverso. Et nota quod Firauf tenet hoc idem in priori loco ubi tractat presentem questionem'.

Therefore, to the article, I say that the will truly is not nobler than the intellect nor *vice versa*, and note that Fitzralph holds the same [view] in the prior place where he treats the present question; but in another question, he says that just as the intellective soul is any of its powers so too is the sensitive soul each of its [own] powers, and that [the soul] is called (*denominatur*) this or that power from the action that it carries out through this or that organ. In the article of his corrected work [titled] 'whether the memory, intellect, and will are distinct from each other', he holds rather that in the human being, the sensitive is distinct from the intellective, yet no sensitive power [is distinct] from [the sensitive], nor [any] intellective [power] from the intellective [soul].[40]

It is useful to keep in mind that, when Wodeham wrote this passage, he was still a bachelor of the *Sentences*, and as such his prowess as a theologian was still subject to evaluation by the regent masters of Oxford. This should help us see that Wodeham is not criticizing FitzRalph or accusing him of vacillation or hedging, as Michałski, Robson and Walsh supposed; far less is there the 'contemptuous scorn' in Wodeham's tone that Robson described.[41] After all, FitzRalph was not only a regent master, but also chancellor of the university. Rather, Wodeham is listing three places in FitzRalph's *Sentences* lectures where he has already espoused positions close to or the same as those of Wodeham himself.[42] These passages – and the first is simply a cross-reference to the *locus*

---

40 I *Ordinatio Oxon.*, d. 1, q. 14, Paris, Université MS 193, fos 72vb–74va, Vatican, BAV Lat. 955, fo. 99v; Mazarine MS 915, fo. 61va–vb; 'Dico igitur ad articulum quod voluntas veraciter non est nobilior (nobilitate *Maz.*) intellectu nec econverso. Et nota quod Firauf tenet hoc idem (non *add.* Maz.) in priori loco ubi tractat presentem questionem <utrum fruitio beatifica sit actus intellectus>, sed in alia questione dicit (dicens *Vat.*) quod tam anima intellectiva est quelibet sua potentia quam anima etiam sensitiva est sua potentia, et quod denominatur talis vel talis potentia (ponitur *Maz.*; vel talis potentia *iter. Vat.*) ab actione quam exercet in tali vel tali organo. In isto articulo correcti operis 'utrum memoria, intelligentia, et voluntas distinguitur ab invicem,' tenet tamen magis quod in homine sensitiva distinguitur ab intellectiva, nulla tamen sensitiva potentia ab ipsa vel intellectiva ab intellectiva. Sed tamen ulterius dicendum quod licet intellectus sit vere voluntas et econtra, verumtamen nobilius est sibi esse voluntatem quam esse intellectum'. See below, n. 42, for passages in FitzRalph, I *Sent.* q. 5, 'Utrum mens humana sit imago trinitatis increate,' art. 1, 'Utrum memoria, intelligentia, et voluntas distinguantur ab invicem realiter'.
41 See above, nn 9–13.   42 See FitzRalph, I *Sent.* q. 5, 'Utrum mens humana sit imago trinitatis increate,' art. 1, 'Utrum memoria, intelligentia, et voluntas distinguantur ab invicem realiter et ab ipsa mente,' Oriel MS 15, fo. 18ra–rb, Paris 15853, fos 27rb–28ra: 'Ideo dico ad primum articulum, cum queritur utrum memoria, etc., quod quelibet istarum intentionum – memoria, intelligentia, et voluntas – accipitur dupliciter ad propositum: uno modo actu, alio modo pro potentia a qua vel in quam est actus, et sic est ad propositum. Unde sic dico quod memoria, intelligentia, et voluntas non sunt distincte realiter in una mente. Et intellego per 'potentiam memorativam' in proposito memoriam intellectivam, non sensitivam, quia de illa non est articulus. ... *Unde quantum ad illud secundum dictum, non videtur quod iste Doctor, salva sua reverentia, dicit verum; sed quantum ad primam partem, scilicet quod omnes potentie sensitive et etiam intellective sunt una res, distincta secundum hoc quod ista potest in varias operationes, scilicet ipsa substantia anime*

citatus earlier in the discussion – do reveal that FitzRalph's view had become more nuanced over time. Later in the same question, Wodeham again cites FitzRalph to buttress his own position, stating that 'to the sixth [argument], Hibernicus responds – and [does so] well – that the act of the will, that is, the act of wanting, which according to the truth is also the act of the intellect ...'.[43]

rationalis in homine, et in brutis ipsa substantia anime brutalis, videtur mihi satis probabile in brutis et in homine similiter, si non sit anima alia sensitiva in homine distincta ab intellectiva et prius generata. ... Sive igitur ponatur una anima tantum in homine, sive due potentie, sensitive dico sunt ipsa anima sensitiva, et potentie intellective sunt ipsa anima intellectiva, et similiter de brutis. Unde videtur mihi melius dicere quod tota anima sensitiva est sua potentia, scilicet virtus imaginativa et virtus sensitiva etc., quam dicere quod pars sensitiva, que est in oculo vel in certa parte eius, est virtus visiva, et alia pars eius sensus communis, et ita de aliis, ex quo tota anima sensitiva totius animalis est una forma indistincta specifice in suis partibus, actio cuiuscumque partis est actio totius per se et partis per accidens tantum. Et ideo tota per se vocatur 'potentia anime' denominata ab illa actione quam exercet per organum certum, et alia potentia quatenus exercet actionem per organum aliud, et ita tota dicitur distincta, sed solum secundum modum loquendi. ... (P 28ra; O 18rb) *Ad primum argumentum in oppositum: cum arguitur in parte sensitive potentie distinguuntur, igitur in parte intellectiva, dico quod non sequitur, quia non est simile de illis cum pars sensitiva sit virtus organica, et ideo habet diversas potencias in diversis organis, sed numquam habet duas potencias distinctas in eadem parte precise, et ideo non sequitur quod iste potentie distinguantur in mente ...*' (note: the arguments in the italicized capitals are omitted by Oriel, so at least here, the manuscript does not appear to contain the *Opus correctum*'s text). 43 Wodeham, I *Sent.* d. 1, q. 14, Mazarine MS 915, fo. 62ra; Paris, Université MS 193, fo. 74rb; Vatican BAV lat. 955, fo. 100r: 'Ad sextum, respondetur (*mg.* Hibernicus) et bene quod actum voluntatis, idest actum volendi – qui secundum veritatem ita est actus intellectus sicut voluntatis – talem actum, inquam, volendi esse magis actum rectum intelligendi contingit esse dupliciter. Uno modo, quod eius rectitudo sit nobilior et magis laudabiliter, et sic actus volendi est magis rectus cum sit nobilior et melior. Alio modo quod eius rectitudo sit prior secundum naturam, et sic propositio est vera quod actus intellectus est magis rectus secundum quod huius quam actus voluntatis in eo quod voluntas. Quia tamen secundum veritatem rectitudo actus intelligendi ordinatur ad rectitudinem et ad bonitatem actus volendi sicut declarat Anselmus, *Cur Deus Homo*, capitulo primo. Et ordine naturali numquam ordinatur nobilius ad vilius, sed econtra, ut patet ex primo *Ethicorum*, ubi per hoc probat Philosophus quod felicitas est actio nobilissima, quia omnes alie operationes humane sunt genera eius'. See, however, FitzRalph, who makes the argument slightly differently: I *Sent.*, q. 2, 'Utrum beatitudo sit actus intellectus vel voluntatis,' a.1, 'utrum voluntas sit potentia nobilior quam intellectus', Oriel MS 15, fo. 11rb; Paris MS 15853, fo. 13va–vb, Troyes MS 505, fo. 4va: 'Dico quod intellectum esse magis rectum voluntate (*om. Paris, Troyes*) intelligitur dupliciter. Uno modo, quia eius rectitudo secundum quod huiusmodi est prior secundum naturam, et sic propositio est vera; sed (et *Oriel, Paris*) non sequitur propter hoc quod intellectus sit nobilior. Alio modo quia eius rectitudo est nobilior ut talis est, et magis laudabilis; et sic rectitudo voluntatis est melior (maior *Troyes*)'. The arguments that come next in Wodeham's text occur several lines before these sentences in FitzRalph's text; thus Oriel MS 15, fo. 11ra; Paris MS 15853, fo. 13rb–va, Troyes MS 505, fo. 4rb: 'Et ratio (responsio *Paris*) ad hanc partem potest esse talis preter predictas rationes: actio intellectus circa aliquod obiectum ordinatur naturali ordine ad actionem voluntatis circa idem obiectum. ... Sed ordine naturali numquam nobilius (nobilissimus *Oriel*) ordinatur ad vilius, sed econverso, ut patet primo *Ethicorum*, quia per hoc probat Philosophus quod felicitas est actio nobilissima, quia omnes alie actiones humane sunt genera ipsius felicitatis. Sequitur ergo quod actio voluntatis sit nobilior, et per consequens, ipsa potentia a qua procedit *est nobilior inquantum talis –dico non quod sit res aliqua nobilior, cum sint eadem res, ut patebit in articulo de hoc* (the words in italicized capitals appear in the Paris manuscript, but are

A little further along, Wodeham writes: 'To the principal arguments ... I respond as above although FitzRalph responds otherwise' and once again, 'to the Master [Peter Lombard] ... FitzRalph (in the aforesaid place cited above) responds as do I ...'.[44] Here, too, Wodeham enlists FitzRalph's authority when possible, and disagrees gently.

When FitzRalph, Wodeham and his fellow socii disputed regarding the human soul and its acts, they joined and advanced controversies already underway among Oxford theologians, having evidently been sparked by Richard Campsall's interpretation of Scotus, probably by 1316.[45] Like many of his fellow disputants, FitzRalph recognized that the various distinctions (real, formal, intentional or of reason) that previous scholastic generations had drawn among the intellective and sensitive substances of the soul, or its 'faculties', or the faculties' diverse acts and habits, were problematic; yet, he also pointed to significant philosophical and theological impediments that would arise from denying *all* distinctions, obstacles that neither he nor his contemporaries had entirely satisfactory means of eluding. Thus, for instance, if there were no distinction whatsoever between the substance of the divinely *created* intellective soul and the substance of the sexually *generated* sensitive soul – a soul that both humans and the other animals possess, and that is generated in their offspring just as the flesh is generated, through conception – then one must resolve a series of dilemmas. On the one hand, human beings must generate the sensitive soul just as do other animals, for if not, then humans would be less capable of generating souls than are living beings that medieval (and many modern) intellectuals considered to have souls and capacities inferior to those of humans. Yet, if humans do generate the sensitive souls of their progeny, how could one defend the conclusion that human beings do *not* generate their offsprings' intellective souls, as what one

---

omitted in Oriel and Troyes; they seem, however, crucial to Wodeham's claim that according to FitzRalph in this discussion, 'the will truly is not nobler than the intellect nor vice versa,' as above, n. 40). **44** Wodeham, I *Sent.* d. 1, q. 14, Mazarine MS 915, fo. 62ra: 'Ad argumenta principalia patet ex iam dictis, tamen contra se potest argui per Augustinum... Respondeo sicut supra tamen aliter respondit Firauf, quod intellegit quod distinguitur ratione sola ... Ad Magistrum ... respondit ut ego Firauf ubi supra'. **45** Richard Campsall, who rejected what he considered unnecessary distinctions (such as those between intellection or volition and the soul, between intuitive and abstractive cognition, or between cognitive acts and their contents), lectured on Lombard's *Sentences* at Oxford at least a year before Ockham. On Campsall as the originator of views that historians have often thought to be Ockham's or Ockhamist, see Tachau, *Vision and certitude in the age of Ockham: optics, epistemology and the foundations of semantics, 1250–1345* (Leiden, New York, København & Köln, 1988), pp 158–66; Tachau, 'The influence of Richard Campsall on Oxford thought' in Anne Hudson and Michael Wilks (eds), *Oxford thought from Ockham to Wyclif*, *Subsidia*, 5 (1986), 109–23; and 'Richard Campsall as a theologian: new evidence' in B. Mojsisch, O. Pluta (eds), *Historia philosophiae medii aevi: Studien zur Geschichte der Philosophie des Mittelalters: Festschrift für Kurt Flasch* (Amsterdam, 1991), 2, pp 979–1002; and Hester Gelber, *It could have been otherwise: contingency and necessity in Dominican theology at Oxford, 1300–1350* (Leiden, 2004), pp 80, 223–66. See also Wodeham, *Lectura secunda*, d. 3, q. 5, in Gedeon Gál and Rega Wood (eds), *Adam de Wodeham, Lectura secunda*, 2, pp 216–30.

calls the 'intellective soul' is identical to the 'sensitive soul?' Or, to reverse the question: how could one defend the conclusion that God *does create* human beings' intellective souls without *eo ipso* creating human and animal sensitive souls, inasmuch as 'intellective soul' and 'sensitive soul' are just two names for one-and-the-same thing?[46] Again, if there were no distinction whatsoever between the intellectual soul's faculties of will and intellect, then presumably a cognition of any given object, as an act of the intellect, would be identical to the will's volition regarding the same object. To accept this conclusion, however, would introduce numerous complications into any theory of whether and how God reveals future contingents, and lead to untenable consequences.[47] None of these is a trivial problem to solve, and the examples that FitzRalph offers, with such posited cases of 'let Socrates know "b" future contingent', are indistinguishable from the *ars obligatoria*-structured arguments to be found in the writings of Strelley, Holcot, Wodeham and nearly every significant Oxford

46 FitzRalph, I *Sent.* q. 5, a. 1, Paris MS 15853, fo. 27va–vb, Troyes MS 505, fo. 15va: 'Videtur tamen quantum ad hominem multo (*om. Troyes*) probabilius esse dicendum quod homo habet anima sensitivam extensam sicut alia animalia; et maxime movet ad hoc quod anima intellectiva creata est, et non producta ab homine; et (*om. Troyes*) ideo nisi homo in generando hominem generaret animam sensitivam, esset ignobilioris conditionis ex se quoad actum generandi, et quoad continuationem sue speciei, quam cetera animalia. Consequens videtur irrationale, tum quia sic natura foret defectiva in necessariis, ut videtur, et maxime in convenientioribus, quod negat Philosophus et Commentator III *De anima* commento 45, tum quia potentia nutritiva est nobilior in homine quam in aliis animalibus ... igitur potentia generativa hominis nobilior est, ergo potentia generativa potest in effectum tam nobilem (ponatur ergo quod in generationem *add. et del. per vacat Paris*) vel nobiliorem sicut potest potentia generativa bruti; sed ista potest in animam sensitivam; igitur potentia generativa hominis potest in animam sensitivam <et> ergo potentia generativa hominis potest in formam tam nobilem. Ponatur ergo quod in generatione hominis Deus non creet animam intellectivam, tunc sequitur quod homo generabit ad hoc verum animal ergo ita faceret quando Deus creat intellectivam animam, cum ista creatio non impediat actionem hominis. (*om. Oriel*). 47 See, for example, FitzRalph, I *Sent.* q. 5, a. 4, Oxford Oriel 15, fos 19vb–20ra, Paris MS 15853, fo. 34rb, Troyes MS 505, fo. 17ra: 'Propter igitur ista argumenta teneo hanc partem, scilicet quod volitio respectu alicuius rei non est cognitio eiusdem, quamvis fortassis volitio alicuius rei sit cognitio suiipsius, propter hoc quod ipsa presens est intellectui, et propter hanc causam voluntas in volendo necessario agit suam actionem sicut quodcumque aliud agens; et ideo actio voluntatis volentis postquam non voluit est aliquid de novo factum in seipsa ex seipsa, non aliquid prius factum antequam ipsa velit. Ad primum argumentum, quando arguitur quod aliter esset possibile aliquam volitionem preteritam non fuisse, dico quod non sequitur. Et ulterius ad argumentum posito isto casu, cum arguitur 'b' non erit, igitur Sortes non vidit in Verbo 'b' esse futurum, igitur Sortes non cognovit 'b', dico quod prima consequentia est bona et secunda non valet. Unde si Deus revelaret Sortem 'b' esse futurum, dico quod hoc facto, Sortes necessario novit 'b', sed non necessario novit 'b' esse futurum sed ita contingenter sicut 'b' est futurum, ita contingenter novit Sortes 'b' esse futurum – ymmo Deus ita contingenter novit 'b' esse futurum. Sed etsi 'b' non foret futurum, adhuc Sortes cognosceret 'b', quia essentia divina representat 'b' sicut aliquis adhuc cognosceret 'b' et non cognosceret 'b' esse futurum, et ideo non sequitur quin Sortes amavit 'b' et quod 'a' volitio Sortes fuit. *De hoc plenius dicetur et melius in articulo de presentia futurorum et in articulo de revelatione futurorum contingentium*' (text in italicized small capitals is omitted in Oriel 15 and Troyes 505, the latter of which also counts this as the third article rather than the fourth).

theologian of the late 1320s–30s.[48] There is nothing here to indicate that FitzRalph possessed a 'conventional' or unoriginal mind, much less any failure to 'participat[e] in, or perhaps more correctly [be] permeat[ed] by, contemporary thinking' on his part.[49]

This is a rather lengthy *improbatio* of an interpretation of Wodeham's attitude toward FitzRalph that began with Michalski. I hope that I have shown that there is another way to read what Wodeham has to say about FitzRalph as neither hostile nor critical. Hence, if we remove Wodeham from the camp of hostile critics to lodge him instead with the friendly witnesses, what Michalski and, even more, Robson took to be Wodeham's denunciation of FitzRalph's indecisiveness was instead Wodeham's recognition (and for us, evidence) that FitzRalph's views had evolved. That, of course, is precisely what a serious seeker of the truth should do when presented with arguments that reveal to him flaws in his position. If he becomes persuaded that his own conclusions are irretrievably flawed, rather than dig in his heals, he should rethink and alter or modify his views. In this way, Chatton persuaded Ockham that his initial theory that the contents of intellectual acts are *ficta* distinct from the acts themselves would require him to accept the same negative consequences as Pierre Auriol's apparently similar theory presented. Not liking those consequences, Ockham abandoned his earlier theory.[50]

Moreover, we should remember that for Wodeham and his contemporaries among the *bachalarii* – a group that included, among others, the Dominicans William Crathorn, Robert Holcot, John Grafton, the Franciscan William Chitterne and a certain Monachus Niger – the job description included formal debates with each other in regular roles (*respondens* and *opponens*) in the presence of regent masters at regular intervals. Undoubtedly, animus sometimes developed over the course of years facing each other in debates, but we should not assume that this happened routinely – especially now that we know that the *sermo finalis* of Holcot, once seen as evidence of mutual antagonism among Dominican *socii* housed, lecturing, and disputing in the same convent, was instead an example of a genre of jocular speeches, delivered at the end of one's years as *Sententiarius*.[51]

Finally, whenever Wodeham quotes FitzRalph, so far as I know, the citations

---

48 For the role of obligational disputation in the theological treatments of contingency, necessity and divine power in the oeuvre of Oxford theologians, see Gelber, *It could have been otherwise*, ch. 4. See also John E. Murdoch, 'Propositional analysis in fourteenth-century natural philosophy: a case study', *Synthèse*, 40 (1979), 117–46; '*Scientia mediantibus vocibus*: metalinguistic analysis in late medieval natural philosophy', *Sprache und Erkenntnis im Mittelalter, Miscellanea mediaevalia*, 13:1 (1981), 73–106.   49 Leff's evaluation, above, at nn 11–12.   50 See Tachau, *Vision and certitude*, pp 135–53, which includes references to the scholars who pieced together the evolution of Ockham's views on the so-called 'fictum theory'.   51 See Tachau, 'Looking gravely at Dominican puns: the "Sermons" of Robert Holcot and Ralph Friseby', *Traditio*, 46 (1991), 337–45.

are reasonably exact, and can be found in manuscripts of the latter's *Sentences* lectures. Indeed, because Wodeham evidently had available both FitzRalph's original lectures (presumably as a *reportatio*) and the *opus correctum*, but does not always specify which one he cites, Wodeham's occasional, apparently inexact quotations could be more accurate than they seem. In the passages we have considered here, Wodeham's information is sufficient to allow us to differentiate the reported lectures from the corrections that FitzRalph had made in preparation for an eventual *Scriptum* that he may never have completed.[52] The year that FitzRalph spent in Paris after his lectures on the *Sentences* and before his ascent to the magisterium, the position that guaranteed that his views would be taken into account by the younger theologians who were bachelors in the early 1330s, may well have offered him the best opportunity to begin revising his *reportatio*. If so, and if FitzRalph left behind him in Paris a copy of questions from that *opus correctum*, then we might be able to explain how it happens that manuscripts probably produced in Paris (today Paris, Bibliothèque Nationale, MS Lat. 6441, fos 62vb–63ra and Troyes, Bibliothèque Municipale, MS 505) rather than from Oxford contain at least some portions of the corrected work.

---

52 See above, nn 28, 33.

Avignon

The rhetoric of Richard FitzRalph's *Defensio curatorum*

TERENCE DOLAN[1]

On Wednesday 8 November 1357, Archbishop Richard FitzRalph addressed the Curia at the papal court in Avignon in the presence of Pope Innocent VI. At that time, the College of Cardinals comprised about twenty members. FitzRalph preached on the theme 'Nolite iudicare secundum faciem, sed iustum iudicium iudicate' (John 7:24): Do not judge by appearances but judge with right judgment.

The *Defensio* is written in a modest style. His intention is to impress through proof, rather than through bombast and consequently he uses a limited range of rhetorical devices, the commonest of which, apart from various types of repetition, are rhetorical questions; for example, 'Annon est istud dampnum grave in clero et populo?'[2] Many of his charges against the friars are hyperbolical, especially concerning their alleged rapacity in buying up books so that his students cannot buy them for their studies.[3] FitzRalph also, in a famous piece, exaggerates the friars' damaging influence on the two thousand subjects he has in his diocese of Armagh who are every year involved in sentences of excommunication because of the sentences passed against wilful homicides (*homicidas voluntarias*), public robbers, arsonists (*incendarios*) and the like, of whom hardly forty in a year come to me or my penitentiaries, and all such men receive the sacraments just like other men and are absolved, or are said to be absolved, nor are they believed to be absolved by any others except the friars, without doubt since no others absolve them.[4] Apart from frequent use of hyperbole, FitzRalph sometimes employs the device of *occupatio* (emphasizing a point by pretending to pass it by) rarely but effectively; for example, *alia plura, si oportebit, adiciam*. At the conclusion of the *Defensio*, he says that he could say much more but, because he does not want to tire the distinguished audience any more,[5] he draws

[1] I wish to commemorate my dear friend, the late Katherine Walsh, whose untimely death has left us all with a sense of both debt and loss. She was a huge help and support to me for my work on FitzRalph over many years since we both graduated in the Sheldonian Theatre, Oxford. I also wish to thank the late Fr Aubrey Gwynn SJ and Fr Ignatius Fennessy OFM for invaluable insights into the workings of the medieval church, in particular FitzRalph. [2] British Library MS Lansdowne 393, fo. 254 v. [3] Ibid., fo. 257r. [4] See Michael Haren, 'Richard FitzRalph of Dundalk, Oxford and Armagh: scholar, prelate and controversialist' in James McEvoy and Michael Dunne (eds), *The Irish contribution to European scholastic thought* (Dublin, 2009), pp 88–110 at p. 91. [5] British Library MS Lansdowne 393, fo. 263v.

his remarks to an end with a final repetition of John 7:24, which is itself ironical since he has spent most of the sermon judging the friars by their appearances and by allegations concerning their lavish churches, consorting with wealthy women and the like, and by continual use of innuendo, gossip and hearsay (*dictum est mihi*), so much so that his claim that he is aiming for a 'just judgment' must be treated with suspicion.

As already noted, this is not a grandiloquent speech, nor an overtly rhetorical one. The traditional course in rhetoric, as prescribed and practised by Cicero involved much more than the use of colourful language. It also helps a speaker with what to say (*inventio*), not just how to say it (*elocutio*).[6] FitzRalph enriches his speech with a copious set of quotations from established authorities that include the Bible, Augustine, Averroes, Bonaventure, Jean de Pouilly, Chrysostom and Aquinas, as well as, most significantly, the Rule and Testament of St Francis. FitzRalph also discreetly refers to the controversial writings of Gerard of Abbeville (d. 1272) and of William of St Amour (*c*.1200–72). He feels that repetition enforces the veracity of his allegations, many of which had already appeared in his London sermons[7] and he takes pleasure in stressing a point: *Dixi et Dico secundo*.[8] FitzRalph organizes the *Defensio* in such a way as to help his audience to comprehend the main steps in his argument, section by section, over nine interconnected divisions.[9] At the conclusion, he apologizes to the pope and the Curia for having gone on so long and perhaps having tired them and their patience: 'Sanctitatem Vestram et Dominorum meorum reverenciam satis vexavi'.[10] They must have been relieved to hear the final repetition of John 7:24 and probably were amused that he had contradicted the sentiment and gist of this quotation with all the charges of wrong-doing he had made against the friars' misuse of privileges, venal use of offerings for burial, confession and the last rites, as well as their buying up huge quantities of books, to the despair of his students. He also plays on his audience's sympathy with vivid images such as the exemplum of the distraught father searching for his 12-year-old son who had allegedly been taken by the friars. This graphic use of the rhetorical device of exemplum is much more effective than the limp paronomasia of 'a verbis pervenitur ad verbera'[11] which he uses elsewhere.[12]

The *Defensio curatorum* is a long work comparable in size to the last of the

---

6 See H. Caplan, 'Rhetorical invention in some medieval tractates on preaching', *Speculum*, 2 (1927), 284–95, esp. 292–3.   7 See T.P. Dolan, 'Richard FitzRalph's *Defensio curatorum* in Transition' in H.B. Clarke and J.R.S Phillips (eds), *Ireland, England and the Continent in the Middle Ages and beyond: essays in memory of a turbulent friar, F.X. Martin OSA* (Dublin, 2006), pp 177–94.   8 British Library MS Lansdowne 393, fo. 249r.   9 See Dolan, 'Richard FitzRalph's *Defensio curatorum* in Transition', pp 188–9. See also T.P. Dolan, 'Richard FitzRalph' in James McGuire and James Quinn (eds), *Dictionary of Irish biography* (Cambridge, 2009), 3, pp 971–3; T.P. Dolan, 'FitzRalph, Richard' in S.J. Connolly (ed.), *Oxford companion to Irish history* (Oxford, 1998), pp 198–9.   10 British Library MS Lansdowne 393, fo. 263v.   11 Ibid., fo. 252r.   12 See T.P. Dolan, 'Richard FitzRalph's *Defensio curatorum* in Transition', p. 178.

London sermons preached on 12 March 1357 before FitzRalph travelled to Avignon, on the theme 'Nemo vos seducat inanibus verbis'. FitzRalph reserves much of his invective for the way that, in his view, friars contrive to obtain privileges (*procurare*) against the explicit wishes of their founder. Hence, he is especially fond of using the rhetorical device of root-repetition or 'polyptoton'; for example, *procuracio, procurata, procurando, procurantes*. Another favourite characteristic of his rhetoric is the ubiquity of *ymmo*, an exclamatory device that takes back what has been said and replaces it with what seems more suitable; for instance, 'Ymmo, nec Deus posset hoc facere'.

The length of the *Defensio* is of interest because Peter Marchant, a mid-seventeenth-century Franciscan commentator, says that the delivery of the *Defensio* stretched over six days:

> Sex totis diebus peroraverit, ut paupertas et mendicitas fratrum minorum et ceterorum mendicantium tolleretur tamquam Christi doctrinae contraria et privilegia confessionalium ipsorum prorsus cassarentur. Duravit haec publica declamatio ab 8 Novemb. usque ad 14 anni 1357 magna nausea summi Pontificis et Cardinalium.[13]

This seems most unlikely, not least because of the obvious hostility of its author to FitzRalph (see 'magna nausea').

The London sermon of 12 March, as we have noted, is about the same length and there is no evidence that it was not all preached in one day. An explanation may be suggested for the discrepancy. Marchant probably misinterpreted the sequence of events happening at Avignon in that month. On 14 November the cardinals decided that FitzRalph's case should be admitted to the curial court. It seems possible that Marchant wrongly presumed that the whole of the time between 8 and 14 November was taken up with the delivery of the sermon. Marchant was hostile to FitzRalph whom he elsewhere calls 'turbinis maleficus excitator' and may have deliberately misconstrued the occasion.

Some of the references FitzRalph draws on to amplify and authenticate his material lie outside the categories of papal, biblical or Franciscan sources. This other set of references includes Hostiensis, Augustine's *De vera et falsa penitentia*, Aristotle's *De anima* and *Posterior analytics*, Averroes on the *De anima*, Chrysostom on Matthew, a letter of St Bernard, Aristotle's *Nichomachean ethics and topics* and Augustine's *De opere monachorum*. All these references help to amplify and support FitzRalph's central theme on the delinquency of friars and indicate how profoundly indebted he is to the rhetorical device of *invention*, which formed one of the five sections of the rhetorical curriculum, which also

---

13 Peter Marchant, *Fundamenta Duodecim Ordinis Fratrum Minorum* (Gandavi, 17 Feb. 1657), p. 29, col. b.

consisted of *pronuntiatio* (delivery) and *dispositio* (arrangement of material). The latter is a particularly important constituent of the syllabus and assists FitzRalph in his strategic division of his sermon into nine conclusions. The rhetorical curriculum offered three levels of style: *gravis* (grand), *mediocris* (middle) and *extenuata* (plain). The *Defensio* is written in a mixture of the middle and plain styles, which are appropriate because of the forensic nature of the address since it is designed to refute the friars' allegations against the speaker.

The *Defensio* is skilfully organized and runs at a vivid pace from the opening quotation (John 7:24) to its conclusion with the same citation. This forms a perfect climax to the speech, exhibiting FitzRalph's impressive manipulation of rhetoric, even though he failed to persuade the papal court of his case. Perhaps they too recognized the irony of the John 7:24 quotation, which warned about the dangers of gossip and hearsay, which, as we have seen, are the main source of the charges he made against the friars (see also 'sit communis infamia' etc.). The *Defensio* is a model of forensic, epideictic and deliberative oratory, an outstanding Philippic in the anti-mendicant tradition.

Conversion, vision and faith in the life and works of Richard FitzRalph

WILLIAM O. DUBA

While fighting the mendicants, Richard FitzRalph heard a rumour that the famed Franciscan, Giovanni Marignola, bishop of Bisignano, was coming to Avignon to defend the cause of the friars.[1] FitzRalph sent him an invitation:

> Reverend Father, and dear friend. What the honorable men, ___ of ___ and ___ of ___ report from you suit neither your age, nor a feeble old man who should be respected. Nor does what Your Reverence intended to suggest by them attest to soundness of mind. Indeed, with the aid of the Lord, and justice supporting us, we have already defeated the flower of your order, ____. We have already seized the desired objective; we are fearlessly arrayed on the Field of Mars. All that remains is for the prize to be given to the victor, and for the favor of God to crown he whom the sought-after triumph adorns. Already the pen expects bountiful fruits, having cleared the briars and thorns from the yard of the Holy Church, and, driving off the deforming errors, opened the way of the Catholic truth. Nor do we fear your coming, Reverend Father, that we should be afraid in any way of your arguments, we who have already entirely destroyed English *sophismata*, for example, of Ockham, Burley and others, who sought to conceal the tunic of falsehood* under the appearance of truth – we stopped their useless barking with the words of the pious truth. Therefore let him come, that inveterate bishop of Bisignano, let him come! Who is he, who in the imperial court pompously calls himself the Apostle of the Orient? Let him come and put to the test how much his daydreams are worth! For, if, when dealing with barking dogs, one needs chains to bind a young one, by our ability and foresight, we will easily take care of tying up a feeble old panting hound, unaided by clarity of voice or depth of knowledge.[2]

---

[1] On this event, see K. Walsh, *A fourteenth-century scholar and primate: Richard FitzRalph in Oxford, Avignon and Armagh* (Oxford, 1981), pp 445–6. [2] Edited in the preface to *Chronicon Joannis Marignolae*, ed. G. Dobner, in *Monumenta historica Boemiae*, 2 (Prague, 1768), pp 68–78 at pp 73–4: 'Reverende Pater et amice Karissime. Non congruunt etati, neque venerando senio, que de Vobis honorabiles Viri _ de _ et _ de _ recitarunt. Neque mentis testantur prudenciam ea, que per ipsos nobis Vestra Reverencia voluit intimari. Nam florem Ordinis Vestri ____, iam

This blustery broadside also contains a reference to FitzRalph's university past: he, who had vanquished menaces the likes of Ockham and Burley, would dispatch with ease a feeble old ignoramus such as Marignola.

FitzRalph specialists have interpreted this reference in light of an autobiographical prayer in which he claims to have undergone a conversion during his six-year stint at Avignon. Referring to the years 1337–43, FitzRalph states in a celebrated passage:

> Nor were You, the Solid Truth, absent from me those six years, but in Your Holy Scriptures You shone upon me as in a certain radiant mirror; whereas in my former years, in the trifles of the philosophers, You had been hidden from me as in a certain dark cloud. For previously, I used to think that through the teachings of Aristotle and certain arguments that were profound only to men profound in vanity – I used to think that I had penetrated to the depths of Your Truth with the citizens of Your Heaven; until You, the Solid Truth, shone upon me in Your Scriptures, scattering the cloud of my error, and showing me how I was croaking in the marshes with the toads and frogs.[3]

This account, according to the common opinion, expresses FitzRalph's rejection of scholasticism. In light of this conversion, some scholars have taken the reference to combating Ockham and Burley as a confirmation of his 'contempt for the schools';[4] yet Walsh points out that such combat would appear to be incompatible with FitzRalph's confession that he had been in thrall to *aristotelica dogmata* before seeing the light of the truth: if, while at the university, the truth were hidden from him, how could he defeat those who tried to pass off the false as true?[5] FitzRalph's autobiographical account presents further problems: his university writings only make vague and implicit references to Burley and

---

auctore Domino, et iusticia nobis suffragante, convicimus, iam in campo Marcio desiderati voti compotes absque formidine militamus. Neque aliud superest, nisi ut detur victori bravium, et quem triumphus desideratus exornat, Dei velit benignitas coronare. Iam calamus fructus exspectat uberes, qui de area sancte Ecclesie vepres et spinas evulsit, et deformantibus erroribus propulsis viam apperuit Catholice veritatis. Neque Vestrum Reverende Pater timemus adventum, ut vestris argumentis terreamur in aliquo, qui iam Anglicana Sophismata, Okkam puta, Burley, et aliorum, qui sub apparencia veri tunicam falso secernerunt (*sic*) contexere, omnino destruximus, latratus eorum inutiles pie veritatis sermonibus compescendo. Veniat igitur inveteratus ille Bisanensis Episcopus, veniat: quis ille, qui se Apostolum orientis in Curia Cesaris ampulose denominat, ut experiatur in opere, quid sompnia sua prodesse valeant. Nam si canum latrancium iuventuti intersit vincula, nostre provisionis industria facile quidem palpitantem senio molossum ligare curabimus, cui iam neque vocis claritatis, neque sciencie habilitas suffragantur'. 3 W.A. Pantin, *The English church in the fourteenth century* (Cambridge, 1955), pp 132–3. 4 J.A. Robson, *Wyclif and the Oxford schools* (Cambridge, 1966), p. 92. 5 Walsh, *Richard FitzRalph*, p. 42.

Ockham, and, in any case, the historical record shows that FitzRalph exaggerated his destruction of English *sophismata*.

Even the claim of conversion seems overblown. During his Avignon period, FitzRalph continued to use scholastic forms. He developed innovative doctrines that built upon the work of other scholastic theologians. He condemned with even greater forcefulness the competing theological opinions of other schoolmen. And, finally, his treatment of topics in treatises does not display any marked difference from how other scholastics engaged the subject. Indeed, the very account of how he knows the 'Solid Truth', the knowledge that constituted his conversion, fits both his university and Avignon discussions of how humans can know God.

This article therefore has two parts. First, the scholastic structure, content and intent of some of FitzRalph's post-conversion works reveal that he did not leave a 'scholastic' approach in favour of a non-scholastic one; indeed, he remained imbued with the techniques and theses of his school training for his entire life. The evidence does however seem to support a conversion from being a person engaged in the Aristotelian philosophy of the arts faculty to one motivated by theological controversy. Second, the discussion of knowing God in the first question of the *Sentences* commentary and the treatment of the beatific vision in book XIV of the *Summa de questionibus Armenorum* demonstrate that, from his university lectures on theology to the autobiographical prayer, FitzRalph adhered to a consistent and coherent doctrine of knowing God, inspired by Henry of Ghent, but placing emphasis on the experience of Paul in the rapture.

NOT A SCHOLASTIC?

Throughout his career, FitzRalph produced texts that were fundamentally scholastic in structure. While we tend to associate the term 'scholastic' with a *quaestio* format featuring arguments *sic* et *non*, citations of *opiniones*, authoritative arguments and syllogistic reasoning, such a description is unfairly limiting: the duty of a medieval master of theology was not merely to dispute the truth, but to lecture on sacred Scripture and to preach to the clergy and the people. Therefore, an interest in exegesis and preaching does not imply the abandonment of scholasticism: these were as much a part of a master of theology's repertoire and duty as disputation.

Richard FitzRalph produced numerous 'thematic' or 'scholastic' sermons.[6] Judging from Walsh's analysis of FitzRalph's sermon diary, he adhered to the

---

[6] M. Dunne, 'A fourteenth-century example of an *Introitus Sententiarum* at Oxford: Richard FitzRalph's inaugural speech in praise of the *Sentences* of Peter Lombard', *Mediaeval Studies*, 63 (2001), 1–27 at 11–15; Walsh, *Richard FitzRalph*, pp 182–238.

standard scholastic model: he develops the theme, derives a moral lesson and often finishes by lamenting current abuses and shortcomings. If anything, his Latin sermons resemble those of Pierre Roger, later Pope Clement VI, a renowned scholastic sermonist.[7] Like Pierre Roger, FitzRalph debates theological issues only rarely and when he does the issues are the same: the Immaculate Conception and the problem of divine foreknowledge and future contingent propositions. In keeping with the principle that sermons are not the place for determining theological truths, both Richard FitzRalph and Pierre Roger hide their opinions on these burning topics behind equivocations or qualifications.[8] On the truth of prophecy, Pierre Roger, in a sermon on St John the Baptist, given some time between 1334 and 1338, states that this subject touches on the big problem of future contingents, but he then avoids any doctrinally decisive statements.[9] Likewise, FitzRalph, in his Ash Wednesday sermon of 1338 (on Walsh's report), presented 'God as being a mirror without a blemish, reflecting from its nature not only existing things, but also all future and possible things'. Yet, Walsh notes, 'the tone is uncertain'.[10]

In short, almost nothing in the structure or content of Richard FitzRalph's sermons, at least his non-polemic ones, suggests a deviation from the standard scholastic structure and content. The only exception comes in his sermon on the Immaculate Conception and there he announces that his view has changed from his commentary on the *Sentences*. In his Immaculate Conception sermons, FitzRalph supports the 'pious doctrine', stating that Mary was not conceived in original sin. He takes an extreme stance, beyond that held by the immaculist on

---

7 L.L. Hammerich, *The beginning of the strife between Richard FitzRalph and the mendicants* (Copenhagen, 1938), p. 31, in respect to a pair of Latin sermons on St Catherine and St Dominic, refers to them as 'very longwinded panegyrics of the same kind as several of the sermons preached by the later Clemens VI'. 8 W. Duba, 'Moral edification, the search for truth, and the papal court: Pierre Roger (Clement VI) and the intellectual atmosphere of Avignon' in J. Hamesse (ed.), *La vie culturelle, intellectuelle et scientifique à la cour des papes d'Avignon* (Turnhout, 2006), pp 303–18. 9 Petrus Rogerii (Clemens VI), *Quis putas puer iste erit* (ed. in prep.), (non) dividing the theme: 'Ergo *quis putas puer iste erit?* Et ut breviter expediam, propter calorem omnia insimul prosequendo, videamus de veritate questionis. Et videtur mihi quod de futuro contingenti, specialiter de actu et statu hominis ex eius libero arbitrio dependente, respondere conantur quandoque nigromantici, quandoque mathematici et naturales philosophi, quandoque prophete, sancti et viri apostolici, sed differenter, quia nigromantici respondent mendaciter et proditorie, mathematici et naturales philosophi fallibiliter et deceptorie, sed prophete, sancti et viri Spiritu Sancto inspirati, veraciter et edificatorie'. After pointing out the fallibility of the first two (sorcery and natural philosophy), Pierre Roger arrives at the third group: 'Desideramus enim habere responsionem de statu futuro huius pueri non mendacem et proditoriam, non fallacem et deceptoriam, sed veracem et edificatoriam. Et videtur michi quod ad istam questionem respondent directe quatuor testes verissimi et omni credulitate digni. Habemus enim de hoc responsum propheticum, apostolicum et evangelicum, divinum et thearchicum, angelicum'. The rest of the sermon carries the proofs, but nowhere does Pierre Roger make clear his position in the ongoing theological debates on why these sources are infallible. 10 Walsh, *Richard FitzRalph*, p. 207.

whose theory he builds, Peter Auriol. Auriol identified three uses of the expression 'original sin': first, for the cause, 'the libidinous and filthy conception of seed', that is the carnal union at the origin of the conception process; second, for its material aspect, the lack of the righteousness with the obligation of having it and the habitual rebellion of the sensitive appetite against the intellective soul; and third, for its formal aspect, the guilt and offense to God.[11] Auriol argued that Mary was immaculate in the material and formal senses, but not the causal sense, for the act that brought her about did have its libidinous and filthy aspects. In his 1342 sermon, FitzRalph states that Mary was immaculately conceived, even in reason of cause.[12] This rare theological innovation, introduced after FitzRalph's so-called conversion, applies to a topic for which no theologian had yet found any explicit biblical support. Moreover, his point of departure, the thought of Auriol, was heavily scholastic, combining Aristotelian etiology and biology to explain the transmission of original sin. In addition, Contrad von Megenberg, a vocal opponent of Ockham, anti-mendicant agitator and a committed Aristotelian natural philosopher, explicitly declares himself a follower of FitzRalph on this doctrine.[13]

Therefore, if FitzRalph meant to reject scholasticism, his rejection did not extend either to an abandonment of all scholastic structures, or to abandoning scholastic ideas and innovations in favour of purely biblical ones. Nor did he cease using Aristotelian ideas and debating with scholastic authors. Indeed, his most popular work, the *Summa de questionibus Armenorum*, is also at heart a fundamentally scholastic exercise, even if it ends with the very autobiographical prayer that describes his conversion.

Arguing that FitzRalph's conversion was more conceptual than concrete and that his approach continued to be scholastic amounts to breaking down a door that Fr Gwynn opened early in the last century: his conversion could not

---

11 Petrus Aureolus, *Tractatus de conceptione Virginis* in *Fr Gulielmi Guarrae, Fr Ioannis Duns Scoti, Fr Petri Aureoli Quaestiones disputatae de Immaculata Conceptione Beatae Mariae Virginis*, ed. A. Emmen (Quaracchi, 1904), pp 36–8. 12 B. Zimmermann, 'Ricardi archiepiscopi Armacani bini sermonis de immaculata conceptione', *Analecta ordinis carmelitarum discalceatorum*, 6 (1931–2), 158–89. 13 In his *Commentarius de laudibus B.V. Mariae*, tractatus secundus, Conrad of Megenberg first summarizes Peter Auriol's immaculist position in eight conclusions, the first and third of which are where Megenberg and FitzRalph have a more extreme stance (Munich, Bayerische Staatsbibliothek, CLM 14190, fo. 20rb): 'Si queritur de conceptione seminis, clarum est quod virgo fuit in originali concepta, sumendo "originale" pro suo causali et pro necessitate contrahendi' and (ibid., fo. 20va): 'Si questio querit de conceptione predicto modo dicto, videlicet, pro carnis formacione et membrorum lineacione, que durat a conceptione seminis usque ad anime infusione, illa massa formabilis non indiget aliqua mundatione'. His response, also cited by Walsh (*Richard FitzRalph*, pp 208–9, n. 71) and S. Krüger (*Konrad von Megenberg. Ökonomik*, 1 (Munich, 1973), p. xv, n. 44) begins (ibid., fo. 29ra): 'Nunc ergo volo in eadem questione contra primam et tertiam conclusiones Aureoli probabiliter arguere, et me iuvare in hac disputacione rationibus et exemplis eiusdem et pariter rationibus reverende memorie domini mei Richardi quondam Armacani archiepiscopi, cuius anima requiescat coram vultu virgineo in deliciis paradisiacis'.

have been one of methodology, and his *Sentences* commentary seems doctrinally too close to his later work for him to have radically changed his ideological orientation.

Gwynn raised the possibility that the conversion was triggered by discussions at the papal court with the Armenian prelates and the Greek abbot Barlaam, and the consequent realization that theological debate could shape the face of Christianity.[14] Indeed, FitzRalph came to Avignon when the power and influence of university theologians over the papal court were at their peak. While FitzRalph was studying at Oxford, Pope John XXII, more than any previous pope, was taking seriously the claims of university-trained theologians to determine matters of faith, and the theological controversies that marked John's papacy figured prominently in FitzRalph's theological career after the university: apostolic poverty and the beatific vision. In making extensive use of theological commissions, appointing theologians to important posts and in determining theological matters, John XXII increased the importance of theology to the governance of Latin Christianity.[15]

The start of Benedict XII's rule appeared to continue this ascendancy: FitzRalph, on what was likely his first trip to Avignon, participated in the commission at Pont-Sorgues that drew up a report on the beatific vision. Benedict used this report as the basis for *Benedictus Deus*, the constitution that resolved the beatific vision controversy by declaring that the souls of the blessed, after the purgation of their sins and before the Last Judgment, have the immediate face-to-face vision of the divine essence. Compared to FitzRalph's experience at Avignon, where theologians submitted reports to the papal *magisterium*, university debates where students, bachelors and masters argued finer points of doctrine without defining dogma must have appeared as the croaking of frogs and toads around a tiny pond.

For FitzRalph, Avignon was a big pond. Writing after his university years, FitzRalph frames his two major dialogues in terms of a disputation, but appealing to the pope to determine the question. In the *Summa de questionibus Armenorum*, Richard FitzRalph declares that he has produced this text and committed it 'to the approval and disproval of our father, Clement VI, *Summus Pontifex* of the universal church'.[16]

---

14 Aubrey Gwynn, 'Archbishop FitzRalph and the friars', *Studies*, 26 (1937), 50–67. 15 S. Piron, 'Avignon sous Jean XXII. L'Eldorado des theologiens', *Cahiers de Fanjeaux*, 45 (2010), forthcoming. 16 Richardus Armachanus, *De questionibus Armenorum*, prologus (ed. Parisius 1512, fo. 1ra; Padua, Biblioteca Universitaria 1439, fo. 1ra): 'Cum vestro tam accepto Deo desiderio resistere non audebam, exactionem spiritualis usure formidans, si de donis a Domino acceptis officium negligerem institoris et iuxta ipsius promissa, qui evangelizantibus dat verbum virtute multa ardenter desideratis ampliora ob hoc recipere ut habendum magis. Nec debent indignari michi maiores, ex quo ipsi per quos melius perfici potuit illud penitus neglexerunt, et ego cum vidua evangelica cupiam minuta que habeo in domini domum offerre, ipso teste confidens humilis orationis suffragio amplius quam subtitilate ingenii scripture difficilia penetrare.

After a *divisio textus* outlining the nineteen books of the *Summa*, Richard explains his choice in structure:

> But because the manner of proceeding by query and response seems much easier, although it is somewhat more lengthy, I have taken one of my favorite students to dispute with me, so that John shall take the role of the one who asks (*vicem querentis*), and Richard the one who delivers the sentence (*sententians*), or rather who responds (*respondens*).[17]

We find similar introductory notes in his later dialogue *De pauperie salvatoris*, submitted to the correction of Innocent VI, where he announces that John will be the *interrogans* and Richard the *sentencians sive suadendo respondens*.[18]

Both dialogues are configured as disputation: as John asks the questions, Richard gives his opinion, or rather acts as a scholastic *respondens*, the name given in a university disputation to a senior bachelor who defends a thesis, and the pope serves as the master determining the question. By playing on this scholastic model, Richard not only can present his thesis and explore extreme positions, but he can underscore and appeal to the authority of the papal *magisterium* in determining matters of faith.

While the 'big pond' theory might explain why he considered his university years pointless bickering and reveal FitzRalph's attitude to his theological writing after leaving the university, it does not suffice as an account of how the truth of Scripture showed FitzRalph that he had been wandering in error before Avignon. Attention to FitzRalph's career and his 'post-conversion' writings suggests a simpler explanation: the years in which Richard FitzRalph thought the truth could be found in the teachings of Aristotle were the years in which he was teaching Aristotle.

Prior to becoming bachelor of theology, FitzRalph was a master in the arts faculty and a fellow of Balliol College. On commencing his studies in theology,

---

Nec maioris correptionem renuo, sed affecto. Et ipsum opus cuius titulum volui esse De questionibus Armenorum, quod in 19 particulas sive libros distinxi, singulibus libris materiam fidei et ipsius capitula premittendo approbationi et reprobationi nostri patris Clementis VI universalis ecclesie summi pontificis in toto et in parte committo'. 17 Ibid. (ed. Parisius 1512, fo. 1va–b; Padua, Biblioteca Universitaria 1439, fo. 1vb): 'Quia vero per interrogacionem et responsionem modus tractandi videtur multipliciter facilior, licet sit aliquantulum prolixior, unum de meis mihi predilectum discipulum mecum disputantem accepi, ita ut Iohannes vicem querentis et Ricardus intelligatur vicem sententiantis vel potius respondentis. Vos igitur reverendi patres opus accipite quod petistis orationis si placet mercedem mihi pro labore pensantes. Hoc opus sic incipit "Iohannes: quia ex litterali sententia scripture sacre".' 18 Richardus Armachanus, *De pauperie salvatoris*, prologue, in R.L. Poole, *Iohannis Wycliffe De dominio divino libri tres, to which are added the first four books of the treatise De pauperie salvatoris by Richard FitzRalph Archbishop of Armagh* (London, 1890), p. 274: 'Hanc opus, primi libelli capitulis prelibatis, sic incipit: "Iohannes. Quia circa rerum propter hominem creatarum", habens hanc formam quod Iohannes censeatur interrogans et Ricardus habeatur sentencians sive suadendo respondens'.

FitzRalph had to quit Balliol, but he did not cease being an arts master. His year in Paris, apparently after reading the *Sentences*, was to accompany John Northwode, who would have been early in his studies in the arts faculty, and FitzRalph appears in Parisian records as having a *discipulus*.[19] Further, secular theology students commonly financed their studies by teaching in the arts faculty.[20] Well into his theological studies, therefore, FitzRalph could have been lecturing and disputing on philosophical topics. This would also explain the combat with Ockham and Burley mentioned in the letter at the outset: Ockham's writings certainly circulated among theologians, but whatever reputation he earned as a teacher of dangerous material was largely in the arts faculty. Burley's philosophical work far outshone his theological texts.[21] The 1339/40 prohibitions of Ockham's work at the University of Paris were enacted by and applied to the arts faculty, partly under the guidance of FitzRalph's future *sequax*, Conrad von Megenberg.[22] Even the term *sophismata* refers primarily to exercises in the arts faculty; indeed, in their Stanford Encyclopedia of Philosophy article on *Sophismata*, Fabienne Pironet and Joke Spruyt conclude that 'it is no exaggeration to say that *sophismata* in the Faculty of Arts were as important as Biblical exegesis in the Faculty of Theology'.[23]

If we assume that his conversion was not overnight – and there are no grounds to suppose it was – then FitzRalph could above all be referring to Aristotelian philosophy in the strict sense, his primary focus in teaching and disputation as an arts master and one that, as Professor Dunne has shown, impinged heavily on the selection of topics for his *Sentences* commentary.[24] We have no reason to doubt or even to qualify FitzRalph's conversion. He went from being a master of arts, teaching and disputing subjects linked to the Aristotelian corpus, to a master of the sacred page, where the Bible was his proof text and the truth disputed was the revealed truth. His conversion was by no means 'an

---

19 Walsh, *Richard FitzRalph*, pp 68–9.   20 Dunne, 'Richard FitzRalph's inaugural speech', 3; Walsh, *Richard FitzRalph*, pp 4–5.   21 M. Vittorini, 'Walter Burley: life and works' in A. Conti (ed.), *A companion to Walter Burley* (Leiden, forthcoming); indeed, Burley's most influential works from his theological teaching at Paris concern themselves with philosophical questions: L.M. De Rijk, 'Burley's so-called *Tractatus Primus*, with an edition of the additional quaestio "Utrum contradictio sit maxima oppositio"', *Vivarium*, 34 (1996), 161–91; W. Duba and T. Suarez-Nani, 'Introduction' in *Francisci de Marchia Reportatio IIA (Quaestiones in secundum librum Sententiarum) qq. 13–27* (Leuven, 2010), pp lxiv–lxx.   22 See the articles collected in W.J. Courtenay, *Ockham and Ockhamism* (Leiden, 2008); J.M.M.H. Thijssen, *Censure and heresy at the University of Paris* (Philadelphia, 1998), pp 57–72; Z. Kaluza, 'Les sciences et leurs langages: note sur le statut du 29 décembre 1340 et le prétendu statut perdu contre Ockham' in L. Bianchi (ed.), *Filosofia e teologia nel trecento: studi in ricordo di Eugenio Randi* (Louvain-la-Neuve, 1994), pp 197–258.   23 F. Pironet and J. Spruyt, '*Sophismata*' in E.N. Zalta (ed.), *The Stanford encyclopedia of philosophy* (summer 2009 ed.), http://plato.stanford.edu/archives/sum2009/entries/sophismata.   24 M. Dunne, 'Richard FitzRalph's *Lectura* on the *Sentences*' in P. Rosemann (ed.), *Mediaeval commentaries on the* Sentences *of Peter Lombard*, 2 (Leiden, 2010), pp 405–37.

utter repudiation of the techniques and ambitions of the schools'; he thought the techniques were just applied to the wrong areas and the ambitions too modest.

This interpretation of FitzRalph's conversion also has the advantage of explaining why comparisons on a given theme in his *Sentences* commentary to his 'post-conversion' work show compatible doctrine and sometimes the same argumentation: the conversion is in the selection of theological topics instead of purely philosophical ones. Therefore, FitzRalph's discussions of the impossibility of knowing in the Word the truth value of future contingent propositions as presented in his Oxford commentary on the *Sentences* and *Quaestio Biblicus* reappear fundamentally unchanged in his *Summa de questionibus Armenorum*. FitzRalph's conversion did not involve abandoning a methodology, just a subject matter he saw fruitless for one that he felt went to the core of Christianity.

FITZRALPH ON KNOWING GOD

In the prayer that describes his conversion, FitzRalph, addressing the solid truth, states 'in Your Holy Scriptures You shone upon me as in a certain radiant mirror; whereas in my former years, in the trifles of the philosophers, You had been hidden from me as in a certain dark cloud'. The image, *in quodam radioso speculo illuxisti*, contrasted to *in quadam tenebrosa caligine*, evokes Paul's seeing through a glass darkly, *per speculum in aenigmate*, only taken in the divided sense: FitzRalph now sees through a mirror brightly, but previously he could not see in darkness. This description precipitates from FitzRalph's epistemology, particularly his doctrine of human contact with God. As is the case for many scholastics, for FitzRalph epistemology has its points of departure and arrival in the vision of the divine essence had in the beatific vision.

Commentary on the Sentences, q. 1, a. 2
FitzRalph addresses the face-to-face vision of the divine essence throughout his *Commentary on the* Sentences. Richard discusses the epistemological status of the beatific vision in relation to human knowledge in the first question on the prologue to book I. The question 'Whether it is possible for a wayfarer to know demonstratively that God exists' divides into three articles, each of them constituting a question in itself. The second article, 'Whether faith and science of the same reality can exist at the same time in the same thing', specifically asks whether rational beings can both have faith that something is the case and know positively that it is so.

The direct background to FitzRalph's question hinges on the nature of theology as a science and its relationship to the beatific vision. The chief boundaries are, on the one hand, the undesirable result that *in patria* the blessed will have both faith and perfect knowledge of the same objects[25] and, on the other, the strong relationship between the knowledge Paul acquired in the rapture, and the faith he had and preached afterwards.[26] FitzRalph presents two understandings of the relationship between faith and scientific knowledge, namely those of Henry of Ghent and John Duns Scotus.

FitzRalph uses Henry of Ghent's discussion in article 13, question 7 of the *Summa quaestionum ordinariarum*, where Henry argues that faith (*fides*) and understanding (*intellectus*) can exist at the same time with respect to the same object, when understanding is taken to mean the knowledge of an object that is not directly present to the intellect. Henry of Ghent takes as his point of departure that faith is the cognition of things that are not apparent, as from Hebrews 9:1, *Faith is the substance of things to be hoped for, the argument for things that are not apparent.*[27] Against those who conclude that one cannot at the same time hold something on faith and know it to be the case, Henry argues that 'understanding' has two meanings. Through 'cognition by sight' (*cognitio per visum, notitia visionis*) the objects of knowledge are apparent to the mind and this knowledge consists in the cognition of the things as they are present to the beatific mind cognizing the divine essence. On the other hand, in 'cognition by intellect' (*cognitio per intellectum, notitia intellectus*), the objects are present only by their intelligible *species*, or by some other *species*.[28]

The knowledge had in the beatific vision completely removes faith, either both the habit and the act of faith, as is the case with the blessed or the act alone,

---

25 Richardus Armachanus, *Lectura super primum* Sententiarum (Oxford, Oriel 15, fo. 2ra): 'Arguitur quod non, quia tunc fides posset manere in patria. Consequens falsum'. **26** Ibid. (Oxford, Oriel 15, fo. 2rb): 'Item, Paulus post raptum scivit articulos fidei, quia ipse dicit 12 <Cor.> quod ipse <scit> *hominem in Christo* et post pauca *et archana que non licet homini loqui* et manifestum est quod postea fuit fidelis et habuit fidem, ergo etc'. FitzRalph presents this as an argument against the compossibility of faith and understanding: Paul knew the articles of faith in the rapture, but afterwards he only had faith. **27** Heb. 11:1: 'Est autem fides sperandarum substantia rerum, argumentum non apparentium'. **28** Henricus Gandavensis, *Summa quaestionum ordinariorum*, a. 13, q. 7 (ed. Parisius 1520, fo. 96r): 'Dictum istorum in primo fundamento de differentia inter fidem et intellectum deficit, quia non faciunt ulterius distinctionem inter cognitionem per visum et per intellectum, sed sumunt intellectum pro visu. Verum est enim secundum quod dicit Augustinus *De videndo Deum* quod illa quae creduntur absentia sunt; sed eis alterius idoneo testimonio assentitur. Illa autem proprie dicuntur videri quae praesto sunt vel animi vel corporis sensibus, quibus intellectus proprio testimonio assentit propter evidentiam veritatis ex natura ipsius rei vel rationis, sed distinguendo notitiam visionis proprie sumptae a notitia intellectus vel scientiae. Proprie dicitur esse notitia visionis quando res est praesto videnti per seipsam, sicut visui corporali praesto sunt in lumine visibilia corporalia, et intellectui angelico et humano in gloria praesto sunt ea quae vident in verbo et luce increata. Proprie autem dicitur notitia intellectus quando res est praesto intelligenti vel scienti per speciem solum suam vel alienam, sicut geometra habet intellectum et scientiam figurarum corporalium ad absentiam earum secundum rem per veridicam rationem quam habet de eis adminiculo specierum suarum apud animam. Secundum quod triplex ista cognitio, fide, visu, intellectu, distincta est in principio quaestio praecedentis in notitia eclipsis solis'.

as with those seized up in the rapture.[29] The knowledge had in this world, the cognition by intellect, is compatible with faith. Henry summarizes his view, saying that there are two ways of knowing what is held on faith:

> either perfectly and by clear cognition, such that nothing remains to be understood of the thing that was previously believed by obscure cognition – and Augustine properly calls this seeing – or imperfectly and by cognition that is not entirely clear, such that somthing of that thing remains to be more clearly understood, which I properly called understanding as distinct from seeing. Understanding in the first way cannot coexist with faith in the same thing, but entirely clears out faith, as was said, and this understanding cannot occur in this life according to the wayfarer-state, and will be only in the afterlife-state.[30]

Henry now says that the second type of understanding is compatible with faith, but he distinguishes between how we talk about such understanding and how it actually is in the cognizer:

> But understanding in the second way can certainly coexist with faith concerning the same thing, but not as it is on the part of the cognizer with respect to the same thing. Indeed, in this understanding there is not the total obscurity of knowledge nor perfect clarity. Insofar as something obscure remains in that cognition, there is faith; insofar as something of the thing is clearly perceived, there is understanding of it, just as the example of corporeal light and darkness can make clear: for at night the air is entirely dark, at noon the air is entirely light, but at the rising and the setting of the sun it is both light and dark, such that the air may be

---

29 Ibid. (fo. 96r): 'De cognitione autem visionis, quia ipsa propter rei praesentiam claram in seipsa, nullam in se patitur obscuritatem, sed est omnino clara et perfecta; certe verum est quod dicunt quod non potest esse simul de eodem et apud eundem scientia vel intellectus cum fide, quia talis notitia intellectus quae proprie visio appellatur non potest haberi in praesenti de illo circa quod non potest in praesenti fides evacuari, ut secundum illud quod est credibile simpliciter et absolute fiat intelligibile visu, quia talis notitia quandocumque advenit, fidem evacuat, vel quoad habitum ut in beatis, vel quoad actum, ut in raptis; quia res visa inquantum huiusmodi statim amittit rationem credibilis, sicut dicunt et bene. Et de tali modo intellectus non intelligo determinasse quod in praesenti credibile possit fieri quocumque lumine spirituali homini intelligibile, ut statim dicetur'.   30 Ibid. (fo. 96r): 'Est igitur intelligendum ad quaestionem dicendo quod intelligere ea quae sunt fidei primo et absolute, quae proprie pertinent ad istam scientiam, de quibus ad praesens principaliter loquimur, contingit dupliciter, vel perfecte et notitia clara, ut nihil lateat intelligendum de re ipsa prius credita cognitione obscura, quod Augustinus proprie appellat videre, vel imperfecte et notitia non omnino clara, ut aliquid restet de ipsa re clarius intelligendum, quod proprie appello intelligere distinctum contra videre. Intelligere primo modo non stat simul in eodem cum fide, sed fidem omnino evacuat, ut dictum est, et non potest contingere in vita ista secundum statum viae et erit solummodo in statu patriae'.

called dark insofar as it has in itself the some of the darkness that will be entirely removed by the noon light; on the other hand, it can be called light insofar as it has the lightness that removes some of the obscurity of the darkness of night, which lightness the noon light will entirely perfect and complete when the darkness of night is entirely removed. Whence, just as from dawn to noon there is a continual increase of light and decrease of darkness, which is entirely gone around noon, so the brightness of the aforesaid intellect concerning things of belief: for after man begins to perceive with the intellect the things that had previously been believed, if he continually advances, his knowledge of those things believed will continually get brighter, ever more and more continually removing the darkness of faith. Yet it can never perfectly remove that darkness until the brightness of noon light comes in the clear vision of the eternal day, so that every single cognition that we have in the present, however much it may help, is only partial with respect to the vision of glory, and this in two ways, both because it is dark, and because it is imperfect. And it is appropriate that what is dark from faith remain until it is removed by the open vision, and what is imperfect be perfected by brightness of the intellect.[31]

In fact, Henry says, while we speak of faith, intellect and vision, in the person there is only knowledge of the object, which is a mixture of faith and understanding: on one end of the spectrum, there is pure faith; on the other, the pure understanding of the beatific vision; between the two points, there is faith mixed with understanding. As a result, this passage seems to support two ways of considering faith and understanding: on the one hand, understanding directly

---

31 Ibid. (fo. 96r–v): 'Intelligere autem secundo modo bene cum eodem et circa idem stat simul cum fide, non tamen quantum est ex parte cognoscentis quoad idem; cum enim in isto intelligere non est omnino obscuritas notitiae nec perfecta claritas, quoad id quod obscurum aliquid manet in notitia illa, stat fides; quoad id vero quod clare de re perceptum est, est intellectus de ea, sicut potest patere exemplum in luce et tenebra corporali; cum enim de nocte aer est omnino tenebrosus; in meridie vero aer est omnino lucidus; in ortu vero solis et occasu simul lucidus et obscurus, ut tunc possit dici aer tenebrosus quoad id quod habet in se obscuritatis evacuandae omnino in plena luce meridiana; possit vero dici lucidus quoad id quod habet luminositatis evacuantis aliquid de obscuritate tenebrarum noctis, quae perficienda est et complenda omnino luce meridiana; evacuatis omnino tenebris noctis; unde sicut ab ortu diei usque ad meridiem semper procedit lucis augmentum et tenebrarum decrementum, quae omnino evacuantur circa meridiem, sic claritas intellectus predicti circa credibilia; postquam enim homo prius credita omnino inceperit intellectu percipere, si proficiendo continue procedat, continue clarescit notitia eius circa credita, semper magis ac magis continue fidei obscuritatem evacuando, quam tamen nunquam perfecte evacuare poterit quousque adveniat claritas lucis meridianae in visione clara diei aeternitatis, ut sic omnis nostra cognitio in praesenti quantumcunque proficiat sit ex parte respectu visionis gloriae, et hoc dupliciter, tum quia obscura, tum quia imperfecta, et opportunum est quod talis maneat quousque visione aperta evacuetur quod obscurum est ex fide, et perficiatur quod imperfectum est intellectus claritate'.

(vision) is incompatible with faith, while understanding mediately (intellection) is compatible; on the other, the darkness of faith progressively mixes with the brightness of knowledge until, in the afterlife, only pure knowledge remains.

Richard FitzRalph summarizes Henry's position, placing the focus on the two types of knowledge and their implications for the beatific vision and the rapture:

> Henry in the *Summa*, article 13, [question] 7, says that there are two types of scientific knowledge: one that is called vision, in the sense of that had by the blessed and those in the rapture; the other that is [not] from the evidence of the thing, but from discursive reasoning. The first knowledge removes faith with respect to its act and habit in the blessed and removes the act, but not the habit, in those in the rapture. Knowledge said in the second way, which is called abstractive, does not remove faith. This is the sense of his position.[32]

Richard FitzRalph implicitly translates Henry's knowledge of vision into intuitive cognition and explicitly associates the knowledge of intellect with abstractive cognition. He also picks up Henry's comment on the difference between those in the rapture and the blessed in *patria* and places it in the foreground.

FitzRalph criticizes Henry of Ghent's position precisely on the grounds of the rapture. His main objection is that the rapture would remove faith; moreover the angels (and the saints) would have only morning cognition and not also evening cognition. In addition to these objections based on the vision of the divine essence, FitzRalph includes one that criticizes Henry's portrayal of faith and understanding as a continuum: the more one advanced in the abstractive science of theology, the less faith one would have, which would seem contrary to the goal of study.[33] In essence, FitzRalph's criticism goes against Henry of

---

[32] Richardus Armachanus, *Lectura super primum* Sententiarum (Oxford, Oriel 15, fo. 2rb): 'Henricus in *Summa*, 13 articulo, 7 (q.) dicit quod scientia est duplex: una que vocatur visio, sicut est in beatis et in raptis, alia que <non> est ex evidentia rei, sed ex discursu. Prima scientia evacuat fidem quoad actum et habitum in beatis, et in raptis evacuat actum et non habitum. Scientia secundo modo, dicta que vocatur abstractiva, non evacuat fidem. Hec est sententia sue positionis'. [33] Ibid.: 'Contra istud: si in beatis scientia evacuaret fidem quoad actum et habitum, hoc esset tantum ex contrarietate eius ad habitum fidei, que est secundum claritatem et obscuritatem, sicut ipse declarat; habitus ergo raptus amittat fidem, cum sua visio sit scientia clara. Et ita sequitur quod ipse post raptum non haberet fidem, posito quod Deus non infunderet novam, ergo nec caritatem, quia caritas non est sine fide, et sic aliquis inimicus sine sua culpa amittat caritatem, quod est falsum, quia talis raptus et quibus* consiliatur*. —Secundo: si illud esset verum, tunc sic: Aliquis adquireret scientiam abstractivam de aliquo articulo in continuo, minueretur habitus fidei in ipso et continue sicut plus perficeret in scientia illius; ita, si des plus, minueretur, et per consequens non expediret proficere in theologia. Et prima consequentia probatur, quia si prima* et perfecta scientia propter contrarietatem eius ad fidem corrumpat fidem totaliter*, sequitur quod scientia minor aliqualiter corrumpat. Unde minuat. Consequentia

Ghent's primary assumption, based on Hebrews 11:1. Faith is not what is removed by perfect knowledge; the two must in some way be compatible. Otherwise it would be difficult to explain how Paul, after the rapture, had faith, an argument for things that are not apparent.

The other contemporary whose opinion FitzRalph considers is that of John Duns Scotus. FitzRalph states:

> The Subtle Doctor, in book III, distinction 24, the only question, says, speaking about scientific knowledge: 'The Philosopher, in *Posterior Analytics* I says that it is impossible that the same person have scientific knowledge and faith of the same thing'. And he replied to the fourth article above about Peter and John [that Peter and John the Evangelist saw the Passion and held it as an article of faith] that, at that moment, during the passion, they did not have faith with regards to this article. And he responded to the second argument [that Christ had perfect knowledge and, because He had hope, He had faith] that, when one has a demonstrative middle term, a dialectical one does nothing, because the demonstrative middle term impedes it.[34]

There are two commentaries on the *Sentences* by Scotus that treat book III, d. 24, and both have a single question: the version recently identified as the *Lectura* III (which also circulated as part of Scotus' *Ordinatio*) and that of the Parisian *Reportatio* III. The arguments are substantially the same in both and, in both cases, Scotus begins his response with a discussion of the senses of *scientia*, concluded with the proper sense, as described in *Posterior Analytics* I, c. 2.[35] Therefore, it is not yet clear whether FitzRalph is citing Scotus from the *Lectura* (or *Ordinatio*) or from the Parisian *Reportatio*, at least as it is published in the Wadding-Vivès edition.[36]

---

ista probatur per similem modum arguendi Philosophi et Commentatoris III *De celo*, commento 12. Dicit quod, si ignis calefacit propter angulos eius acutos, calefacit aliqualiter, quia dicit Commentator a causis diversis secundum magis et minus proveniunt necessario causata diversa secundum magis et minus. —Tertio contra eum: tunc in angelis non essent due tales cogniciones, sicut est in primo argumento istius articuli, scilicet matutina et vespertina, quia ex quo mat<ut>ina est clara, ipsa corrumpit obscuram et non patitur aliam obscuram cum ea secundum ipsum'. 34 Ibid. (Oxford, Oriel 15, fo. 2rb–va): 'Doctor Subtilis, III libro, d. 24, q. unica dicit, loquendo de scientia, sic: Philosophus I *Posteriorum* sic est <im>possibile quod idem de eodem scientiam habeat et fidem. Et respondet ad quartum argumentum de Petro et Iohanne quod tunc in passione non habuerunt fidem de isto articulo. Et respondet ad secundum argumentum quod, habito medio demonstrativo, medium dialecticum nichil operatur, quia impeditur a medio demonstrativo. Hec'. 35 For a full discussion of Scotus' views in III, d. 24, see A. Poppi, 'La virtù della fede in Giovanni Duns Scoto: *Lectura III* e *Reportationes Parisienses III*' in R. Quinto (ed.), *Fides virtus: the virtue of faith in the context of the theological virtues: exegesis, moral theology and pastoral care from 12th to early 16th centuries* (Münster, forthcoming). 36 Iohannes Duns Scotus, *Reportata Parisiensia* III, d. 24, q. un (ed. Vivès, xxxiii), pp 446–59.

Indeed, in the *Lectura*, in response to the question 'Whether someone can have at the same time science and faith of revelations that are to be believed, speaking of science in the sense of every certain knowledge from the evidence of reality', Scotus declares that one cannot have at the same time and with respect to the same object both faith and scientific knowledge, scientific knowledge properly understood according to the *Posterior Analytics* definition, as being certain, necessary, evident and discursive. Bible study, theological research and even the reception of truths directly from God all in some way fall short of this definition. They are not scientific knowledge, but can coexist with faith. The last type of non-scientific knowledge, the reception of truths directly from God, will be criticized by FitzRalph. Scotus argues:

> But if those things that Scripture treats were apprehended clearly and intuitively, they would generate certain cognition without any doubt, and this cognition, because it is evident, would be called scientific knowledge; but God can cause, without any motion of the object, certain cognition without any doubt; therefore one who has such a revealed-by-God cognition could not doubt its truth. And it is believed that the Prophets had this sort of cognition, and many other Saints in Scripture, and that such people had a habit that produced great assent, so that, with that habit, they were unable not to assent to the truth. But that truth was not evident from the evidence of reality, because then it would be a contradiction for this sort of knowledge and faith to exist together.[37]

In effect, Scotus distinguishes between 'certain cognition without any doubt' and 'certain cognition without any doubt from the evidence of the thing'. For God can and does bring about the former in the minds of some people and this

37 Iohannes Duns Scotus, *Lectura* III, d. 24, q. un. (ed. Vaticana, xxi), pp 148–9: 'Sed si loquamur de tertio modo, qualem certitudinem habuerent "montes" et rapti in Ecclesia (ut Paulus et Ioannes) et prophetae illi quibus veritas Scripturae primo revelabatur, dico quod omnem effectum quem Deus potest facere cum causa effectiva secunda, potest facere immediate. Sed si res ipsae, de quibus Scriptura tractat, essent clare apprehensae et intuitive, generarent notitiam certam absque omni dubitatione, <et haec notitia, quia evidens est, diceretur scientia; sed Deus absque motione obiecti potest sic causare notitiam certam absque omni dubitatione>. Ergo habens talem notitiam revelatam a Deo, non posset dubitare de veritate illius. Huiusmodi notitiam creditur prophetas habuisse, et multos alios Sanctos in Scriptura, et illi habuerunt habitum praebentem magnum assensum, ita quod – illo stante – non potuerunt non assentire veritati. Tamen illa certitudo non fuit evidens ex evidentia rei, quia tunc contradictio esset quod huiusmodi notitia et fides simul starent; fuit tamen certitudo illa ita firma, sicut est certitudo scientialis, quae causatur ex principiis notis ex evidentia terminorum – sed non causabuntur a talibus principiis, sed aliunde; ideo scientia ex evidentia rei dici non potuit; fuit tamen maior certitudo quam sit certitudo fidei, quia fides non excludit omnem dubitationem, sed potest aliqua stare cum fide'. The interpolated passage comes from the Wadding-Vivès edition of '*Ordinatio III*'; from the context, it appears that the *Lectura* edition includes an *omissio per homoioteleuton* in this passage.

certain cognition can coexist with faith; but if that cognition is 'from the evidence of reality', it is then scientific knowledge and removes faith. In the *Lectura* version, Scotus mentions the rapture specifically: God created in Paul a cognition that was indistinguishable from the direct vision of the divine essence, but was not itself the direct vision. Therefore, Paul's faith was compatible with the rapture. Whatever the case may be concerning this passage,[38] elsewhere Scotus provides another interpretation: Paul saw directly the divine essence and remembered what he saw. Scotus' wording, in the context of whether angels have natural knowledge of the divine essence, provides a different solution: the cognition was only intuitive and then only from the evidence of the thing during the rapture. Therefore, during the rapture, Paul did not have faith, but afterwards he believed what he saw to be true.[39]

FitzRalph does not believe a solution like this can hold and against Scotus he argues,

> Against him [Scotus]: If he should say 'whence it follows that Paul in the rapture lost his faith', therefore after the rapture he did not have faith, assuming that God did not re-create it. Consequently, after the rapture, because he saw God, he was unfaithful. In the same way one could argue about Thomas the Apostle.

FitzRalph deems this result unacceptable. Moreover, the argument that Peter and John did not hold the crucifixion on faith is beside the point, since the crucifixion in itself is not an article of faith. Articles of faith are things that one cannot sensibly perceive: that God was made man, that the pile of accidents over there does not have a subject and so on.[40]

---

38 The mention of Paul and John in the *Lectura* does not have a parallel in the *Reportatio*, nor does it even appear in the Wadding-Vivès edition of the question as '*Ordinatio*' III, d. 24; the edition of *Lectura* III is based on three fifteenth-century manuscripts, two of which are by the same copyist; much of the manuscript tradition for this text, therefore, has not been considered.
39 Iohannes Duns Scotus, *Ordinatio* II, d. 3, pars 2, q. 1 (ed. Vaticana, vii, pp 556–7): 'Secundo persuadetur per hoc quod aliquis – raptus – videns transitorie essentiam divinam, cessante illo actu videndi potest habere memoriam obiecti, et hoc sub ratione distincta (sub qua erat obiectum visionis), licet non sub ratione praesentis actualiter, quia talis praesentia non manet post actum, in ratione cognoscibilis; ergo per aliquam rationem perficientem intellectum talem potest obiectum istud – illo modo – obiective esse praesens, et ita non est contra rationem essentiae quod species illius sit in aliquo intellectu, distincte repraesentans eam. Ergo nec videtur tale negandum ab intellectu perfectissimo creato: nihil enim videtur debere negari ab intellectu summo creato, quod non repugnat alicui intellectui creato in naturalibus, quia non est perfectio excellens nimis. – Assumptum potest declarari per raptum Pauli, qui, transeunte illo raptu, recordabatur illorum visorum, secundum quod ipse scribit, ad Cor.: *Scio,* inquit, *hominem ante annos quattuordecim, sive in corpore sive extra corpus, nescio, Deus scit* etc., qui *audivit arcana verba, quae non licet homini loqui.* Quod autem post raptum possit species distincte manere, videtur, quia hoc est perfectionis in intellectu quod potest conservare speciem obiecti cessante praesentia obiecti'. 40 Richardus Armachanus, *Lectura super primum* Sententiarum (Oxford, Oriel 15, fo.

Conversion, vision and faith in the life and works of Richard FitzRalph 119

In criticizing both Henry of Ghent and John Duns Scotus, Richard FitzRalph's objections centre on Paul's rapture. In resolving the question, Richard makes explicit the centrality of Paul:

> I reply in the affirmative to this article, because scientific knowledge and the habit of faith are not in themselves incompatible, as the arguments adduced against the Solemn Doctor (Henry) proved, and because of the fact that Paul, as he himself testifies, II Corinthians 12, *heard secret words which it is not granted to man to utter*, where the Gloss states that he perceived a notification concerning the secret essence of God. Therefore he recounted that he had seen such things, and consequently that he knew them; therefore at that time he knew that he knew; therefore when he missionized, he knew.[41]

Paul's authority comes from the rapture, from the fact that he remembered it, and thus his writings and teachings reflect the scientific knowledge of vision of the divine essence. That he had faith is also indisputable. FitzRalph implicitly adopts most of the epistemology of Henry of Ghent: he only differs with Henry in stating that the knowledge obtained in the vision is compatible with faith and appears to leave room for abstractive knowledge. Richard continues his resolution of the problem with statements that appear – the only manuscript witness presents a rather opaque text on this point – to confirm this affiliation with Henry and, for that matter, Augustine:

> I say, however, that [the habit of faith] will not *de facto* remain in the afterlife, but will be corrupted – not by a science as by a contrary, but by God, because if faith were to exist, without doubt it would be superfluous as there would be clear cognition, since at that time with respect to the same object [the blessed] will have another immediate cognition,

---

2va): 'Secundo, aliquis potest adherere propter auctoritatem ita firmiter sicut alius per demonstrationem, et firmius medium est quam alius de facto adheret per demonstrationem, ergo si talis adquirat per demonstrationem plus adhuc operabitur medium dyalecticum quam demonstrativum. —De hoc quod dicit ad quartum argumentum quod Petrus et Iohannis non habuerunt fidem de illo articulo, quia quod hoc quod ipsi sciverunt per visum non fuerit articulus fidei, scilicet quod ipse homo visus fuit crucifixus; sed quod Deus homo fuit, sicut patet in symbolo, quod sciverunt tunc manifestum est, tum quia nesciverunt utrum accidentia que ibi videbantur fuerunt sine subiecto, tum quia nesciebant utrum Christus aliquem alium in tantum quod non posset ab eo descrivi loco sui statuisset non plura ut breviter transeam'. 41 Ibid. (Oxford, Oriel 15, fo. 2vb): 'Ad istum articulum dico quod sic, quia habitus fidei et scientia non repugnant secundum se, sicut probant argumenta adducta contra Doctorem Solempnem et propter hoc quod Paulus, ut ipse testatur, II Cor. 11, *scivit multa archana que non habet (leg. licet) homini loqui*, ubi glossa dicit quod ipse intimacionem percepit de secreta Dei essentia. Ipse ergo recoluit se talia vidisse, et per consequens scivisse; ergo tunc scivit se scivisse; ergo tunc scivit quando coluit'.

which is *per se* and prior. I say this on account of the morning cognition of angels, because certainly morning cognition is not the cognition *per se* and primarily of creatures, but it is immediately of God. And since God is cognized immediately by this cognition, as a result of God Himself being cognized, creatures are cognized. Augustine states this throughout the fourth book of *The Literal Interpretation of Genesis*. Hence certainly the other cognition, namely evening cognition, is not superfluous, since there is no other first and immediate cognition with respect to creatures.[42]

De facto, faith will not coexist with the beatific vision, because as such it would be superfluous: the *viator* knows God via faith and the beatific vision is knowing God clearly. Faith and vision are both immediate, but vision is also clear and so the darkness of faith is left without much of a role. Since, however, there can be both direct and indirect knowledge of creatures in the afterlife without one removing the other, all the more can there be faith and knowledge of the divine essence.

In summary, FitzRalph re-proposes Henry of Ghent's distinction between abstractive knowledge and knowledge of vision, and his 'rejection' of Henry's view constitutes a slight modification: rather than positing faith as compatible with abstractive knowledge and incompatible with knowledge of vision, one should say that there is no formal incompatibility among the three types of knowledge. That said, in the afterlife, God will probably remove faith since it would play no useful role.

In his *Sentences* commentary, Richard FitzRalph builds his position on the compatibility of faith and understanding in reaction to Henry of Ghent's discussion in the *Summa quaestionum ordinariarum* and to John Duns Scotus' statements in his *Sentences* commentary. He takes from Henry of Ghent the notion that abstractive knowledge and the knowledge of vision are distinct and compatible types of knowledge about God. Like Scotus, FitzRalph took issue with Henry's model of knowledge as a continuum, starting with faith and ending with perfect scientific knowledge, and therefore insists with Scotus that faith, abstractive and intuitive cognition are different ways of knowing the same thing. Against both Henry and Scotus, FitzRalph argues that faith and perfect knowl-

---

42 Ibid.: Dico tamen quod non manebit in patria de facto sed corrumpetur – non a scientia tamquam a contrario, sed a Deo, quia si esset, sine dubio superflueret ut fieret cognitio clara, ex quo nunc respectu eiusdem obiecti habebit aliam cognitionem, immediatam et per se et prius. Hoc dico propter cognitionem matutinam angelorum, quia certe ipsa non est cognitio creature primo et immediate, sed est immediate cognitio Dei et ex hoc quod per istam cognitionem cognoscitur Deus immediate, ex consequenti per ipsum Deum cognitum cognoscuntur creature. Istud declarat Augustinus diffuse, IV libro *Super Genesim ad litteram*, propter hoc certe alia cognitio, scilicet vespertina, non superfluit, cum non alia ab illa prima cognicio respectu creaturarum et immediata in angelis preter illam.

edge are not in themselves exclusive. The apostle Paul proves this: he saw the divine essence in the rapture and he knew and preached what he saw.[43]

Summa de questionibus Armenorum, XIV

FitzRalph's theology in the *Sentences* takes as indisputable that Paul saw the divine essence and remembered what he saw, and he rejects those positions that appear to render having seen the divine essence clearly and directly incompatible with having faith. Paul wrote and taught with the authority of one who knew directly the divine essence. In the Latin tradition, the writings believed to have been produced by Paul's disciple, Dionysius the Areopagite, were imbued with the authority of Paul's teaching. In this way, a corpus of mystical writings in the finest tradition of Greek negative theology came to constitute for fourteenth-century Latins a body of knowledge derived from the positive, direct vision of God. Probably from his discussions with Barlaam the Calabrian, Richard FitzRalph became aware that modern Greeks subscribed to a negative theological tradition, denying the beatific vision or any vision of God, and used Dionysius' writings to support this view.

FitzRalph dedicates book XIV to the conflict. His student, John, asks:

> Modern Greek doctors, and even some of the Armenians hold that no creature can be united to the divine nature such that it cognizes that nature by a bare and clear (*nuda et clara*) vision. They also say that our final beatitude in the future and the beatitude of the angels and the saints in the present does not consist in this sort of bare and clear vision of the divine substance, but rather they affirm that the final beatitude of a rational creature consists in this: that it, being supernaturally illuminated, cognize perfectly that God is not some being but rather is above all beings and is entirely invisible, without the creature seeing Him clearly or bare. They ascribe their assertion to their ancient doctors, and particularly to Blessed Dionysius in his writings. Many arguments from Scripture and from reason seem to have been made in favor of this assertion, and I deem them very difficult to resolve. And yet the sound teaching of all Latins appears to go against this assertion. Therefore I ask that you first refute their assertion, and then to treat the sayings of Dionysius on this matter, since it does not seem true that such a holy and distinguished doctor would speak contrary to the truth in this matter, and I ask also that you resolve his sayings and my objections.[44]

---

[43] Richard FitzRalph's near-contemporary at the University of Paris, Francis of Meyronnes (d. c.1328), held a similar position with regards to faith and understanding, making the additional step of arguing that, *de facto*, in the afterlife, faith will coexist with the understanding achieved in the beatific vision. See W. Duba, 'Faith in Francis of Meyronnes' *De Virtutibus* and commentary on the third book of the *Sentences*' in *Fides virtus*, forthcoming. [44] Richardus Armachanus,

book XIV follows the plan as outlined by FitzRalph's student: first, FitzRalph discusses how the Bible supports the bare and clear vision of God, and that Paul and Moses had such a vision; then he addresses how the writings of the [Pseudo-] Dionysius can be interpreted in support of a positive vision of the divine essence.[45]

At the structural and conceptual centre of book XIV lies the hermeneutical discussion in which Richard explains how to understand Dionysius' repeated statements that God cannot be seen. In chapter fourteen, concluding the discussion of how biblical passages support the beatific vision, Richard asks his student, 'tell me what you have got against this'.

John replies by referring to Paul: 'Against this the Apostle says, concerning God, that *He inhabits light inaccessible, whom no man has seen nor can see*'.

After citing a series of other biblical passages concerning the invisibility of God, John gets to Dionysius:

> And Saint Dionysius so says that God is invisible to all, unnamable, hidden to all, Whom nobody sees nor will see, and He is not apparent, unsearchable and many similar things. He often says so in *On the Celestial Hierarchy*, *On the Divine Names*, *On Mystical Theology* and in his letters. All these statements, and many more like them in Scripture, clearly appear to hold that God cannot be seen bare (*nude*) in his divine substance by any creature.[46]

Summa de questionibus Armenorum, 1. 14, c. 1 (ed. Parisius 1512, fo. 110rb; Padua, Biblioteca Universitaria 1439, fo. 161rb): 'Iohannes: tenent Grecorum doctores moderni et etiam Armenorum aliqui quod nulla creatura potest ita divine nature uniri ut nuda et clara visione intuitiva eam cognoscat, nec nostram beatitudem finalem in futuro aut angelorum et sanctorum beatitudinem in presenti dicunt consistere in huiusmodi nuda et clara visione divine substantie, sed affirmant finalem creature rationalis beatitudinem in hoc esse: quod cognoscat perfecte, supernaturaliter illuminata, quod Deus non est aliquid entium sed est super omnia, omnino invisibilis sine hoc quod ipsum clare aut nude videat. Et hanc suam assercionem ascribunt suis antiquis doctoribus et precipue Beato Dyonisio in suis opusculis. Pro qua assercione michi multa videntur facere in scriptura et rationes ut puto multum difficiles, et nichilominus econtrario huic assercioni obviat, ut michi videtur, consona omnium latinorum doctrina. Peto ergo ut istam sententiam primo reffellas et consequenter dicta Dyonisii de materia ista pertractes, quoniam non est verosimile tam sanctum et tam eximium doctorem in hoc dixisse contrarium veritati et etiam eius dicta et meos obiectus absolvas'.   45 Such a reading of the Pseudo-Dionysius is not novel: around 1324, the Franciscan Francis Meyronnes, who, as noted above, shared with FitzRalph the belief that faith and understanding could coexist with respect to the same object, produced a collection of the Pseudo-Dionysius' writings along with a commentary that argued for the same positive vision. See J. Barbet, 'Le prologue du commentaire dionysien de François de Meyronnes', *Archives d'histoire doctrinale et littéraire du Moyen Age*, 29 (1954), 183–91.   46 Richardus Armachanus, *Summa de questionibus Armenorum*, XIV, c. 14 (ed. Parisius 1512, fo. 113vb; Padua, Biblioteca Universitaria 1439, fo. 169rb): 'Ricardus: Dic tu quid contra hoc habes. —Iohannes: Contra hoc dicit Apostolus de Deo quod <1 Tim 6:16> *lucem habitat inaccessibilem quam nullus hominum vidit sed nec videre potest* ... Et sanctus Dyonisius sic dicit quod Deus est omnibus invisibilis, innominabilis, occultus omnibus quem nullus vidit neque videbit et est

In addition to authoritative arguments, John brings in arguments from reason, starting with *Metaphysics* II's famous allusion to the eyes of bats (or, in Latin, of night-ravens) to the sun.

Richard replies:

> Although you do not know how to resolve your objections, as perhaps you are not able to explain all the doubts that you may have concerning the simple infinite Trinity, the mystery of the incarnation of Lord Jesus Christ and the sacrament of the altar, just as I confess I don't know how to resolve them, nevertheless you should not oppose such a clear assertion of infallible Scripture, but rather admire its loftiness and leave to the doctors the solving of this sort of difficult question. Nevertheless, take what God has allowed me presently to see. For, besides the common usage according to which we say something is invisible because it cannot be seen with a corporeal eye, in the holy writings from Scripture of the doctors, saints and philosophers, it seems to me that 'invisible God' is said in many ways.[47]

Richard outlines four such ways: in the first way, God is said to be invisible because those who live in flesh cannot see him clearly and bare (*clare et nude*) by an intellectual vision; in the second way, God is said to be invisible because no creature can on its own see God *nude et clare*; third, although a creature can see God *clare et nude* when given some supernatural aid, because of God's infinity, a creature cannot fully see all of God. Fourth, and finally, God is said to be invisible, unknowable, unspeakable and not capable of being understood because we, in the normal course of life, cannot attain the simple cognition of His divine essence.[48]

inapparibilis, investigabilis et multa similia. Sepe dicit in *De celestia ierarchia* et in *Divinis nominibus* et in *De mistica theologia* et in suis epistolis. Que omnia cum multis dictis similibus in scriptura videntur manifeste pretendere quod Deus non potest in sua divina substantia nude videri ab aliqua creatura'. 47 Ibid., XIV, c. 15 (ed. Parisius 1512, fo. 114rb; Padua, Biblioteca Universitaria 1439, fo. 169vb): 'Ricardus: Quamvis ignores hec obiecta tua dissolvere, sicut forte non omnia nosci explicare dubia que possunt suscitari tibi inter trinitatem simplicem infinitam et misterium incarnationis domini Ihesu Christi et circa sacramentum altaris, sicut fateor me nescire, non tamen debes tam patenti assertioni scripture infallibilis repugnare, sed potius eius altitudinem admirari et dissolutionem huiusmodi difficilium questionum doctoribus reservare. Verumtamen, accipe quod Deus pro presenti michi videre concessit. Videtur michi enim, preter communem usum quo dicimus aliquid invisibile quia oculo corporali videri non potest, in sacris litteris ex scripturis doctorum, sanctorum et philosophorum, quod multipliciter Deus invisibilis dicitur'. 48 Ibid. (ed. Parisius 1512, fo. 114rb-va; Padua, Biblioteca Universitaria 1439, fos 169vb-170ra): 'Uno modo, quia a carnaliter viventibus nude et clare visione intellectus videri non potest. —Secundo modo, quia per nullam naturalem diligentiam ad eius nudam et claram visionem potest creatura attingere. —Tertio modo, quod, licet clare et nude videri posset a creatura supernaturaliter adiuta, tamen propter eius infinitatem, plene secundum illud quod est sive perfecte sive proportionaliter nobilitati sue et infinite sue essentie a creatura videre non

Richard groups large quantities of Dionysian citations under each sense of invisibility. Each way God is said to be invisible implies a way in which Dionysius intends God can be seen. He concludes the description of the first way of not seeing by an appeal to abstractive knowledge, referring to *On the divine names*, c. 7: 'In this passage, [Dionysius] means that in this mortal life we cognize God abstractively, that is, by cognition caused by His effects, not intuitively, that is bare and clearly (*nude et clare*)'.[49] Knowing God abstractively in this passage correlates to the terms of the *Sentences* commentary used to describe Henry of Ghent's position: abstractive knowledge is the knowledge of God from his effects, that is reasoning from creation and not directly from God.

Also like in the *Sentences* commentary, FitzRalph here focuses on the possibility of seeing the divine essence before the beatific vision, just not according to the common course of events. On his reading of Dionysius, there are two types of direct union with God: At the end of book XIV, he declares:

> Moreover, it is also clear from the texts adduced above that this saint's intention was that in this union above the intellect, when it is had, we see bare or uncovered. But his intention was that there are two modes of this union: one for the perfect wayfarers, and another for the *comprehensores*, that is for the Blessed properly speaking. The first mode is dark and cloudy, although it is bare, because it is by faith.[50]

---

potest, ad quem modum pertinet modus invisibilitatis et impalpabilitatis et inaccessibilitatis que dicuntur contrapassive, de quo loquitur beatus Dyonisius in *De divinis nominibus*, capitulo septimo, dicens huiusmodi dicta de Deo non significant privationem, sed potius excellentiam....
—Quarto modo dicit a sanctis patribus quod Deus invisibilis, incognoscibilis et indicibilis et non intelligibilis, scilicet quia a nobis in hac vita de cursu communi nulla potest haberi simplex cognitio que essentialiter et univoce representat eius essentiam. Cuius causa est quia omnis nostra cognitio simplex est generata a naturis creatis, et ideo nulla talis simplex competit creationi univoce, sicut iuxta sancti Dyonisii dicta inferius ostendetur, sed potius significat primo divinos effectus seu processus, non ipsorum auctorem iuxta hos modos invisibilitatis, incomprehensibilitatis et inaccessibilitatis Dei intelliguntur omnia per te adducta superius et quecumque alia de dictis sancti Dyonisii precedentia quod Deus a creatura nude et clare videri non potest'.
49 Ibid., XIV, c. 16 (ed. Parisius 1512, fo. 114vb; Padua, Biblioteca Universitaria 1439, fo. 170ra): 'Ubi vult dicere quod in hac vita mortali Deum cognoscimus abstractive, scilicet per cognitionem causatam a suis effectibus, non intuitive, scilicet nude, sed clare videndo eum. Hec cognitio est super omnem intellectum nostrum et rationem, nec haberi potest nisi supernaturaliter in vita futura. Unde consequenter dicit quod est ipsius ut intelligentia et ratio et scientia et intellectus et opinio et fantasia et natura et alia omnia et nec intelligitur nec dicitur nec nominatur. Ita hoc modo intelliges'. **50** Ibid., XIV, c. 27 (ed. Parisius 1512, fo. 118ra; Padua, Biblioteca Universitaria 1439, fo. 175va–vb): 'Patet insuper ex hiis que superius adducuntur quod intentio istius sancti erat quod in hac unione super intellectum, cum haberetur, videmus nude sive incircumvelate. Quod tamen hec unio duplicem habet modum – unum apud viatores perfectos et alium apud comprehensores, scilicet apud vere beatos – quorum primus est obscurus et caliginosus, licet sit nudus, quia est per fidem'.

FitzRalph explains where, in the *De divinis nominibus* and *De mystica theologia*, Dionysius discusses this type of vision.

> Whence according to Dionysius' judgment this vision is had in this life (*in via*), but, although it is had without covering, it is not had perfectly or clearly, because the soul is weighed down by the corrupted body that prevents it from having the full pull. For the soul joined to the body always has carnal affection, which as long as it fills the soul, the soul is not suited to take up the divine light so perfectly that it is illuminated clearly to see God or the divine light.[51]

The difference is the body: since the blessed soul is not weighed down by bodily concerns, beatitude consists in a union to the second degree, namely bare and clear. The vision had by perfect wayfarers is bare, that is direct but not clear, for it is by faith.

Richard finishes book XIV by bringing together the knowledge of the perfect wayfarers with that of rapture:

> What I have adduced above from the sayings of this saint show sufficiently that the bare and clear vision of the divine essence is not only possible for angels now and humans in future, but moreover they set forth clearly the intention of this saint in this, as some statements affirm that there is the bare and clear vision, others perhaps only the bare vision, each of which affirmations is clearly against the opinion of the Greeks.[52]

FitzRalph's discussion of the vision of God in the *Summa de questionibus Armenorum* makes clear his position in the *Sentences* commentary: there are three ways of knowing God: faith, abstractive knowledge and the knowledge of vision. The knowledge of faith taken to the extreme by those 'perfect wayfarers' leads to a direct (bare) but obscure vision of God; abstractive knowledge is reasoning from God's effects back to the cause, providing a clear but indirect

---

51 Ibid. (ed. Parisius 1502, fo. 118ra; Padua, Biblioteca Universitaria 1439, fo. 175vb): 'Unde constat quod habetur in via secundum eius sententiam, sed non perfecte aut clare, licet invelate, propter aggravationem anime a corpore quod corrumpitur et eam ab integro conamine prohibente. Habet enim anima corpori coniuncta semper affectionem carnalem, que quamdiu animam replet, non est apta divinum lumen suscipere sic perfecte ut illustratur clare ad Deum sive divinum lumen videndum'. 52 Ibid.,1. 14, c. 29 (ed. Parisius 1512, fo. 118va; Padua, Biblioteca Universitaria 1439, fo. 176va): 'Rycardus: illa que ego supra adduxi de dictis sancti istius satis ostendunt visionem nudam et claram divine essentie non solum esse possibilem angelis in presenti et hominibus in futuro, sed insuper clare pretendunt intencionem istius sancti esse ad hoc quorum aliqua affirmant visionem nudam et claram, aliqua fortasse nudam duntaxat, quorum utrumque est plane contra Grecorum sententiam'.

understanding; and the knowledge of vision is the bare and clear vision of the divine essence had in the beatific vision, or in those souls that are seized up to Heaven in rapture. In book XIV, as in the first question of the *Sentences* commentary, FitzRalph concentrates on faith and the vision of the divine essence, and he explains how faith can be superfluous but not contrary to vision: both, he says in the *Sentences*, bear upon the same object: the divine essence, in the same way and, he clarifies in the *Summa*, the perfect viator, through faith, accedes to the vision *nude* to God, a step below the vision *nude* et *clare*. Theology, the abstractive knowledge of God, is clear, but mediated through creation.

CONCLUSION

In the autobiographical prayer, FitzRalph refers to his conversion with the same terminology: 'in Your Holy Scriptures You shone upon me as in a certain radiant mirror; whereas in my former years, in the trifles of the philosophers, You had been hidden from me as in a certain dark cloud'. In contrasting the *radioso speculo* with the *tenebrosa caligine*, Richard brings in again the Dionysian terminology: earlier, in contrasting the beatific vision with the vision of faith, he called the former *nuda et clara et beatifica* and the latter *nuda et caliginosa*.[53] When he refers to knowledge of the truth in a bright mirror, he introduces another combination: *circumvelata* (that is, *non nuda*) *et clara*, which, he argues, constitutes the perfect abstractive knowledge obtained through Scripture. As master of arts, he had the knowledge of faith, the direct but dark knowledge of God. Only when he began studying and teaching theology did he begin reasoning from the Sacred Page, acquiring through Scripture the clear knowledge of God. The statements in his autobiographical prayer reveal his opinion that Latins like himself had privileged access to this abstractive knowledge of God, confirming Dunne's observation that Richard FitzRalph is 'closest in spirit' to Henry of Ghent, but 'his thought is his own'.[54] The continuation of his prayer attests to an implicit rejection of Scotus' claim that understanding scripture is separate from belief:

> For until I had You, the Truth, to lead me, I had heard, but did not understand, the tumult of the philosophers chattering against you, the pertinacious Jews, the paganizing Greeks, the carnal Saracens and the unlearned Armenians, who all falsely and shrewdly flayed Your

---

[53] Ibid.,1. 14, c. 17 (ed. Parisius 1512, fo. 115ra; Padua, Biblioteca Universitaria 1439, fo. 171ra): 'Ecce quod dicit quod solis incircumvelate manifestatur que omnia immunda derelinquerunt. Idem est incircumvelate et nude. Non tamen puto eum hic loqui de visione eius clara et nuda et beatifica, sed de nuda et caliginosa'. [54] M. Dunne, 'Richard FitzRalph's *Lectura* on the *Sentences*', p. 422.

Scripture, so that it, as if pregnant with sense, by their various rhetorical tricks would give birth and bear unto them numerous abortions.[55]

Midway through his life, Richard FitzRalph underwent a religious conversion, inspired by his study of Paul, Augustine and the Pseudo-Dionysius. This conversion was not away from scholastic theology, but towards it. FitzRalph adapted Henry of Ghent's thought, on the one hand to bolster the authority of Paul, who, on his reading, had the most perfect knowledge of God available to humans, and had this knowledge along with faith. On the other hand, FitzRalph used Henry's distinction between faith, abstractive knowledge and knowledge of vision to interpret the writings of the Pseudo-Dionysius. His eminently scholastic epistemology permeates even the prayer in which he describes his conversion. FitzRalph's post-university career was not a rejection of scholasticim, but rather the application of it to the burning issues confronting Latin Christianity.

---

55 Armachanus, *Summa de questionibus Armenorum*, 1. 19, c. 35 (in L.L. Hammerich, *The beginning of the strife between Richard FitzRalph and the mendicants*, pp 20–1): 'Audiveram quippe, sed non noveram nisi te Veritate ductrice contra te Veritatem garrientium philosophorum, pertinacium Iudeorum, simigentilium Grecorum, carnalium Sarracenorum, atque indoctorum Armenorum tumultum qui fraudulenter et callide decorticabant Tuam Scripturam ut ipsa quasi fetus sensus eis coloris variis perturiret et peperit eis plurimos abortivos'.

Richard FitzRalph on the *Filioque* before and after his conversations with Barlaam the Calabrian

CHRIS SCHABEL*

When we find philosophers and theologians modifying their positions or even changing their minds as a result of external factors, such as lawsuits, regime changes, conciliar decisions or papal proclamations, this casts doubt on our certainty about the sincerity of all their opinions. When we discover thinkers divided into camps depending on their places of origin and cultural traditions, this hinders the search for independent rational thought. Richard FitzRalph constitutes an interesting and perhaps unique case of a major fourteenth-century Latin theologian – arguably the top secular theologian of the first half of the fourteenth century – who dealt with the contemporary doctrine of another 'camp', that of the Byzantine Greeks, in writings composed both before and after the author had direct personal contact with a Greek theologian, in this case the famous Barlaam the Calabrian. Before meeting Barlaam, FitzRalph was misinformed about Greek doctrine, approving what he thought they believed and condemning in harsh terms what they in fact maintained. When Barlaam set him straight, FitzRalph became critical, yet he abandoned some of the vehemence of his earlier remarks.

As bachelor of theology at Oxford in the late 1320s, Richard FitzRalph lectured on the standard textbook for systematic theology in the western universities, the four books of Peter Lombard's *Sentences*. The master of the *Sentences* had touched on issues of conflict between contemporary Greek and Latin theologians primarily in books I and IV. In the written commentary on the *Sentences* stemming from his Oxford lectures, FitzRalph intended to treat the Greek positions on the *Filioque*, unleavened bread and purgatory, three of the four main points of disagreement between Greek and Latin doctrine at the time, the fourth being papal primacy. Unfortunately, as Michael Dunne's study of FitzRalph's *Sentences* commentary has shown, according to the surviving manuscripts, the *Doctor Hibernicus* only managed to complete the section on the *Filioque* in book I, leaving the issue of unleavened bread unresolved and failing to reach the subject of purgatory as he had announced, since these last two topics were traditionally discussed in commentaries on book IV of the *Sentences*.[1]

---

* I would like to thank William Duba, Thomas Izbicki, the City Pride Reading Group, Tia Kolbaba, Michael Dunne, and the ILL office at the University of Cyprus for their assistance.
1 For dating, manuscripts, and questions, see now M. Dunne, 'Richard FitzRalph's *Lectura* on

Elsewhere, I have surveyed the known Oxford positions on the *Filioque* between 1300 and 1330, when the university discussion over the subject died.[2] Outside the Oxford context, however, FitzRalph had reason to return to the issue later. By the time he wrote the great dialogue entitled *Summa de quaestionibus Armenorum* in the late 1340s, much had happened in western theology and in FitzRalph's personal life. FitzRalph was in Avignon in 1334–6, during much of the controversy over the Beatific Vision, definitively decided in Pope Benedict XII's *Benedictus Deus* from 29 January 1336. From 1337/8 to 1343/4, FitzRalph was again in Avignon, where he participated in negotiations for church union with the Armenians and in doctrinal conversations with Barlaam, the famous Greek theologian and abbot from Calabria.[3] In his *Summa* on the dogmatic differences with the Armenians, therefore, FitzRalph took the opportunity to confront Greek theology on topics where both Armenians and Greeks opposed the Latins, especially the *Filioque*, papal primacy, purgatory and now the Beatific Vision. In his essay in this volume, William Duba covers the Beatific Vision. Although I will present some remarks on unleavened bread, my essay focuses on the *Filioque*.

THE *SENTENCES* COMMENTARY

By the 1320s, western theologians facing the issues of the procession of the Holy Spirit and the type of bread employed in the sacrament of the Eucharist generally understood that both had provoked controversy between what we now call Greek Orthodox and Roman Catholic theologians. By the beginning of the second millenium, Greeks were communing with ordinary leavened bread, while Latins used unleavened bread for the sacrament, each side believing that it followed Christ's example. We are uncertain of the real historical roots of the difference in rite, but westerners believed that the entire church had begun with unleavened bread but switched to leavened bread to combat the Ebionite heresy, which insisted on following Jewish rituals, in this case the use of unleavened bread. Once the heresy ceased to be a problem, the story went, the Roman church returned to unleavened bread, but the Greeks stayed with the new usage.[4] Thus, in the incomplete question one of his commentary on book IV of

the *Sentences*' in P. Rosemann (ed.), *Mediaeval commentaries on the* Sentences *of Peter Lombard*, 2 (Leiden & Boston, 2010), pp 405–39. 2 See C. Schabel, 'Attitudes toward the Greeks and the history of the *Filioque* dispute in fourteenth-century Oxford' in P. Piatti (ed.), *The fourth crusade revisited: Atti della conferenza internazionale nell'ottavo centenario della IV Crociata 1204–2004. Andros (Grecia) 27–30 maggio 2004*, Pontificio Comitato di scienze storiche, Atti e Documenti, 22 (Vatican City, 2008), pp 320–35. 3 The most extensive survey of this period in FitzRalph's life is K. Walsh, *A fourteenth-century scholar and primate: Richard FitzRalph in Oxford, Avignon and Armagh* (Oxford, 1981), pp 85–181. 4 For the history of the dispute, see J. Mabillon, *Dissertatio de pane eucharistico, azymo, ac fermentato* (1673), PL CXLIII, cols 1225–78; J.H.

the *Sentences*, the last extant question of the entire work, FitzRalph remarks that 'at one time the Roman church indifferently used leavened and unleavened bread, and on account of this early custom the church of the Greeks still uses solely leavened bread'.[5]

We know considerably more about the history of the *Filioque* quarrel. Latin theologians maintained that many church fathers, both Greeks and Latins, assumed and sometimes defended the procession of the Holy Spirit from both the Father and the Son, *ex Patre Filioque*, but that when this was defined explicitly in the Roman church, for various reasons – obstinacy being one of them – the Greeks refused to go along and asserted that the Holy Spirit proceeds from the Father alone.[6]

For the specific case of Richard FitzRalph, there is one more piece to this background puzzle. At the Second Council of Lyon of 1274, which Pope Gregory X convoked for church union, the Greek representatives accepted the procession of the Holy Spirit from both the Father and the Son. They also admitted the validity of the Latins' use of unleavened bread, which many Greeks had considered heretical, although the Latins had virtually always deemed the Greek ritual with leavened bread valid.[7] Now, within a decade of Lyon II, the Greeks had explicitly and emphatically repudiated the agreement,

Erickson, 'Leavened and unleavened: some theological implications of the Schism of 1054', *St Vladimir's Theological Quarterly*, 14 (1970), 155–76; M.H. Smith III, *And taking bread ... Cerularius and the azyme controversy of 1054* (Paris, 1978); G. Avvakumov, *Die Entstehung des Unionsgedankens. Die lateinische Theologie des Mittelalters in der Auseinandersetzung mit dem Ritus der Ostkirche* (Berlin, 2002), pp 29–159 and passim; idem, 'Der Azymenstreit–Konflikte und Polemiken um eine Frage des Ritus' in P. Bruns and G. Gresser (eds), *Vom Schisma zu den Kreuzzügen: 1054–1204* (Paderborn, 2005), pp 9–26; C. Schabel, 'The quarrel over unleavened bread in western theology, 1234–1439' in M. Hinterberger and C. Schabel (eds), *Greeks, Latins and intellectual history, 1204–1500* (Leuven, 2011), pp 85–127. **5** M. Dunne (ed.), http://philosophy.nuim.ie/projects-research/projects/richard-fitzralph/text (§10): 'aliquando Ecclesia Romana utebatur indifferenter fermentato et azymo. Adhuc Ecclesia Graecorum utitur fermentato solo propter illam primam consuetudinem'. **6** Some western medievalists who are theologians still blame the 'stubborn' Greeks. The bibliography on the *Filioque* dispute is substantial. See recently P. Gemeinhardt, *Die Filioque-Kontroverse zwischen Ost- und Westkirche im Frühmittelalter* (Berlin & New York, 2002), for the period up to the twelfth century and for thirteenth- and fourteenth-century developments A. Papadakis, *Crisis in Byzantium: the Filioque controversy in the patriarchate of Gregory II of Cyprus (1283–1289)* (Crestwood, NY, 1997); Schabel, 'Attitudes towards the Greeks'; R.L. Friedman, *Intellectual traditions in the medieval university: the use of philosophical psychology in trinitarian theology among the Franciscans and Dominicans, 1250–1350* (Leiden, 2012). **7** For Lyon II and the Greeks, see D.M. Nicol, 'The Byzantine reaction to the Council of Lyons, 1274' in idem, *Byzantium: its ecclesiastical history and relations with the western world* (London, 1972), no. VI; D.J. Geanakoplos, 'Bonaventura, the two mendicant orders and the Greeks at the Council of Lyon' in idem, *Constantinople and the West: essays on the late Byzantine (Palaeologan) and Italian Renaissances and the Byzantine and Roman churches* (Madison, WI, 1989), no. III, pp 183–211 (*Studies in church history*, 13 [1976]); J. Gill, *Byzantium and the papacy, 1198–1400* (New Brunswick, 1979), pp 97–185; Papadakis, *Crisis in Byzantium*; T. Kolbaba, 'Repercussions of the Second Council of Lyon (1274): theological polemic and the boundaries of orthodoxy' in Hinterberger-Schabel, *Greeks, Latins and intellec-*

which is probably why the council plays no role in the *Filioque* discussions of the fifteen Oxford theologians active in the first three decades of the fourteenth century whose pertinent writings survive,[8] with one exception: Richard FitzRalph. When asking 'whether the Holy Spirit proceeds from the Father and from the Son', question four of book I in most manuscripts,[9] FitzRalph's final preliminary argument against the *Filioque* is that, if the *Filioque* were true and the Holy Spirit did proceed from the Father and from the Son,

> then the entire Church of the Greeks would be heretical, since it holds that the Holy Spirit does not proceed from the Son; and yet the [Greeks] are considered faithful; therefore [what they believe] is true and not erroneous. Thus John of Damascus says, in the first book of *De fide orthodoxa*, chapter 8, that 'we do not say that the Holy Spirit is from the Son, but we call It the Spirit of the Son'.[10]

FitzRalph's brief third article provides his response:

> This is why the decretal in the *liber sextus*, 'On the Highest Trinity and the Catholic Faith', the chapter *Fideli et devota*, was done. As the gloss says there, the reason for the publication of this decretal was that at one time the Greeks held that the Holy Spirit proceeds from the Father

---

tual history, pp 43–68. 8 See Schabel, 'Attitudes towards the Greeks', based on editions in *Ioannis Duns Scoti Opera Omnia* V, C. Balic (ed.) (Vatican City, 1959), pp 1–24; *Guillelmi de Ockham Opera Theologica* III, G.J. Etzkorn (ed.) (St Bonaventure, NY, 1977), pp 345–73; *Adam de Wodeham Lectura secunda* III, ed. R. Wood and G. Gál (St Bonaventure, NY, 1990), pp 164–73; Walter Chatton, *Reportatio super Sententias, Liber I, distinctiones 10–48*, J.C. Wey and G.J. Etzkorn (eds) (Toronto, 2002), pp 14–25; R.L. Friedman, 'Trinitarian theology and philosophical issues [I]: trinitarian texts from the late thirteenth and early fourteenth centuries', *Cahiers de l'Institut du moyen-âge grec et latin (CIMAGL)*, 72 (2001), 89–168 (William of Nottingham, Robert Cowton and Thomas of Sutton); C. Schabel and R.L. Friedman, 'Trinitarian theology and philosophical issues III: Oxford, 1312–1329: Walsingham, Graystanes, FitzRalph and Rodington', *CIMAGL*, 74 (2003), 39–88; R.L. Friedman and C. Schabel, 'Trinitarian theology and philosophical issues IV: English theology ca. 1300: William of Ware and Richard of Bromwich', *CIMAGL*, 75 (2004), 121–60; C. Schabel and R.L. Friedman, 'Trinitarian theology and philosophical issues V: Oxford Dominicans: William of Macklesfield and Hugh of Lawton', *CIMAGL*, 76 (2005), 31–44; Henry of Harclay, *Ordinary questions I–XIV*, M.G. Henninger (ed.) (Oxford, 2008), pp 252–81; Walter Chatton, *Lectura super Sententias, Liber I, distinctiones 8–17*, J.C. Wey and G.J. Etzkorn (eds) (Toronto, 2009), pp 197–239. 9 'Utrum Spiritus Sanctus procedat a Patre et a Filio'. Article one, 'Utrum Spiritus Sanctus distingueretur a Filio, posito quod non procederet ab eo', is edited in Schabel-Friedman, 'Trinitarian theology and philosophical issues III', pp 74–9, but in this essay the same editors' on-line edition of the complete question will be cited by paragraph number: http://philosophy.nuim.ie/projects-research/projects/richard-fitzralph/text. 10 [§10] 'Ad principale, tunc tota Ecclesia Graecorum esset haeretica, cum teneat quod Spiritus Sanctus non procedit de Filio; et tamen reputantur fideles; ergo hoc est verum et non erroneum. Unde Iohannes Damascenus dicit, libro primo *Sententiarum*, capitulo 8, quod "Spiritum Sanctum non ex Filio dicimus, sed Spiritum Filii nominamus"'.

alone, and at that time, as the gloss says, they were heretics. And this is Guido [de Baysio]'s gloss. But later, in the General Council of Lyon, as Jean Lemoine's gloss states, all the Greeks agreed to this definition through their nuncios, and so now they are faithful.[11]

So FitzRalph concludes the whole question by repeating this, asserting that 'the Church of the Greeks' is not opposed to the *Filioque* now, after the Second Council of Lyon, although 'once they were in the wrong and then they were heretics, as Guido [de Baysio]'s gloss says'. Then, concerning the Damascene, FitzRalph continues, 'I say that John of Damascus was mistaken in this – indeed, if he held this obstinately, he was a heretic'.[12]

FitzRalph's understanding of Greek doctrine is a half century out of date. Indeed, to make matters worse, in the four manuscripts of what is known as the 'Full Text', immediately we find another response to John of Damascus before FitzRalph proceeds to the next question:

> Or it can be said, just as the master says at the end of book I, distinction 11, that later on, in his *Homilies*, John Chrysostomos agreed with us, as the master adduces via various passages of his, and he revoked that dictum for the later one.[13]

Now, since the three manuscripts of the 'Short Text' do not include this passage, either FitzRalph himself wrote it in haste, conflating the fourth-century church

---

11 [§78] 'Ad hoc enim facta est Decretalis in VI libro, "De summa Trinitate et fide catholica", capitulo "Fideli ac devota". Causa autem editionis illius decretalis erat, sicut ibidem dicitur in glossa, quia Graeci aliquando tenuerunt quod Spiritus Sanctus procedat a solo Patre. Et tunc, sicut dicit glossa ibi, fuerunt haeretici. Et est glossa Guidonis. Postea tamen in consilio generali Lugdunensi, sicut dicit glossa Iohannis Monachi, omnes Graeci per suos nuntios in istam sententiam consenserunt, et ita nunc sunt fideles. Ideo absque ambiguitate tenendum est quod Spiritus Sanctus procedat de Patre et Filio, sicut dicit Anselmus in *De processione Spiritus Sancti*, et probat hoc per rationem et per auctoritates varias Novi Testamenti satis evidenter'. 12 [§89] 'Ad decimum argumentum, cum arguitur quod tunc tota Ecclesia Graecorum esset haeretica quia tenet quod Spiritus Sanctus procedit a solo Patre, dico – sicut dixi in positione – quod Ecclesia Graecorum hoc non tenet nunc, quia in consilio generali Lugdunensi per nuntios suos consenserunt integre nobiscum in isto articulo, sicut dicit glossa illius capituli "Fideli", ut dixi in positione quaestionis. Aliquando tamen erraverunt, et tunc fuerunt haeretici, sicut dicit glossa Guidonis, ut allegavi in positione. Et de hoc quod additur, quod Iohannes Damascenus dicit quod "Spiritum Sanctum non ex Filio dicimus, sed Spiritum Filii nominamus", dico quod Iohannes Damascenus in hoc erravit, immo fuit haereticus, si pertinaciter hoc sustinuit etc'. 13 [*Additio*] 'Vel potest dici, sicut dicit Magister, libro primo, distinctione 11 in fine, quod Iohannes Chrysostomus postea in *Homeliis* suis consensit nobiscum, sicut allegat Magister ibi per diversas auctoritates suas, et illud dictum alio posteriori dicto revocavit' (actually, as Brady notes in the *apparatus criticus* to Petrus Lombardus, *Sententiae in IV libris distinctae*, I, ed. I. Brady [Grottaferrata, 1971], p. 117, the author is not even John Chrysostomos, but John Mediocris, bishop of Naples!).

father with the eighth-century theologian he had just mentioned by name, and then he wisely removed it later, or some foolish scribe added this in compiling the 'Full Text'.[14]

The source of FitzRalph's confusion about Lyon II may be that he goes out of his way to cite canon law in this context, which is somewhat unusual. Jean Lemoine and Guido de Baysio published their works in their final form around 1300, well after the agreement of Lyon II had collapsed. FitzRalph appears to have cobbled together from Guido the idea that 'many, like the Greeks, and it is a wonder that they said this, namely that they denied that the Holy Spirit proceeds from both ...', and many lines later, 'we declare as heretics ...', and finally a few lines afterwards, 'and these statements are against the Greeks, who refuse to be subject to the Apostolic See'.[15] True, Jean Lemoine does state that 'at the Council of Lyon all Greeks agreed to this opinion through their nuncios', but he does not say 'now they are faithful'.[16] FitzRalph's Oxford contemporaries do not seem to suffer from the same confusion and perhaps as a result most of them avoid explicitly calling the denial of the *Filioque* heresy. Secure in his belief that modern Greeks are faithful, FitzRalph is free to declare any opposition to the *Filioque* heretical. Although we do not have his determination on the issue of eucharistic bread, FitzRalph does write that 'the Church of the Greeks is considered faithful, so the body of Christ can be brought about legitimately with leavened bread'.[17] We can guess that his determination would have been sympathetic, based on the Second Council of Lyon.

14 If Michael Dunne's *stemma codicum* is accurate ('Richard FitzRalph's *Lectura* on the *Sentences*', p. 420), this passage must be a later addition to a subfamily (F1F2P1V1) of manuscripts of 'version 1' of the commentary (the others being O1V3). It should be noted that P1 (Paris, BnF, lat. 15833), sometimes considered the best, has large omissions *per homoeoteleuton* and does not provide a reliable text on its own.   15 Guido de Baysio, *In Sextum Decretalium commentaria* (Venice, 1577), fo. 3rb: 'Sed quia nonnulli, ut Graeci, sed mirum fuit quare hoc dixerunt, scilicet quia negabunt [*pro* negabant?] Spiritum Sanctum procedere ab utroque ... Damnamus, id est haetericos declaramus ... et haec sunt contra Graecos, qui Sedi Apostolicae subiici recusant'.   16 Iohannes Monachus, *Glossa aurea nobis priori loco super Sexto Decretalium libro addita* (Paris, 1535; repr. Aalen, 1968), fo. 14a: 'Vel dic quod in concilio Ludunensi omnes Greci per nuncios proprios in hanc sententiam consenserunt'.   17 What was accomplished is as follows (Dunne (ed.), §10): 'Praeterea, si Christus sit sub speciebus sacramenti, tunc hoc est quia per verba sacerdotis conficitur corpus Christi ex pane et sanguis ex vino. Aut ergo potest illa consecratio fieri ex solo pane azymo aut ex fermentato. Non ex solo azymo, quia aliquando Ecclesia Romana utebatur indifferenter fermentato et azymo. Adhuc Ecclesia Graecorum utitur fermentato solo propter illam primam consuetudinem, sicut dicit Thomas, IV libro, distinctione 11. Sed Ecclesia Graecorum reputatur fidelis. Ergo corpus Christi potest confici legitime de fermentato. Nec videtur dicendum quod corpus Christi potest confici de fermentato, quia pari ratione posset sanguis Christi confici de aceto vel de vino non puro sed mixto. Cuius oppositum tenet Ecclesia. Et similiter pari ratione posset corpus Christi confici de alio pane quam de pane triticeo. Consequentia patet, quia Christus vel consecravit in cena sua de azymo tantum vel de fermentato solum. Ergo nullus postea potuit de alio conficere nisi posset mutare modum. Et si posteriores poterunt mutare modum quo ad panem, pari ratione poterunt mutare modum consecrationis de vino et possent consecrare de vino albo vel de aceto et de pane hordeaceo vel alio,

This form of argumentation appears elsewhere in FitzRalph's treatment of the Greeks. FitzRalph's discussion of the eternal procession of the Holy Spirit takes up close to five hundred lines of text in a normal format. He never once refers to Scripture, except to say that Anselm proved the *Filioque* 'clearly enough through argument and various New Testament passages'.[18] Instead, FitzRalph bases himself on Augustine's *De Trinitate* and Anselm's *De processione Spiritus Sancti*, citing them fifteen times apiece, with four references each to Aristotle, Peter Lombard, Henry of Ghent and John Duns Scotus, and a couple to Thomas Aquinas, Giles of Rome and Godfrey of Fontaines, although he mentions the Decretals and related glosses on ten occasions. The only Greek who shows up is John of Damascus, three times.

The internal western discussion of the *Filioque* was thus a philosophical one. As Russell Friedman has shown,[19] since the mid-thirteenth century, university theologians generally asked two questions, one *de facto*: 'does the Holy Spirit proceed from the Father and from the Son?'; the other counterfactual: 'if the Holy Spirit did not proceed from the Son, would the Holy Spirit be distinct from the Son?' Given that even the Greeks now accept the *Filioque*, or so he thinks, FitzRalph devotes all of a dozen lines to the unphilosophical *de facto* question, his article three, where scriptural passages would have been important. The more philosophical counterfactual question had arisen because of the Greek position: is it merely an error, or does it entail a heretical denial of the Trinity? Since FitzRalph believes that the Greeks no longer reject the *Filioque*, the fact that he focuses almost all of his attention on this issue, his article one, must be due to his interest in the internal western philosophical discussion. Indeed, in contrast to what FitzRalph would say in the *Summa*, his emphasis on the counterfactual issue in the *Sentences* commentary meant that, except in passing, he omitted the main philosophical justification for the *de facto* validity of the *Filioque*, that divine simplicity and unity entail that the Father communicates to the Son everything that is not repugnant to the latter's personal identity, including the active spiration of the Holy Spirit.

By FitzRalph's time, western theologians were entrenched in two opposing camps over the counterfactual question (*in hoc contrariantur doctores*), roughly corresponding to the two main mendicant orders and their followers.[20] FitzRalph was no friend of the mendicants, of course, but on theological issues

---

quod falsum est'. 18 [§78] 'Ideo absque ambiguitate tenendum est quod Spiritus Sanctus procedat de Patre et Filio, sicut dicit Anselmus in *De processione Spiritus Sancti*, et probat hoc per rationem et per auctoritates varias Novi Testamenti satis evidenter'. 19 See R.L. Friedman, 'Divergent traditions in later-medieval trinitarian theology: relations, emanations and the use of philosophical psychology, 1250–1325', *Studia Theologica*, 53 (1999), 13–25; Friedman, *Medieval trinitarian thought from Aquinas to Ockham* (Cambridge, 2010); Friedman, *Intellectual traditions in the medieval university*. 20 [§12] For the Franciscan and Dominican positions, see the works of Friedman cited in the previous note, for example, *Medieval trinitarian thought* and Schabel, 'Attitudes toward the Greeks'.

this does not seem to have bothered him and here he presents both sides. The Franciscans stressed an emanationist account of the Trinity and for them the differing ways of emanation of the Son and the Holy Spirit from the Father would be sufficient to preserve the distinction between the Son and the Holy Spirit in the counterfactual case without the *Filioque*. The Franciscans employed the distinction between the divine attributes intellect and will as an explanation for both the distinction between the second and third persons of the Trinity and for the fact that there is a Trinity at all. The Son emanates as the Word by way of nature or intellect, while the Holy Spirit proceeds as Love by way of will. They thus have disparate relations of origin with the Father, even ignoring the procession of the Holy Spirit from the Son. Moreover, the two attributes help explain why there is a Trinity: one is unemanated, one is emanated by intellect, one is emanated by will. FitzRalph presents elements of the Franciscan position via Henry of Ghent and John Duns Scotus, himself coming out in favour of the Franciscan stance, which was rather sympathetic to the Greek doctrine.[21]

The Dominicans, on the other hand, took as their starting and ending point the opposition of relations within the Trinity. FitzRalph remarks that Thomas Aquinas, Giles of Rome, Godfrey of Fontaines and 'many others' argue that the Holy Spirit would not be distinct from the Son without its procession from the Son, since the opposing relation of origin between the two is the only basis for their distinction: 'There is only a distinction of origin between the Son and the Holy Spirit, because there is only one distinction between them. So with that removed, there would not be any distinction between them'.[22] This would be tantamount to denying the Trinity. Indeed, FitzRalph continues, 'other moderns' maintain that the article's hypothesis that the Holy Spirit does not proceed from the Son includes a contradiction.[23]

FitzRalph argues at length against the Dominicans and their 'modern' supporters. He does employ the Franciscans' reasoning, but his first argument is of a different nature and involves the Greeks. If these 'moderns' mean that plainly and simply the hypothesis of no *Filioque* includes contradictories, 'they speak falsely, it seems, because the greatest doctors of the Greeks would not have spoken thus, since none of the great doctors has ever said anything expressly and formally entailing contradictories, because this would be very stupid'.[24] Thus the argument mentioned above stemming from the Greeks' fidelity appears in a

21 §§21–33: [§24] 'Henricus tenet hanc partem et probat illam multipliciter'; [§33] 'Haec Henricus, et concordat cum eo Iohannes in hoc articulo'. 22 [§34] 'Sed beatus Thomas, Aegidius, Godefridus, et multi alii tenent contrariam partem, et tamen non arguunt ad illam sicut isti arguunt ad istam partem, sed videntur maxime fundare se super hoc quod inter Filium et Spiritum Sanctum est sola distinctio originis, quia non est inter ipsos nisi una distinctio. Ergo illa remota non esset inter ipsos aliqua distinctio'. 23 [§35] 'Alii moderni dicunt in isto articulo quod iste articulus supponit unum quod claudit contradictoria, scilicet Spiritum Sanctum non procedere a Filio'. 24 [§§36–37] 'Haec positio videtur multis habere evidentiam, et ideo arguo contra istam positionem multipliciter. Primo sic, cum dicunt illam positionem claudere contradictoria, aut intelligunt quod formaliter in suo intellectu expresse importet contradictoria aut

new form: the great doctors of the Greeks were not stupid, so if they denied the *Filioque*, this denial cannot entail contradictories.

While FitzRalph devotes much attention to the counterfactual issue, the basic philosophical argument for the validity of the *Filioque* itself merely arises in connection with FitzRalph's response to an opening argument: 'if it were not repugnant for the Holy Spirit to be, and [yet] not to be from the Son, Anselm would not prove in *De processione Spiritus Sancti* that the Holy Spirit proceeds from the Son solely because It proceeds from God'.[25] FitzRalph replies that this was not Anselm's only basis, but he also used the principle that 'unity holds its consequent where opposition of relation does not impede', that is, whatever the Son can share with the Father He does share with the Father, unless His filiation precludes it.[26]

It is this tenet, mentioned in passing, that FitzRalph would make the cornerstone of his discussion in the *Summa*. Yet in the *Sentences* commentary, perhaps secure in his belief that the Greeks held to the *Filioque*, FitzRalph had just undermined this very dictum a few lines earlier in responding to another argument:

> The principle that 'unity holds its consequent where opposition of relation does not impede' is not a *propositio per se nota*. Indeed it would be denied by someone who said that the Holy Spirit does not proceed from the Son. And so he would have to deny this consequence: 'The Holy Spirit proceeds from God the Father and the same God is the Father and the Son, therefore the Holy Spirit proceeds from the Son'[27]

— which a Greek would deny.

quod importet contradictoria cum aliquibus aliis principiis extraneis adiunctis. Si intelligant primo modo, falsum dicunt, ut videtur, tum quia tunc non dixissent sic maximi doctores Graecorum, cum numquam aliquis maximorum doctorum dixit aliquid importans expresse et formaliter contradictoria, quia hoc esset nimis stultum; tum quia tunc ad probandum istam positionem numquam occurrerent argumenta tam evidentia, sicut sunt iam adducta ad Henricum et Ioannem, quae multum sunt evidentiora, ut videtur, quam ad partem oppositam; tum quia tunc habita fide de hoc quod Spiritus Sanctus procedit a Patre, non indigeremus fide nec instructione ad hoc credendum, ex quo suum oppositum includeret formalem repugnantiam ad alium articulum. Ergo non potest dici quod illa hypothesis includat formaliter contradictoria'. 25 [§20] 'Septimo sic: si non repugnaret Spiritui Sancto esse et non a Filio, non probaret Anselmus in libro *De processione Spiritus Sancti* quod Spiritus Sanctus procedat a Filio ex hoc solo quod procedit de Deo'. 26 [§52] 'Ad septimum, cum accipitur quod, nisi repugnaret Spiritum Sanctum esse et non esse a Filio, non probaret Anselmus in *De processione Spiritus Sancti* contra Graecos quod ex hoc quod procedit de Deo necessario procedit de Filio – dico quod sic, sed non ex hoc solo demonstrat illam conclusionem, sed cum illo principio quod "unitas tenet suum consequens ubi non obviat oppositio relationis"'. 27 [§50] 'Unde ad probandum illam repugnantiam ipse accipit hoc principium quod "unitas tenet suum consequens ubi non obviat oppositio relativa", quae propositio non est nota per se, immo neganda esset ab illo qui diceret Spiritum Sanctum non procedere a Filio, et ideo ipse deberet negare hanc consequentiam: "Spiritus Sanctus procedit a Deo Patre et idem Deus est Pater et Filius, ergo procedit a Filio"'.

In fact, repeatedly stating that the propositions 'the Holy Spirit is distinguished from the Son' and 'the Holy Spirit does not proceed from the Son' are not *formally* contradictory,[28] he also asserts that 'it is *not* expressed in Holy Scripture that the Holy Spirit proceeds from the Son, and so, if the Holy Spirit did not proceed from Him, there would still be something found in Scripture by which the Holy Spirit would be distinguished from the Son, namely because the Holy Spirit proceeds from the Father and is not the Son, both of which are in Scripture'.[29] For these reasons, FitzRalph's contemporary Adam Wodeham put FitzRalph in the Franciscan camp of Henry of Ghent, Scotus and Ockham.[30]

Of course, for FitzRalph, *de facto*, although not formally, the propositions 'the Holy Spirit is distinguished from the Son' and 'the Holy Spirit does not proceed from the Son' are necessarily repugnant because it is *de facto* of the very essence of the Holy Spirit that It proceeds from the Son, just as it is of the very essence of the Son that He spirates the Holy Spirit and *de facto* it cannot be otherwise. Moreover, *de facto* the *Filioque* is the basis for their distinction. In this *de facto* sense, although Henry of Ghent and Scotus were right about the lack of formal repugnancy, Aquinas, Godfrey and Giles were also correct.[31] Still, if someone were not to accept the scriptural basis for this *de facto* claim, he would find philo-

---

28 E.g. [§44] 'Primum patet, scilicet quod non repugnat formaliter "Spiritus Sanctus distinguitur a Filio" et "non procedit ab eo", quia non repugnat formaliter "Spiritus Sanctus procedit a Patre per modum amoris" et "Spiritus Sanctus non procedit a Filio", et per consequens nec alia duo repugnant formaliter, cum ista sequantur formaliter ex istis. Assumptum patet quia illa duo non plus repugnant formaliter: "Spiritus Sanctus procedit a Patre per modum amoris" et "Spiritus Sanctus non procedit a Filio", quam ista duo repugnant formaliter: "Filius procedit a Patre per modum naturae" et "Filius non procedit a Spiritu Sancto", quae non repugnant. Ergo nec alia duo'. 29 [§46] 'Sed non est expressum in scriptura sacra quod Spiritus Sanctus procedat a Filio, et ideo, si non procederet ab isto, adhuc esset aliquid inventum in scriptura sacra unde distingueretur a Filio, scilicet quia procederet a Patre et non est Filius, quorum utrumque est in scriptura'. 30 Wodeham, *Lectura Secunda* I, d. 11, ed. Wood and Gál, p. 164: 'Quaero utrum Spiritus Sanctus posset distingui a Filio si non procederet ab eo ... Hic tenent quod non Chatton, Thomas, Aegidius, Godefridus; contrarium Gandavensis, Scotus, Ockham, FitzRalph'. Wodeham seems to be mistaken in his placement of Chatton, however. 31 [§43] 'Ad istum articulum, cum quaeritur utrum Spiritus Sanctus distingueretur a Filio posito quod non procederet ab eo, dico quod videtur mihi quod quaestio quaerit de repugnantia istorum duorum: "Spiritus Sanctus distinguitur a Filio" et "Spiritus Sanctus non procedit a Filio". Unde – quia repugnantia est duplex, una necessaria, licet per accidens, sicut ista repugnant necessario: "Deus est" et "Deus non est trinus"; et alia est repugnantia necessaria per se, ubi unum ex suo formali intellectu infert oppositum alterius, sicut sequitur "Sortes est homo, ergo Sortes est animal" consequentia formali simpliciter, et ideo ista duo per se repugnant necessario: "Sortes est homo" et "Sortes non est animal" – ideo dico ad articulum, si quaeratur de repugnantia formali et necessaria, quod stant simul, et non repugnant quod Spiritus Sanctus distinguatur a Filio et quod non procedat ab eo; et sic dicunt et loquuntur Doctor Solemnis et Doctor Subtilis in isto articulo. Si vero quo modo intelligatur de stare simul vel repugnare per accidens et necessario, sic dico quod non stant simul, sed repugnant; et hoc – videtur mihi – intelligunt ipsi doctores, scilicet Thomas, Godefridus, et Aegidius ... [§45] Secundum patet quod dictum est in positione, scilicet quod ista repugnant necessario, etsi non formaliter et per se: "Spiritus Sanctus distinguitur a Filio" et "non

sophical support in FitzRalph himself: Anselm's proposition is not *per se nota* and could be denied.

THE *SUMMA DE QUAESTIONIBUS ARMENORUM*

After Richard FitzRalph's tenure at Oxford, most issues in trinitarian and eucharistic theology disappeared from debate at the English university in the following decades, to judge from surviving writings. Different circumstances led FitzRalph to return to the Trinity and the Eucharist in his *Summa de quaestionibus Armenorum* in the late 1340s. There was no need for FitzRalph to deal with the specific issue of the bread of the Eucharist in the *Summa*, however, because the Armenians, like the Latins, employed unleavened bread. In fact, it has been argued convincingly that the Greeks came to oppose the Latin custom because they had already linked the Armenian sacrament with elements of their Christology that the Greeks considered heretical. The Latins agreed with the Greeks on the Christological issue, yet the Greeks applied their related censure of the Armenian sacrament to the Latins in the mid-eleventh century.[32]

If FitzRalph could avoid the issue of unleavened bread while treating the Eucharist in book IX of the *Summa*, he had to face the fundamental difference over papal primacy in book VII. Although in general FitzRalph puts forth an uncompromising papalist position, at the end of chapter sixteen he does support the interesting idea that the pope should be in Jerusalem. Perhaps hinting at a Petrarchian criticism of the papal practice of living in Avignon,[33] replying to John, his interlocutor in the dialogue, Richard relates:

> But as far as the other thing you objected, on the glory of the place of Jerusalem, you speak the truth and you conclude something true, namely that there is no doubt to any Christian that it would be fitting for the highest pontiff of Christ's Church to reside there insofar as it is from the head. But other factors stand in the way[34]

procedit ab eo", quia nunc necessarium est absolute quod inter Filium et Spiritum Sanctum non sit alia distinctio realis nisi distinctio originis, et ideo si illa distinctio non esset distinctio originis, omnino non esset Filius neque Spiritus Sanctus, et per consequens non distinguerentur tunc'. **32** T.M. Kolbaba, 'Byzantine perceptions of Latin religious "errors": themes and changes from 850 to 1350' in A.E. Laiou and R.P. Mottahedeh (eds), *The Crusades from the perspective of Byzantium and the Muslim world* (Washington DC, 2001), pp 117–43 at pp 122–5. See also Kolbaba, *The Byzantine lists: errors of the Latins* (Urbana & Chicago, 2000). **33** Barlaam, at least, knew Petrarch well, but we have no reason to believe that FitzRalph did: Walsh, *A fourteenth-century scholar and primate*, pp 156, 177. **34** Richard FitzRalph, *Summa de quaestionibus Armenorum* VII, c. 16, J. Sudoris (ed.) (Paris, 1511), fo. 48bis(49)va: 'In alio vero quod obicis de gloria loci Hierosolimitani, verum dicis et verum concludis, scilicet quod ibi quantum est ex illo capite nulli dubium Christiano summo pontifici Ecclesiae Christi summa congrueret residere. Sed obstant alia, scilicet tam subvertio populi illius a fide tunc futura in proximum

— namely, the rule of the Sultan.

Aside from his entertaining ignorance about contemporary Greek theology, 'Richard FitzRalph on the Trinity in his *Sentences* commentary' would not constitute a very interesting essay, and indeed in Russell Friedman's monumental survey of western trinitarian doctrine at the universities, 1250–1350, FitzRalph is given a mere paragraph under the rubric 'Traditional treatments and waning interest'.[35] FitzRalph's stay in Avignon forced him to reevaluate the issue comprehensively.

In Avignon, FitzRalph came into contact with the colourful Bernardo Massari, a Greek from Seminara near Reggio di Calabria, who took the monastic name Barlaam when he professed as a monk at the nearby Greek-rite monastery of St Elias of Capassino. Until the late 1320s, he was in the spiritual jurisdiction of Rome, but then, at about 35 years of age, he went to Thessaloniki and afterwards to Constantinople, became abbot of the Holy Saviour and for a decade represented Emperor Andronikos III in negotiations with the west. In Constantinople in 1334–5, Barlaam met with two Dominican representatives of Pope John XXII in discussions over church union.[36] As a result of his talks with Francis of Camerino and Richard of England, he composed several anti-Latin treatises in Greek, published recently by Antonis Fyrigos.[37]

We have at least three basic sources for Barlaam's views on the *Filioque*: a Latin report of discussions over church union, Barlaam's Greek writings and FitzRalph's own report in the *Summa*. The irony is that, despite the fact that Barlaam spent four decades in the west, much of it in a Greek religious context, until 1334 he was as ignorant about the Second Council of Lyon as FitzRalph was about the Greeks' repudiation of the council. Until 1334, it seems that Barlaam had no idea about fundamental doctrinal decisions made at the council, and although his discussions in Constantinople with two Dominican papal representatives in 1334 must have made him aware of these developments, there is no clear evidence that he understood them completely before 1339, when Barlaam visited Pope Benedict XII at the Papal Curia in Avignon to discuss the possibilities for the reunion of the church, probably with FitzRalph himself in attendance.[38] The

---

quam imperatoria potentia supradicta etc'. Earlier in the chapter (rb), John mentioned the present powers: the Khan, the Persians, the Sultan ...   35 Friedman, *Intellectual traditions in the medieval university*, ch. 11, section 4. G. Leff, *Richard FitzRalph: Commentator of the Sentences, a study in theological orthodoxy* (Manchester, 1963), makes no mention of this question.   36 On Barlaam, see Walsh, *A fourteenth-century scholar and primate*, pp 152–8, and the essays in A. Fyrigos (ed.), *Barlaam Calabro: l'uomo, l'opera, il pensiero: atti del convegno internazionale Reggio Calabia – Seminara – Gerace 10–11–12 dicembre 1999* (Rome, 2001), along with the literature cited there.   37 Barlaam Calabro, *Opere contro i Latini*, A. Fyrigos (ed.), 2 vols, Studi e Testi 347–8 (Vatican City, 1998), for dating, i, pp 211–18; see also A. Fyrigos, 'Considerazioni sulle *Opere contro i Latini* di Barlaam Calabro' in *Barlaam Calabro: l'uomo, l'opera, il pensiero*, pp 119–40.   38 The controversial issue of when Barlaam learned about Lyon II is treated in A. Fyrigos, 'Quando Barlaam Calabro conobbe il Concilio di Lione II (1274)?' *Rivista di studi bizantini e neoellenici*, n.s., 17–19 (1980–2), 247–65, which I follow here.

resulting Latin report[39] emphasized that at the Second Council of Lyon Patriarch John (John Beccos – although this is incorrect, as he was not yet patriarch) and Emperor Michael Palaiologos sent their representatives, who agreed to union, accepting the Latin position on the *Filioque*. Unlike FitzRalph earlier, the report then states that the Greeks backslid, 'damnably retreating from their profession [of faith] and returning to their vomit'.[40] Barlaam's response is reported in direct discourse:

> But if someone should say that these things have already been dealt with at the General Council in Lyon, where the Greeks were present as well, he should know that no one can humble the Greek people such that they accept this council without [having] another council. Why? Because those Greeks that attended that council were sent neither by the four patriarchs who govern the Eastern Church nor by the people, but by the emperor alone, who was trying to make the union through force and not voluntarily.[41]

Barlaam's suggestion was for the west to help Byzantium militarily and then to convoke an ecumencial council where the *Filioque* would be discussed openly. The Latins repeated that this had been done at Lyon already, and Barlaam replied that the Greeks and Latins could be allowed to hold their different beliefs. The Latins answered that a double-faith is impossible, but rather than a council of discussion, perhaps a council of instruction would suffice. Barlaam responded that examining what is in doubt has always been the way forward, so why should the Latins fear such an examination, if they are correct?

The report on the discussion – which went nowhere – gives no arguments or authorities for either side's position on the *Filioque*. Barlaam had attacked the *Filioque* in writing already, but it is doubtful that FitzRalph would have taken the time to have Barlaam's Greek works translated (but see below) when he had access to the man himself, not only in 1339–40, but also in 1341–2, when Barlaam was back in Avignon before Pope Clement VI (with Petrarch's good word) made him bishop of Gerace, again in southern Calabria, in which capacity he died in 1348.[42] Book VI of the *Summa* concerns the *Filioque*, about twice the length of

39 There are editions in Leo Allatius, *De perpetua consensione* ... (Cologne [Amsterdam], 1648), and *Patrologia Graeca* 151. I use *Acta Benedicti XII (1334–1342)*, A.L. Tautu (ed.), Pontificia Commissio ad redigendum codicem iuris canonici orientalis, Fontes 3, vol. 8 (Vatican City, 1958), no. 43 (pp 85–97), from Reg. Vat. 134. Apparently F. Mosino, 'Le orazione avignonesi di Barlaam Calabro nel Registro 134 dell'Archivio Segreto Vaticano', *Divptuca*, 4 (1986), 149–62, is the latest edition.   40 *Acta Benedicti XII*, p. 86.   41 Ibid., pp 87–8.   42 See E. d'Agostino, 'Barlaam di Seminara Vescovo di Gerace' in *Barlaam Calabro:l'uomo, l'opera, il pensiero*, pp 67–77. During his second visit, however, Barlaam was undergoing a sort of partial conversion to Latin views: see T.M. Kolbaba, 'Conversion from Greek Orthodoxy to Roman Catholicism in the fourteenth century', *Byzantine and Modern Greek Studies*, 19 (1995), 120–34, and M. Hinterberger, 'Από το

the treatment in the *Sentences* commentary, perhaps around one thousand lines. John, Richard's student and interlocutor in the dialogue, opens as follows:

> By firm faith I hold that the Holy Spirit proceeds, is spirated, or exists *a Filio* or *ex Filio* just as *a Patre* or *ex Patre*. The Greeks and some Armenians do not assert this with us, however, although they do assert, just as we do, that the Holy Spirit is spirated and proceeds and exists *a Deo* and *a Patre* and is the Spirit of the Father and the Spirit of God, and is sent and given by God, and even proceeds *a Patre* and is the Spirit of the Son or of the Word and is sent and given *a Filio* to us [that is, in time], just as John of Damascus plainly puts forth. So, on the basis of Holy Scripture and of those things that the Greeks and the Armenians confess along with us, I would like you to show me by plain and clear deduction that the Holy Spirit *exists* thus and thus *proceeds a Filio* just as It proceeds *a Patre, as you pledged to that Greek doctor Barlaam*.[43]

Katherine Walsh has quoted from this passage and remarked elsewhere that FitzRalph's treatment of the Beatific Vision in the *Summa* was also at Barlaam's request, while Barlaam was again FitzRalph's source for the Greek stance on the issue of Purgatory.[44] Although Anselm has done a sufficient job proving the *Filioque*, John continues, 'because you promised that doctor of the Greeks to do this', he asks Richard to oblige.[45]

The *Summa* is not quite a polemical treatise and in book VI FitzRalph really appears to be trying to convince a sceptic to accept the *Filioque*, which was hardly an issue in his *Sentences* commentary. To do this, FitzRalph needs to deal with potential and real objections of a scriptural, conciliar, patristic and philosophical

ορθόδοξο Βυζάντιο στην καθολική Δύση. Τέσσερις διαφορετικοί δρόμοι' in *Το Βυζάντιο και οι απαρχές της Ευρώπης* (Athens, 2004), pp 11–30 at pp 17–20. 43 *Summa*, VI, c. 1 (Paris fo. 39ra; corrected as noted with Padova, Bibliotheca Universitaria 1439, which lacks numeration of the folios): 'Iohannes: Quamvis firma fide teneam Spiritum Sanctum procedere, spirari, sive esse a Filio sive ex Filio, sicut a Patre aut ex Patre, quia tamen Graeci et Armeni aliqui hoc nobiscum non asserunt, licet [1] affirment sicut nos Spiritum Sanctum spirari et procedere et esse a Deo et a Patre et esse Spiritum Patris et Spiritum Dei, et mitti a Deo et dari, et etiam procedere a Patre et esse Spiritum Filii sive Verbi, et a Filio mitti et dari nobis, sicut Iohannes Damascenus, libro *Sententiarum* suarum primo, 7, 10, et 12 capitulis, plane exponit, vellem tamen ut mihi ex Sacra Scriptura et ex his quae Graeci et Armeni nobiscum confitentur plana et clara deductione ostenderes, sicut illi doctori Graeco Barlam spopondisti, quod Spiritus Sanctus ita est et ita procedit a Filio sicut procedit [2] sive spiratur a Patre'. [1] non *add.* Ed. | | [2] a Filio sicut procedit *om. per hom.* Ed. 44 Walsh, *A fourteenth-century scholar and primate*, pp 102, 151–2. It should be noted that Walsh quotes from two Vatican manuscripts (see p. 152, n. 77), but her quotation includes the edition's omission cited in the previous note. We certainly need a critical edition of this text. 45 *Summa*, VI, c. 1 (Paris, fo. 39ra; Padova): 'Quamvis enim venerabilis Anselmus subtiliter et sufficienter hoc egerit, quia tamen hoc facere huic doctori Graecorum promiseras, et mihi etiam in [1] similibus valere illud poterit, ut promissa perficias eiusdem Spiritus amore deposco'. [1] et mihi etiam in] aut quia mihi etiam et mihi Ed.

nature. Because FitzRalph has this specific goal in mind and a plan to reach it, I have decided that it is best to follow FitzRalph's own path in my essay.

Walsh has written that FitzRalph's treatment of the *Filioque* in the *Summa* places overwhelming emphasis on Scripture,[46] which, as we have seen, is in extreme contrast to his procedure in the *Sentences* commentary. Walsh is certainly correct, and the reasons are obvious, since Scripture is the main common ground of the three sects: Armenians, Greeks and Latins. Yet, as William Duba shows in his paper, this does not entail a rejection of scholasticism in the *Summa*. Indeed, before FitzRalph offers any scriptural defence of the *Filioque*, he begins by stating a rule of faith that can only be seen as a reflection of the western philosophical, neo-Platonic view of divine simplicity:

> First I suppose a rule of faith that the Greeks and Armenians cannot deny: that whatever applies to or is attributed to God or to one person [of the Trinity], consequently also applies to the three divine persons separately on account of the identity of the simple essence of the persons, unless by reason of personal property this is repugnant to any person; *e converso*, whatever applies to or is attributed to any divine person or to two persons together or to three, applies to God and is attributed to Him; because each person is God and every two persons are God.[47]

The remainder of the first chapter of book VI FitzRalph devotes to proving this supposedly undeniable rule via a dozen or so passages from Scripture, most not surprisingly from the Gospel according to John. FitzRalph repeats this rule at the end of the chapter and then opens chapter two by reiterating that, 'From this rule of the Catholic faith, which the Greeks acknowledge', the *Filioque* follows, since the Father's active spiration of the Holy Spirit is not repugnant to the personal property of the Son.[48] FitzRalph does not mention the Armenians

---

46 Walsh, *A fourteenth-century scholar and primate*, pp 147, 172–3, although her claim that FitzRalph has no Greek patristic or conciliar references is an exaggeration. Her statement that the Greeks and Armenians 'deleted' the *Filioque* from the Creed (p. 149) is, one assumes, merely an extrapolated paraphrase from FitzRalph.   47 *Summa*, VI, c. 1 (Paris, fo. 39ra; Padova): 'Suppono primo pro [1] regula fidei, quam Graeci et Armeni negare non possunt: quod quicquid convenit sive attribuitur Deo aut uni personae convenit consequenter et divisim tribus personis divinis propter identitatem simplicis essentiae personarum nisi illud ratione proprietatis personalis alicui personae repugnet, et e converso quicquid convenit aut attribuitur alicui divinae personae aut duabus communiter seu tribus convenit Deo et sibi attribuitur, quia unaquaeque persona est Deus et omnes duae personae sunt Deus'. [1] Suppono primo pro] Supposito pro illa Ed.   48 *Summa*, VI, cc. 1–2 (Paris, fo. 39rb; Padova): 'Sic igitur est in istis exemplis positis [1] sicut fatemur in omnibus esse quae Deo vel alicui personae divinae conveniunt, scilicet quod duabus aut tribus personis divisim aut [2] communiter conveniunt, et e converso, nisi ea propter proprietatem personalem [3] alicui aut aliquibus personis repugnarent, etc. [ch. 2] Ex hac regula catholicae fidei, quam nobiscum Graeci fatentur ..'. [1] positis *iter*. Ed. | | [2] aut *om*. Ed. | | [3]

here, because book VI concentrates on the Greeks. Yet it is by no means apparent that the Greeks would admit this rule, a variation on Anselm's rule that FitzRalph had expressly called not *per se nota* in his *Sentences* commentary, a rule that he even admitted would be denied by someone who also rejected the *Filioque* itself. On the contrary, Greeks had consistently argued that the Latins' philosophical emphasis on divine simplicity 'relativizes the reality of personal, or hypostatic, existence in the Trinity', to use John Meyendorff's phrasing.[49] While the Latins worried that the Greeks focused too much attention on the 'three' in 'triune' to the detriment of the 'one', the Greeks argued that the Latins neglected the reality of the three persons. If Barlaam had been able to obtain and read a copy of FitzRalph's earlier work, it could have proved embarrassing.

In the *Sentences* commentary, FitzRalph remarked that Scripture never explicitly endorses the *Filioque*. Chapter two of book VI of the *Summa*, in contrast, focuses on showing that Scripture does not explicitly deny the *Filioque*, nor does Scripture explicitly state that the spiration of the Holy Spirit applies more to the Father than to the Son, so according to the *ars obligatoria*, any passage affirming the spiration from the Father is *impertinens*, despite what John of Damascus might claim.[50] What Scripture does say, FitzRalph argues in chapter three, is that man has been made in God's image, an issue that FitzRalph had addressed in his lost questions *De imagine Dei in anima humana*.[51] In his *Sentences* commentary, FitzRalph devoted the question following the one on the procession of the Holy Spirit to the issue 'whether the human mind is an image of the uncreated Trinity', but in his lengthy treatment of this and related topics he did not emphasize the psychological model of the Trinity in order to prove the *Filioque*.[52] To quote Russell Friedman, 'FitzRalph was simply not interested in pursuing the possible trinitarian ramifications of this material'.[53] Indeed, by the 1340s the psychological model had gone out of fashion, but now in the *Summa* FitzRalph finds it useful against the Greeks.

For humans, according to FitzRalph, we have a *verbum mentis* with respect to the thing known. When a *verbum vocale* arises when we speak, our mind can love that thing. It is like this with God: 'since our word spirates love, it follows that God's Word spirates Love'. In speaking or thinking, God says or gives birth to the Word, that is, the Son, so in loving Himself He spirates or produces Love, that is, the Holy Spirit. For FitzRalph, it is clear that God first speaks and then loves, and not the other way around, so spiration presupposes generation. To say

---

personalem] personaliter Ed.   **49** J. Meyendorff, *Byzantine theology: historical trends and doctrinal themes* (New York, 1974), p. 92.   **50** *Summa*, VI, c. 2 (Paris, fo. 39vb; Padova): 'illa Sancti Iohannis assertio, quod Spiritus a Patre procedit, de Filio spirationem non negat [1], sed esse impertinens constat'. [1] negat] negaret Ed.   **51** Walsh, *A fourteenth-century scholar and primate*, pp 48 and 53.   **52** In Dunne, 'Richard FitzRalph's *Lectura* on the *Sentences*', p. 410, the question 'Utrum mens humana sit ymago trinitatis increate' is number 6 in book I, while number 10, 'Utrum amor procedat ab aliqua notitia', is also pertinent.   **53** Friedman, *Intellectual traditions in the medieval university*, ch. 11, section 4.

the reverse would be 'stupid', according to FitzRalph. It is also clear to him that the Word is the principle of the one who is spirated.[54] The psychological model thus comes in quite handy, and in chapter four FitzRalph puts forth what might be called his second *regula*, which depends on this model: one person must be from the other person; the Son cannot be from the Holy Spirit; therefore the Holy Spirit is from the Son:

> The generation of the Son is prior in origin to the spiration of the Holy Spirit, because the Father does not spirate nor love unless beforehand, at least in origin, He speaks the Word. This cannot be the case unless the Holy Spirit proceeds from the Son. For if the Son is not the productive principle nor the cause of the Holy Spirit more than the other way around, then He is not more presupposed in the Holy Spirit by origin and essence than the other way around, rather they are completely disparate with respect to priority and posteriority of origin.[55]

---

54 *Summa*, VI, c. 3 (Paris, fos 39vb–40ra; Padova): 'Richardus: Etenim non dubium quin mens humana sit trinitatis creatricis imago ... Constat autem in mente humana Deum aut [1] aliud cognoscente actualiter et cogitante et illud amante quod [2] a specie rei cognoscibilis in mente velut apparente [3] gignitur cogitatio actualis sive verbum eiusdem rei cognitae et ab utroque amor respectu [4] eiusdem rei procedit sive spiratur, nec sine cogitatione actuali quam propinquissimum "verbum mentis" nostrae respectu rei cognitae appellamus, cum ab eo sit verbum vocale sic dictum potest mens rem illam amare ... Certum est ergo ex quo fecit e contra quod sic est in Deo quo ad processiones sicut in sua creata [5] imagine invenitur ... Cum ergo verbum nostrum spiret amorem sive dilectionem [6], consequitur quod Verbum divinum spiret Amorem sive Caritatem quam "Spiritum" appellamus. Alias enim iuxta modum suum Verbum Dei esset in hoc deficientius verbo nostro. Item, non puto quemquam [7] posse negare quin sicut Deus se dicendo sive cogitando dicit sive gignit aut parit Verbum, ita se amando sive diligendo spirat sive producit Amorem. Et praecipue non potest quisquam hoc negare, quia sic esse reperit apud [8] se ipsum in Dei imagine. Aut ergo ideo Deus se diligit quia se dicit sive cogitat aut actu cognoscit, aut e contra, ideo se dicit aut cogitat [9] sive cognoscit actu quia se diligit, vel haec sunt penitus disparata. Stultum autem nimis videtur asserere quod ideo Deus se cogitat aut dicit aut actu cognoscit quia se diligit, cum nihil possit amari nisi actu praecognitum. Per idem patet quod non sunt haec penitus disparata. Igitur [10] relinquitur quod ideo se diligit quia se dicit aut cogitat, et per consequens ideo Amorem spirat quia gignit seu dicit aut parit Verbum, et per consequens Genitus sive Verbum est Spirati principium. Aliter enim spiratio non praesupponeret generationem sive dictionem [11] ut causam sive principium, quod est falsum'. [1] aut] autem Ed. || [2] et illud amante quod] illud a mente et Ed. || [3] apparente] a parente Ed. || [4] amor respectu] amore spiritum Ed. || [5] creata] creatura Ed. || [6] dilectionem] dilectione Ed. || [7] quemquam] quemquem Ed. || [8] apud *om*. Ed. || cogitat] cogit Ed. || [10] Igitur] Ideo Ed. || [11] dictionem] productionem Ed.   55 *Summa*, VI, c. 4 (Paris, fo. 40rb; Padova): 'Si ergo dicatur, sicut oportet, quod [1] dicitur essentialiter Spiritus Filii, et ob hoc quia generatio Filii est prior origine quam spiratio Spiritus Sancti eo quod Pater non spirat nec amat nisi prius saltem origine Verbum dicat, istud stare non potest nisi Spiritus procedat a Filio. Si enim Filius non est principium productivum nec causa Spiritus Sancti magis quam e contra, non magis ei praesupponitur originaliter et essentialiter quam e contra, sed [2] sunt penitus disparati quantum ad prioritatem et posterioritatem originis'. [1] quod] quo Ed. || [2] sed] si Ed.

It is difficult to imagine a Greek considering such arguments as convincing, or even pertinent, and FitzRalph's efforts at biblical exegesis were probably no more successful. In the *Sentences* commentary, FitzRalph was apparently unaware of the main difficulty of proving the *Filioque* via Scripture. Article two of his question on the *Filioque* in the *Sentences* commentary deals exclusively with 'the temporal procession of the Holy Spirit, that is, His mission' – how the Holy Spirit comes to us in our lives after the incarnation – and this is not the same as the Holy Spirit's eternal procession, which involves the Holy Spirit's very existence.[56] In the extremely brief article three *ad quaestionem*, which was 'whether the Holy Spirit proceeds from the Father and the Son', before his short appeal to the authority of the Second Council of Lyon quoted above, FitzRalph answers as follows:

> I say that [the Holy Spirit does proceed from the Father and the Son], whether the question is understood concerning the Holy Spirit's temporal procession, about which the previous article spoke, or concerning the Holy Spirit's eternal procession, by which the Holy Spirit is eternally spirated by the Father and the Son.[57]

Now, the problem is that not only did the Greeks agree that the Holy Spirit proceeds, in some way, from the Father and the Son as regards the Holy Spirit's temporal mission, but they also traditionally interpreted any passages that the Latins used to prove the Holy Spirit's *eternal* procession *ex Patre Filioque* as applying instead to the Holy Spirit's temporal mission.[58] This was hardly a concern in the *Sentences* commentary, when FitzRalph believed that the Greeks were obediently following the Latin dogma. Indeed, it was slightly unusual that he combined the eternal procession and the temporal mission of the Holy Spirit into one question. By the time he composed the *Summa*, however, FitzRalph was aware that he had to refute the Greeks' interpretation of all pertinent scriptural passages as applying to the temporal mission and not the eternal procession.[59]

Chapters five through eight thus deal with scriptural exegesis, of the sort that

---

56 [§12] 'Secundo, quia processio Spiritus Sancti duplex est, scilicet aeterna et temporalis, de processione eius temporali, scilicet eius missione, erit secundus articulus utrum Spiritus Sanctus mittatur sive detur a Patre et Filio. [§65] Ad articulum istum, cum quaeritur utrum Spiritus Sanctus detur vel mittatur a Patre et a Filio, dico ... quod missio Spiritus Sancti, quae est eius processio temporalis ...'.   57 [§77] 'Ad quaestionem principalem, cum quaeritur utrum Spiritus Sanctus procedat a Patre et Filio, dico quod sic, sive intelligatur quaestio de processione illius temporali, de qua dictum est in ultimo articulo, sive de processione eius aeterna, qua aeternaliter spiratur a Patre et Filio'.   58 See, for example, Meyendorff, *Byzantine theology*, pp 93–4. Barlaam himself argues thus; for example, Tractatus B, IV, §1 (Barlaam Calabro, *Opere contro i Latini*, II, p. 344).   59 *Summa*, VI, c. 5 (Paris, fo. 40vb; Padova): '... nisi forte Graeci dixerint quod in omnibus his Apostolus accepit Spiritum sic dici propter missionem vel dationem aut traditionem temporalem'.

the Greeks would be unlikely to find compelling. For example, FitzRalph believes that some passages at least refer to the Holy Spirit's mission from the Son at creation, well before the incarnation, and he tries to interpret these as indicative of the eternal procession. But the Greeks would have simply said that this is still temporal. FitzRalph also maintains that only five biblical passages prove the Holy Spirit's procession from the Father and only one of these does not also include the Son. For FitzRalph, this means that if Scripture is the Greeks' basis for their claims about the relationship between the Father and the Holy Spirit, then most of this basis also supports the *Filioque*.[60]

FitzRalph does mention in passing the differing ways of emanation of the Son and the Holy Spirit, which he discussed at length in the counterfactual article one of the question in the *Sentences* commentary. Naturally this discussion is largely omitted in the *Summa*, beyond what was stated about man being created in God's image, since the arguments could be used to support the Greek tradition. Yet FitzRalph has enough intellectual honesty, or perhaps practical wisdom, not to retreat to the reasoning of Thomas Aquinas, Giles of Rome and Godfrey of Fontaines, according to which the *only* way to preserve the distinction between the Son and the Holy Spirit, and thus to preserve the Trinity itself, is to assert that the one comes from the other, that is, that the Holy Spirit proceeds from the Son.

Secure in his belief that the Latin position on the *Filioque* has the support of Scripture, FitzRalph in chapters nine through eleven turns to the question of church tradition, that is, the fathers and the councils, both on offence and on defence. The Greeks always objected that adding the *Filioque* without the consent of an ecumenical council, as they defined it, was illegitimate and FitzRalph's chapter nine opens with his interlocutor John offering Greek objections based on conciliar history. The Council of Nicaea, called to combat the 'Arian heresy that posited an inequality between the Father and the Son', is correctly placed in the reigns of Constantine the Great and Pope Sylvester I, but dated vaguely 'around 350', twenty-five years off. The often flawed Paris 1511 printed edition omits a phrase contained in the Padua Antoniana manuscript that I use, relating that the Council of Nicaea 'was the first of those four councils which our Church venerates like the four gospels'. Then the first Council of Constantinople is dated 'around 426', forty-five years too late, although the emperor, Theodosios the Elder, and the pope, Damasus I, are correctly identi-

---

60 Ibid., c. 6 (Paris, fo. 41ra; Padova): 'Item, si considabimus [1] Scripturam attentius, inveniemus quinque capitula et non plura ex quibus videri potest divisim aut saltem communiter probari posse quod Spiritus Sanctus procedit a Patre, quorum quodlibet probat aeque de Filio sicut de Patre, uno dumtaxat excepto, quod est insufficiens de se ad hoc quod probandum de Patre. Aut igitur ex Sacra Scriptura spiratio eius esse a Patre probari non potest, quod et Graeci negant et respuit religio Christiana, aut sicut probari potest eius spiratio esse a [2] Patre, sic potest probari esse a Filio'. [1] considerabimus] consideremus Ed. | | [2] a *om*. Ed.

fied, as is the heresy against which the council was called, that of the Macedonians 'who asserted that the Holy Spirit is not God'. In these councils, 'creeds were composed with the common assent of the Latins and the Greeks', maintaining the Holy Spirit's procession from the Father, saying nothing about the Son in connection with the procession and anathematizing any other teaching on this matter – which creed Pope Leo III caused to be inscribed on a silver table around the year 800 and which has remained in common use, except for the Latins' addition of the *Filioque*.[61]

Richard replies that the Greeks themselves specified church doctrine afterwards in ways that had not been and were not later expressed in the Creed, listing the [Third] Council of Constantinople of 'around 715' (really 680) under Constantine IV, the Council of Chalcedon of 'around 470' (really 451) under Pope Leo I and the Emperor Marcian and finally the [Second] Council of Constantinople of 'around 560' (really 553) under Pope Vigilius.[62] So FitzRalph continues:

> If the Greeks are correct in arguing that we are bound by the aforesaid sentence [of anathema] because of an addition that we made that is not contrary to the words that have been fixed, then neither can they excuse

61 Ibid., c. 9 (Paris, fo. 42va; Padova): 'Iohannes: Obiciunt nobis Graeci quod in Concilio Niceno, quod fuit primum illorum quatuor conciliorum quae nostra Ecclesia velut quatuor evangelia veneratur, quod scilicet Nicenum Concilium fuit [1] sub papa Silvestro et magno Constantino imperatore celebratum [2] circa annum Domini 350 propter heresim Arianam, quae posuit inaequalitatem inter Patrem et Filium ... et consequenter in Consilio primo Constantinopolis celebrato sub Damaso papa et Theodosio seniore imperatore circa annum Domini 426 propter heresim Macedonii confutandam qui asseruit Spiritum Sanctum Deum non esse, symbola edita fuerunt de communi assensu Latinorum et Graecorum, in quibus symbolis assertum est Spiritum Sanctum procedere a Patre, nihil penitus quo ad illam processionem expresso de Filio, et in fine subiunctum erat, "Qui aliud docuerit et aliud praedicaverit anathema sit". Et papa Leo tertius in tabula argentea ob amorem fidei Romae relinquit symbolum commune illorum duorum conciliorum quod symbolum usque in praesens cantatur apud nos in missis, cum illa tamen condicione ibi non posita: 'Filioque' [3]. Tu ergo primo [4] huiusmodi anathematis ligamentum a nobis alienum ostende quod Graecorum aliqui nos asserunt [5] incurrisse'. [1] quod fuit ... Nicenum Concilium fuit *om. per hom.* Ed. || [2] celebrato] celebratum Ed. || [3] Filioque] Filio quoque Ed. || [4] primo] primus Ed. || [5] asserunt] assentiunt Ed.
62 Ibid.: 'Unde si intellexisset per ly "aliud" quodcumque distinctum [1], Graeci seipsos esse ligatos negare non possent, cum in Concilio Constantinopolitano circa annum Domini DCCXV [2] sub Constantino quarto de eorum assensu fuerat definitum duas voluntates esse in Christo, quod nullatenus in symbolis est expressum. Item, in Concilio Calcedonensi sub papa Leone primo et Martiano imperatore circa annum Domini 470 contra Euticem [3] abbatem Constantinopolis et Dyoscorum Alexandrinum episcopum de Graecorum etiam assensu fuerat definitum in Christo esse duas naturas in una persona. Item, in [4] Constantinopolis Concilio circa annum Domini 560 sub papa Vigilio [5] et imperatore contra Theodorum asserentem Beatam Virginem Mariam solum hominem genuisse, de Graecorum assensu fuerat definitum quod ipsa genuit Deum et hominem, quorum nullum in illis symbolis est expressum'. [1] per ly ... distinctum] aliud quodcumque Ed. || [2] DCCXV] DII 15 Ed.; CCXV Padova || [3] Euticem] Entitem Ed. || [4] in *om.* Ed. || [5] Vigilio] Virgilio Ed.

> themselves for the aforesaid additions and many others made in later councils with their consent.[63]

Besides, according to FitzRalph, even before the *Filioque* was defined 'by the Latins at the [Fourth] Lateran Council under Innocent III around 1213', it had been defended by many holy doctors, both Greeks and Latins, and FitzRalph names Hilary, Ambrose, Jerome, Augustine, Gregory the Great and Anselm on the Latin side and Athanasius, Didymus, Cyril and John Chrysostomos for the Greeks, and no major Greek doctor opposed the *Filioque* in his writings. (Actually, the Athanasius and Chrysostomos *auctoritates*, at least, are apocryphal.) This was the case, FitzRalph declares quite wrongly, up until 'those times', supposedly the time of Lateran IV, and afterwards it was defined 'on the authority of the successor of the Prince of the Apostles, Peter, namely Gregory X, in whom the authority resides with respect to defining things concerning the faith'.[64] Winning few Greek friends, FitzRalph then remarks:

> Consequently, at the [Second] Council of Lyon, with Patriarch Germanos of the Greeks [actually former patriarch] and other prelates of theirs [actually only one more] present and agreeing, the definition of the same article was approved and it was defined with the assent of their Greek prelates that the Holy Spirit proceeds from the Father and the Son with a unique spiration as from one principle, not as from two principles.[65]

Somewhat in anger, FitzRalph cannot see how the Greeks can keep fighting against the truth. And if the Greeks complain that they should have been invited

---

63 Ibid.: 'Igitur si Graeci nos recte arguunt sententia praefata ligatos propter additionem non contrariam verbis definitis quam fecimus [1], nec ipsi se ipsos propter praetactas additiones et alias quamplures factas in posterioribus conciliis de ipsorum consensu excusare possunt'. [1] fecimus] facimus Ed.   64 Ibid. (Paris, fo. 42vb; Padova): 'Ante definitionem huius articuli per Latinos in Lateranensi Concilio sub Innocentio tertio circa annum Domini 1213, per multorum annorum curricula turba doctorum [1] sanctorum miraculis choruscantium tam Latinorum quam Graecorum, videlicet Hylarus [2], Ambrosius, Ieronimus, Augustinus [3], Gregorius, Anselmus, etiam Athanasius Graecus, Didimus Graecus, Cyrillus Graecus, et Iohannes Crisostomus Graecus hunc articulum de processione Spiritus Sancti a Filio in suis litteris plenissime et planissime affirmaverunt, nullo doctorum maiorum Graecorum aut Latinorum usque in illa tempora in aliqua terrarum suarum contrarium exprimente. Et ob hoc quod auctoritate successoris Principis Apostolorum Petri, videlicet Gregorii X, in quo ad definiendum ea quae fidem concernunt auctoritas residet'. [1] doctorum] dictorum Ed. | | [2] except for the first name, which is in the accusative, the edition has the list in the indicative, the Padova manuscript in the accusative, because of the awkward grammar. | | [3] Augustinus *om*. Ed.   65 Ibid.: 'Consequenter in Lugdunensi Concilio, praesentibus et consentientibus Germano patriarcha Graecorum et aliis praelatis eorum, definitio eiusdem articuli fuerat approbata, et quod Spiritus Sanctus unica spiratione tanquam ab uno principio, non tanquam a duobus principiis, procedit a Patre et Filio de eorum praelatorum Graecorum assensu fuerat definitum'.

to Lateran IV as in ancient times, that may be, but it makes no difference, since they were invited to Lyon II for this article of faith.[66] Parenthetically, some of FitzRalph's contemporaries claimed that the Greeks were angry because they were not invited to a 'nearby' council, without naming the council. I had guessed that they referred to the Council of Frankfurt of 794, since they usually placed the doctrinal split in Charlemagne's time.[67] Perhaps, however, they were completely confused and thought that there had been no Greek–Latin debate before the definition of Lateran IV. In any case, given FitzRalph's tone, it would have been interesting to be present when he first learned that the Greeks had long ago repudiated the agreement of Lyon II, especially if Barlaam himself was the bearer of the news.

Besides the general disagreement about where the stress should be, on the one essence or on the three hypostases, the Greeks' main theological difficulty with the *Filioque* was that 'it destroys the monarchy of the Father', to use John Meyendorff's words again.[68] In chapters ten and eleven, FitzRalph confronts quotations from the pseudo-Dionysius that assert that the Father is the only source or fountain of divinity, while John of Damascus appears to reject the *Filioque* explicitly. FitzRalph offers a benign interpretation of the pseudo-Dionysian passages, but as far as the Damascene is concerned, his first reaction is in keeping with what he had declared in the *Sentences* commentary: 'If this doctor asserted this, it would seem that he is to be rejected',[69] since his opinion is opposed by many Greek and Latin doctors, mainly the ones that FitzRalph had mentioned earlier. This is already a lighter 'sentence' than FitzRalph's charge of heresy in the *Sentences* commentary, however, and then he adds a further, traditional justification for John of Damascus' statement:

> But it does not seem to me that this doctor's intention was to deny this article entirely, but he only meant to deny that in his time or that of his Fathers it was among the articles of the faith defined by the Church or even explicitly handed down in the canonical scriptures.[70]

Indeed, FitzRalph continues, at that time it was not even defined by 'our Latin Church'.[71]

---

66 Ibid.: 'Et desistant amodo tam praeclaram veritatem et catholicam impugnare. Si vero dixerint quod, ut fieri solebat [1] per patres antiquitus, ad Lateranense Consilium vocari debebant, fateor, sed acceleratio definitionis ipsius articuli ad praecludendum viam diversis erroneis dogmatibus etiam difficultas forsitan tunc mittendi in Graeciam non permisit, et ob hoc, cum oportunitas vocationis eorum se obtulit, vocati fuerunt pro illo articulo et alio subtracto ad Concilium Lugdunense'. [1] fieri solebat] si cur solebant Ed. 67 Schabel, 'Attitudes towards the Greeks', pp 324–5. 68 Meyendorff, *Byzantine theology*, p. 92. 69 *Summa*, VI, c. 11 (Paris, fo. 43rb; Padova): 'Richardus: Si iste doctor sic asseruisset, videretur negandus'. 70 Ibid.: 'Verumtamen non mihi videtur intentionis istius doctoris fuisse articulum istum omnino negare, sed tantum negare intendit tempore suo aut patrum suorum ipsum fuisse de articulis fidei ab Ecclesia definitum aut etiam expresse traditum eis in Scriptura canonica'. 71 Ibid.: 'Insuper et

Having dealt with the potential Greek resistance to the *Filioque* on the basis of scriptural exegesis, patristic authority and conciliar tradition, FitzRalph has saved Barlaam's philosophical objections to the *Filioque* for last. Antonis Fyrigos has shown that Barlaam's anti-Latin treatises, formerly thought to number twenty-one separate works, actually constitute an early and somewhat brief *Syntagma* about four hundred lines in length, two versions of a much longer treatise, the more mature one being some 2,600 lines in the edition, and two short dialogues, all dating before Barlaam's contact with FitzRalph. With the exception of some remarks on the position of the pope, virtually all of this material deals directly with the *Filioque*, but the main arguments are found in the *Syntagma* and developed in the longer treatise.[72] There are a number of interesting aspects of Barlaam's treatises, not least the fact that he seems to have been the first Greek to react directly to Thomas Aquinas, even before the Dominican's works were translated into Greek. He firmly rejects Aquinas' claim that relative opposition of original is necessary for the distinction between the Son and the Holy Spirit. Although he argues, as many Franciscans accepted, that the different ways that the Son and Holy Spirit emanate from the Father are sufficient to distinguish between them, Barlaam attacks the claim popular among the Minorites that the divine attributes, will and intellect, help account for the Trinity. Not only are they interesting writings, but over fifty manuscripts preserve portions of these texts, so they were rather popular and presumably quite influential. In a volume dedicated to FitzRalph, our focus is rather narrow, but Barlaam's writings deserve more attention from historians of both the Latin and the Greek traditions.[73]

Popular as his anti-Latin treatises were, however, Barlaam was not necessarily the best source of information for Greek theology at the time.[74] In 1341, just two years after Barlaam's Avignon presentation, and before FitzRalph composed the *Summa*, Gregory Palamas engineered Barlaam's condemnation in Constantinople for his opposition to Hesychasm, in part for his view on the Holy Spirit. It is possible to interpret Byzantine doctrine on the Holy Spirit as having moved in the direction of the Latin position after the Second Council of Lyon, since most Byzantines now asserted that the Holy Spirit's 'eternal manifestation' is via the Son. Since the Greeks did not have this interpretation and Barlaam did not agree with this development, it need not detain us here. But Palamas also criticized

nostra Latina Ecclesia tunc fecit similiter, quia tunc non fuerat ab Ecclesia definitus ille articulus'.   72 See Fyrigos' introduction to Barlaam Calabro, *Opere contro i Latini*, i, esp. pp 11–28.
73 For the manuscripts, see Barlaam Calabro, *Opere contro i Latini*, i, pp 7–9. For explicit refutations of Thomas Aquinas, see, for example, Tractatus A IV, §§8–11 (II, pp 560–2); against the necessity of relative opposition (mainly associated with Dominicans), for example, Tractatus B, VI, §§27–37 (pp 436–42); for the different ways of coming from the Father, for example, Tractatus B, II, §§31–36 and VI, §§29–32 (pp 296–302, 436–8); against the utility of the will and intellect distinction (often employed by Franciscans), Tractatus B, VI, §§3–26 (pp 416–36).
74 Walsh, *A fourteenth-century scholar and primate*, p. 157, also points this out.

Barlaam for being too philosophical, too Aristotelian, in his theology – a charge that was levelled at the Latins also. Most Greek theologians took issue with the Latin's unauthorized addition to the Creed, their destruction of the Father's monarchy, their focus on relations and their failure to determine which biblical passages concerned the Holy Spirit's eternal procession and which applied to the temporal mission. In contrast, Barlaam's objections were more philosophical.[75]

The arguments FitzRalph cites as Barlaam's are found in both versions of the longer treatise, but this contains much material that FitzRalph would hardly have ignored had he had access to it. In contrast, some of what FitzRalph presents as Barlaam's is not in the *Syntagma*, yet the *Syntagma* too has a principle that FitzRalph should have taken into account: whatever the Son shares with the Father because of consubstantiality of essence (ομοούσιος), the Son must also share with the Holy Spirit; whatever one person of the Trinity does not share with any other person of the Trinity is an unshared personal property (χαρακτηριστικόν εστιν υποστάσεως).[76] If it is shared, it is essential; if it is not, it is personal. If the Father and the Son share active emanation, it is essential and the Holy Spirit should also share it; but since the Holy Spirit does not share active emanation, it is personal and belongs to only one of the hypostases. To Anselm's rule, Barlaam responds with his own.

It is thus unlikely that FitzRalph had access to any of Barlaam's extant writings, but he may have had a Latin summary of some sort. Chapter twelve of the *Summa* begins with John affirming his belief in the *Filioque* 'even if it were not defined by the Church', but feeling unable to respond to the objections of 'that doctor, the Greek abbot Barlaam'. John gives seven objections, but the last three are supposedly John's own, beginning, 'If I can object ...' (*Item, si possem obicere* ...), even if echoes are in Barlaam.[77] Only the first four are from Barlaam, and the fact that the arguments are presented 1, 2, 3 and 4, but refuted 1 and 2 together, then 4, and finally 3, suggests that FitzRalph may have had some sort of (now lost) text in mind.

According to John, Barlaam's main philosophical complaints are 'that we put in God a quaternity of persons and even that we reduce the Trinity to a duality of persons'. Before Lyon II, the Greeks had claimed that the *Filioque* entailed a 'double procession', so, as quoted above, at the council it was spelled out that the Father and Son together act as one principle, not two. In his writings, sometimes

---

75 For the new Byzantine view, see Papadakis, *Crisis in Byzantium*; Meyendorff, *Byzantine theology*, pp 93–4. For how the doctrine relates to the Latin position, see W. Duba, 'The afterlife in medieval Frankish Cyprus', Επετηρίδα του Κέντρου Επιστημονικών Ερευνών, 26 (2000), 167–94 at 175–8; G. Geréby, 'Hidden themes in fourteenth-century Byzantine and Latin theological debates: monarchianism and crypto-dyophysitism' in Hinterberger-Schabel, *Greeks, Latins and intellectual history*, pp 183–211. 76 *Syntagma*, §31 (Barlaam Calabro, *Opere contro i Latini*, II, p. 654). 77 *Syntagma*, §§33 (#6) and 37 (#5) (Barlaam Calabro, *Opere contro i Latini*, II, pp 656–60). The seventh simply claims that the *Filioque* is not explicitly in Scripture, often found in Barlaam.

Barlaam accuses the Latins of holding that the Holy Spirit has two principles or that the Holy Spirit emanates from the Father through or by way of (μέσον, διά του μέσου) the Son, suggesting ignorance of Lyon II.[78] In FitzRalph's *Summa*, however, Barlaam asserts that every single act in number is from one hypostasis in number, and yet spiration is not from any single of the three hypostases alone, therefore there is a fourth; second, if the Father and Son share active spiration, then they constitute one hypostasis, not two.[79] For these first two objections, FitzRalph simply denies the premise that unity of action in God must stem from one hypostasis, 'although it is otherwise with creatures'.[80]

Barlaam's third objection is that, because of the shared active spiration of the Father and the Son, the Latins posit a greater identity between the Father and the Son than between the Father and the Holy Spirit.[81] FitzRalph replies that this identity statement might apply where there is not already the 'highest identity', but not in God, where there is this highest identity 'among the three and between any two divine persons'. More forcefully, perhaps, FitzRalph adds that one could just as easily argue that there is a greater *convenientia* between the Son and Holy Spirit than between either of them and the Father on account of their having a principle and the Father having none.[82]

78 *Syntagma*, §27 (Barlaam Calabro, *Opere contro i Latini*, II, p. 652). 79 *Summa*, VI, c. 12 (Paris, fo. 43va; Padova): 'Iohannes: Quamvis huic articulo propter praemissa fidem perhiberem indubiam etiam si non esset ab Ecclesia definitus, non tamen est mihi in promptu quid ad motiva contraria quae obiciuntur respondeam. Ideo quaeso te ut ea plano sermone dissolvas, saltem sicut ipsa materia permittit, quae omnis creaturae mentem excedit. Obicit doctor ille Graecus abbas Barlaam quod nos ponimus in Deo quaternitatem personarum et etiam trinitatem ad [1] dualitatem personarum restringimus. De primo dicit sic [2]: omnis actio una numero est alicuius unius suppositi sive hypostasis numero, aliter enim actio non esset una numero. Spiratio ergo, cum sit actio una numero, est alicuius unius suppositi numero dumtaxat. Non Patris, nec Filii, nec Spiritus Sancti, secundum nos. Igitur est quartae [3] hypostasis. Item, ex eodem [4] medio, quod omnis actio una numero est alicuius suppositi sive hypostasis unius numero dumtaxat, cum hoc quod spiratio est communiter Patris et Filii, sequitur quod de Patre et Filio sit una hypostasis in numero, et sic in Deo non sunt nisi duae hypostases'. [1] ad] et Ed. (Walsh, *A fourteenth-century scholar and primate*, p. 152, includes this error, citing two Vatican manuscripts, n. 78) || [2] sic] sicut Ed. [3] quartae] esse alterius Ed. || [4] eodem] eo Ed. Cf. Barlaam, Tractatus B IV, §19 (#2); *Confutazione* (#2); Tractatus A II, §§7 (#2) and 8 (#1); *Syntagma*, §§32 (#2) and 33 (#1) (Barlaam Calabro, *Opere contro i Latini*, II, pp 362, 488, 534, 656). 80 *Summa*, VI, c. 13 (Paris, fo. 43vb; Padova): 'Primum et secundum te turbare non debent, quoniam unitas actionis in Deo non est minor propter pluralitatem hypostasum, licet in creaturis sit aliter, quia tanta unitas est Patris et Filii simul, licet sint duo supposita, quanta est unitas unius ipsorum ad se, cum sit summe unum, quod nusquam in creatis suppositis poterit inveniri. Unde non est verum ...'. 81 Ibid., c. 12 (Paris, fo. 43va; Padova): 'Item, dicit tertio quod nos ponimus maiorem identitatem inter Patrem et Filium quam inter Patrem et Spiritum Sanctum, quia propter identitatem essentialem quae aequalis est utrobique dicimus Filium cum Patre habere identitatem spirationis activae, quae non est communis Spiritui Sancto. Igitur secundum nos maior identitas [1] Patris cum Filio quam cum [2] Spiritu Sancto'. [1] communis ... identitas *om.* Ed. || [2] Filio quam cum *om.* Ed. Cf. Barlaam, Tractatus B IV, §§13–16, 18–19; Tractatus A II, §§3–5 (Barlaam Calabro, *Opere contro i Latini*, II, pp 356–8, 364, 530–2). 82 *Summa*, VI, c. 13 (Paris, fos 43vb–44ra; Padova): 'Pro tertio tibi constat quod convenientia sive identitas in relatione maiorem

Barlaam's final objection is that every single simple relation is between two hypostases alone, otherwise there would be an imbalance with more than one extreme on one end of the relation; since spiration is one simple relation between spirator and spirated, there is no room for a third hypostasis.[83] Again, FitzRalph answers that this may be true in creatures, but not in God. Besides, every relation between God and creature involves the three hypostases anyway, FitzRalph claims, so if the Greeks are correct, 'it would follow that God is not one in the supreme way, which no Christian, Jew or even Saracen would allow'.[84]

CONCLUSION

Unfortunately, we have no surviving reaction from Barlaam. He soon fell out with the Greeks and quickly accepted a Greek-rite bishopric from the pope. Perhaps he was required to accept the *Filioque*, in which case it would be ironic that his anti-*Filioque* writings became so popular and continued to be copied into the eighteenth century, but we shall probably never know.

Richard FitzRalph's *Sentences* commentary was by no means forgotten,[85] but it had nowhere near the circulation of the *Summa de quaestionibus Armenorum*. As with other such writings, like the anonymous Dominican tract *Contra graecos* composed in Latin Constantinople in 1252, FitzRalph's *Summa* became a classic partly as a result of the Council of Florence.[86] Of the almost forty manuscripts

identitatem non arguit nisi ubi non est summa identitas. Ubi autem est summa identitas, sicut est inter tres et quascunque duas divinas personas, nihil mundi identitatem potest maiorem arguere sicut convenientia in processione sive in essendo ab alio inter Filium et Spiritum Sanctum, quae non est inter Patrem et eorum aliquem [1], potest maiorem convenientiam inter se ad ipsos arguere quam ad Patrem. Uterque enim principaliter ab alio et Pater non, tamen omnes tres aeque conveniunt et aeque sunt idem'. [1] aliquem *om.* Ed.   83 Ibid., c. 12 (Paris, fo. 43va; Padova): 'Item, quarto dicit sic: omnis relatio una et [1] simplex suppositorum sive individuorum sive hypostasum est medium inter duo supposita vel inter duas hypostases dumtaxat. Aliter enim ex uno extremo illius relationis esset plures hypostases sive plura supposita quam ex alio extremo, et sic non est simplex unitas illius relationis, cum eius unitas et simplicitas sit ab extremis. Cum igitur spiratio sive relatio spirantis ad spiratum [2] qua ad invicem referuntur sit una simplex inter supposita divina sive divinas hypostases, sequitur quod ex neutro extremo habeat pluralitatem suppositorum sive hypostasum'. [1] et *om.* Ed. | | [2] spiratum] spiritum Ed. See Barlaam, Tractatus B IV, §8 (Barlaam Calabro, *Opere contro i Latini*, II, p. 352).   84 *Summa*, VI, c. 13 (Paris, fo. 43vb; Padova): 'Pariter dico ad quartum, scilicet quod pluralitas suppositorum in uno extremo ubi illa supposita sunt summe unum non amplius plurificat rationem mediam extremorum aut eius unitatem minuit quam unitas suppositi in altero relationis extremo, licet sic esse in creaturis non poterit reperiri. Alias enim relatio inter creatorem et creaturam non esset summe una ex parte creditoris, cum in illo extremo sint tria supposita, ex quo sequitur Deum non esse summe unum, quod nullus recipit Christianus, Iudeus, aut [1] etiam Saracenus'. [1] aut] ac Ed.   85 Even at the University of Paris it became a classic text: Walsh, *A fourteenth-century scholar and primate*, pp 61–3.   86 See A. Dondaine, '"Contra Graecos": premiers écrits polémiques des dominicains d'Orient', *Archivum Fratrum Praedicatorum*, 21 (1951), 320–446; Walsh, *A fourteenth-century scholar and primate*, pp 130–1 (noting that Juan de Torquemada OP

of the work, a number were either purchased or produced within the context of the council, when the Latins sought to accumulate arguments against the Greeks. Thus, FitzRalph's rather mild treatment of the Greeks in his *Sentences* commentary did not have as much impact as the concluding remarks in the chapters on the *Filioque* and papal primacy in the *Summa*. At the end of book VII, FitzRalph declares that whoever does not obey the Roman Pontiff incurs damnation and this even with respect to the form of conferring orders, the times and ages for receiving orders, observing fasts, the separation of the people from the clergy and the priest celebrating in the church, following the correct forms of the various masses, even having *studia* of theology and everything else of this sort.[87] Since this applies as much to the Armenians as to the Greeks, I add the words FitzRalph had to say concerning the Modern Greeks – as opposed to the wise fathers, who, according to FitzRalph, were not stupid – in his own conclusion to book VI, on the *Filioque*:

> Is it clear from these things that this procession of the Holy Spirit follows from scripture expressly, evidently and by unbreakable argument. Nor on the whole do I think that this evidence is unknown to the Greeks at present, although it was unknown to them and to us before the holy doctors labored for a very long time concerning this to express or extract this evidence from various scriptural passages. That at the present time the Greeks pretend to deny this article [of faith] is either the obstinacy of someone who shuts his eyes or an invention of the mouth against the judgment of the mind and contrary to the glory of the [superior] wisdom that they used to have over the Latins in ancient times, which they seem to be losing and to have lost up until now.[88]

Historians will never be certain about the cause of the *Filioque* quarrel. One can easily argue that acceptance or rejection of the *Filioque* depended on deeply rooted theological differences between Greek and Latin Christendom that were already manifest in the writings of the church fathers in the fourth and fifth

owned a copy), 469–75. 87 *Summa* VII, c. 26 (Paris, fo. 52rb): 'Constat autem eos qui in mandatis licitis et honestis non obediunt Romano pontifici primati totius Ecclesiae Romanae damnationem incurrere, et sic quo ad formam conferendi ordines, quo ad tempora, quo ad aetatem ordinandorum, insuper quo ad ieiunia observanda, et quo ad separationem populi a clero et sacerdote celebrante in ecclesia, quo ad formam missarum et distinctionem ipsarum, quo ad studia theologiae habenda, et quo ad unitatem patriarchae sui, et cuncta similia'. 88 Ibid., c. 13 (Paris, fo. 44rb; Padova): 'Ex quibus patuit quod haec processio Spiritus Sancti expresse et evidenter ac infrangibili ratione sequitur ex Scriptura. Nec puto ex toto hanc evidentiam Graecos in praesenti latere, licet latuerit suos et nostros antequam sancti doctores circa hanc evidentiam exprimendam sive extrahendam ex variis Scripturae particulis [1] diligentius laboraverunt. Quod autem in praesenti hunc articulum Graeci se negare praetendunt aut est pertinacia excaecantis aut fictio oris contra mentis iudicium et gloriam sapientiae quam supra Latinos habebant antiquitus, quam amittere videantur et hactenus amisisse'. [1] particulis] titulis Ed.

centuries. Yet, one could also make a claim that, under different circumstances, the *Filioque* could have arisen as a Greek addition later rejected or perhaps accepted by the papacy and Latin theology. In any case, in the second millennium, the lines were already drawn. Ignorant of the details of the doctrinal proclamation of Lyon II, in his anti-Latin treatises Barlaam the Calabrian attacked the Latins for their 'double procession'. Ignorant of the Greeks' repudiation of Lyon II, in his Oxford *Sentences* commentary Richard FitzRalph felt safe within an internal Latin debate to make certain statements that would have weakened his arguments had he repeated them in his *Summa*. At the same time, in the *Sentences* commentary FitzRalph condemned as heresy what, unbeknownst to him, the Greeks really believed. In the *Summa*, FitzRalph did not himself change his mind about the *Filioque* of course, although both his reasoning and his responses to Barlaam had changed: the Greeks are wrong, FitzRalph asserts, but he avoids accusing them of heresy. No longer ignorant, FitzRalph and Barlaam still continued to adhere to the party lines. It is difficult to see how either side would have given in without outside pressure, and this impression remains today.

Reputation and aftermath

Richard FitzRalph and John Wyclif: untangling Armachanus from the Wycliffites

STEPHEN LAHEY

There is a long history of connection between Archbishop Richard FitzRalph and Wycliffism. Wyclif himself is responsible for this; his theological outlook led him to cite relatively few scholastics as authoritative positions. His allegiance was to the theology of the twelfth century rather than that of the period of Aristotelian synthesis and his writings are interlarded with admiring references to Anselm, the Victorines, Bernard and most especially Robert Grosseteste, his intellectual *beau idéal*.[1] Aquinas receives frequent praise, but later thinkers almost none. The two exceptions are Thomas Bradwardine and FitzRalph; Bradwardine's *De causa Dei*, a compendium of arguments directed against Ockhamist theology of divine foreknowledge and the relation of grace and merit, had a tremendous impact on early fourteenth-century Oxford. Bradwardine's position occasionally teetered on the precipice of an excessive determinism, although the haphazard structure of *De causa Dei* does not make it simple for contemporary readers to map out the details. What was clear was Bradwardine's dedication to a conservative theological ideal in determined opposition to Ockhamism and likely to Thomism and Scotism as well. Richard FitzRalph had acquired a similar reputation by virtue of his celebrated defence of the traditional Latin church against the Greeks, the Jews and the Muslims in *Summa quaestionibus Armenorum*, and his subsequent vigorous opposition to the friars in *De pauperie salvatoris*. By the time Wyclif entered Oxford in the 1350s, both had acquired reputations as defenders of old-fashioned Latin orthodoxy in the face of threats from without and within. It did not hurt that both had attained archiepiscopal rank, even if Bradwardine enjoyed it for only a month.[2]

Wyclif's enthusiasm for FitzRalph was not an eccentricity; Armachanus enjoyed a particularly strong reputation among secular scholars through the 1360s and '70s, a fact that certainly aided Wyclif in the controversy that arose

[1] See R.W. Southern, *Robert Grosseteste: the growth of an English mind in medieval Europe* (Oxford, 1986), pp 298–309. [2] See J.A. Robson, *Wyclif and the Oxford schools* (Cambridge, 1966); William Courtenay, *Schools and scholars in fourteenth-century England* (Princeton, 1987); Heiko Oberman, *Archbishop Thomas Bradwardine: a fourteenth-century Augustinian* (Utrecht, 1958). For a fuller bibliography on Oxford in the fourteenth century, see my *John Wyclif* (Oxford, 2009). See also Michael Dunne, 'Richard FitzRalph's *Lectura* on the *Sentences*' in Phillip Rosemann (ed.), *Medieval commentaries on the sentences of Peter Lombard* (Leiden, 2010), pp 405–38 for an updated bibliography on FitzRalph's thought.

over his *De civili dominio* in the mid-1370s. It is not difficult to imagine secular scholars, particularly the younger ones who already had begun to refer to their champion as 'Doctor Evangelicus', delighting in the friars' rage at the reappearance of FitzRalph's *De pauperie* in a new, politically incendiary avatar. FitzRalph may have used his theory to combat the friars, but Wyclif used it to attack the pope as well. Nicholas Hereford, an influential early disciple of Wyclif, commented in a sermon on Ascension Day 1382 that just as Christ's work had a greater effect after his ascension, so FitzRalph's writings against the friars were having a greater effect now than when they had been written.[3] It is difficult to trace the beginnings of vernacular Wycliffism and most scholars agree that it is impossible to determine which of the early Wycliffite writings, if any, are the work of Wyclif himself.[4] Still, by 1389 FitzRalph had become firmly associated with the Wycliffite movement, as evidenced by the Apocalypse commentary known as *Opus arduum*. Here, both Grosseteste and FitzRalph are referred to as worthy of beatification but because their writings fail to correspond to the present biases of the curia, the faithful can expect no immediate movement towards sainthood for either.[5] Still, there was no harm in holding forth hope. In one tract, the argument is against the friars' tendency to keep the holy books from the people and the clergy, for 'as seynt Richard primat of irland witnesseþ, þei casten to distroie clergie of seculeris and trewe techynge of þe peple'.[6] It is important to remember, though, that not all cases of FitzRalph celebration in late fourteenth-century Oxford were necessarily Wycliffite. John Trevisa, a contemporary of Wyclif's, translated FitzRalph's *Defensio curatorum*, the famous sermon delivered at Avignon in the 1350s. His motives were not necessarily Wycliffite, even if they were distinctly antimendicant.[7]

A DIALOGUE BETWEEN JON AND RICHARD

Conversely, not all instances of FitzRalph name-dropping in Wycliffite literature are evidence of Fitzrovian thought. The dialogue, whether in Latin or English, was a popular genre for fraternal and antifraternal dispute and three examples remain in the vernacular Wycliffite tradition: the Upland series ('Jack Upland', 'Friar Daw's Reply' and 'Upland's Rejoinder'), 'Piers the Plowman's Crede' and 'Dialogue between Jon and Richard'. The latter dialogue is especially relevant

---

3 Anne Hudson, *The premature reformation* (Oxford, 1986), pp 70–1.   4 See ibid., ch. 2, 'The establishment of the Wycliffite movement', pp 60–120; also her *Studies in the transmission of Wyclif's writings* (Farnham, Surrey, 2008) for a valuable collection of Prof. Hudson's post-1991 work on the relation of Wyclif to the beginnings of Lollardy and Hussite thought.   5 Anne Hudson, 'A neglected Wycliffite text' in *Lollards and their books* (London, 1985), p. 49.   6 F.D. Matthew (ed.), *The English works of Wyclif*, Early English Text Society O.S.74, 2nd ed. (1902), 'Of clerks possessioners', p. 128.   7 David C. Fowler, *The life and times of John Trevisa, medieval scholar* (Seattle, WA, 1995), p. 228.

here because of its obvious allusion to FitzRalph, who used these two names for his interlocutors in both *Summa quaestionibus Armenorum* [*SCA*] and *De pauperie salvatoris* [*DPS*]. This dialogue is rich in Wycliffite ideals: the gospels provide the basis for the law of Christ, the perfect morality for any Christian; human reason allows any man, whether Jew, Christian or pagan, to assess papal claims of authority; popes who live in poverty and turn from the riches of this world are worthy, while those who embrace this world are antichrist.

The chief aim of the dialogue is criticism of the friars and it is helpful to follow the conversation to understand the difference between FitzRalph and Wyclif. In FitzRalph's dialogues, Jon is the student and Richard is the master. Here, the roles are reversed. Richard begins by suggesting that the friars truly follow Christ by being poor, chaste and obedient, to which Jon responds that their rule is manmade and not from Christ. Given that they rely more on the pope than the founders of their rule, he continues, they may as well be considered followers of the pope rather than Francis or Dominic. What good is giving up worldly goods if there is no poverty of spirit involved? If they imagine themselves to be following Christ, surely they are leading him with their fine chapter houses, the excesses of their order and the identification of their religion with habits and other such affectat. Richard counters: but surely the friars do more than other Christians do? Jon scoffs at this: if Christ was meek, should not the friars be even meeker than he? Ask anyone who has been critical of them whether the friars are gentle to those who criticize them! The friars preach the gospel though, Richard continues, which elevates them above the average Christian layman. Jon admits that maybe the friars do manage to do some good work, 'but not so miche as fendes and damned men'.[8] Lazy secular priests make it possible for the friars to do any good; if they were to actually do what they should, the friars would be without any purpose whatsoever, superfluous as butterflies. Their preaching is really only in hopes of receiving material payment and is full of 'enuey, and sclander and of bacbytynge' [486]. When they take on the duties of priests by hearing confession and offering absolution, they downplay contrition and penance and emphasize their own powers. The requirement that the faithful should confess only to a priest is one of the better papal ordinances, even if Christ can forgive sins without priestly intercession. It would have been better had 'schrifte' not been instituted, but now that it is a sacrament it should be in the hands of priests alone.

Do the friars please God in building churches? If the friars had no churches, but instead occupied themselves with preaching the gospel anywhere, they would do more good, Jon suggests. As to the ornaments and decorations they provide in churches, 'orrnamentis of vertues in a mannes soule ben more preciouse þan ournamentis of bodi' [752]. As to keeping God's law, it seems that

---

8 Fiona Somerset (ed.), *Four Wycliffite dialogues* (Oxford, 2009), p. 15.447.

they are more wedded to their own order's rule and divorced from God's ordinances: 'but nowe a frere may trespas aʒens Goddis lawe as myche as he wole and be not clepid apostate ... But for a litel trespas aʒens þis clouted beggar [Francis] he schal be prisouned and defamed as he hadde killed Crist!' [785]. Richard asks why friars do not love their rule as other men love their wives, which gives Jon the chance to discourse on the right ordering for all human love. All things on earth should be loved as they pertain to God: 'if þou loue any wordley þing, loue it in God, þat is to sei, in þat ordre and mesure þat it helpeth to loue þi God more' [844]. It is perfectly understandable that friars attempt to place their rule above God's, since this is the fallen human nature; far better, then, simply to cast aside anything that is not God's as useless: 'God hath ʒeuen a sufficient reule, as oure feith techiþ, þat is more liʒt and more fre to iche Cristen man to holde' [876]. The teachings of Francis, Dominic and Bernard add nothing to the rule that is the wellspring of their own moral purity: 'but soþli alle þese sectis ben damnpnable foles, siþen a reule of Christ sufficed for hem alle, and God axit of hem keping of þt reule, as he axiþ of us, and þer wille excueþ not' [891].

Richard has one more argument in his quiver. If God's law is all that man needs, what is the use of any human law? Of obedience to a prelate? Of the Salisbury rite, or papal command? Jon responds that he is certainly not suggesting the overthrow of human authority:

> men schulde obeische to alle men and more to þe pope, but for him do not but þat God biddeþ. And so to alle prelatis schulde we obeysche as to ministeries of God or to Goddes seruantis. If any man biddeþ þee do contrarie to Godes law, fle þat as venym siþen ʒow art Goddes seruantis [945]

Grosseteste provides a fine example of this, rendering due obedience to his pope, except for when he was asked to do what he knew ran afoul of God's law.[9] This is particularly true with obedience to secular lords; if a secular priest somehow commands what is counter to God's law, or prevents its implementation: 'stonde stifly in wille to suffering of deþ' [978]. It would be a very good thing indeed for secular lords to ask friars to prove that Christ begged as they do and to force them to stick to Gospel values as other Christians do. Priests would likewise do well to police the friars' teachings and prevent the faithful from giving them alms [1025].

The friars were a favourite subject for Wycliffite preaching and polemics and this dialogue appears typical in its catalogue of arguments against the fraternal

---

9 Reference is likely to Grosseteste's 1253 refusal to confer a benefice in Lincoln on a nephew of the pope. See James McEvoy, *Robert Grosseteste* (Oxford, 2000), p. 47.

orders.[10] The friars rightly emphasize poverty, but their abuses and their insistence on placing their own rule before that of Scripture defeat their purpose. The emphasis is on the precedence of God's law to fraternal rules and points to the generally antisectarian nature of Wyclif's thought. Whether it is indicative of a Fitzrovian influence is a different matter altogether. The use of Jon and Richard may be simply tribute to 'Seint Richard', or an attempt to convince less educated Lollards of FitzRalph's precedence. Whatever the case, the dialogue provides a useful example of the differences between Wyclif's criticisms and FitzRalph's, as will become evident.

THOMAS NETTER AND THE HERETICIZATION OF FITZRALPH

The revival of interest in orthodox theology at Oxford did not end with Wyclif; indeed, orthodoxy so came to define post-Wyclif Oxford as to preclude innovation altogether.[11] Thomas Netter of Walden was the Carmelite friar at the forefront of the reaction to Wycliffism in the early fifteenth century. At the command of Henry VI in 1426, Netter assembled the *Doctrinale*, a three-volume compendium of all the errors associated with Wyclif and Wycliffism, including its Bohemian variant, the Hussite movement.[12] The first volume of *Doctrinale* addresses Wyclif's philosophical errors as they appeared in the *Summa de ente*, while the second and third are concerned with the theological errors that define Wycliffism: the errors regarding eucharist, the papacy, the other sacraments, holy orders and the relation of church to secular power each receive a detailed and vigorous refutation grounded in Scripture, the fathers and the canon law tradition. Like Wyclif, though, Netter rarely refers to more recent schoolmen in his arguments; the weight of ancient authority appears sufficient to smother the flames of heresy.

FitzRalph figures as an unwitting accomplice to Wyclif for Netter. In places, his errors are taken up and magnified by Wyclif and in others Wyclif departs from them in favour of even greater ones. Examples of the latter can be found in Netter's refutation of Wyclif's confusion about the sacraments. FitzRalph erroneously claims that the Armenians embrace confirmation in the way that the

---

10 See Pamela Gradon and Anne Hudson (eds), *English Wycliffite sermons* (Oxford, 1996), 4, pp 121–45, for an overview of Wycliffite antisectarian and antifraternal literature. 11 See Jeremy Catto, 'Oxford after Wyclif' in *The history of the University of Oxford: 2, late medieval Oxford* (Oxford, 1992). 12 The eighteenth-century edition of this remains the standard; see *Thomae Waldensis Carmelitae Anglici Doctrinale antiquitatum fidei catholicae ecclesiae*, B. Blancotti (ed.) (3 vols, Venice, 1757–9). For Netter, see Johan Bergstrom-Allen & Richard Copsey (eds), *Thomas Netter of Walden: Carmel in Britain, 4* (British Province of Carmelites, 2009). See also Robson, *Wyclif*, pp 231–46. An important recent publication is Kevin J. Alban, *The teaching and impact of the 'Doctrinale' of Thomas Netter of Walden (c.1374–1430)* (Turnhout, 2010).

Roman church does and mistakenly interprets the biblical account of Ananias having laid hands on Paul as meaning that lower orders may confirm the faithful. Again, he argues that the apostles did not receive the power of forgiving sins after the resurrection, but at the formation of the Apostolate at Pentecost. These may be erroneous positions but surely they are better than Wyclif's rejection of the two sacraments![13]

Netter reports Wyclif as having claimed that the only order of clergy truly necessary is simple priests, who should be able to ordain one another as necessary. FitzRalph, he continues, knew better, but argued very harmfully using biblical precedent in the *Summa de quaestionibus Armenorum* book eleven, in such a way as to have misled Wyclif. Armachanus cites Old Testament precedent in the Aaronic priesthood of lesser priests offering sacrifices on behalf of ailing high priests, which seems to allow him to say that deacons can do the work of priests in time of need. He can be read, Netter continues, as having envisioned deacons celebrating mass, forgiving sins and other priestly offices; small wonder that Wyclif would conclude that bishops are not really necessary! Within several sentences, Netter drops all pretense of following the argument in the *Armenian questions* and assumes Armachanus as having truly believed that ordained powers are equal:

> the powers of the ordained are equal, and only the restrictions of reason have led to the reduction of the execution of power and jurisdictive authority; there would not remain such which reasonably could so restrict without a superior Pontifex; therefore, the common law of God makes it suitable for inferior priests to carry out their assigned ministry.[14]

FitzRalph is receiving an exceptionally harsh reading here, assuming that Netter is reading *Summa de quaestionibus Armenorum* book eleven, chapter seven, in which FitzRalph explores the relation of Dionysius' reasoning in *De [ecclesiastica] hierarchia* to scriptural precedent. FitzRalph admits that, if somehow all bishops died, lesser priests could conceivably ordain one from their number to be a bishop. Further, understanding the scriptural precedent for Episcopal powers of consecration and ordination might be a case of recognizing that bishops accept these sacred powers just as other holy people have done in the church, in which case it is legitimate to restrict these actions to bishops as expressed in holy writ. Armachanus hastily adds that he could well be wrong about this and he is, as always, open to correction. This is a long way from the position that all ordained power is essentially the same thing.

Netter then uses FitzRalph to refute Wyclif's position that the Episcopal

---

13 See *Doctrinale*, 1, cols 670, 803. See also Christopher O'Donnell, 'A controversy on confirmation: Thomas Netter of Walden and Wyclif' in Bergstrom-Allen & Copsey (eds), *Thomas Netter of Walden*. 14 *Doctrinale*, 3, cols 382–92.

office is unnecessary because it is extra-biblical, with an interesting critique of the two erring theologians' use of Scripture as an authority. FitzRalph is represented as suspecting that the power of ordination and consecrating churches is restricted to bishops simply because of scriptural precedent, without a real theological foundation. It is no wonder that Wyclif's approach, which is to limit authority to Scripture and living reason alone, would lead him to dismiss the need for bishops and higher orders altogether: 'Wyclif surpasses Richard in liberality, because he would give assent to reason beyond Scripture, while Richard admits only to what Scripture brings ... and thus whatever would be the law of God that is not written in the book by the Evangelists is condemned by both'.[15] The topic of FitzRalph and Wyclif on Scriptural authority will receive a fuller exploration below, wherein the accuracy of Netter's unfriendly assessment will be apparent.

The two areas where one might expect a wealth of connections between FitzRalph and Wyclif are in the arguments against the mendicants and the arguments regarding just dominion. Curiously, Netter avoids connecting the two thinkers in both instances. In Netter's refutation of Wyclif's arguments regarding grace as a necessary condition for just civil dominion, FitzRalph is never mentioned. And in his much longer analysis of Wyclif's antimendicancy, William of St Amour plays the role of Wyclif's mentor, with FitzRalph receiving a brief mention at the beginning of the section and making a brief appearance at the end: 'I do not doubt that they sin wildly, this first author Armoraeorum and his son Richard Armachanus, and third, the damnable Wyclif, against grammar in their perverse interpretation of vocabulary, but much more do they do so against the Catholic faith of the mendicancy of our Lord Jesus Christ'.[16] That Wyclif and FitzRalph disagree regarding Christ's mendicancy and that Wyclif mines *De pauperie salvatoris* for many of his arguments receives nary a mention. Netter's relationship to William Woodford OFM, Wyclif's opponent and the author of *De dominio civili clericorum*, the initial response to Wyclif's dominion theory, has been a matter of disagreement for scholars. Until recently, the assumption was that Woodford's death in 1397 pre-dated Netter's years at Oxford, but recently Richard Copsey has suggested that the two may have become acquainted in London.[17] It is possible that Netter's relatively brief treatment of the dominion issue can be explained by his having believed that Woodford had done enough to refute the position already.

Whatever the case, the association between FitzRalph and Wyclif had been made by the forces determined to stamp out Wycliffism. It had become so firm as to allow Cardinal Robert Bellarmine to condemn Armachanus for an association he doubtless would have been astonished to learn that he had made. Bellarmine describes FitzRalph in his catalogue of late medieval theologians:

---

15 Ibid., col. 392. 16 Ibid., 1, col. 825. 17 Richard Copsey, *Thomas Netter of Walden: a biography*, in Bergstrom-Allen & Copsey, *Thomas Netter of Walden: Carmel in Britain, 4*, p. 31.

> Richard Radulfus, chancellor of Oxford Academy in England and Irish archbishop, commonly called Armachanus, died in the year 1359, whose books should be read with caution, he sinned in many things, they have been written from him by many in many places and swallowed by John Wyclif and by his followers Jan Hus and Jerome of Prague, who were condemned at the Council of Constance.[18]

Katherine Walsh commented that the availability of the Wycliffite corpus made possible in the past century has helped to propagate this distortion and suggested that a critical study of Wyclif's debt to FitzRalph in relation to his debts to Bradwardine, Ockham and Wodeham would certainly help to redress matters.[19] In what follows, I will attempt to pick up Prof. Walsh's gauntlet, both to continue in her own work of clearing FitzRalph of a reputation he likely would have regarded with horror and to help in my own project of understanding Wycliffism as Wyclif himself seems to have envisioned it. Rather than survey the whole of Wyclif's thought, I will direct attention to three areas in which the connections seem to be the strongest: use of the Bible, grace-founded dominion and antimendicancy. While FitzRalph appears occasionally as a respected authority in numerous works of Wyclif, it is in these three areas that his reputation is most associated with Wycliffism. This reputation has been fostered most recently in Malcolm Lambert's study of medieval heresy, where FitzRalph's arguments elide gracefully into Wyclif's. Describing the Aegiddian argument of grace and dominion, Lambert has FitzRalph turning the argument

> against the friars, his *bêtes noirs*, by arguing more generally that all rights of authority and possession derived from God, and were thus dependent upon the holder being in a state of grace; the friars, who were not, thus did not justly exercise the rights which they held within the Church. Wyclif simply took over this argument ...[20]

Much rests on the offhand comment that FitzRalph supposed the friars not to have been in a state of grace. Had he thought this, it would have been easy for Wyclif simply to lift the argument from Armachanus and substitute 'the Caesarian clergy' for 'the friars'. This would make Wyclif's opposition to the friars appear to be a part of his overall opposition to clerical excess. But Wyclif's

---

[18] Robertus Bellarminus, *De scriptoribus ecclesiasticus*, ed. P.Labbé (Paris, 1660): 'Ricardus Radulfus, Oxoniensis Academiae in Anglio Cancellarius ab Archiepiscopatu Hibernico dictus vulgo Armachanus, obiit anno 1359 cuius libri caute legend, in pluribus enim peccavit, multosque ut plerique scripserunt, errors ab eo Iohannes Wiclefus, quique eum sequuti sunt Iohannes Hus et Hieronymus Pragensis in Concilio Constantiensi damnati, hauserunt', p. 290.   [19] Katherine Walsh, *A fourteenth-century scholar and primate: Richard FitzRalph in Oxford, Avignon and Armagh* (Oxford, 1981), p. 465.   [20] Malcolm Lambert, *Medieval heresy* (3rd ed., Oxford, 2002), p. 259.

opposition to the friars is nothing like FitzRalph's; in fact, the two positions are so thoroughly different as to bear only passing resemblance to one another.

Demonstrating this dissimilarity entails analysis of the two theologians' respective understanding of the authority of Scripture in addressing the friars, because both relied on it almost to the exclusion of all other authorities in making their arguments. The only exceptions to this are the relevant papal bulls having to do with the friars, which receive some mention in both, although less attention in Wyclif. This is relevant to the argument not because we need to consider the two as interpreters of papal ruling: for FitzRalph, they have a much more solid foundation as authoritative than they do for Wyclif, as will become clear below. We will make brief mention of the theory of grace and dominion, which Wyclif did indeed develop from FitzRalph's thought, but given my earlier comparison of the two versions of the theory elsewhere, this will only be to show how FitzRalph used it to limit fraternal privilege and that Wyclif used it only as the beginning point for a very different argument against the friars.[21] This will allow contrasting the two theologians' arguments against the friars, with the aim of demonstrating that FitzRalph's arguments are as similar to Wyclif's as chalk is to cheese.

THE AUTHORITY OF SCRIPTURE

Before exploring the relation of FitzRalph to Wyclif regarding the friars, it is important to contrast their differing understandings of the nature of biblical authority. Both theologians are notable for basing their arguments against the friars almost exclusively on Scripture. Both make reference to the papal bulls establishing and challenging the friars, but their arguments rest in general on Scripture and not on the precedence of church fathers, doctors or glossators. Alistair Minnis argued that the two theologians had notably different understandings of how the Bible's teachings were to be understood and established that the two uses of its authority were sufficiently unlike as to require differentiation in understanding the hermeneutic theory of the Lollard Bible prologue.[22] The difference lies in their understanding of the ontology of Scripture: Wyclif believed the physical Bible to be the final iteration of a universal the primary reality of which lies in God's eternal understanding, while FitzRalph had the more mundane view that it is a divinely inspired book written by men.[23] Both tended towards a very conservative hermeneutical stance, denying any inherent

---

[21] Stephen Lahey, *Metaphysics and politics in the thought of John Wyclif* (Cambridge, 2003). [22] A.J. Minnis, '"Authorial intention" and "literal sense" in the exegetical theories of Richard FitzRalph and John Wyclif: an essay in the medieval history of biblical hermeneutics', *Proceedings of the Royal Irish Academy*, 75 (Mar. 1975). [23] See also Ian C. Levy, *John Wyclif: scriptural logic, real presence and the parameters of orthodoxy* (Milwaukee, WI, 2003), pp 81–122.

ambiguity and downplaying the emphasis of allegory above the 'literal sense' of the letter, in effect championing a 'strict constructionist' reading of Scripture. Until the coming of Ockhamism, the emphasis had always been on the force of tradition and the reliability of the fathers as hermeneutic guides. Minnis describes Ockham's logical analysis of Scripture as text bound to the intention of the author as challenging this older method and FitzRalph understood himself to be at the forefront of the older method's defence.[24] FitzRalph understood Scripture as unencumbered by the four layers of meaning traditionally studied by masters of the sacred page and argued for two literal senses: what the author intended in relating the content and, where necessary, what the Holy Ghost intended the place of the content to be in the greater scheme of revealed truth.[25] Wyclif followed FitzRalph's emphasis on the need for grace in the right understanding of Scripture, but the degree to which grace exceeds every other means by which to understand it is much higher. Wyclif argued that the author of Scripture is unmediatedly divine and that grace is absolutely necessary for understanding the divinely intended sense inherent as primary in the text; it connects the reader to the eternal understanding that contains Scripture's archetype. The difference between the two thinkers then rests on two points: the nature of Scripture as crafted by man or by God and the extent to which grace is necessary for understanding it.

But what gives Scripture its primary authority? On the face of it, this might seem a moot question for a discussion of medieval theology; the Bible was taken to be the bedrock authority by all medieval theologians, whatever their other disagreements might have been. But the difference between FitzRalph and Wyclif on the basis for scriptural authority lies at the heart of their respective responses to the friars. FitzRalph's more conventional approach led him to what one scholar has characterized as a *de facto* defence of the Spiritual Franciscan ideals, while Wyclif's understanding led him to attack not only the friars, but any species of man-made division or sect within the church.[26]

The place to begin for FitzRalph is *Summa de quaestionibus Armenorum* eighteen. Here, he examines the nature and structure of Scripture's authority as it holds between the Old and New Testaments and in relation to other ecclesiastical authorities in preparation for his analysis of the authority of Qu'ran. It makes no difference who is the author of a given book of Scripture, because the ultimate author of any one of its books is God. Moses is frequently thought to be the author of Pentateuch, but he is only the mediate author. We find Christ citing Pentateuch in the gospels, which points to the divine authority underlying the books of Moses. Peter, Paul and other apostles all cite the law of Moses,

---

24 FitzRalph was not alone here; Bradwardine also represented a conservative reaction to this new approach. See *De causa Dei* II.31, pp 601–10. 25 See *Summa de quaestionibus Armenorum* I.3. 26 James Doyne Dawson, 'Richard FitzRalph and the fourteenth-century poverty controversies', *Journal of Ecclesiastical History*, 34:3 (July 1983).

emphasizing this authority. The authority of the New Testament does not cancel out that of the Old; the ties between the two canons all show the intrinsic cohesiveness of the whole of the Bible. As a result, a Christian can justly use any book of the Old Testament in arguing with a Muslim, for 'they [the books] have spread as the Jews have spread, and are likely to be known throughout the world' [c.6]. The Muslim law certainly cites Jewish law with approval. Regarding the canonicity of the accepted New Testament, the decretal of the church has established this sufficiently for anyone's purposes.

So far, we have a fairly circular argument for Scripture's authority: the whole of the Bible's authority is based in the authority of the New Testament and its appropriation of the Old. Those wishing for arguments for the New Testament's authority should turn to the legislation of the church, the ongoing human participation in the historical events described in the New Testament. FitzRalph recognizes this and describes competing authorities, whether they are Jewish, Saracen, Tartar or gentile, as likely to have doubts [c.8]. Is there sufficient reason available to make the New Testament canon authoritative in the face of the denials of non-Christians? 1 Peter 3:13-14 provides the basis for a response:

> I admit that it seems to me that Peter understands that we should be prepared to give a reason about our faith and hope to all men who desire it, just as it appears to me that you should prudently add the decretal of the church, whether it be to the universal Christian church beyond [Rome] or indeed for Christian teaching to those seeking the reason of the authority of our scripture, or why the faith is not able to be sufficient ... [c.8]

And if the command of the church is not enough, the merit of acquiescence to authority, as suggested in 1 Peter 3, should tip the balance. Anyone living under any species of God's law, indeed, any legal system whatsoever, should see the force of this argument.

FitzRalph is unable to surpass the circularity of his approach and the reader will not be much surprised to find his critique of Qu'ran assuming the shape of a comparison and contrast with the New Testament. What is of value in Qu'ran is what comes into it from the New Testament, whether directly or indirectly, and all else is dross. The juridical authority of the New Testament, and the Old Testament thereby, appears axiomatic in the *Armenian questions*.[27] Katherine Walsh makes note of this, emphasizing FitzRalph's willingness to engage in ecumenical or interreligious dialogue.[28]

27 Book 19 of the *Armenian questions* continues with a similar analysis in discussion of the nature of the literal sense in observing the law.   28 Katherine Walsh, 'Preaching, pastoral care and *Sola Scriptura* in later medieval Ireland: Richard FitzRalph and the use of the Bible', *Studies in Church History*, Subsidia, 4 (1985), 251-68.

FitzRalph's grace-based dominion theory provides a way past this apparent impasse by referring back to the prelapsarian state and the need for juridical authority there. In *Armenian questions* book eight he begins his description. We were created just initially and reason was sufficient to regulate behaviour, both in our loving relations with one another and with God; this was the basis for prelapsarian justice. We would not have been placed as custodians of Paradise had we not been wise and just, nor would God have given us commands had we not had some conception of right and wrong. It is this to which Hosea refers when he speaks for God, saying, 'I was like a foster-father of Ephraim, I carried them in my arms, and they knew not that I healed them; I will draw them with the cords of Adam, with the bands of love' [Hos 11:3–4]. The gifts of the Spirit, of wisdom, justice and love were ours there as an inheritance, and all that we did was according to that law of life. With sin, all of this was lost and it is only through grace that these gifts, which are necessary for justice and just legislation, can be recovered.[29] In *De pauperie salvatoris*, written two decades after his *Summa*, he takes up the question of just *iurisdictio*, this time beginning with Sirach 15:14–18 ('God made man from the beginning, and left him in the hand of his own counsel. 15 He added his commandments and precepts. 16 If you will keep the commandments and perform acceptable fidelity for ever, they shall preserve you. 17 He has set water and fire before you: stretch forth your hand to which you will. 18 Before man is life and death, good and evil, that which he shall choose shall be given him'). FitzRalph reasons that we were so constituted by God that, by keeping his commandments, everlasting life will be the natural result. This we cannot do without grace. Again, FitzRalph cites Hosea 11:3–4 and as he had earlier, he discusses the 'band of love' binding Adam to God. The initial band uniting Adam to God may have been a band of love, but sin has severed this for the species. Better to understand Hosea to be speaking of the connection of Christ to Mary, or the tie between Jeremiah or John the Baptist, or other prophets, to God. This, he recognizes, is evidence of grace; grace connected Adam to God in Eden and this same grace was the basis for Edenic human dominion. Adam lost this through sin and in so doing 'he lost all the virtues that he had by his delinquency, and his rational soul as well, condemning him to eternal death …'[30] Not all grace was taken though; we retained control over our physical body and sufficient grace remained in us whereby through Christ's assistance we could be saved. It is through Christ that the testament in which the elect are promised eternal life is given us:

> They had from the beginning the power of inheriting the aforementioned gifts, just as all of their descendants from the beginning had the law of life, namely the hereditary right, and through God's justice they

[29] *SQA* 8, cc. 20–1. [30] *De pauperie salvatoris* II.7, p. 353.22–25.

knew His justice, and they even knew the eternal testament, namely, that had the eternal pact of happiness. Whence the church in the given canon calls the blood of Christ the blood of the eternal testament, because by its mediating, it is made a testament made to the fathers of the promised blessing, and so eternal life is given to the elect.[31]

This accounts for the assumption that the rest of Scripture is justified through the example of the Old Testament's use in the New, but there is an important opening remaining within FitzRalph's reasoning that is expressly ruled out by Wyclif. Very simply, FitzRalph is willing to envision extra-scriptural sources for legislation and governance within the church. He composed three main works against the friars: the *Unusquisque*, a short sermon given on 5 July 1350, *De pauperie salvatoris*, written between 1351 and 1356, and *Defensio curatorum*, a sermon delivered at Avignon on 8 November 1357.[32] In the final work, FitzRalph makes mention of the Franciscan claim that God gave Francis the order's rule:

> Again, since Francis asserted in these words, that God gave him purely and simply this rule and these words: to speak and write, then either for a great lie at the end of his life they claimed that he was damned, or that the Lord truly spoke to him, that he should tell the friars and his disciples that God gave this command to them; and so with the fact that they are not held to preserve this law by reason of the fact that Saint Francis gave it to them, still they should hold to this command because it is a command of God given to them through Saint Francis. The friars may choose whichever they like of these two; I imagine that they will choose the affirmative, and say that he held this without the sin of lying. Thus it follows that by procuring Apostolic letters, the friars acted against the command of God and were disobedient to their own rule.[33]

---

31 *SQA* 8.21, Ex quibus verbis ostenditur quod potestatem habebant ab ortu heriditandi suas in donis predictis ita, ut omnes posteri sui ab origine habuerunt legem vite, scl. Iure hereditario et etiam iudicia dei, scirent iusticiam et testamentum eternum, scl. Pactum eterne felicitatis haberent. Unde ecclesia in canone missa dicit sanginem Christi etiam sanguinem testamenti eterni quia eo mediante testamentum factum patribus de benedictione praemissa impletur, et datur electis beatitudo eterna. 32 See L.L. Hammerich, 'The beginning of the strife between Richard FitzRalph and the mendicants, with an edition of his autobiographical prayer and his proposition *Unusquisque*', *Det Kgl. Danske Videnskabernes Selskab Historisk-filologiske Meddeleiser* XXVI.3 (Copenhagen, 1938); John Wyclif, *De Dominio Divino*, ed. R.L. Poole, Wyclif's Latin works (London, 1890), containing *De pauperie salvatoris*, bks 1–4; R.O. Brock, 'An edition of Richard FitzRalph's *De pauperie salvatoris*, books V, VI and VII' (PhD, U Colorado, 1954); *Defensio curatorum* in M. Goldast, *Monarchia S.Romani Imperii* (Frankfurt, 1612), tomus 2, pp 1394–410; see also John Trevisa, *Dialogus inter militem et clericum*, ed. A.J. Perry (Oxford, 1925), 'Richard FitzRalph's sermon: Defensio curatorum', Middle English translation, pp 39–93. 33 'Item, cum in his verbis Franciscus affirmet, quod Dominus dedit sibi simpliciter & pure

Whether or not God actually gave Francis the rule is not the issue here; it is the story that the friars will tell that will convict them for relying so heavily on a letter from the pope. What is significant is that FitzRalph does not dismiss the possibility that God might give an extra-scriptural rule to an order that could serve as sufficiently authoritative to regulate an order of friars. As we will see in our discussion of his criticisms of the friars, his issue is with the privileges the friars enjoy and not the existence of the friars as such.

For Wyclif, the nature of Scripture's authority lies at the base of his argument that the fraternal orders should not even exist. The ontology of Scripture is grounded securely in his conception of God's eternal understanding. Wyclif explains in *De veritate Sacrae Scripturae* that the physical Bible is but an instantiation of the eternal exemplar of the Book of Life described in Revelation twenty and twenty-one.[34] This gives him an entirely different perspective on the relation of the human author of a biblical text to the divine inspiration behind it. While FitzRalph, and the majority of biblical scholars of the period, were interested in considering the human hand behind the text as at least having some relevance to understanding the meaning of Scripture, Wyclif dismisses this, saying, 'it is futile to quarrel over who might have been the scribe, the composer of the manuscript, or the Lord's reed-pen, whom God infused with divine knowledge'.[35] But it is not enough simply to say that the eternal exemplar for Scripture exists immutable and perfect in the divine understanding. Levy argues that Wyclif's identification of Scripture with the divine understanding, indeed with Christ, the second person of the Trinity, is so strong as to make it feasible to say that Wyclif imagined a genuine personhood for Scripture. Hence, when Christ teaches how a Christian ought to live in the gospels, the teachings have the force of Scripture explaining itself, elucidating its hidden meaning for the improvement of the faithful. The juridical authority of Scripture that follows from this is far more than simply the privileged position of a text containing revealed truth, to be preferred over the written products of the rational mind. It is immutable, living truth articulated in human language and written in ink on parchment, the living Word in flesh (of a sort). Other books containing the reasoned philosophies and juridical codes proceeding from human thought and

---

hanc regulam, & hac virba dicere & scribere: aut propter tantum mendacium in exitu huius vitae dicent eum damnatum, aut quod vere Dominus dixit sibi, quia & ita diceret Fratribus suis: & sic ipse divinum mandatum in hoc Fratribus suis dixit: & per consequens non obstante quod illud tstamentum ratione mandati sancti Francisci non teantur Fratres servare, nihilominus quia est mandatum Dei eis per sanctum Franciscum suum instituorem expressum, istud servare tenentur. Eligant Fratres, quod voluerint ex duobus: & puto quod eligent affirmare, quod sancte sine tantorum mendaciorum peccatis decessit. Et sequitur quod Fratres procurando literas Apostolicas contra mandatum Dei & suae regulae se peccato inobedientiae infecerunt'. *Defensio curatorum* 1401. **34** See *De veritate Sacrae Scripturae*, I, ch. 6; see also the earlier *De civili dominio*, III.19, pp 403–4. **35** *De veritate Sacrae Scripturae*, ch. 10, p. 218, cited and translated in Levy (2003), p. 83.

experience are no more comparable to the Bible than human artifacts are to beings created by God *ex nihilo*. Authority, Wyclif explains, is either from faith in Scripture, in reasoning or in the testament of some other witness. The fact that Scripture is the witness of God, in addition to the fact that all that is reasonable and true is contained within it, make Scripture the primary authority for all creation. Hence, while every truth may be as true as any other truth, it is not logical to assume that every authority is as authoritative as every other; the one authority that contains all others, in addition to revealed truth not otherwise available, must surpass all the rest. By this reasoning, no one part of Scripture is preeminent; there is no primary element within the primary authority. This obviates FitzRalph's argument that Christ's use of the law lends weight to the authority of the Old Testament.[36]

In Wyclif's understanding, the justice that is possible to postlapsarian man is expressly through grace and is restricted to the law given in Scripture. Extrabiblical law is not a source of real justice unless it corresponds to something within Scripture. This is evident in the opening tag of *De civili dominio* and throughout the rest of the work: 'Divine law is presupposed by civil law; natural dominion is presupposed by civil dominion'.[37] This is not to say that every just human law has a correlate in Scripture, but the basis of *ius* that underlies a just human law certainly is. This is because the property ownership brought about by the Fall necessitates laws for postlapsarian man that exceed the specific scope of Scripture. The many cases in which the need for legislation arises within civil dominion, such as feudal arrangements, commercial transactions and so on, may not be explicitly described in the Bible, but the justice that makes it possible for us to do good in these cases can be found there.[38]

The relation of the church to civil dominion is not of one institution to another, but of what Wyclif calls evangelical to civil dominion. He wrote extensively on civil dominion, but only referred to evangelical dominion in discussions of natural and civil dominon.[39] His conception of the church has everything to do with the uncertain nature of evangelical lordship. On the one hand, the church was founded by Christ and should ideally be a body of apostolically poor Christians living in communal harmony and protected by a just civil lord, while on the other, the church is the body of the elect and no one can know who is truly a member. This makes it seem as though one can know how to be a member of the church and so how to be an evangelical lord, but one can never know whether one *is* a member. Critics of Wyclif's thought from the time of Constance onwards have used this paradox to dismiss his ecclesiology as impracticible. This problem is worth pursuing, but not here; for our argument, what matters is the jurisdictive foundation for evangelical dominion, which is Scripture alone.[40]

36 *DVSS*, Levy translation, pp 201–10. 37 *De civili dominio*, I, p. 1. 38 See Lahey, *Philosophy and politics in the thought of John Wyclif*, pp 147–63. 39 Ibid., pp 119–24. 40 *De ecclesia*, c. 7, p. 173.12, '*Nullum est verum privlegium ecclesi, nisi de quanto fundatur, doctetur vel*

Wyclif is clear that any addition to Scripture in governing the church is an imposition on the purity of the institution and a hindrance in its mission of salvation. This is especially the case for those who carry out its main office, which is preaching; as will be evident, Wyclif's position is that man-made legal codes in addition to Scripture, such as fraternal rules, are theologically inadmissable. Given the divine foundation of Scripture, Wyclif reasons in *De potestate pape*, it must be the case that God is the chief author while the apostles and evangelists are but mediate causes of the books. Hence, God himself speaks in Scripture's pages; anyone who imagines that their own writings have some kind of parity with scriptural authority at the least purports to be living in as pure and perfect a matter as the apostles or the evangelists. Such a person would presume to suggest that God gave the apostles a half-formed, incomplete law that would someday, twelve or thirteen centuries later, need supplementation! While this appears in his criticism of papal claims to speak with scriptural authority, it applies equally well to support his argument against the very idea of a fraternal rule.[41]

FITZRALPH AND WYCLIF AGAINST THE FRIARS

Despite being the two chief antifraternal writers in Britain in the fourteenth century, the arguments FitzRalph and Wyclif use are profoundly different. FitzRalph's arguments are ecclesiastically centred and are directed at the privileges the friars enjoy, while Wyclif's arguments are chiefly metaphysical and are aimed at the very nature of sectarianism itself. Penn Szittya's 1986 study features the two theologians' arguments and rightly makes this distinction, but more remains to be said.[42] Szittya's description of Wyclif's position characterizes him as opposed to friars who associate themselves with Ockhamism, which, while true, does not get at the root of Wyclif's rejection of fraternal orders. Further, Wyclif's apparent plan for a cohort of poor preachers, evidence for which runs throughout his later writings, receive no mention in Szittya's study; had FitzRalph known of what probably was a band of mendicant preachers championing 'Saint Richard' as one of their patrons, he might have been apoplectic with rage.

Szittya characterizes FitzRalph's antifraternalism as primarily ecclesiological in substance and intent; the arguments he presents in the main antifraternal works, *De pauperie salvatoris*, *Defensio curatorum* and *Unusquisque* are grounded in attention to ecclesiastical function and intended to force the friars into a more suitable place in the standing ecclesiastical structure. FitzRalph's objections are

---

elicitur ex scriptura. Patet sic: Omnis lex utilis sancte matri ecclesie docetur explicite vel implicite in scriptura ...'. See also Augustine, *De doctrina Christiana*, c. 42. **41** *De potestate pape*, c. 6, pp 108–9. **42** Penn Szittya, *The antifraternal tradition in medieval literature* (Princeton, 1986).

less to the friars' existence than they are to the privileges they claim for themselves, including preaching and administering sacraments, which rightly are the duties of priests functioning under the supervision of bishops. The arguments in *DPS* have none of the antifraternal polemic quality of William of St Amour, but develop from within his philosophically complex analysis of the proprietary elements of *dominium*. Mendicant friars making claims of apostolic poverty must understand that the poverty they suppose is what they share with Christ and his apostles is a fiction. FitzRalph's definitions rely on Aegiddian arguments that grace is necessary for just dominium and entail an understanding of the prelapsarian state that the friars assume can be recreated by papal fiat.

Szittya perceives the full force of his argument arising at *DPS* VI, where he argues that Christ and his apostles did not beg and that while they may have enjoyed apostolic poverty, it was not because of any vow they had taken, nor was it expected that any of their successors would be likewise paupers. 'Christ and the twelve were poor', Szittya summarizes, 'but Scripture shows that they kept some things in reserve for future use and that they did not beg; therefore the friars' claim to imitate the poverty of Christ was false'.[43] Hence, Szittya argues, mendicancy is neither given a New Testament precedent nor is it an acceptable state for anyone capable of working, whether lay or ordained.[44] FitzRalph's commitment to an absolute rejection of mendicancy for anyone preaching the gospels is apparent throughout his antifraternal writings and should be understood to be a central tenet of his arguments against the friars.[45]

Not all scholars interpret *De pauperie* as entailing the equation of antifraternalism and antimendicancy. James Doyne Dawson interpreted FitzRalph as opposing not the friars nor even their claims of poverty, but the pastoral offices to which they laid claim. This made FitzRalph a 'new and improbable defender' of the Spiritual Franciscans, who had similarly envisioned mendicants ministering to the poor, but unencumbered by the duties of presbyters.[46] FitzRalph had earlier attacked the friars' preaching privilege in *Unusquisque*, when he had argued that the exercise of pastoral offices of any sort without episcopal supervision was too easily abused.[47] Dawson reasons that FitzRalph envisioned the friars as ministering to the poor, engaging in manual labour for their sustenance. The attack on mendicancy, he argues, arose later, in *Defensio curatorum*, when the tenor of the argument with the friars became much more bitter.

[43] Ibid., p. 126, referring to *DPS* VI.4.   [44] *DPS* VI.29.   [45] See Szittya, *The antifraternal tradition*, p. 141, n. 68. Also, *Defensio curatorum*, 1399.60–1400.10 in M. Goldast, *Monarchia S. Romani Imperii* Tomus II (Frankfurt, 1614). See also *Unusquisque, 420–46*, in L.L. Hammerich, 'The beginning of the strife between Richard FitzRalph and the mendicants with an edition of his autobiographical prayer and his proposition *Unusquisque*', *Det.Kgl. Danske Videnskabernes Selskab.Historisk-filologiske Meddelelser XXVI 3* (1938).   [46] Doyne Dawson, 'Richard FitzRalph and the fourteenth-century poverty controversies', 333.   [47] Hammerich, 'The beginning of the strife', pp 69–72.

The issue of when FitzRalph shifted from attacks on the preaching and pastoral privileges of the friars to attacks on their mendicancy is important not only in understanding his own evolving attitude toward the friars, but also in showing Dawson to have been right in assessing the earlier FitzRalph to be in agreement with the spirituals. Szittya reads the arguments of *Defensio curatorum* back onto the discussion of the nature of the apostolic example in *DPS* VI.4, understanding FitzRalph to have believed that mendicancy was not imitation of Christ at this point. In fact, FitzRalph's argument here is wholly on what Christ and the apostles possessed and not about how they obtained it. He argued that the apostolic band had to have had more than was absolutely necessary, otherwise why would Christ have advised them to abandon satchel, shoes, extra clothing, silver and gold when going out to preach among the people in John 12:6? 'The witness of the gospel appears to me to be replete with examples of Christ and His apostles frequently preserving things for the future needs of others and for themselves'.[48] How they obtained what they stored up for themselves is not a part of the discussion. Again, the discussion in *DPS* VI.29 is not condemnatory of mendicancy, but of the argument that only the friars claiming the highest degree of poverty are truly imitating Christ; one is a disciple of Christ through keeping his command that we love one another as he has loved us and not through any other species of justice. FitzRalph refers to begging, '*mendicantur humiliter*', as a means of obtaining necessary provisions, second in legitimacy to hard work, several times in *De pauperie* V and VI.[49]

Eventually, FitzRalph turned against mendicancy in *Defensio curatorum* to drive a wedge between the preaching and pastoral activities of the friars and those of parochial priests. The latter exist, he explains, to provide the sacraments because he is 'ordained by God's precepts and for his church by a common law'.[50] Which common law FitzRalph has in mind is not clear; he cites Scripture, canon law and papal bulls, and refers to the authority of Augustine, Aquinas, Bonaventure and other 'glossators and doctors'.[51] Since Aquinas and Bonaventure were both friars actively engaged in preaching and administering the sacraments, it is not surprising that they only receive a fleeting mention in this context. The unspecificity about law is one of FitzRalph's apparent blindspots; he refers to the natural law at the base of prelapsarian dominium as distinct from subsequent civil law without further account.[52] God is described as having given man his commands and laws from the beginning: 'If you wish to preserve these commands, they will preserve you and make an endless, faithful peace'.[53] Man seems not to have needed a set law code in paradise. FitzRalph argues in both *DPS* and *SQA* that man was created with sufficient wisdom to

---

48 *DPS*, VI.4, *Immo videtur michi evangelium testimoniis huiusmodi esse plenum quod dominus noster Ihesus et eius apostolos atque discipulis sepissime ultra sibi necessaria pro sua et aliarum futura indigincia conservebant.* 49 Ibid., V, c. 12, c. 33; VI, c. 11, c. 9. 50 Goldast, *Monarchia S. Romani Imperii*, 1393.57. 51 Ibid., 1396.14. 52 *DPS*, V.14. 53 Ibid., II.6, p. 346.

exercise morality with virtue, but 'Adam lost all the virtues he had through his delinquency, and his rational soul as well, condemning him to eternal death'.[54] FitzRalph's references to God's law predominate in his condemnation of mendicancy and his arguments rest entirely on scriptural precedent. Job 5:7 teaches that man is born to labour and FitzRalph argues that nowhere in Scripture is there evidence that Christ begged. Mendicancy is outright covetousness of one's neighbour's goods and certainly Christ never disobeyed the Mosaic code! Among the collection of arguments that Armachanus collects from the examples of Christ, Paul and the early church to establish the absolute prohibition against begging is a remarkable one. Any preacher who presumes to beg for alms demonstrates his lack of regard for the Paternoster, for in praying it we ask that we not be led into temptation: 'what greater occasion for temptation is there than mendicancy?'[55]

WYCLIF AGAINST THE FRIARS

On the face of it, the friars would seem to be the logical allies for Wyclif. Both Wyclif and the Franciscans were dedicated to a radical conception of poverty, a recreation of the life of Christ and the apostles in a world that seemed not to have changed very much in the past fourteen centuries. Wyclif held a passion for preaching Scripture in common with all four orders of friars, for teaching the morality of Christ to the people without concern for episcopal authority. Wyclif could rival the Dominicans in his rage against the misuse of philosophical innovation to make the faith fit into an Aristotelian mold. And most remarkable of all, at the end of his life Wyclif seems to have actually initiated an order of poor preachers, itinerant teachers of Christ's law meant to refresh and rejuvenate a faltering Christianity, just as Francis and Dominic had done.[56]

Indeed, there is a sense in which Wyclif stands with the friars against William of St Amour and Richard FitzRalph. William had been a secular theologian at the University of Paris when the friars made their debut in the theology faculty and his antipathy for the friars found its roots in biblical warnings of pseudo-prophets and false apostles, especially in 1 Cor. 1–4. William relies on the biblical idea of prophecy to attack the friars and ridicules the claims of apostolic poverty on similar, scriptural grounds: he could see no theological necessity for poverty. The rest of the laundry list of William's criticisms would apply to anyone taking advantage of clerical status: profitting from sacraments, false preaching, political manoeuvering and the rest. William's antipathy resulted in his defeat; he lost

---

[54] Ibid., II. Cc. 6–8; *SQA* VIII cc. 21–3; citation p. 353.22–5.   [55] *DC*, Goldast, *Monarchia S. Romani Imperii*, 1409.25.   [56] See Michael Wilks, 'Wyclif and Hus as leaders of religious protest movements', *Studies in Church History*, 9 (1972), 109–30; repr. in Anne Hudson (ed.), *Wyclif: political ideas and practice* (Oxford, 2000), pp 63–84.

benefices and authority and ultimately saw his writings condemned by Alexander IV. One characteristic that FitzRalph and William share is an inability to understand the friars from within; neither of them gives evidence of having considered the benefits of a simple, fraternal life dedicated to preaching the gospel and doing good works. This is where Wyclif's antifraternalism stands out. Given his devotion to apostolic poverty, his approval of mendicancy, his enthusiasm for preaching, his willingness to countenance a degree of eschatology in his hermeneutics and his deep frustration with papal and episcopal abuses, had he become a friar while still young he might have been another Bonaventure or Olivi.[57] Why, then, was Wyclif's antifraternalism so pronounced? After all, for sheer volume of titles, Wyclif's antifraternal output far exceeds William's and FitzRalph's.[58] The question is itself poorly formed and, once corrected, the answer, I will argue, has everything to do with an element of Wyclif's thought that has until recently received relatively little scholarly attention.

Previous discussions of Wyclif's opposition to the friars have centred on two subjects: realist metaphysics and the heresies of the friars. Both Margaret Aston and Penn Szittya rightly point out that antifraternalism was by no means Wyclif's starting position; in the 1360s and through most of the '70s, some of Wyclif's best friends were friars. Aston notes that the shift came after friars joined with the bishop of London and the archbishop of Canterbury in opposing Wyclif's reasoning about ecclesiastical divestment, the result of papal condemnation in 1376.[59] Szittya marks the turning point at Wyclif's ultimate rejection of transubstantiation as a tenable explanation for what happens at Eucharist and the friars' angry reaction to this.[60] Both Aston and Szittya provide well structured accounts and taken together they provide a very thorough overview of the effects of Wyclif's antifraternalism: his later work is filled with scriptural references and quasi-millenialist warnings about the dire threat of CAIM to the church.[61] Indicative of this antifraternal energy in Wyclif's later life is the Supplement to the *Trialogus* (*c*.1382), a part of what was probably his best known work in the centuries to come, which is filled with attacks on the friars' mendicancy, sacramental theolgy and the letters of fraternity.[62]

---

[57] While he was certainly no disciple of Joachim of Fiore, Wyclif's attention to eschatology was real; see Michael Wilks, 'Wyclif and the wheel of time', *Studies in Church History*, 33 (1997), 177–93; repr. in Hudson (ed.), *Wyclif: political ideas and practice* (2000), pp 205–21.   [58] Williel Thomson lists twenty titles expressly against the friars and the sects in his *The Latin writings of Wyclyf*, Pontifical Institute of Medieval Studies (1983); the vigorous arguments that crop up in other, especially later, works such as *Trialogus* would increase the number of titles significantly. [59] Margaret Aston, 'Caim's castles: poverty, politics and disendowment' in *Faith and fire: popular and unpopular religion, 1350–1600* (London, 1993), pp 95–132.   [60] Szittya, *The antifraternal tradition*, pp 152–82.   [61] The acronym CAIM stands for Carmelites, Austyns, Jacobites, Minorites, the four orders of friars, commonly used by Wyclif and his followers. The Jacobites are the Dominicans, so named because of their Paris chapter of St James.   [62] See John Wyclif, *Trialogus cum supplementum trialogi*, ed. Gotthard Lechler (Oxford, 1869), esp. pp 361–85.

Two problems confuse matters. If Aston is correct and Wyclif's antifraternalism was catalyzed by the friars turning on him in the late 1370s, one could ask why Wyclif did not also attack Oxford University. After all, the university administration turned on him because of the same cynically political necessities.[63] Wyclif never lost his enthusiasm for championing the import of philosophy and logic for the Scripture scholar; unlike FitzRalph he clearly never felt that his days in the classroom had been wasted.[64] Secondly, I do not believe that Wyclif's realism compelled him to reject transubstantiation; I have argued elsewhere that it was his spatio-temporal atomism that lay at the base of his conclusion that Aristotelian metaphysics could not account for what Innocent III claimed for it.[65] This atomism is not necessarily connected to realism; prior to Wyclif, its most important endorser was Walter Chatton, a Franciscan Ockhamist.[66] We are left wondering just what exactly it was about the friars that bothered him so in Wyclif's later years.

The Lollard compilations of Wycliffism known as the *Floretum* and the *Rosarium* serve as quick preacher's guides for where to find the material for a good sermon. The works of Wyclif most frequently cited are: *Sermons*, *Trialogus*, *Opus evangelicum* and *De mandatis divinis*.[67] Of these, the three latter titles were the product of Wyclif's later years; *Trialogus* can be dated precisely to 1382, *Opus evangelicum* was left unfinished at his death in 1384 and the *Sermons* appear to have been delivered earlier but reworked into a set of exempla for Wycliffite preachers. *De mandatis divinis* seems out of place though; it is listed in Thomson's catalogue as the first treatise of Wyclif's *Summa theologie*. It appears to be an extended survey of the basis for the Old Law, with an exploration of the roots of *ius* and *iustitia* as preparation for the extended argument that all just human law is dependent upon divine law for justice. The treatise is obviously patterned on Robert Grosseteste's *De mandatis* and a brief overview leaves one with the impression of an unremarkable survey of the Decalogue.

While the treatise seems to have begun in this way, a more careful reading reveals that Wyclif has reworked it, expanding and elaborating his analysis of the foundation for the law of God to create a homiletic manual for Wycliffite preachers. After the rather dry section on *ius*, Wyclif asks why human beings should obey laws in general and God's laws in particular. The answer is jarring: the disobedience of sin harms not only the sinner and not only the created

---

63 J. Catto and R. Evans, 'Wyclif and Wycliffism at Oxford 1356–1430', *The history of the University of Oxford: 2, late medieval Oxford* (Oxford, 1992), pp 175–261; Joseph Dahmus, *The prosecution of John Wyclyf* (New Haven, CT, 1952). 64 For FitzRalph's later repudiation of his scholastic studies, see his autobiographical prayer in *SCA* 19.35, edited in Hammerich, 'The beginning of the strife', p. 20.74–80. 65 Stephen Lahey, *John Wyclif* (Oxford, 2009), pp 102–34. 66 Christophe Grellard and Aurelien Robert (eds), *Atomism in late medieval philosophy and theology* (Leiden, 2009). 67 Anne Hudson, *The premature reformation* (Oxford, 1986), pp 103–10.

universe in a general sense, but each instance of a human being sinning affects the divine idea of that human being.

Not everyone grasps my word that my sin detracts from all the stars, but they should know with wonder how every part of the world is ordered to its perfection, because all ordinately serve God according to primary institution; this order some philosophers call the 'golden chain', which is certainly disrupted each time a creature sins. So as a consequence, any creature is rendered imperfect to a certain extent in its proper ordering by sin, which destroys it. And it is clear that it is not possible for any creature to sin mortally without thereby sinning against any neighbor and God, unless he sins against every creature, injuring the whole world.[68]

This touches upon the profoundly tangled issue of Wyclif's determinism, which I will avoid here. The popular image of Wyclif having been a strong determinist to the point of nullifying human free will is profoundly erroneous: he used a complex metaphysical apparatus to prove that God's necessary and eternal understanding of the elect or damned state of each human being is brought about by the contingent and temporal actions of that human being.[69] The divine idea of each human being is connected to the divine idea of each other human being that ever has lived or ever will live. So what one person does eternally touches the divine understanding not only of that person but of every other member of the species as well.

Wyclif's understanding of the interrelation of the divine ideas is complex and necessarily entails the explanation of how a multiplicity of ideas can exist in the absolute unity of the divine being.

> All things of particular natures are in the same genus one according to one confused union, although they are distinct progressively from potency into act according to shapes and particular differences. And thus philosophers say that a genus is matter because it contains in itself, as Lincolniensis says, with equal potentiality and univocally [G 62ra] all its subjective parts, just as matter contains in itself, indistinctly, [M 98vb] every form producible from its potency. Likewise God unites in Himself every creature not in such a way that there could be many essences within

---

[68] *De mandatis divinis*, ch. 5 '[P]atet quod astra et omnes partes mundi que istud faciunt mandati Dei implecionem licet inculpabiliter impediunt. Nec capiunt omnes hoc verbum quod peccatum meum imperficit omne astrum, sed notent mirantes quomodo de perfeccione secunda cuiuslibet partis mundi est, quod omnes ordinate serviant Deo suo secuncum institucionem primariam; quem ordinem quiddam philosophorum vocarunt cathenam auream que indubie in qualibet creatura dirumpitur per peccatum, et per consequens quelibet creatura in tanto bono ordinis quoddammodo ex peccato imperficitur, dum hoc perdit. Et patet quod non est possibile aliquem hominem peccare mortaliter, nisi eo ipso peccet in quemcunque proximum et in Deum; immo nisi iniuriando toti mundo peccet in quamlibet creaturam'. p. 39.3–17. [69] See Lahey, *John Wyclif*, pp 169–98.

Him, but everything there is one essence, one life, as Augustine says in *On the Trinity* VI, chapter 27.[70]

Put very simply, when I lie to someone, that act has a negative effect on the divine idea of Marie Antoinette, the apostle Paul and Charlie Chaplin.[71] This means that Wyclif needs to explain how created action in time can have an effect on an eternal idea of something in God's mind. I have explored his use of modal metaphysics to do this elsewhere and can only refer the reader to this and other discussions of the topic.[72] This makes ethics a very serious matter in the Christian life.

What has this to do with the friars? Peckham's reforms had regularized the catechesis of the laity in England and Archbishop Thoresby's catechism had been translated while Wyclif was a young man. In fact, Wyclif himself may have been involved in the translation, although this is likely to remain undemonstrable. But the day-to-day business of the Christian moral life requires regular instruction and inspiration and this is the place of the sermon and the confessional. Increasingly, the friars had come to play a very important role in both and their abuses of preaching and penitential authority were quick to rival the misdeeds of secular clergy. Wyclif's criticisms are not based in a reaction against these abuses nor were they founded in a rejection of the life of poverty the friars espoused, nor in a rejection of mendicancy as such. Further, Wyclif's criticisms were hardly against the friars' freedom from episcopal oversight; his own band of poor preachers went out into the countryside without episcopal approval as well. The problem is deeper than any of the antifraternal criticisms that had preceeded Wyclif: it lies in the existence of sects as such.

The moral truth necessary for salvation is contained wholly and perfectly in Scripture; any situation the wayfarer might face in this pilgrimage on Earth has its model or its ethical maxim in the Bible.[73] The eternal arbiter of divine justice became one of us and founded a new religion that did not supersede Judaism, but instead folded its wisdom and law traditions into the complete perfection of the law of Christ. The perfect life of Christ serves as an exemplar for all human action and we are meant to pay as close attention to his actions as described in the gospels as to his words. The unity and interconnected reality of the human

---

70 *De ideis*, p. 20, forthcoming trans. of ed. by Herold and Mueller.   71 See Stephen Lahey, 'Of divine ideas and insolubles: Wyclif's explanation of God's understanding of sin', *Modern Schoolman*, 86 (Nov. 2008/Jan. 2009), 211–32. Fiona Somerset has kindly pointed out to me that Peter the Chanter held a position evocative of this in *verbum abbreviatum* c. 84: '... quod peccatum unius redundat in multitudinem et peccatum multitudinis redundat in singulos'. PL 205, p. 538. A fuller description of Wyclif's understanding of this will be possible with the publication of an edition of *De sciencia Dei*, now in preparation by Ivan Mueller.   72 See Lahey, *John Wyclif*, pp 169–86; Levy, 'Grace and freedom in the soteriology of John Wyclif', *Traditio*, 60 (2005), 279–337; see Wyclif, *De logica* III, pp 178–97.   73 *DVSS*, I.15; see *John Wyclif on the truth of holy Scripture*, trans. Ian Levy (Kalamazoo, MI, 2001), pp 197–215.

species has Christ as its centerpoint in the divine understanding and this means that the sect Christ founded, the Christian religion, is the means through which every member of the species can understand what is right and just.[74]

We are to note very carefully that Christ's teachings do not cease with the ascension; while each epistle may have come from the hand of an apostle, every word in them is more than divinely inspired: every word is eternal, universal truth. So the fact that the threat of pseudo-apostles crops up in the letters of Paul, of Peter and of James is important. Even more important is the fact that none of these men attempted to start their own version of Christianity. Their patron and the author of their rule of life was Christ and none of the apostles presumed to add upon his words with their own innovations or ideas. A sect, Wyclif explains, is a 'group of men following one patron, professing one rule'.[75] They recognized the divine authority with which Christ guided the formation and the continuation of the Christian life and submitted themselves to it as every Christian is meant to do. So as Christ is the exemplar for human perfection, the lives of the apostles are exempla for lives devoted to the service of Christ. This is the argument of Wyclif's *De fundatione sectarum*, one of the longer of his antifraternal pieces; given the frequency of mention of the Bishop Despenser crusade in Flanders in this tract, it can be dated with some certainty to 1383 or 1384.

When a saintly person who lives by the rule of Christ guides other Christians, it is always on the understanding that the saintly person has absolutely nothing to add to the eternal truth of Christ's law. But when such a person strays into the place of patron or legislator, the spectre of blasphemy threatens the religion. Wyclif explains that

> whether Benedict, or Dominic, or Francis or anyone else gathers together a new sect, he ought not be praised, nor ought he be followed; this is even more the truth for a sect imagining itself to have another patron or some worthless history behind it, as is true of the Augustinians or the Carmelites.[76]

The fact that such prophets as Elijah and Elishah encouraged this sort of thing, Wyclif argues in *Purgatorium sectae Christi*, is not evidence of a change in the

---

74 See *De fundacione sectarum* in *Polemical works*, ed. R. Buddenseig (1883), 1. See also *Trialogus III*, cc. 30–1; for Wyclif's christology, see Lahey, 'Wyclif's christology and trinitarian theology' in Ian Levy (ed.), *A handbook to John Wyclif, late medieval theologian* (Leiden, 2006). 75 *De fund. sect.*, p. 21.20. 76 Ex istis colligitur, quod sive Benedictus, sive Dominicus sive Franciscus vel quivis alius novam sectam supra christianam collegerit, non in hoc est laudandus nec persona ipsum sequens sectaliter, sed culpanda, et multo magis secte fingentes false se habere patronos vel extravagantes superflue sine illis, ut de Augustinensibus et Carmelitis supponitur: ibid., p. 20.20–5.

religion; it is, rather, evidence of a need to be careful in the traditions included in the authoritative structure of the church.[77]

Wyclif acknowledges that others have laboured to overturn the newly introduced orders, mentioning FitzRalph and Ockham 'with many other faithful friars [who strove] for the purgation of their brothers who had fallen away from the old rule'. William of St Amour and Grosseteste, at the end of his life, also worked to stop the rise of the friars. Now, monks are loud in their denunciation of the friars, making the same sorts of arguments that Bonaventure and Ockham had made. But, in truth, the friars and the monks are equally at fault in their departures from the law of Christ.[78]

One of Wyclif's arguments stands out from the rest; here he employs his metaphysical framework directly to show the illicit nature of constructing particular additions to Christ's religion.

Our God neither makes nor can make anything without a probable reason. So, despising a vacuum, he implemented an analogum of being through created substance and accidents with a being of reason, which mediates between these. So from every kind, down to the most particular species and to the individuals that participate in them, by which the whole universe is knit together to is final perfection at the Day of Judgment. Just as God is full of ideas, so it is fitting that none of them are superfluous or baseless. Since these orders are ordained to assist and to encourage in following Christ in behaviour, it seems amazing how a habit and a perceptible ritual pertain to that end.[79]

It should by now be clear that Wyclif is not simply antifraternal. He is antisectarian, rejecting monks, nuns and anchorites as well as the friars; in other pieces Wyclif even warns that the possessioners, the cloistered monks and nuns living in rich and long-established houses, are as much a danger to Christianity as are the friars.[80] The friars' special problem is that when they are preaching about Christ's law they are actively engaged in preaching a moral code they do not actually practice. Their arguments that Francis or Dominic only augment the perfection of Christ's law with a means by which his faithful servants might more effectively teach it are wholly illogical. Had Jesus been but a man, it would be sensible and logical that another man might come along to make it easier to teach the thoughts of Jesus; people do that with Aristotle's ethics all the time.

---

77 *Purgatorium sectae Christi* in *Polemical works*, 1, pp 299–300. 78 *De ordinatione fratrum* in Buddenseig, 1, pp 92–3. 79 Constat quidem ex principiis fidei, quod d eus noster nec fecit nec facere potuit aliquid nisi probabili racione. Ex hoc enim odiendo vacuum implevit analogum entis per substanciam creatam et accidens cum ente racionis, quod mediat inter ista. Et sic de omni genere, usque ad speciem specialissimam et de individuis que ipsa participant, quo usque tota creata universitas ad suam perfeccionem ultimam in die iudicii sit redacta. Sicut enim deus est plenus ydeis, sic oportet, quod nulla illarum sit superflua sine causa. Et cum isti ordines ad sequendum Cristum in moribus et ad acuendum alios ad hoc ordinentur, mirandum videtur, quomodo habitus et ritus sensibiles pertinent ad hunc finem. *De fundatione sectarum*, pp 25.17–26.7. 80 *De quattuor sectis novellis* in Buddenseig, 1, pp 245–6.

But we are not Jesusans, followers of Jesus the man; we are Christians, followers of the divine legislator whose laws need no augmentation even for those who would teach the law: 'Jesus is the proper name of our abbot who does not save us unless we preserve our religion. So, lest we overextend ourselves from propriety or presume about our confirmation, we are not called Jesusans, but, that we may cognize the habitus of grace and communicate this in all things, are called Christians, and not equivocally'.[81] A rule instituted to facilitate following the law of Christ does nothing but draw those it regulates away from Christ: 'Such an ordering blasphemes directly against God, and so regulates the ordering of God away from eternal cognition, but what greater blasphemy could there be?'[82] Note how hard Jesus was on the Pharisees, Wyclif comments; they were a sect founded apart from the Old Law to facilitate its promulgation. That such sects be allowed to thrive in Christ's church is a sin far more grave than the existence of the Pharisees![83]

Earlier I said that Wyclif's association with the friars was much closer than the relations of FitzRalph or William to the orders. This is because of his conviction that a pure and perfect species of Christ's law exists to be preached to the laity and that the duty of the clergy, the evangelical lords as he calls them in *De civili dominio*, is first and foremost to bring this law to the laity.[84] Sacraments are of secondary importance in this logic and episcopal authority and the material success of the body that provides the preachers their support is so marginal as to be of no import whatever: 'Preaching the gospel exceeds prayer and administration of the sacraments to an infinite degree'.[85] Hence, his many arguments against papal authority and the canonical power of the hierarchy are merely aspects of his understanding of the first responsibility of a servant of Christ, which is to instruct the laity in the law of Christ.

This is a relatively new picture of Wyclif the antifraternal polemicist. At almost every point it looks as though Wyclif is setting himself up to be another, better Francis or Dominic. His careful construction of a moral system is indebted to the structure of Thomas' *Summa Theologiae* and the *Compendium Theologiae* as well. His departure from the safety and security of the university and his subsequent exile to Lutterworth suggest the wanderings of the prophet Elijah, the purported founder of the Carmelites. His tireless arguments for apostolic poverty and the substance of his moral theology, framed primarily on what he calls the law of love, strongly suggest the ideals of Francis and Bonaventure. The fact that he gathered together disciples and sent them out into

---

81 *De civili dominio III*, c. 2, p. 15.16–23.   82 *De perfectione statuum* in Buddenseig, 2, pp 468.29–469.2.   83 *De triplici vinculo amoris* in Buddenseig, 1, p. 174.   84 For evangelical lordship, see Lahey, *Metaphysics and politics in the thought of John Wyclif*, pp 119–24.   85 See *De officio pastoralis*, II.2, Ford Lewis Battles (trans.), *Advocates of reform from Wyclif to Erasmus*, ed. Matthew Spinka (Westminster, 2006), p. 49; see also Gotthard Lechler, *Iohannis de Wiclif Tractatus de officio pastoralis* (Leipzig, 1863), p. 32.

England to preach and live a life of apostolic exemplary purity sounds very much like the founding of another order of preaching friars. This is why he works so hard to denounce them. Each of the friars' patrons was so close to the apostolic ideal but erred grievously in creating a rule with which to gild the lily of Christ's perfect law. Wyclif's idea was to free the friars and ultimately all the sects from their self-imposed exile from the body of Christ.

Despite Wycliffite and anti-Wycliffite assertions, it is clear that FitzRalph's position that developed against the friars is entirely different from Wyclif's position. While using the term 'antifraternal' to describe both is not wholly inaccurate, it obscures the important elements of each position. FitzRalph can be understood as never having advocated the absolute dissolution of the friars but only restricting their privileges, from preaching and shriving to mendicancy. Wyclif, on the other hand, cannot conceive of allowing any factions within the Christian religion, whether monastic or fraternal. FitzRalph's arguments are based in ecclesiology and his use of Scripture follows an unremarkable hermeneutic consonant with the conservative approach of his day. Wyclif's arguments are grounded in a formal theology of ideas, a topic of no apparent interest to FitzRalph, and are associated with a Scripture hermeneutic quite different from any other approach of his time. So, understanding FitzRalph and Wyclif to be of one mind in arguing against the friars is akin to saying that Adam Smith and Karl Marx thought that economics are central to an understanding of the nature of history.

De Vitoria on FitzRalph: an adequate assessment?

GRAHAM McALEER

When Tony Blair visited Dublin in September 2010, he was pelted with shoes and eggs. Those doing the pelting accused Blair of being a war criminal. Blair, well-known for his familiarity with Catholic ideas, defended the Iraq War by recourse to just war theory. As the Irish scholar Cian O'Driscoll has pointed out, although Tony Blair is a lawyer he did not so much rely on contemporary categories of international law for his justification, but rather ideas basic to classical and Thomistic just war jurisprudence.[1] During the debates leading to the Iraq War, the archbishop of Canterbury, Rowan Williams, argued that national governments have no authority to declare war. He insisted that, according to Aquinas, the authority to make war is vested in a public authority with a care for the common good; since each nation pursues national gain in war, nations act like a private authority – like you and I in our daily lives. The archbishop's conclusion: the only genuine public authority with war making powers is the United Nations.[2]

The debate between the prime minister and the archbishop is familiar to everyone: it is as old as Christianity itself. Explaining why Rome fell, the French Catholic anarchist Proudhon argued that Rome's 'public objects of veneration' were blood and luxury and though these gods served Rome well for a millennium, they faltered when confronted by the new demand for purity made by Christianity.[3] The logic of Archbishop Williams repeats this demand: nations are not pure enough to licitly wage war; driven by parochial interests, national authorities are incapable of serving the common international good. It is likely too much to say that the archbishop of Canterbury is applying the ideas of the archbishop of Armagh, Richard FitzRalph, but he is channelling their shared intuition that Christian judgment about the world must defer to a high standard of purity and holiness.

In the Middle Ages, and up into early modernity,[4] Richard FitzRalph was well known for his signature thesis that legitimate authority (*dominium*) requires grace:

---

[1] Cian O'Driscoll, 'Re-negotiating the just war: the invasion of Iraq and punitive war', *Cambridge Review of International Affairs*, 19:3 (Sept. 2006), 405–21. [2] R. Williams and G. Weigel, 'War and statecraft: an exchange', *First Things*, 141 (Mar. 2004), 14–21. [3] P.-J. Proudhon, *What is property?* (Cambridge, 2007), pp 24–6. [4] See the references to FitzRalph in J. Kraye & R. Saarinen (eds), *Moral philosophy on the threshold of modernity* (Dordrecht, 2005).

No: for as stated at Ephesians (ii.3) all are born *sons of anger* and as the Apostle testifies at Romans (iii. 22, 23) *for all have sinned and come short of the glory of God*, whence all of us in our personal origin, until we have grace, are denuded of lordship; so, that lordship previously had by our first parent no one receives, though each should have succeeded to it in time, accepted that lordship, and been conformed to justice or justifying grace (344).[5]

Francisco de Vitoria, who died a few months after Martin Luther in 1546, feels the pressure of this intuition for purity but disagrees utterly with FitzRalph's analysis of legitimacy.

A Spanish Baroque Dominican, de Vitoria is one of the Catholic Church's greatest moral theologians.[6] The depth of his disagreement with FitzRalph explains some of his choice words about Richard but also clarifies what is distinctive about the Thomistic approach to moral theology and, in light of the comparison, gives us significant insight into Richard's basic positions. In my opinion, de Vitoria did not understand these basic positions well. Richard's thinking about legitimate authority and property stems from a theological anthropology that is unusual for his time. In light of this originality, de Vitoria's arguments fail to hit their target and his assessment of Richard FitzRalph is thus inadequate. I will conclude this essay with some brief thoughts about moral theology and whether it is best served by Thomism or Richard's theological anthropology.

This essay documents what separates Richard from Thomism but there is one significant continuity that ought to be noted at the outset. In the great fourteenth-century debates about the legitimacy of property, FitzRalph defended the position that lordship is original to the human condition and thus the Franciscan claim that property is ungodly is false. Aquinas famously held that property, although a function of human arrangement, was congruent with natural law. This was a departure from ancient tradition, which held that property was a concession to sin necessary to help humans muddle along. After Aquinas, ancient tradition was vigorously defended, for example by Peter John Olivi, one of the most original Franciscan thinkers of the period, who believed that any kind of lordship whatsoever was contrary to natural law. He argued that things held individually or communally robbed humans of the grandeur of their

---

5 'Non, quia omnes *filii ire* nascuntur, Eph. ii. 3; et *Non est distinccio, omnes enim peccaverunt et egent Gloria Dei*, testante apostolo, ad Romanos iii. 22, 23: unde in nostra origine personali omnes, donec graciam habeamus, sumus isto dominio denudati; ita quod dominium istud nemo recipit antequam suo primo parenti, cui debet succedere pro tempore quo dominium istud acceperat, in iusticia seu iustificante gracia conformetur' (Richard FitzRalph, *De pauperie salvatoris* in John Wycliffe, *De Dominio divino* (London, 1890)). 6 For extensive commentary on de Vitoria, see G.J. McAleer, *To kill another: homicide and natural law* (London, 2010).

being ('aliquo modo altitudo naturalis libertatis contrahitur et coartatur per dominium divitiarum communium vel propriarum').[7] Richard is far closer to Aquinas, but he adds an interesting twist. R.O. Brock is more or less right when he says that, for Richard, property is acquired in the civil state, with the limitation in the right of use (*ius utendi*) not a part of original dominion.[8] This is partially right, but there is a sense in which Richard is more radical than Thomas. Richard does appear to argue that a right of occupation is original to Paradise. He argues that even if Adam and Eve had never been expelled from Paradise, on account of their fertility a shortage of the finest land would have had to be resolved by later generations taking up other lands less suited to human development. Less suited: because the operations of the planets and the earth's humours create certain geographical limitations in the earth's fecundity (372).

De Vitoria is nonetheless a good witness that Thomists read FitzRalph with some dismay. De Vitoria tells us that Richard subscribes to 'one lunatic heresy' (243) despite his being 'a man of otherwise blameless character and intelligence' (18). For, says de Vitoria, FitzRalph 'certainly argues' (18) 'not merely unbelief but any mortal sin impedes any kind of power or dominion (*dominium*) or jurisdiction, either public or private' (18). Note the scope of de Vitoria's presentation of the thesis that any mortal sin – any offence against charity that is – cancels any kind of authority and this in either the public or private domain. This does seem a fair summary of Richard's most basic legal and political thinking. Richard writes:

> Civil lordship, just as original lordship (without question), is given to men by God so that the one empowered can stand in rightful obedience to God; accordingly, when someone sins mortally, the person loses and forfeits original lordship, equally, and for equal reason, the person forfeits civil lordship.[9]

Granting de Vitoria's perspective for now: what drove Richard to lunacy? De Vitoria thinks he knows: Richard argues his case, says de Vitoria, 'in the mistaken belief that the true title and foundation of all power is grace'. What does this mean? Having edited the latter parts of FitzRalph's *On the poverty of the saviour*, Brock gives us a handy image: 'Armachanus, then, would insist on every judge holding the Holy Scripture before his books of civil law'.[10] Many would indeed

---

7 For this material, I rely on the excellent article of Roberto Lambertini, 'Poverty and power: Franciscans in later medieval political thought', *Moral Philosophy on the Threshold of Modernity*, 57:2 (2005), 141–63.   8 R.O. Brock, 'An edition of Richard FitzRalph's *De pauperie salvatoris*, books V, VI and VII' (PhD, U Colorado, 1954), p. lvi.   9 'Civile dominium, sicud original dominium (non dubium) datum est a Deo hominibus pro prestando debito Deo obsequio ab eo cui est datum; igitur, cum quis peccat mortaliter, per hoc perdens ac forefaciens originale dominium, pariter et pari racione forefacit civile dominium' (Brock, 'An edition of Richard FitzRalph's *De pauperie salvatoris*', p. lvi).

agree that the route to lunacy is, for example, the review of property law by some biblical judicial review, perhaps derived from passages where the prophets condemn greed as an offence against the love of God and neighbour. It is worth pointing out that not all would be fazed by Richard's commitment to divine positive law.

A Thomist like de Vitoria might be spooked by this commitment but many leading theologians certainly are not. Consider this passage from Benedict XVI's 2008 encyclical, *Charity in truth*: 'charity does not exclude knowledge, but rather requires, promotes, and animates it from within. Knowledge is never purely the work of the intellect. Deeds without knowledge are blind, and knowledge without love is sterile'. Indeed (quoting Pope Paul VI), 'the individual who is animated by true charity labors skillfully to discover the causes of misery, to find the means to combat it, to overcome it resolutely'.[11]

And this, from one of the world's leading theologians: John Milbank, writing in 2005:

> it is fair to say that contemporary Catholic theology, if it is to avoid both a liberalism and a conservatism that are predicated on the idea of an autonomous pure nature, needs to recover the authentic and more radical account of the natural desire for the supernatural as offered by de Lubac ... This account is articulated in terms of spirit always orientated to grace ... the cosmos as lured by grace through humanity.[12]

A close collaborator with John Milbank, the well-known theologian Graham Ward, makes the political implications plain. In the section of his 2009 *The politics of discipleship* titled *So just what is wrong with theocracy?*, Ward writes: 'But in principle if not always in fact, every act, every intuition, every emotional response, every thought is to be submitted to God, to be ruled by God – terrifying and liberating as this inevitably is. So, as a people of God, we are theocratic'.[13]

Of course, a Thomist also thinks human life is only rightly understood in the light of God's love and the revelation of that love in Scripture. Yet some profound difference is at play here. Contrast the centrality of grace, charity and mortal sin in Richard's thinking with the following passage from de Vitoria:

> Fourth, I say and conclude that by that commandment [Do not kill] there is prohibited every homicide which, *by the law of nature alone*, is evil and irrational. And it is *only* to this that we must look, and not to

10 Brock, 'An edition of Richard FitzRalph's *De pauperie salvatoris*', p. lvii. 11 Benedict XVI, *Charity in truth*, para. 30. 12 J. Milbank, *The suspended middle: Henri de Lubac and the debate concerning the supernatural*, (Grand Rapids, MI, 2005), pp 107–8. 13 G. Ward, *The politics of discipleship: becoming postmaterial citizens* (Grand Rapids, MI, 2009), p. 299.

exceptions or permissions given in divine law. For all of these are only judicial, and have ceased to obtain, or if they are moral are explanatory of the natural law. Accordingly, when it is lawful to kill and when it is not must be *ultimately* referred to this. However, it does help to *consult* the Scriptures (emphasis added).[14]

Scripture is a useful tool to consult, says de Vitoria, but judgments must ultimately defer to, as he puts it, 'the law of nature alone'. Following Aquinas, de Vitoria understands 'the law of nature' to be a participation in the eternal law where emphasis is placed on the rationality of God and, relatively speaking, less weight placed on God's will and love.

The theologians cited above, like Richard, all have an Augustinian sensibility. The lure of the Platonic form is felt strongly in this sensibility. It explains, I think, the interest in purity (346). It is at least true of Richard's *On the poverty of the saviour* that his thought bears again and again on the creation narrative. God's original loving relationship with Adam offers the best window into the definition of human being. In that original personal relationship, Adam was the pristine form of man. For Richard, lordship begins and ends in a love relationship. Richard writes:

> You think me a little unclear about whether the lordship of God is really the same as that which God gives to Adam for him to exercise. Let me respond: without completely denying that there is some genuine difference between their lordships, they had one and the same charity, through which God loved Adam and Adam loved God [...] so they had really one lordship by which God was the lord of Adam and the things gifted to him, and by which Adam was the lord of these things; Adam did not have that lordship so fully, because he was unable to possess it so perfectly as God for he could not have had as perfect charity as the Holy Spirit (310).[15]

Instead of stressing the relationship between God and Adam, much contemporary theology emphasizes the relationship between Adam and Eve, or even the relationship between Christ and the church, and in Aquinas focus is on the incarnation and the cross. There is nothing obvious, therefore, about Richard

14 F. de Vitoria, *On homicide* (Milwaukee, WI, 1997), p. 83.   15 'Quia tamen te puto ambigere, nunquit realiter sit idem Dei dominium quod in Adam Deus constituit et sibi retinuit, an diversum; ecce tibi respondeo, non negando diversa realiter ipsos habuisse dominia, quod sicut unam caritatem habebant, scilicet, qua Deus Adam dilexit et Adam Deum dilexit [...] ; ita habebant realiter unum dominium quo Deus dominatus est Ade et rebus sibi donatis, et quo Adam dominatus est rebus eisdem, quod dominium non ita plene habebat Adam, quia nec ita perfecte illud capere poterat sicut Deus, sicut nec ita perfecte caritatem que est Spiritus sanctus capere poterat aut habebat' (310).

privileging the creation narrative. Perhaps this captures some of the difference between FitzRalph and the Thomist tradition. Christian reflection on the incarnation and the cross has proven complex on account of how to think the link between two different orders: the spiritual reality of the Word and the seemingly contained realm of the passions, human body and nature. One of the distinctive features of Thomism is its valorization of the natural. Richard believes a mortal sin is a preference for cupidity and while a Thomist also believes a mortal sin is an offence against charity, a Thomist is likely to resist the claim that failures in charity are also preferences for cupidity; and this on account of a pretty rigorous account of natural virtue, a confidence in rationality and a belief that, in principle at least, evolved social, political and legal institutions can be rightly ordered through human effort. For Aquinas, a life without grace is a diminished life, but it is not a human life shattered. Richard does appear to think otherwise, perhaps impressed by a passage like the following from Augustine:

> For the things which you fill by containing them do not sustain and support you as a water-vessel supports the liquid which fills it. Even if they were broken to pieces, you would not flow out of them and away. And when you pour yourself out over us, you are not drawn down to us but draw us up to yourself: you are not scattered away, but you gather us together.[16]

Something like the preceding helps explain, I think, the central dispute between de Vitoria and Richard on the place of Roman law in moral theology. Part of de Vitoria's reputation rests on his accommodation of Roman law in natural law thinking, but Richard rejects three central planks of Roman law. He rejects the Roman law definition of property and also its ideas of the person and freedom. These three things stand together and profoundly so. Richard's thought does appear to be quite original and perhaps it is so because it represents a break with the Roman tradition which de Vitoria later restores. This point is crucial to why de Vitoria reacts with such dismay to FitzRalph's position.

Proudhon begins the seminal work of anarchism, *What is property?*, with a denunciation of the Justinian definition of ownership, this being 'the right to use and abuse a thing within the limits of the law' ('jus utendi et abutendi re sua, quatenus juris ratio patitur').[17] Roman law permits a man 'to let his crops rot underfoot, sow his field with salt, milk his cows on the sand, turn his vineyard into a desert'. Proudhon echoes FitzRalph: rejecting this definition from Roman law, Richard writes:

---

[16] St Augustine, *Confessions*, trans. R.S. Pine-Coffin (London, 1975), p. 22. [17] Proudhon, *What is property?*, p. 35.

> The power to abuse and insatiable cupidity in no way pertains to dominion but rather attaches to tyranny. As God is always and necessarily without these things, for God cannot abuse things nor be stained by reprehensible cupidity, God would be unable to have dominion (308).[18]

This departure from the Roman law definition of property relies on an equally significant departure from the Roman conception of the person and liberty. What is so interesting about Richard's thought is that loss of original lordship evacuates the legal or civil title of property not because someone transgresses natural *law* but because of an abandonment of a person's very nature. What is significant is not that Richard makes lordship intrinsically normative, therefore. He certainly does hedge power round with normativity and explains this powerfully. Legitimacy is an attribute of God on account of God's goodness and not a function of sheer power. Since God has lordship over creation, the question is raised whether God could annihilate a creature (a person). Richard denies this, saying:

> It follows from this that God has the power of annihilation, just as God has the power of conserving, so it is understood that in God there is a power or faculty of annihilation should God wish this, but annihilation is hateful to God, in fact, because incompatible with God's omnipotent goodness (299).[19]

Stating the normative account of ownership, Richard writes:

> Neither sufficiency nor abundance in the human use of things, is, or can be, measured by insatiable cupidity, for the abuse of things is inseparable from sin. The measure of use is rather happiness whether natural need or, more properly, personal need (308).[20]

Richard's is not a law based conception of ethics but one rooted in an account of the human person.

Richard's mentors in moral theology are not easily discerned. Aubrey Gwynn

---

18 'Potencia ad abusum et insaciabilitas cupiditatis nequaquam ad dominium pertinent, set tirannidi annectuntur; alioquin Deus necessario ac semper hiis carens, qui nec rebus potest abuti nec cupiditate reprehensibili maculari, dominium non haberet'. 19 'Et ob hoc ita Deus habet adnichilandi potenciam, sicut habet potenciam conservandi, intellige quod in Deo est potencia sufficiens sive facultas adnichilandum si vellet, quamvis adnichilacio, que odii esse videtur, Deo de facto propter suam omnipotentem bonitatem non congruat' (299). 20 'Non enim habet aut debet affluencia seu sufficiencia rerum pertinencium ad usum hominis cupiditate insaciabili mensurari, cum non possit, nec reum abusu quo semper peccatur, set pocius commoditate seu indigencia naturali vel verius personali' (308).

De Vitoria on FitzRalph: an adequate assessment?

SJ argues that FitzRalph's thesis respecting *dominium* is a tweaking of Giles of Rome's claim that dominion is only licitly held by those faithful to the church.[21] Giles' position relies on Augustine's claim that the riches of the world belong to the faithful.[22] Brock insists that FitzRalph's thesis is more original than Gwynn credits since Giles' position that the church's authority is supreme spiritually and temporally seems a far cry from Richard's insistence that lordship relies on grace. Brock comments: 'the difference is so great, and its implications so manifold, that it is difficult to understand how the two theories could be confused'.[23]

Brock is certainly right about this because the originality of FitzRalph's thesis about legitimate authority and ownership is underwritten by what strikes me as an original anthropology. It is certainly unlike anything found in Giles of Rome.[24] Philosophically, this anthropology is curious, being both thick and thin, so to say, at the same time. The human person is thickly social. Cupidity separates the person from a proper regard for others and grace is lost because cupidity forsakes the social character of charity. A human life is one woven into the lives of others. Defining of the very meaning of human being is a life not only woven into the lives of others, but a life of service and generosity to others. Citing pseudo-Dionysius, Richard dwells on God's generosity as God communicates goodness, power and beauty to creation (309–10). Human solidarity is a function of this generosity. To be a human in the image and similitude of God is to be an agent who communicates goodness, power and beauty to others. Only such an agent has legitimate authority. Those with a preference for cupidity remain in the image of God but no longer hold a similitude of God: as an image of God they retain the material cause of lordship but not the formal cause (363).

Departing from solidarity, mortal sin is also a radical diminishment of the person for, in Richard's conception, the core of the person is the will's orientation either to grace or cupidity. This now is a thin anthropology, for here human standing seems to hinge on the will's orientation. Unlike in Aquinas, the fact of being appears to add no safety net for false choices, nor do the inclinations of natural law, nor the embryonic goodness of the passions. The following passage strikes me as remarkable:

> You understand the point well: because, whoever has put above the act of free will, the law of cupidity, or the rule of natural affection, has sold himself with the result that such acts always exclusively happen for the sake of his own carnal pleasure. When the will's act is principally for the

---

21 A. Gwynn SJ, *English Austin friars in the time of Wyclyf* (Oxford, 1940), pp 60–1. 22 Brock, 'An edition of Richard FitzRalph's *De pauperie salvatoris*', p. xxxvi. 23 Ibid., p. xxxvii. 24 See McAleer, 'Sensuality: an avenue into the political and metaphysical thought of Giles of Rome', *Gregorianum*, 82 (Jan. 2001), 129–47. For my sense of Giles' political thought, see 'Giles of Rome on political authority', *Journal of the History of Ideas*, 60 (Jan. 1999), 21–36.

glory of God, not only is cupidity restrained as though with a collar or bridle, but more accurately the carnal passions – sorrow, joy, fear, love – and natural affection itself, what is called 'cupidity,' in its nature or essence is diminished, just as the subject or essence or nature of moral vice is diminished by the growth of moral virtue (327).[25]

To sell oneself to cupidity is to fall away from personhood: Richard can make this claim because he does not rely on a broadly Aristotelian conception of the make-up of the human being. Instead, there is a marked existentialism about Richard's conception, with the will's every choice radical and decisive in its consequences. This might seem an anachronistic formulation but the texts do point this way and I see it as a mark of Richard's originality.

I think it is Richard's originality here that earns him the opening pages of one of the most consequential texts of the entire Catholic intellectual tradition. The opening argument of Francisco de Vitoria's *On the American Indians* is a discussion of FitzRalph's ideas of property and government. De Vitoria's text is perhaps the single most important text of the Catholic just war tradition. It defends Aquinas' natural law account of war but significantly amplifies Aquinas' brief words about the legitimacy of war. The text is most famous for its positive recommendation of what is now termed 'humanitarian intervention'. Dating to 1539, *On the American Indians* is the attempt to assess international political action by the norms of law, philosophy, history, ethnology and moral theology. In terms of scope and complexity, it was the first attempt of its kind and has led some to speak of the Spanish Dominican as the 'father of international law'. The greatest jurist of the twentieth century, the infamous Carl Schmitt, speaks of de Vitoria's 'almost mythical renown' in international law.[26] It should be noted that the Catholic theory of just war is only one of a number of theories about war and as Schmitt points out in his 1950 treatise on international law, *The nomos of the Earth*, Enlightenment thinkers developed international law in opposition to some fundamental tenets of de Vitoria's thinking. However, Schmitt's effort in *The nomos of the Earth* is to show that international law in the twentieth century – especially under the influence of American jurists – has returned to the basic principles of de Vitoria after these had been dismantled by Enlightenment thinkers. Tony Blair and the Iraq war seem to warrant Schmitt's assessment.

---

25 'Prudenter ista intelligis: quoniam, cum lex huius cupiditatis sive affeccionis seu naturalis imperii, quod quiscunque habet super actus sue libere voluntatis, sibi vendicat ut actus talis propter commodum proprium carnale principaliter semper agatur; cum actus ipse propter Dei gloriam precipue exercetur, non solum quasi chamo seu freno constringitur ipsa cupiditas, et veraciter tam carnales passiones tristicie, leticie, timoris, atque amoris, quam eciam ipsa naturalis affeccio, que vocatur cupiditas, in sua natura sive essencia minuitur, sicut subiecta sive essencia seu natura vicii moralis minuitur crescente virtute morali' (327).   26 C. Schmitt, *The nomos of the Earth in the international law of the Jus Publicum Europaeum* (New York, 2003), p. 115.

De Vitoria on FitzRalph: an adequate assessment?

Since we can safely assume that de Vitoria paid heed to Thomas' warning – 'a small error in the beginning of something is a great one at the end' – it is of real intellectual, and not merely historical, interest how FitzRalph figures at the start of de Vitoria's seminal work.

FitzRalph is discussed four times by de Vitoria. He twice addresses his ideas on lordship and also Richard's arguments in defence of the temporal rule of Israel by Jesus, a rule inherited from Mary's bloodline and his arguments for when exactly Christ gave to the church the keys of spiritual authority. De Vitoria appears to have known two works: Richard's *De paupertate salvatoris* (1350–6)[27] and his *Summa de quaestionibus Armenorum*. Since de Vitoria enjoys calling Richard a heretic here and there, one might think that he does not take Richard's ideas especially seriously. This is far from true. Not only does he thoroughly document the arguments of Richard, he has also read what other commentators have said about him. In the modern edition of de Vitoria's works, his discussion of FitzRalph's thinking on Jesus as the temporal king of Israel covers six pages and on the matter of when Christ gave the keys of spiritual authority to the church, three pages. True, on first mentioning FitzRalph in his 1528 relection *On civil power*, de Vitoria dismisses Richard's position as not worthy of serious attention. He has read Richard, but after stating his essential position, he briskly concludes: 'Nevertheless, the authorities and arguments which he adduces to try to prove the assertion are so weak and unworthy of consideration for the solution of this problem [whether non-Christians are legitimate sovereigns] that I shall not waste time over them'. Ten years later, in the relection that concerns us, matters stand otherwise. Listing six arguments of Richard's, de Vitoria combats each in turn. In the modern edition of de Vitoria's *On the American Indians*, this discussion covers four pages.

On the American Indians is about the massive land-appropriations made by the Spanish in coming into contact with the New World. The text is about colonization, but de Vitoria's arguments must not be casually dismissed on this account. Very briefly, de Vitoria's argument is that the Aztecs do genuinely own their land. FitzRalph is rejected because his theory would imply that the Aztecs cannot be true owners and their land can simply be assumed without fault. Richard is clear: the grace of baptism is necessary for anyone to have original lordship (362). By contrast, de Vitoria writes: 'so neither Christian sovereigns nor the church may deprive non-Christians of their kingship or power on the grounds of their unbelief, unless they have committed some other injustice' (18). The Aztecs have true dominion of their lands, insists de Vitoria, and only the laws of war can justify replacing their rule with that of the Spanish. What could be grounds for war? Famously, de Vitoria dwells on the cannibalism and human sacrifice pervasive in

---

27 For the dates of the text and other good background, see Brock, 'An edition of Richard FitzRalph's *De pauperie salvatoris*', p. xii.

Aztec culture, but this is not his basic argument. Rather, he argues that communication is basic to human existence: inclined to seek friendship, trade and the expression of religion, under natural law humans may licitly press the laws of war against those who constrain these foundational forms of communication. Rejecting these forms of communication, the Aztecs lost their lordship as a consequence of losing the war with the Spanish, concludes de Vitoria.

De Vitoria's text has four parts. The first addresses the question whether it is appropriate for theology to address Spanish policy, the second asks whether the Indians genuinely owned their lands before the arrival of the Spanish – this is the section where de Vitoria and FitzRalph clash – and the third and fourth sections discuss the unjust titles to the Spanish land appropriation and the just titles, respectively. The second section on the original right of ownership of the Indians, considers five matters: can dominion be held by sinners, unbelievers, irrational beings, children or the mad? He discusses these five as the Indians were classed by some in one or all of these categories. FitzRalph's ideas provide the content for the discussion of whether lordship can be held by sinners. Others, like the Poor Men of Lyon, or the Waldensians, and John Wycliff, are cited, but serious consideration is reserved for FitzRalph.

Quick to point out that the Council of Constance condemned as error the proposition that 'no one is a civil master while he is in a state of mortal sin', de Vitoria nonetheless reviews FitzRalph's arguments. These are:

> 1. A human prince would not tolerate rebellion, but remove the rebels from their property, likewise God.
> 2. Proof of this is that God has cast down some from their thrones, e.g. Saul.
> 3. Made in the image of God, humans were given lordship of the earth. The image is not in the sinner and without the image there is no legitimate authority.
> 4. The sinner commits the crime of lese-majesty and thus ought to lose lordship.
> 5. The sinner, says Augustine, is not even worthy of the bread he eats, thus even less worthy of lordship.
> 6. Adam was deprived of dominion on account of sin; we are sinners, therefore etc.
> The second, fourth and fifth arguments are judged inconclusive since biblical witness contains counterexamples. Solomon, for example, though an 'evil sinner', holds the title 'king' in Scripture but none can be a king unless they have legitimacy.

The response to the sixth is historically freighted: de Vitoria arguing that since mortal sin does not deprive one of spiritual jurisdiction, it certainly does not remove civil jurisdiction; the latter is less dependent on grace than the former. De Vitoria was well aware that intense controversy surrounded this reasoning.

The responses that show the depth of disagreement between de Vitoria and FitzRalph, and that de Vitoria did not genuinely address Richard's arguments, are those to the first and the third. To the third, de Vitoria says that the human being is in the image of God 'by his inborn nature, that is by his rational powers'. Being in mortal sin does not alter this nature. We saw above that Richard just does not accept this: being human demands that our wills cleave to God in a personal loving relationship; less than this and our very natures corrode. In his first response, de Vitoria returns to Roman law. He reasons: natural dominion is a gift of God and if one loses civil dominion by offending God, natural dominion would be lost for the same reason; however, this is false because the human never loses lordship 'over his own acts and body'. Note what Richard says, however. Addressing the argument that if our natures corrode upon the loss of grace then so must our legal standing (*ius*), he writes:

> Careful. You do not rightly infer from the loss of cupidity some loss of right in this case, even though cupidity in itself is diminished; because natural lordship, which the will has over its own intrinsic acts [...] is not intrinsic to cupidity. That lordship, the will over its own acts, the confirmed angels have, and we will have *in patria*. Cupidity is one stock of this natural lordship and grace is the other stock of it. Lordship follows free will, as if a natural property of a just rational nature ... but it does not follow upon cupidity (328).[28]

Richard denies what de Vitoria assumes: the ontological fixity of the capacity for self-mastery (see 354; 363).

CONCLUSION

De Vitoria never engages the deeper ontological and normative insights animating FitzRalph's thought. His basic arguments cannot be judged a success, therefore. Indeed, De Vitoria's argument against FitzRalph has a paradoxical tone: progress or failure in charity is not important enough to determine

---

28 'Cave ne non recte inferas cupiditatis amitti ius aliquod in hoc casu, quamvis in se ipsa cupiditas minuatur; quoniam dominium naturale, quale habet voluntas super intrinsecos actus suos (...), non est intinseca cupiditas; quoniam istud dominium est in angelis confirmatis, et erit in nobis in patria; set cupiditas est unum instrumentum istius naturalis dominii, et gracia est aliud instrumentum ipsius. Dominium enim consequitur liberam voluntatem, tanquam proprietas naturalis iuste nature racionalis ... ; non autem ita eam consequitur ista cupiditas' (382).

property disputes. This must raise an eyebrow. On the other hand, surely FitzRalph would be discomforted if pressed on the problem of the Aztecs. If Christian ethical life is made basic to moral and political life, if grace is necessary for right social order, including the distribution of property, then the Aztecs would have to be judged as having no lordship. In principle, a godly settler could assume Aztec lands. This would not be seizure: the lands would be unowned.

Deference to Roman law grants property holding to the ungodly and forbids seizure. Why are our two thinkers so different on the matter of this deference? Goodness and generosity define the human being, insists Richard. De Vitoria is a moral theologian; he would not disagree. The difference turns on how social the human is understood to be: solidarity is basic to Richard. Compromise solidarity and a person corrodes her freedom. De Vitoria wants to argue that liberty is as basic as solidarity. This is not a liberty of indifference, the appeal of the good registers. It is to carve out a place for the individual, however. If de Vitoria experienced dismay on reading the archbishop of Armagh, he would have relished the ideas of a famous Dubliner, Edmund Burke.

John Foxholes OFM Armachanus (†1474): a note on his logical treatises formerly attributed to Richard FitzRalph

MICHAEL W. DUNNE

INTRODUCTION

In the *Bulletin* of the SIEPM,[1] I announced my intention to edit some logical treatises that were attributed to Richard FitzRalph as part of my general interest in his scholastic works. Here I shall argue that the attribution of these works to FitzRalph is a mistake, being based upon the fact that these texts are by an Armachanus but not FitzRalph. Rather, these texts are to be attributed to another archbishop of Armagh, John Foxholes OFM.

FITZRALPH'S SCHOLASTIC WORKS

FitzRalph's career as a lecturer at Oxford begins after 1322 when he was master of arts and continued when he began lecturing on the *Sentences* in 1328. After spending a year at Paris, where he was also qualified to teach, he returned to Oxford. His inception as doctor seems to have taken place in the summer of 1331. His academic career presumably ended when he, like many others, chose a career in university administration and was elected chancellor in 1332.

The following is a list of works assigned to FitzRalph's time as lecturer in Oxford:

1. The Logical Treatises:
   a) Magistri Ricardi filii Radulfi de Ybernia, *Tractatus de distinctionibus et formalitatibus* (contained in Pisa, Bibl. del Seminario Arcivescovile S. Caterina, 159ff 11r–55v; Roma, Biblioteca Angelica 563 (F.3.15), 49–81);

---

[1] In my original announcement of my intention to edit the *Lectura* of FitzRalph in *Bulletin de philosophie medieval*, 39 (1997), 100, following Walsh (see n. 2 below), I included the Pisa manuscript, Bibl. del Seminario Arcivescovile S. Caterina, 159, as containing some of the *quaestiones* from the Lectura. I later announced my intention to edit these logical treatises in *Bulletin de philosophie medieval*, 43 (2001), 48–9.

b) Id., *Tractatus de continentia singularis*, Pisa, Bibl. del Seminario Arcivescovile S. Caterina, 159ff 59r–79v;

c) Id., *Tractatus de praxi*, Pisa, Bibl. del Seminario Arcivescovile S. Caterina, 159ff 83r–114bisvb;

d) Id., *Tractatus de triplici genere actionum*, Pisa, Bibl. del Seminario Arcivescovile S. Caterina, 159ff 155r–121r;

e) Id., *Tractatus de propositione per se nota* (Pisa, Bibl. del Seminario Arcivescovile S. Caterina, 159ff 121r–128r; Roma, Bibl. Angelica 563 (F.3.49–15), 49–81;

f) Id., *Tractatus de productione verbi*, Pisa, Bibl. del Seminario Arcivescovile S. Caterina, 159ff 130r–178v;

2. A *Commentary on the physics* (c.1322–8; now lost, but referred to by FitzRalph himself – something of it may be possible to reconstruct from references by contemporary authors such as Kilvington, or a flavour gained from his own later comments on infinity, motion etc.).

3. The *Commentary on the* Sentences (lectures given in 1328–9 and then partially edited by FitzRalph as the *Opus correctum* of the *Sentences* in 1330–2).

4. A tractatus *De ymagine Trinitate* referred to by Wodeham probably part of the *Sentences* commentary circulating as a separate work.

5. The *Questio Biblica* (1329), which was given immediately after the *lectura* before FitzRalph left for Paris and later incorporated (by him, or others) as part of the *Opus correctum*.

6. *Quaestiones disputatae* contained in Vienna, Osterreichische Nationalbibliothek, CVP 5076ff 65r–69r, as noted by Walsh and repeated by R. Sharpe. The questions are as follows:
   - Queritur utrum creatura racionalis clare videns Deum necessario diligat ipsum;
   - Queritur utrum dampnati in inferno ante iudicium videntes gloriam beatorum post iudicium omni luce privati penitus excecentur;
   - Queritur utrum essenciam proportionatam caritatis (vie) succedit pro premio proportionaliter magnitudo gloriae;
   - Queritur utrum persone divine in mentes proprias ad sanctificandum eas invisibilis missio sit operacio propria emitatur.

The problem here, however, is that whereas these quaestiones follow on from some sermons of FitzRalph, the first seems to be attributable to Adam Wodeham and the second is identical to material contained in the Augustinian library of Klosterneuburg and attributed to Petrus de Pirichenwart and dating from 1424. Much of the content is a reply to the Ockhamist theory regarding the intensification and remission of forms. However, the authorship of at least one of the determinations is contested. See J.-F. Genest, 'Les premiers écrits théologiques de Bradwardine: textes inédits et découvertes récentes', *Medieval Commentaries*, 1, 395–421. On pp 404–7, Genest argues that no. 1 should be attributed to Bradwardine.

7. The *determinationes Ybernici* (given after he returned from Paris in 1330 when he was regent master in theology) are referred to by Adam Wodeham. A number of *determinationes* are contained in a manuscript in Florence. There are seven *determinationes*, which follow FitzRalph's *lectura* in Firenze, Conv. soppr. A.III.508.

At the bottom of fo. 109vb: *Hic incipiunt determinationes ybernici*. They are followed by a table of contents of the lectura on fo. 138vb, which finishes: *Expliciunt tituli questionum ybernici siue phyraph*. They are:

1. fo. 109vb *Utrum cuiuscumque actionis meritorie sit caritas principium effectivum*;
2. fo. 113va *Utrum per omnem actum meritorium augmentata caritate minuatur caritas*;
3. fo. 120ra *Utrum ammitata caritate necessario minuatur cupiditas*;
4. fo. 120vb *Utrum cupiditas possit augeri*;
5. fo. 121ra *Utrum per omnem actum augmentandem caritatem minuatur cupiditas*;
6. fo. 121vb *Utrum caritas et cupiditas in eadem anima possint simul augeri* ;
7. fo. 129ra *Utrum sit possibile antichristum fore bonum pro omni tempore quo conversabitur in terra*.

THE LOGICAL TREATISES

Katherine Walsh refers in her book to a Pisa manuscript, Seminario Arcivescovile MS 159, as containing individual *quaestiones* drawn from the *Lectura* on the *Sentences*.[2] When I examined the manuscript some years ago, it was immediately apparent that the works in it were not *quaestiones* belonging to the *Lectura*, but were instead logical treatises. The manuscript, which is made up of paper leaves, has already been catalogued and dated to the fifteenth century.[3] On fo. 10r a title is given in an eighteenth-century hand: 'Tractatus et distinctiones Archiepiscopi Armachani'. On the verso of the end cover, a sixteenth-century hand has provided an index of the volume as follows:

2 K. Walsh, *A fourteenth-century scholar and primate, Richard FitzRalph in Oxford, Avignon and Armagh* (Oxford, 1981), p. 38, n. 12. 3 *Catalogo di Manoscritti Filosofici nelle Biblioteche Italiane*, I, Firenze, Pisa, Poppi, Rimini, Trieste, a cura di T. De Robertis, D. Frioli, M.R. Pagnoni Sturlese, L. Pinelli, E. Staraz, L. Sturlese (Florence, 1980), pp 64–6.

In hoc volumine continentur infrascripti tractatus / Archiepiscopi armachani De distinctionibus / De continentia singularis / De praxi / De triplici genere actionis / De propositione per se nota / De productione verbi / De latitudine specierum Iohannis de ripa / Alberti Magni De principiis motus localis animalium / De principiis corporum animalium.

The editors of the catalogue of the Pisa manuscripts made the mistaken, if understandable, conclusion that the Armachanus in question was Richard FitzRalph. I too was convinced at one stage that these were works that possibly dated from before the time FitzRalph lectured on the *Sentences* and after he became a master in arts and so to the years 1322–8. Based on internal evidence, however, one of these works at least cannot belong to the fourteenth century, since in the *Tractatus de continentia singularis* the author refers to a 'karissimus frater Georgius de Macedonia'.[4] The most likely candidate is Georgius Benignus de Macedonia (Juraj Dragišić), also known as Georgius Benignus Salviati, who was born around 1444 in Srebrenica in Ragusa.[5] Srebrenica had become part of the Ottoman Empire in 1440 and so, having joined the Conventual Franciscans, he went to Italy for his studies, being ordained priest in Bologna in 1469. Salviati was in the circle of Cardinal Bessarion in Rome in the early 1470s, at the court of Federico of Montefeltro in Urbino between 1472 and 1482, and in the Florence of Lorenzo de' Medici from around 1486 until 1494. He obtained his doctorate in theology at Rome around 1474 and was then master of theology in Urbino, Florence, Pisa and Rome. He became bishop of Cagli in 1507 and then archbishop of the Church of the Blessed Virgin at Nazareth in Barletta. He died in Rome in 1520.[6] George was trained in scholastic philosophy, and he especially mentions one of his teachers, John Foxholes (1415/16–75), whom Edelheit describes as 'an English theologian and philosopher in the Scotist tradition'.[7] Foxholes wrote an extensive commentary on Scotus' *Questions on Porphyry's Isagoge* as well as on one of the *Questions on the metaphysics* of Antonius Andreas. Could Foxholes perhaps be the author of this text, which refers to his fellow Franciscan, George of Macedonia?

4 Bibl. del Seminario Arcivescovile S. Caterina, MS 159, fo. 59r.   5 George wrote a reply to George Trapezuntius' *Obiectiones*.   6 See Girard J. Etzkorn (ed.), *De arcanis Dei. Card. Bessarion eiusque socii anno 1471 disputantes: card. Franciscus de la Rovere OFM Conv, Joannes Gattus OP, Fernandus de Cordoba et Joannes Foxal OFM Conv. Secretarius: Georgius Benignus Salviati OFM Conv.* (Rome, 1997), p. 12. A recent article on George's thought is to be found in A. Edelheit, 'Human will, human dignity, and freedom: a study of Giorgio Benigno Salviati's early discussion of the will, Urbino 1474–1482', *Vivarium*, 46 (2008), 82–114.   7 A. Edelheit, 'Human will ...', p. 85. The *Tractatus de continentia singularis* is well within the Scotist tradition and refers to the *Questions on the metaphysics* of Antonius Andreas (1280–1320). George Salviati also wrote an introduction to logic, his *Dialectica nova* published in Rome in 1488 (see G.J. Etzkorn, *De arcanis Dei*, p. 12, n. 27) and it would make an interesting study to trace the possible influences between these treatises and Salviati's text.

John Foxholes, also known as also Foxhalls and Foxall and Iohannes Anglicus, was a member of the Conventual Franciscans.[8] He was perhaps from Yorkshire and was ordained priest at Lichfield in 1441. He was at Oxford friary in 1450 and afterwards taught at Cologne and Erfurt. He was next in Bologna after 1465 where he was lector in the great Franciscan stadium at San Francesco and where he would have had George Salviati as a student. Foxholes made the acquaintance of Francesco della Rovere OFM as participants in a theological debate on divine foreknowledge presided over by Cardinal Bessarion on 1 June 1470 or 1471 and at which George Salviati fulfilled the role of secretary.[9] It was della Rovere who, having been elected Pope Sixtus IV on 9 August 1471, elevated Foxholes to the see of Armagh on 16 December 1471, and so he became 'Armachanus'.

Another Vatican manuscript, Biblioteca Angelica 563, copied at Bologna in 1467, contains some logical treatises with the same titles as some of those contained in our Pisa manuscript and which in the Vatican manuscript are attributed to Iohannes Anglicus, which is how Foxholes was referred to in academic circles. A list of thirteen separate writings has been compiled by Girard Etzkorn[10] and to which Benignus Millett has added three more.[11] Some of these texts are to be found in another Vatican manuscript, Vat. lat. 9402, but neither Etzkorn or Millett seems to have been aware of the Pisa manuscript and its contents. Of the works contained in the Pisa manuscript, the *De distinctionibus*, *De triplici genere actionis* and *De propositione per se nota* appear in the Etzkorn/Millett list, but not the *De continentia singularis*, *De praxi* and *De productione verbi*, which, it seems, may well be hitherto unattributed works of Foxholes.

Foxholes, it would appear, did not have a happy time as Dominus Armachanus. The previous incumbent, Archbishop Bole, had left the diocese bankrupt and so Foxholes found that he could not pay the fees to the Curia in order to obtain the pallium. He had to borrow 1,100 gold florins from some Italian bankers, but he died in 1474 before paying them back. The bankers brought a case to court to compel the diocese to pay the money back, but it seems that Foxholes never actually obtained the papal bull providing him to the archdiocese and so never in fact truly became Armachanus.

---

8 See Benignus Millett OFM, 'John Foxholes, Franciscan, archbishop of Armagh, 1471–74', *Seanchas Ardmhacha: Journal of the Armagh Diocesan Historical Society*, 18:1 (1999/2000), 22–9. 9 See G.J. Etzkorn, *De arcanis Dei*, p. 11. 10 G. Etzkorn, 'John Foxhall OFM: his life and writings', *Franciscan Studies*, 69 (1989), 17–24 at 20–4. 11 B. Millett, 'John Foxholes', 28–9.

Bibliography of primary and secondary sources

Alban, K.J., *The teaching and impact of the 'Doctrinale' of Thomas Netter of Walden (c.1374–1430)* (Turnhout, 2010).
Anselmus Cantuariensis, *De humanis moribus per similitudines* in R.W. Southern and F.S. Schmitt (eds), *Memorials of Saint Anselm* (London, 1969).
Aristotle (ed.), *Aristoteles Latinus* (Bruges-Paris, 1961).
Aston, Margaret, 'Caim's castles: poverty, politics, and disendowment' in *Faith and fire: popular and unpopular religion, 1350–1600* (London, 1993), pp 95–131.
Augustine, *Confessions*, trans. R.S. Pine-Coffin (London, 1975).
Averroes [Ibn Rushd], *In Aristotelis de anima librum primum*, ed. S.F. Crawford (Cambridge MA, 1953).
Avvakumov, G., *Die entstehung des unionsgedankens: Die lateinische heologie des Mittelalters in der Auseinandersetzung mit dem Ritus der Ostkirche* (Berlin, 2002).
Avvakumov, G., 'Der Azymenstreit Konflikte und Polemiken um eine Frage des Ritus' in P. Bruns and G. Gresser (eds), *Vom Schisma zu den Kreuzzügen, 1054–1204* (Paderborn, 2005), 10–26.
Bakker, P.J.J.M., *La raison et le miracle: les doctrines eucharistiques (c.1250–c.1400). Contribution à l'étude des rapports entre philosophie et théologie* (Nijmegen, 1999).
Bakker, P.J.J.M., 'Durandus of Saint-Pourçain on Eucharistic presence: with a three-fold edition of Durandus' question: *Utrum totus Christus sit in sacramento eucharistie* (Sent. IV, d. 10, q. 2)' in R. Forrai, G. Geréby and I. Perczel (eds), *The Eucharist in theology and philosophy: issues of doctrinal history in East and West from the Patristic Age to the Reformation* (Leuven, 2005), pp 229–39.
Barbet, J., 'Le prologue du commentaire dionysien de François de Meyronnes', *Archives d'histoire doctrinale et littéraire du Moyen Age*, 29 (1954), 183–91.
Bellarminus, Robertus, *De scriptoribus ecclesiasticus*, ed. P. Labbé (Paris, 1660).
Bennett, N. (ed.), *The registers of Henry Burghersh, 1320–1342* (Woodbridge, 2003).
Benrath, G.A., *Wyclifs Bibelkommentar* (Berlin, 1966).
Bergstrom-Allen, Johan & Richard Copsey (eds), *Thomas Netter of Walden: Carmel in Britain* (4 vols, Faversham, 2009), iv.
Blancotti, B. (ed.), *Thomae Waldensis Carmelitae Anglici Doctrinale antiquitatum fidei catholicae ecclesiae* (3 vols, Venice, 1757–9).
Bliss, W.H. (ed.), *Calendar of entries in the papal registers relating to Great Britain and Ireland: papal letters* (London, 1895).
Brock, R.O., 'An edition of Richard FitzRalph's *De pauperie salvatoris*, books V, VI and VII' (PhD, U Colorado, 1954).
Buddenseig, R. (ed.), *De fundacione sectarum* in *Polemical works* (London, 1883).
Buescher, G., *The Eucharistic teaching of William Ockham* (New York, 1950).
Caplan, H., 'Rhetorical inventio in some medieval tractates on preaching', *Speculum*, 2 (1927), 284–95.
Catto, Jeremy, 'Oxford after Wyclif' in *The history of the University of Oxford, 2: late medieval Oxford* (Oxford, 1992), pp 240–6.

Catto, Jeremy & R. Evans, 'Wyclif and Wycliffism at Oxford, 1356–1430' in *The history of the University of Oxford, 2: late medieval Oxford* (Oxford, 1992), pp 175–261.

Clarke, H.B. & J.R.S. Phillips (eds), *Ireland, England and the Continent in the Middle Ages and beyond: essays in memory of a turbulent friar, F.X. Martin OSA* (Dublin, 2006).

Copsey, Richard, 'Thomas Netter of Walden: a biography' in Johan Bergstrom-Allen & Richard Copsey (eds), *Thomas Netter of Walden: Carmel in Britain* (vol. 4, Faversham, 2009), pp 23–111.

Courtenay, W.J., *Adam Wodeham: an introduction to his life and writings* (Leiden, 1978).

Courtenay, W.J., 'Between despair and love: some late modifications of Augustine's teaching on fruition and psychic states' in Kenneth Hagen (ed.), *Augustine, the harvest and theology, 1300–1650* (Leiden, 1990), pp 5–19.

Courtenay, W.J., *Ockham and Ockhamism* (Leiden, 2008).

Courtenay, W.J., *Schools and scholars in fourteenth-century England* (Princeton NJ, 1987).

Dahmus, J.H., *The metropolitan visitation of William Courteney, archbishop of Canterbury, 1381–1396* (Urbana IL, 1950).

Dahmus, J.H., *The prosecution of John Wyclyf* (New Haven CT, 1952).

Dawson, J.D., 'Richard FitzRalph and the fourteenth-century poverty controversies', *Journal of Ecclesiastical History*, 34:3 (July 1983), 315–44.

de Baysio, Guido, *In sextum decretalium commentaria* (Venice, 1577).

de la Torre, B.R., *Thomas Bradwardine and the contingency of futures: the possibility of human freedom* (Notre Dame IN, 1987).

de Rijk, L.M., 'Burley's so-called *Tractatus Primus*, with an edition of the additional quaestio "Utrum contradictio sit maxima oppositio"', *Vivarium*, 34 (1996), 161–91.

Chronicon Joannis Marignolae in Dobner, G. (ed.), *Monumenta historica Boemiae* (6 vols, Prague, 1768), ii.

Dolan, T.P., 'Richard FitzRalph's *Defensio curatorum* in Transition' in H.B. Clarke and J.R.S Phillips (eds), *Ireland, England and the Continent in the Middle Ages and beyond: essays in memory of a turbulent friar, F.X. Martin OSA* (Dublin, 2006), pp 177–94.

Dolan, T.P., 'Richard FitzRalph' in James McGuire and James Quinn (ed.), *Dictionary of Irish biography* (Dublin and Cambridge, 2009).

Dolan, T.P., 'FitzRalph, Richard' in S.J. Connolly (ed.), *Oxford companion to Irish history* (Oxford, 1998).

Dondaine, A., '"Contra Graecos": premiers écrits polémiques des dominicains d'Orient', *Archivum Fratrum Praedicatorum*, 21 (1951), 320–446.

Duba, W., 'The afterlife in medieval Frankish Cyprus', Επ ετηρίδα του Κέντρου Επ ιστημονικών Ερευνών, 26 (2000), 167–94.

Duba, W., 'Moral edification, the search for truth, and the papal court: Pierre Roger (Clement VI) and the intellectual atmosphere of Avignon' in J. Hamesse (ed.), *La vie culturelle, intellectuelle et scientifique a la cour des papes d'Avignon* (Turnhout, 2006), pp 303–19.

Duba, W. & T. Suarez-Nani, 'Introduction' in *Francisci de Marchia Reportatio IIA (Quaestiones in secundum librum Sententiarum) qq. 13–27* (Leuven, 2010), pp xii–xiii.

Dunne, Michael, 'Richard FitzRalph's *Lectura on the Sentences*' in P. Rosemann (ed.),

Medieval commentaries on the Sentences of Peter Lombard (vol. 2, Leiden & Boston, 2010), ii, pp 405–37.

Dunne, Michael, 'A fourteenth-century example of an *Introitus sententiarum* at Oxford: Richard FitzRalph's inaugural speech in praise of the *Sentences* of Peter Lombard', *Medieval Studies*, 63 (2001), 1–29.

Dunne, Michael, 'FitzRalph, Richard' in T. Duddy (ed.), *Dictionary of Irish philosophers* (London, 2006), pp 129–32.

Edelheit, A., 'Human will, human dignity and freedom: a study of Giorgio Benigno Salviati's early discussion of the will, Urbino 1474–1482', *Vivarium*, 46 (2008), 82–114.

Emden, A.B., 'Northerners and southerners in the organization of the university to 1509' in *Oxford studies presented to Daniel Callus* (Oxford, 1964), pp 1–30.

Erickson, J.H., 'Leavened and unleavened: some theological implications of the Schism of 1054', *St Vladimir's Theological Quarterly*, 14 (1970), 3–24.

Etzkorn, G.J. (ed.), *Guillelmi de Ockham Opera Theologica* III (St Bonaventure NY, 1977).

Etzkorn, G.J., 'John Foxhall OFM: his life and writings', *Franciscan Studies*, 69 (1989), 17–24.

Etzkorn, G.J. (ed.), *De arcanis Dei. Card. Bessarion eiusque socii anno 1471 disputantes: card. Franciscus de la Rovere OFM Conv., Joannes Gattus OP, Fernandus de Cordoba et Joannes Foxal OFM Conv. Secretarius: Georgius Benignus Salviati OFM Conv.* (Rome, 1997).

FitzRalph (see Radulphi, Ricardus).

Fowler, D.C., *The life and times of John Trevisa, medieval scholar* (Seattle WA, 1995).

Friedman, R.L., 'Trinitarian theology and philosophical issues [I]: trinitarian texts from the late thirteenth and early fourteenth centuries', *Cahiers de l'institut du moyen-âge grec et latin*, 72 (2001), 89–168.

Friedman, R.L., 'Divergent traditions in later-medieval trinitarian theology: relations, emanations and the use of philosophical psychology, 1250–1325', *Studia Theologica*, 53 (1999), 13–25.

Friedman, R.L., *Medieval trinitarian thought from Aquinas to Ockham* (Cambridge, 2010).

Fyrigos, A. (ed.), *Barlaam Calabro. L'uomo, l'opera, il pensiero. Atti del convegno internazionale Reggio Calabia – Seminara – Gerace 10–11–12 dicembre 1999* (Rome, 2001).

Fyrigos, A. (ed.), *Barlaam Calabro Opere contro i Latini* (2 vols, Vatican City, 1998).

Geanakoplos, D.J., 'Bonaventura, the two mendicant orders and the Greeks at the Council of Lyon' in idem, *Constantinople and the west: essays on the late Byzantine (Palaeologan) and Italian Renaissances and the Byzantine and Roman churches* (Madison WI, 1989), pp 55–83 (*Studies in Church History*, 13 [1976]).

Gemeinhardt, P., *Die Filioque-Kontroverse zwischen Ost- und Westkirche im Frühmittelalter* (Berlin & New York, 2002).

Georgedes, K., 'The serpent in the tree of knowledge: enjoyment and use in fourteenth-century theology' (PhD, Wisconsin-Madison, 1995).

Gill, J., *Byzantium and the papacy, 1198–1400* (New Brunswick, 1979).

Gradon, Pamela & Anne Hudson (eds), *English Wycliffite sermons* (Oxford, 1996).

Grellard, Christophe & Aurelien Robert (eds), *Atomism in late medieval philosophy and theology* (Leiden, 2009).
Gualterus Chatton [Walter Chatton], *Reportatio super Sententias, Liber I, distinctiones 10–48*, ed. J.C. Wey and G.J. Etzkorn (Toronto, 2002).
Gualterus Chatton, *Lectura super Sententias, Liber I, distinctiones 8–17*, ed. J.C. Wey and G.J. Etzkorn (Toronto, 2009).
Gwynn, A., 'Richard FitzRalph at Avignon', *Studies*, 22 (1933), 591–607.
Gwynn, A., 'Richard FitzRalph, Archbishop of Armagh', *Studies*, 25 (1936), 8–96.
Gwynn, A., 'The sermon-diary of Richard FitzRalph, archbishop of Armagh', *Proceedings of the Royal Irish Academy*, 1C (1937), 39–41.
Gwynn, A., 'Archbishop FitzRalph and the friars', *Studies*, 26 (1937), 50–67.
Gwynn, A., *English Austin friars in the time of Wyclyf* (Oxford, 1940).
Gwynn, A., 'Two sermons of Primate Ric. FitzRalph', *Archivia Hibernica*, 14 (1949), 50–65.
Hammerich, L.L., *The beginning of the strife between Richard FitzRalph and the mendicants* (Copenhagen, 1938).
Haren, M.J., 'Bishop Gynwell of Lincoln, two Avignonese statutes and Archbishop FitzRalph of Armagh's suit at the Roman curia against the friars', *Archivum Historiae Pontificiae*, 31 (1993), 275–92.
Haren, M.J., 'The will of Master John de Belvoir, official of Lincoln (d. 1391)', *Medieval Studies*, 58 (1996), 119–47.
Haren, M.J., 'Montaillou and Drogheda: a medieval twinning' in A. Meyer, C. Rendtel and M. Wittmer-Butsch (eds), *Päpste, Pilger, Pönitentiarie: Festschrift für Ludwig Schmugge zum 65. Geburtstag* (Tübingen, 2004), pp 435–56.
Haren, M.J., *Sin and society in fourteenth-century England: a study of the* Memoriale presbiterorum (Oxford, 2000).
Haren, M.J., 'Richard FitzRalph of Dundalk, Oxford and Armagh: scholar, prelate and controversialist' in James McEvoy and Michael Dunne (eds), *The Irish contribution to European scholastic thought* (Dublin, 2009), pp 88–110.
Haren, M.J., 'Richard FitzRalph and the friars: the intellectual itinerary of a curial controversialist' in J. Hamesse (ed.), *Roma, magistra mundi. Itineraria culturae medievalis: mélanges offerts au Père L.E. Boyle à l'occasion de son 75e anniversaire* (3 vols, Louvain-la-Neuve, 1998), i, pp 349–67.
Haren, M.J., 'The interrogatories for officials, lawyers and secular estates of the *Memoriale presbiterorum*' in P. Biller and A.J. Minnis (eds), *Handling sin: confession in the Middle Ages* (Woodbridge, 1998), pp 123–64.
Haren, M.J., 'Confession, social ethics and social discipline in the *Memoriale presbiterorum*' in Biller and Minnis (eds), *Handling sin: confession in the Middle Ages* (Woodbridge, 1998), pp 109–22.
Henricus Gandavensis [Henry of Ghent], *Summa quaestionum ordinariarum* (Paris, 1520).
Henricus Gandavensis, *Quodlibeta* in R. Macken and R. Wielockx (eds), *Henrici de Gandavo opera omnia* (Leuven-Leiden, 1979–present).
Henricus de Harclay, *Ordinary questions I–XIV*, ed. M.G. Henninger (Oxford, 2008).
Highfield, J.R.L., 'The English hierarchy under Edward III', *Transactions of the Royal Historical Society*, 5:6 (1956), 115–38.

Hingeston-Randolph, F.C. (ed.), *The register of John de Grandisson, bishop of Exeter, AD1327–1369* (London, 1894).
Hinterberger, M., 'Απ ό το ορθόδοξο Βυζάντιο στην καθολική Δύση. Τέσσερις διαφορετικοί δρόμοι', in *Το Βυζάντιο και οι απ αρχές της Ευρώπ ης* (Athens, 2004).
Hirvonen, V., *Passions in William Ockham's philosophical psychology* (Dordrecht, 2004).
Holopainen, T.M., 'William Ockham's theory of the foundations of ethics' (PhD, Helsinki, 1991).
Hudson, Anne, 'A neglected Wycliffite text' in *Lollards and their books* (London, 1985), pp 43–65.
Hudson, Anne, *The premature reformation* (Oxford, 1986).
Hudson, Anne, *Studies in the transmission of Wyclif's writings* (Oxford, 2008).
Iohannes Duns Scotus, *Opera omnia*, ed. Wadding (Lyon, 1639; repr. Paris, 1891–5).
Iohannes Duns Scotus, *Opera omnia*, ed. Balic (Vatican City, 1950–).
Kaluza, Z., 'Les sciences et leurs langages : note sur le statut du 29 décembre 1340 et le prétendu statut perdu contre Ockham' in L. Bianchi (ed.), *Filosofia e teologia nel trecento: Studi in ricordo di Eugenio Randi* (Louvain-la-Neuve, 1994).
Kekes, J., *Enjoyment: the moral significance of styles of life* (Oxford, 2008).
Kitanov, S.V., 'Peter of Candia on demonstrating that God is the sole object of beatific enjoyment', *Franciscan Studies*, 67 (2009), 427–89.
Kitanov, S.V., 'Durandus of St-Pourçain and Peter Auriol on the act of beatific enjoyment' in S.F. Brown, T. Dewender and Th. Kobusch (eds), *Philosophical debates at Paris in the early fourteenth century* (Leiden, 2009), pp 163–78.
Kitanov, S.V., 'Beatific enjoyment in scholastic theology and philosophy, 1240–1335' (PhD, Helsinki, 2006).
Kitanov, S.V., 'Peter of Candia on beatific enjoyment: can one enjoy the divine persons separately from the divine essence?', *Mediaevalia Philosophica Polonorum*, 35:1 (2006), 144–66.
Kitanov, S.V., 'Displeasure in heaven, pleasure in hell: four Franciscan masters on the relationship between love and pleasure, and hatred and displeasure', *Traditio*, 58 (2003), 287–340.
Kitanov, S.V., 'Bonaventure's understanding of *fruitio*', *Picenum Seraphicum*, 20 (2001), 137–81.
Knowles, D., *Great historical enterprises and problems in monastic history* (London, 1962).
Knuuttila, S., *Emotions in ancient and medieval philosophy* (Oxford, 2004).
Kolbaba, T., 'Repercussions of the Second Council of Lyon (1274): theological polemic and the boundaries of orthodoxy' in M. Hinterberger and C. Schabel (eds), *Greeks, Latins and intellectual history* (Leuven, 2011), pp 43–68.
Kraye, J. & R. Saarinen (eds), *Moral philosophy on the threshold of modernity* (Dordrecht, 2005).
Krüger, S., *Konrad von Megenberg. Ökonomik* (Munich, 1973), i.
Ladurie, E. Le Roy, *Montaillou: Cathars and Catholics in a French village, 1294–1324* (London, 1980).
Lahey, S., *John Wyclif* (Oxford, 2009).
Lahey, S., *Metaphysics and politics in the thought of John Wyclif* (Cambridge, 2003).
Lahey, S., 'Of divine ideas and insolubles: Wyclif's explanation of God's understanding of sin', *Modern Schoolman*, 86 (Nov. 2008/Jan. 2009), 211–32.

Bibliography of primary and secondary sources

Lahey, S., 'Grace and freedom in the soteriology of John Wyclif', *Traditio*, 60 (2005), 279-337.

Laiou, A.E. & R.P. Mottahedeh (eds), *The Crusades from the perspective of Byzantium and the Muslim world* (Washington DC, 2001).

Laiou, A.E. & R.P. Mottahedeh (eds), *The Byzantine lists: errors of the Latins* (Urbana & Chicago IL, 2000).

Lambert, M., *Medieval heresy* (London, 1977; Oxford, 1992).

Lambertini, R., 'Poverty and power: Franciscans in later medieval political thought', *Moral Philosophy on the Threshold of Modernity*, 57:2 (2005), 141-63.

Lechler, G. *Iohannis de Wiclif Tractatus de Officio Pastoralis* (Leipzig, 1863).

Leff, G., *Richard FitzRalph: commentator on the Sentences: a study of theological orthodoxy* (Manchester, 1963).

Levy, I., *A companion to John Wyclif, late medieval theologian* (Leiden, 2006).

Levy, I., *John Wyclif: scriptural logic, real presence and the parameters of orthodoxy* (Milwaukee WI, 2003).

Lombardus, Petrus, *Sententiae in IV libris distinctae*, ed. I. Brady (vol. 1, Grottaferrata, 1971).

Lumby, J.R. (ed.), *Chronicon Henrici Knighton vel Cnitthon, monachi Leycestrensis* (London, 1895).

Mabillon, J., *Dissertatio de pane eucharistico, azymo, ac fermentato* (1673).

MacIntyre, A., *Three rival versions of moral enquiry: encyclopaedia, genealogy and tradition* (Notre Dame IN, 1990).

Marchant, Peter, *Fundamenta Duodecim Ordinis Fratrum Minorum* (Ghent, 1657).

Matthew, F.D. (ed.), *The English works of Wyclif* (London, 1902).

Maurer, A., *The philosophy of William of Ockham in the light of its principles* (Toronto, 1999).

McAleer, G.J., *To kill another: homicide and natural law* (London, 2010).

McAleer, G.J., 'Sensuality: an avenue into the political and metaphysical thought of Giles of Rome', *Gregorianum*, 82 (Jan. 2001), 129-47.

McAleer, G.J., 'Giles of Rome on political authority', *Journal of the History of Ideas*, 60 (1999), 21-36.

McEvoy, J., *Robert Grosseteste* (Oxford, 2000).

McFarlane, K.B., *Lancastrian kings and Lollard knights* (Oxford, 1972).

McGrade, A.S., 'Enjoyment at Oxford after Ockham' in A. Hudson and M. Wilks (eds), *From Ockham to Wyclif* (Oxford, 1987), 63-88.

McGrade, A.S., 'Ockham and Valla on enjoyment' in I.D. McFarlane (ed.), *Acta conventus neo-Latini sanctandreani: proceedings of the fifth international congress of neo-Latin studies* (Binghamton NY, 1986).

McGrade, A.S., 'Ockham on enjoyment: towards an understanding of fourteenth-century philosophy and psychology', *Review of Metaphysics*, 33 (1981), 706-28.

Megenberg, Conrad of, *Commentarius de laudibus B.V. Mariae* (Munich, Bayerische Staatsbibliothek, CLM 14190).

Meyendorff, J., *Byzantine theology: historical trends and doctrinal themes* (New York, 1974).

Michałski, Konstanty, 'Le problème de la volonté à Oxford et Paris au XIVe siècle',

Studia Philosophica, 2 (1937), repr. in idem, *La philosophie au XIVe siècle* (Frankfurt-am-Main, 1969), pp 281–412.

Milbank, J., *The suspended middle: Henri de Lubac and the debate concerning the supernatural* (Grand Rapids MI, 2005).

Millett, B., 'John Foxholes, Franciscan, Archbishop of Armagh, 1471–74', *Seanchas Ardmhacha: Journal of the Armagh Diocesan Historical Society*, 18:1 (1999/2000), 22–9.

Minnis, A.J., '"Authorial intention" and "literal sense" in the exegetical theories of Richard FitzRalph and John Wyclif: an essay in the medieval history of biblical hermeneutics', *Proceedings of the Royal Irish Academy*, 75C (Mar. 1975), 1–31.

Monachus, Iohannes, *Glossa aurea nobis priori loco super Sexto Decretalium libro addita* (Paris, 1535; repr. Aalen, 1968).

Mosino, F., 'Le orazione avignonesi di Barlaam Calabro nel Registro 134 dell'Archivio Segreto Vaticano', *Divptuca*, 4 (1986), 149–63.

Nicol, D.M., 'The Byzantine reaction to the Council of Lyons, 1274' in idem, *Byzantium: its ecclesiastical history and relations with the western world* (London, 1972), 113–46.

Oberman, H., *Archbishop Thomas Bradwardine: a fourteenth-century Augustinian* (Utrecht, 1958).

Ockham, Guillelmus de, *Scriptum in librum primum Sententiarum*, ed. Gedeon Gál and Stephanus Brown (St Bonaventure NY, 1967).

Ockham, William of (Guilelmus de Ockham), *Quaestiones in librum secundum Sententiarum*, ed. Gál and Wood (St Bonaventure NY, 1981).

O'Donnell, C., 'A controversy on confirmation: Thomas Netter of Walden and Wyclif' in Bergstrom-Allen & Copsey (eds), *Thomas Netter of Walden: Carmel in Britain* (4, British Province of Carmelites, 2009), 317–22.

O'Driscoll, C., 'Re-negotiating the just war: the invasion of Iraq and punitive war', *Cambridge Review of International Affairs*, 19:3 (2006), 405–20.

Olson, L., 'Reading Augustine's *Confessiones* in fourteenth-century England: John de Grandisson's fashioning of text and self', *Traditio*, 52 (1997), 201–57.

Orme, N., 'Bishop Grandisson and popular religion', *Reports and Transactions of the Devonshire Association for the Advancement of Science, Literature and Art*, 134 (1992), 107–18.

Pantin, W.A., *The English church in the fourteenth century* (Cambridge, 1955).

Papadakis, A., *Crisis in Byzantium: the Filioque controversy in the patriarchate of Gregory II of Cyprus, 1283–1289* (Crestwood NY, 1997).

Petrus Aureolus, *Tractatus de conceptione Virginis* in *Fr Gulielmi Guarrae, Fr Ioannis Duns Scoti, Fr Petri Aureoli Quaestiones disputatae de Immaculata Conceptione Beatae Mariae Virginis*, ed. [A. Emmen] (Quaracchi, 1904).

Piana, C., 'Un sermone inedito su l'assunzione della Vergine di Riccardo FitzRalph, Primate d'Irlanda (+1360)', *Studi Francescani*, 20 (1948), 115–25.

Piron, S., 'Avignon sous Jean XXII. L'Eldorado des theologiens', *Cahiers de Fanjeaux*, 45 (2010), 17–85.

Pironet, F. and J. Spruyt, '*Sophismata*' in E.N. Zalta (ed.), *The Stanford encyclopedia of philosophy* (summer 2009 edition), http://plato.stanford.edu/archives/sum2009/entries/sophismata.

Poppi, A., 'La virtù della fede in Giovanni Duns Scoto: *Lectura III* e *Reportationes Parisienses III*' in R. Quinto (ed.), *Fides virtus: the virtue of faith in the context of the theological virtues: exegesis, moral theology and pastoral care from 12th to early 16th century* (Münster, forthcoming).

Proudhon, P.J., *What is property?* (Cambridge, 2007).

Radulphi, Ricardus [Richard FitzRalph, 'Armachanus'], *Summa de questionibus Armenorum*, ed. Johannis Sudoris (Paris, 1511).

Radulphi, Ricardus [Richard FitzRalph, 'Armachanus'], *Prosposicio 'Unusquisque'* (see Hammerich).

Radulphi, Ricardus [Richard FitzRalph, 'Armachanus'], 'Sermons' (see Gwynn, Piana, Zimmermann).

Radulphi, Ricardus [Richard FitzRalph, 'Armachanus'], *Defensio curatorum* (printed Louvain, 1475, Paris, 1485, Rouen, 1485, Lyon, 1496, Paris, 1627, Paris, 1633; in Goldast, *Monarchia s. Romani imperii*, ii, pp 1393–410; Brown, Fasciculus rerum expetendarum, ii, pp 466–86).

Radulphi, Ricardus [Richard FitzRalph, 'Armachanus'], *De pauperie salvatoris*, bks I–IV, ed. R.L. Poole in John Wyclif, *De dominio divino libri tres to which are added the first four books of the treatise De pauperie salvatoris by Richard FitzRalph Archbishop of Armagh* (London, 1890), pp 257–476.

Robson, J.A., *Wyclif and the Oxford schools: the relation of the 'Summa de ente' to scholastic debates at Oxford in the later fourteenth century* (Cambridge, 1966).

Rose-Troup, F., *Bishop Grandisson, student and art lover* (Plymouth, 1929).

Salviati, George, *Dialectica nova* (Rome, 1488).

Steele, M.A., 'A study of the books owned or used by John Grandisson, bishop of Exeter, 1327–1369' (PhD, Oxford, 1994).

Salter, H.E., *The Oxford deeds of Balliol College* (Oxford, 1913).

Salter, H.E., *Snappe's formulary* (Oxford, 1923).

Schabel, C., 'Attitudes toward the Greeks and the history of the *Filioque* dispute in fourteenth-century Oxford' in P. Piatti (ed.), *The Fourth Crusade revisited: Atti del conferenza internazionale nell'ottavo centenario della IV Crociata, 1204–2004. Andros (Grecia) 27–30 maggio 2004*, Pontificio Comitato di scienze, Atti e Documenti, 22 (Vatican City, 2008), 320–35.

Schabel, C., 'Attitudes towards the Greeks' in R.L. Friedman, *Intellectual traditions in the medieval university: the use of philosophical psychology in trinitarian theology among the Franciscans and Dominicans, 1250–1350* (forthcoming).

Schabel, C., 'The quarrel over unleavened bread in western theology, 1234–1439' in M. Hinterberger and C. Schabel (eds), *Greeks, Latins and intellectual history, 1204–1500* (Leuven, 2011).

Schabel, C. & R.L. Friedman, 'Francis of Marchia's commentaries on the *Sentences*: question list and state of research', *Medieval Studies*, 63 (2001), 31–106.

Schabel, C. & R.L. Friedman, 'Trinitarian theology and philosophical issues III: Oxford, 1312–1329: Walsingham, Graystanes, FitzRalph and Rodington', *Cahiers de l'institut du moyen-âge grec et latin*, 74 (2003), 39–88.

Schabel, C. & R.L. Friedman, 'Trinitarian theology and philosophical issues IV: English theology ca. 1300: William of Ware and Richard of Bromwich', *Cahiers de l'institut du moyen-âge grec et latin*, 75 (2004), 121–60.

Schabel, C. & R.L. Friedman, 'Trinitarian theology and philosophical issues V: Oxford Dominicans: William of Macklesfield and Hugh of Lawton', *Cahiers de l'institut du moyen-âge grec et latin*, 76 (2005), 31–44.

Schmitt, C., *The nomos of the Earth in the international law of the Jus Publicum Europaeum* (New York, 2003).

Smith III, M.H., *And taking bread ... Cerularius and the azyme controversy of 1054* (Paris, 1978).

Somerset, Fiona (ed.), *Four Wycliffite dialogues* (Oxford, 2009).

Southern, R.W., *Robert Grosseteste: the growth of an English mind in medieval Europe* (Oxford, 1986).

Spinka, Matthew (ed.), *De officio pastoralis: advocates of reform from Wyclif to Erasmus*, trans. Ford Lewis Battles (Westminster, 2006).

Sylla, E., 'The academic context of Walter Burley's *Tractatus Primus*', forthcoming in the acts of the 12th International Congress of the Société Internationale pour l'Etude de la Philosophie Médiévale (2007).

Szittya, P., *The antifraternal tradition in medieval literature* (Princeton NJ, 1986).

Tachau, K.H., *Vision and certitude in the age of Ockham: optics, epistemology and the foundation of Semantics, 1250–1345* (Leiden, 1988).

Tachau, K.H., 'Looking gravely at Dominican puns: the "Sermons" of Robert Holcot and Ralph Friseby', *Traditio*, 46 (1991), 337–45.

Tachau, K.H., 'Introduction' in P.A. Streveler and K.H. Tachau (eds), *Seeing the future clearly: questions on future contingents by Robert Holcot* (Toronto, 1995), 1–27.

Thijssen, J.M.M.H., *Censure and heresy at the University of Paris* (Philadelphia, 1998).

Thomas Aquinas, *Opera omnia*, Commissio Leonina, 1888–.

Thompson, A.H., 'The will of Master William Doune, archdeacon of Leicester', *Archaeological Journal*, 72 (1915), 233–84.

Thomson, J.A.F., 'Orthodox religion and the origins of Lollardy', *History*, 74 (1989), 39–55.

Thomson, W., *The Latin writings of Wyclyf* (Toronto, 1983).

Trevisa, John, *Dialogus inter Militem et Clericum*, ed. A.J. Perry (Oxford, 1925).

Vitoria, F. de, *On homicide* (Milwaukee WI, 1997).

Vittorini, M., 'Walter Burley: life and works' in A. Conti (ed.), *A companion to Walter Burley* (Leiden, forthcoming).

Walsh, K., *A fourteenth-century scholar and primate: Richard FitzRalph in Oxford, Avignon and Armagh* (Oxford, 1981).

Walsh, K., 'Der Becket der irischen Kirche: der "Armachanus" Richard FitzRalph von Armagh (+1360), Professor – Kirchenfürst – "Heiliger"', *Innsbrucker Historische Studien*, 20/21 (1999), 1–58.

Walsh, K., 'FitzRalph, Richard (b. before 1300, d. 1360)', *Oxford dictionary of national biography* [Oxford] (2004).

Walsh, K., 'Preaching, pastoral care and *Sola Scriptura* in later medieval Ireland: Richard FitzRalph and the use of the Bible', *Studies in Church History: Subsidia*, 4 (Oxford, 1985), 251–68.

Ward, G., *The politics of discipleship: becoming postmaterial citizens* (Grand Rapids MI, 2009).

Wilks, M., 'Wyclif and Hus as leaders of religious protest movements', *Studies in Church History*, 9 (1972), 109–30; repr. in Anne Hudson (ed.), *Wyclif: political ideas and practice* (Oxford, 2000), pp 63–84.
Wilks, M., 'Wyclif and the wheel of time', *Studies in Church History*, 33 (1997), 177–93.
Williams, R. & G. Weigel, 'War and statecraft: an exchange', *First Things*, 141 (Mar. 2004), 14–21.
Wood, R., 'Introduction' in R. Wood and G. Gál (eds), *Adam de Wodeham, Lectura secunda in librum primum Sententiarum* (3 vols, St Bonaventure NY, 1990).
Wood, R. & G. Gál (eds), *Adam de Wodeham Lectura secunda* III (St Bonaventure NY, 1990).
Wyclif, John, *De dominio divino*, ed. R.L. Poole (London, 1890).
Wyclif, John, *On the truth of holy scripture*, trans. Ian Levy (Kalamazoo MI, 2001).
Wyclif, John, *Trialogus cum supplementum trialogi*, ed. Gotthard Lechler (Oxford, 1869).
Yarnold, E., 'Transubstantiation' in R. Forrai, G. Geréby and I. Perczel (eds), *The Eucharist in theology and philosophy: issues of doctrinal history in east and west from the Patristic Age to the Reformation* (Leuven, 2005), pp 381–94.
Zimmermann, B., 'Ricardi archiepiscopi Armacani bini sermonis de immaculata conceptione', *Analecta ordinis carmelitarum discalceatorum*, 6 (1931–2), 158–89.

ONLINE MATERIALS

M. Dunne (ed.), http://philosophy.nuim.ie/projects-research/projects/richard-fitzralph/text.
The Adam Wodeham Critical Edition Project at *http://www.bc.edu/sites/adamwodehamcriticaledition/*.

Index of ancient, medieval and Renaissance names

Adam Wodeham, 2–5, 11–12, 28–9, 56–78, 79–95, 131, 137, 166, 200, 201
Albert the Great, 56, 202
Ambrose of Milan, 148
Andronikos III, emperor, 139
Anselm of Canterbury, 64, 67, 68, 89, 134, 136, 138, 141, 143, 148, 151, 159
Antonius Andreas, 202
Areopagite, ps. Dionysius, 5, 121, 122n, 124, 125, 127, 149, 164, 193
Aristotle, 13, 23, 26, 27, 47, 56, 58, 61, 62, 64, 65, 69, 72n, 74, 75, 89, 101, 104, 109, 134, 183
Arnold of Strelley, 93
Athanasius, 148
Augustine, 5, 21, 32, 34, 40, 56, 58, 89, 100, 101, 113, 119, 120, 127, 134, 148, 174n, 176, 181, 191, 193, 196
Averroes [Ibn Rushd], 56, 75, 100, 101

Barlaam the Calabrian, 6, 108, 121, 128–55
Basilios Bessarion, cardinal, 202, 203
Benedict, St, 182
Benedict XII, pope, 15, 33, 39, 108, 129, 139
Berengar of Tours, 15
Bernard, St, 101, 159, 162
Bernardo Massari, 139
Boethius, 67, 68
Bonagratia of Bergamo, 15
Bonaventure, St, 86, 100, 176, 178, 183, 184,

Charlemagne, 149
Cicero, 39
Clement VI, pope, 106, 108, 140
Conrad of Megenberg, 107, 110
Constantine the Great, pope, 146
Constantine IV, pope, 147
Cyril of Alexandria, 148

Didymus, 148
Damasus I, pope, 146
Dominic, St, 161
Durandus of Saint-Pourçain, 15

Federico of Montefeltro, 202
Francesco della Rovere, 203
Francis, St, 161

Francis of Camerino, 139
Francis of Marchia, 27n
Francis of Meyronnes, 121n, 122n
Francisco de Vitoria, 7, 186–98

Georgius Benignus Salviati, 202
Gerard of Abbeville, 100
Giles of Rome, 14, 134, 135, 137, 146, 193
Godfrey of Fontaines, 134, 135, 137, 146
Gratian, 16
Gregory Palamas, 150
Gregory of Rimini, 82n
Guido de Baysio, 132, 133

Henry Burghersh, bishop, 39
Henry le Despenser, bishop, 182
Henry of Ghent, 2, 5, 19, 21, 24, 82n, 86, 105, 112, 115, 119, 120, 124, 126, 127, 134, 135, 137
Henry Knighton, 31, 45
Henry of Segusio, 'Hostiensis', 101
Henry Totting of Oyta, 2, 28, 57
Hilary of Poitiers, 148
Hugh de Courtenay, 31
Hugh of St Cher, 20

Innocent III, pope, 148, 179
Innocent VI, pope, 99, 109

Jacques Fournier, 15, 32, 33, 34
Jean Lemoine, 132, 133
Jean de Pouilly, 100
Jean Quidort, 12
Jerome, St, 148
Jerome of Prague, 166
Joachim of Fiore, 178n
John de Belvoir, 46
John Bole, archbishop, 203
John Chrysostom, 100, 101, 132, 148
John Damascene, 132, 149
John Duns Scotus, 2, 4, 14, 19, 21, 23–5, 27, 29, 39, 64, 66, 71, 72n, 80, 82n, 83–6, 89, 92, 112, 116–20, 126, 134, 135, 137, 202
John Foxholes, 7, 199–203
John Grandisson, bishop, 2–3, 15, 30–55
John Hus, 166

Index

John of Marignola, 103
John de Northwode, 38, 110
John Peckham, archbishop, 181
John Scottus Eriugena, 56
John of Thoresby, archbishop, 181
John Wyclif, 6, 7, 29, 45, 59, 81, 82, 84, 92, 104, 109, 159–85, 187, 196

Leo I, pope, 147
Leo III, pope, 147
Lorenzo de' Medici, 202

Marcian, 147
Michael of Cesena, 15

Pelagius, 39
Peter Auriol, 94, 107
Peter John Olivi, 14, 178, 187
Peter Lombard, 13, 16, 20, 28, 58, 59, 61, 63, 78, 82n, 89, 92, 128, 134
Peter of Tarantaise, 14n
Petrarch, 138, 140
Petrus de Pirichenwart, 200

Richard Campsall, 76n, 92
Richard Kilvington, 200
Richard Middleton, 14
Richard(?) Reppes, 11

Robert Grosseteste, 159, 160, 162, 179, 183
Robert Holcot, 4–5, 11, 63n, 76n, 79–95

Thomas Aquinas, 2–4, 12–15, 19, 21, 22, 24, 56, 61–3, 64n, 65, 68, 71, 79, 81–3, 86–8, 89n, 100, 104, 135, 137, 146, 150, 159, 176, 186–8, 190, 191, 193, 194
Thomas Bradwardine, 39n, 82n, 159, 166, 168n, 201
Thomas Netter of Walden, 6, 163–5
Thomas Walsingham, 31
Theodosius the Elder, emperor, 146

Vigilius, pope, 147

Walter Burley, 103, 104, 110
Walter Chatton, 11, 28, 29, 94, 179
William of Auxerre, 20n
William Courtenay, archbishop, 45
William Crathorn, 94
William Doune, 37, 42, 46
William of Ockham, 2, 4, 12, 14, 15, 23, 25, 26, 28, 29, 57, 61, 65n, 69, 72, 73, 76, 77, 80, 85, 88n, 92n, 94, 103–5, 107, 110, 137, 159, 166, 168, 174, 179, 183, 200
William of St Amour, 100
William Skelton, 11, 29

Index of modern names

Alban, K., 163n
Aston, M., 178

Bakker, P.J.J.M., 13n, 14–16, 28
Bellarmine, R., 165
Benedict XVI, pope, 189
Buescher, G., 25, 26
Brady, I., 132n
Brock, R.O., 188, 193, 195n
Burke, E., 198

Copsey, R., 165
Courtenay, W., 2, 4, 11, 12, 29, 57, 61, 63n, 82n, 83, 84

Dolan, T.P., 1n, 5, 99–102
Doyne Dawson, J., 175
Duba, W.O., 5–6, 103–27, 128n, 129, 142, 151n
Duddy, T., 56
Dunne, M.W., 1, 2, 7, 11–29, 56, 59n, 77n, 110, 126, 128, 133n, 199–203

Edelheit, A., 202
Etzkorn, G.J., 203

Fennessy, I., 99n
Friedman, R.L., 1, 134, 139, 143
Fyrigos, A., 139, 150

Gelber, H., 92n, 94n
Genest, J.F., 1, 57, 201
Gwynn, A., 4, 40n, 41n, 79, 99n, 107, 108, 192, 193

Hammerich, L.L., 4, 79, 179n
Haren, M., 2–3, 30–55, 57
Highfield, J.R.L., 30
Hingeston-Randolph, F.C., 31, 32

Kekes, J., 78
Kitanov, S., 3–4, 56–78, 87n, 88n
Knowles, D., 31
Kolbaba, T., 128n

Lahey, S., 1, 6–7, 159–85
Lambert, M., 166
Lambertini, R., 188n

Leff, G., 4, 57n, 63n, 64n, 76n, 82–4, 94n, 139n
Lubac, H. de, 189
Luther, M., 187

McAleer, G., 7, 186–98
MacFarlane, K.B., 46
MacIntyre, A., 56, 57n
Marchant, P., 101
Mair, J., 57
Marx, K., 185
Meyendorff, J., 143, 149
Micha_ski, K., 4, 63, 76n, 79, 80, 81, 82n, 83–90, 94, 210
Milbank, J., 189
Millett, B., 203
Minnis, A., 167, 168

O'Driscoll, C., 186
Olson, L., 32

Pantin, W.A., 37, 39
Pironet, F., 110

Robson, J., 4, 63n, 79, 81–4, 88n, 89n, 90, 94

Schabel, C., 1n, 6, 18, 128–55
Schmitt, C., 194
Smith, A., 185
Somereset, F., 181n
Spruyt, J., 110
Steele, M., 32
Streveler, P., 86
Szittya, P., 174–6, 178

Tachau, K.H., 4, 63n, 79–95
Thomson, J.A.F., 46
Thomson, W., 178n, 179
Trevor-Roper, H., 41

Wadding, L., 57
Walsh, K., 4, 7, 32, 35, 36, 56, 63n, 83, 84, 86, 90, 99n, 141, 166, 169, 201

Zalta, E.N., 110, 210
Zimmermann, B., 107, 211, 213